An Annotated Guide

to BIBLICAL
RESOURCES
for Ministry

An Annotated Guide

to BIBLICAL
RESOURCES
for Ministry

DAVID R. BAUER

HENDRICKSON
PUBLISHERS

Hendrickson Publishers, Inc.
P. O. Box 3473
Peabody, Massachusetts 01961-3473

Printed in the United States of America

First Printing — March 2003

Library of Congress Cataloging-in-Publication Data

Bauer, David R.
    An annotated guide to biblical resources for ministry / David R. Bauer.
      p. cm.
    Includes bibliographical references and index.
    ISBN 1-56563-723-2 (pbk. : alk. paper)
    1. Bible—Criticism, interpretation, etc.—Bibliography. 2. Bible—Bibliography.
I. Title.
Z7770.B38 2003
[BS540]
016.22—dc21   2003001526

TABLE OF CONTENTS

INTRODUCTION

The interpretation of the Bible is a central concern to all Christian ministers, for integrity demands that all ministers, in whatever capacity they serve, be professionally informed and personally shaped by the message of the Scriptures. The interpretation of the Bible involves, first of all, direct, firsthand study of the text. But it must also include, at the proper time, the use of various kinds of secondary sources. These resources are the indispensable tools of the biblical interpreter. I have compiled the following bibliography with these considerations in mind.

Although this book includes approximately twenty-two hundred titles by thirteen hundred scholars, it is still a highly selective bibliography, containing only a fraction of works that could have been included. Inclusion of individual items was based on one or more of the following considerations: (1) usefulness for the theological interpretation of the Bible within the context of the faith of the church; (2) significance in the history of interpretation; and (3) representation of evangelical and especially evangelical Wesleyan scholarship. I have annotated those items deemed most helpful, approximately six hundred in number.

I readily concede that any attempt to develop a bibliography and to identify within that bibliography works deserving special attention is a matter of individual judgment; no two scholars would agree on the selection. Thus, I present this bibliography as a suggestion, a place to start, inviting students to test the worth of these items in the process of the interpretive task.

I have prepared this volume for use primarily by seminary students and ministers. For that reason, almost everything included here is in English. But I also hope that scholars will find help here in identifying major works in areas outside of their specialization. This bibliography is intended, first of all, to acquaint students with major works, significant publishers, and prominent scholars in biblical studies. Its second purpose is to help students develop their personal libraries. The inclusion of many titles that are presently out of print should alert the student to the importance of stores and distribution houses that trade in theological used books. The ultimate purpose of the bibliography, however, is to direct students to those works that will be most helpful in interpreting the Bible for preaching and teaching in the church and for personal formation in Christian discipleship. I emphasize interpretation, since all of these works assist in the *exegetical* process. I have not included essentially homiletical or devotional volumes, not because they lack value as such, but because they stand outside the exegetical focus of this bibliography.

I have operated throughout on the basis of a number of assumptions. The first assumption, of course, is that biblical interpretation is foundational for both ministry and personal discipleship and is therefore to be pursued with all seriousness. I also assume that although the direct study of the text should be given priority in the interpretive process, this process necessarily involves the employment of secondary sources, in order (1) to aid in the direct study of the text itself (e.g., the use of concordances); (2) to provide knowledge of background (both semantic and historical) that will lead to a "competent" reading, i.e., a reading that makes use of the kind of knowledge the original biblical writer assumed his readers possessed; and (3) to enter into dialogue with the community of interpreters, recognizing that, in the final analysis, interpretation is a task that God has given to the church as a whole and must be done within the context of the church's struggle to understand these texts. This final point, however, must not lead to the conclusion that we should consult only those authors who write from the perspective of faith, for all serious and accurate study of the Bible illumines the meaning of the text and is thus helpful for the use of the Bible within the community of faith.

Finally, I assume that there is value in encountering interpreters from various periods and theological traditions. While affirming the necessity of understanding the Bible according to contemporary issues and the importance of teaching and preaching the Bible to our own age, we should recognize that the parameters of our specific historical existence limit our ability to understand dimensions of the text that were perhaps much clearer to persons who lived in a different age. And while celebrating our participation in our own theological traditions, we should recognize that the meaning of biblical passages is often larger than the construals of individual theological communities, so that our interpretations can be enhanced by insights from those whose theological commitments differ from our own. Hence, I have included authors from a variety of theological traditions, while giving some special consideration at points to evangelical Wesleyan scholarship. And I have incorporated items that represent or discuss interpretive work from different periods, though of necessity giving primary attention to current scholarship, which builds on the interpretation of the past and carries it forward.

I hope this book will provide assistance to all who work in the area of biblical studies. But I developed this bibliography specifically for the benefit of my own students, and it is to them that I affectionately dedicate it.

My thanks go to Dr. James Ernest, editor at Hendrickson Publishers, who has been gracious and helpful at every point; to Asbury Theological Seminary, which provided both a sabbatical and a grant to underwrite some of the research for this volume; and to Mr. Andrew Gilmore, who gave excellent assistance in bibliographic research and compiled the author index.

1

THE WHOLE BIBLE

1.1 Bibliographic Helps: General

H I G H L Y   R E C O M M E N D E D

1.1.1 Allison, Joe. *Swords and Whetstones: A Guide to Christian Bible Study Resources*. 3d ed. Nappannee, Ind.: Evangel, 1999. 217pp.

An introduction to biblical studies resources that also explains clearly how to use each type of Bible reference work. Especially helpful is the guidance provided for selecting an English translation. Contains highly selective bibliography with annotations. Written from a conservative perspective for a primarily evangelical readership, but fair and balanced both in the works selected and in the evaluation of these works.

1.1.2 Danker, Frederick W. *Multipurpose Tools for Bible Study*. Rev. ed. Minneapolis: Fortress, 1993. 330pp.

Has been the benchmark of bibliographic guides to the Bible since the first edition in 1960. Contains specific descriptions of the various resources (including works from the entire history of the church, not simply the modern period), along with discussion on the use of these works in interpretation, often with examples from one or two selected passages. The only serious limitation is its failure to list commentaries on specific biblical books, though it does discuss commentary series. A must for all Bible students.

1.1.3 Fitzmyer, Joseph A. *An Introductory Bibliography for the Study of Scripture*. Studia Biblica 3. 3d ed. Rome: Biblical Institute Press, 1990. 154pp.

From a leading Roman Catholic biblical scholar, it contains paragraph-long annotations of major scholarly works in the various areas of biblical studies but gives relatively little attention to commentaries on individual biblical books. Discusses works produced in a variety of languages, especially German and French; English works comprise fewer than half of those cited.

Essential for academic research but of relatively limited usefulness for those engaged in regular teaching and preaching in the church.

See also Elenchus of Biblica (§1.2.9)

A L S O   S I G N I F I C A N T

1.1.4 Marrow, Stanley B. *Basic Tools of Biblical Exegesis: A Student's Manual.* Rome: Biblical Institute Press, 1976. 91pp.

1.1.5 Moo, Douglas J. *An Annotated Bibliography on the Bible and the Church.* Deerfield, Ill.: Trinity Evangelical Divinity School, 1986. 70pp.

1.1.6 Stuart, Douglas. *A Guide to Selecting and Using Bible Commentaries.* Waco, Tex.: Word, 1990. 131pp.

1.2 Periodicals

1.2.1 *Bible Review.* 1985–. Quarterly.

This journal, produced by the Biblical Archaeology Society in Washington, D.C., provides studies in which some of the most prominent scholars address questions about biblical passages or biblical issues that trouble or concern nonspecialists. Articles represent almost all methods, and contributors include scholars of virtually all faiths (and secularists who shun religious commitment entirely). The orientation is, in fact, generally secular. It contains much informed and fresh insight, and is of value to specialists, but it is more useful to seminary students and trained pastors. Language: English. Book reviews: very few.

1.2.2 *The Bible Today: Scripture for Life and Ministry.* 1962–. 6 issues/year.

Produced by the Order of St. Benedict in Collegeville, Minnesota, this Roman Catholic publication seeks to translate for the nonspecialist the results of serious scholarly investigation into the Bible, with special emphasis on clarifying the meaning of difficult biblical passages and concepts. Although written for laypersons, the academic reputation of its contributors and the high quality of its articles make it profitable for the seminary student and trained pastor. It is consistently reverent in handling the text and attentive in a pastoral way to issues of faith that are of concern to its Christian readers. Language: English. Book reviews: few and very brief (practically book notices).

1.2.3 *Biblica.* 1920–. Quarterly.

Produced by the Pontifical Biblical Institute in Rome, it is one of the oldest and most prestigious journals given to serious biblical scholarship. Articles deal meticulously with meaning and background of specific biblical passages, employing almost exclusively the traditional historical-critical method. Excellent for serious, in-depth study. Language: All European languages (Latin prominent in the earlier volumes), with English articles comprising approximately a third of the total. Book reviews: moderately few, but extensive in length. *See also* the related bibliographic annual, *Elenchus of Biblica* (§1.2.9)

1.2.4 *Biblical Interpretation: A Journal of Contemporary Approaches.* 1993–. 3 issues/year.

In response to the predominance of the historical-critical orientation of most periodicals in biblical studies, this journal, produced by Brill Academic Publishers in Leiden, the Netherlands, offers interpretations of particular texts and theoretical hermeneutical discussions centering on the new and emerging methods in interpretation, e.g., poststructuralism, semiotics, feminism, liberation hermeneutics, reader-oriented criticism, psychological and ecological readings. Contributions are consistently original and creative. Articles often illumine the methods employed more than the text itself, at least the text understood as canonical scripture with its normative role in relation to the faith of the church. Yet there are exceptions, articles offering fresh, powerful, and compelling insights into the biblical text. Language: English. Book reviews: very few.

1.2.5 *Biblical Theology Bulletin: A Journal of Bible and Theology.* 1971–. Quarterly.

In spite of its name, this journal, produced by Biblical Theology Bulletin, Inc., in Wilmington, Delaware, does not deal primarily with larger issues of biblical theology (e.g., salvation-history, kingdom of God) but rather explores the meaning of specific biblical passages and books using a variety of methods, especially new, emerging methods such as cultural anthropological and literary approaches. Articles are uneven in terms of their ability to serve as the basis of theological insights useful for preaching and teaching. In general, solid and helpful contributions by leading scholars in these emerging methods of interpretation. Language: English. Book reviews: few.

1.2.6 *Bulletin for Biblical Research.* 1991–. Annual.

The Institute for Biblical Research (IBR), which is the organization of evangelical biblical scholars responsible for producing this journal in Winona Lake, Indiana, accurately describes it as "both fully critical, yet supportive of the Christian faith." In many ways the American equivalent of the *Tyndale Bulletin,* its articles are in accord with the evangelical convictions of the IBR but employ contemporary critical methods—in many cases in a masterful way. Unlike *Tyndale Bulletin,* however, it publishes mostly the work of established, senior scholars. Language: English. Book reviews: few.

1.2.7 *The Catholic Biblical Quarterly.* 1939–. Quarterly.

Next to the *Journal of Biblical Literature,* probably the most authoritative journal for serious academic study of the whole Bible. Published by the Catholic Biblical Association in Washington, D.C., its articles tend to avoid the kind of obscure and arcane issues that often occupy *JBL* and instead focus on significant questions of interpretation. Consequently, its articles rather consistently provide basis for theological reflection useful for preaching and teaching. Language: English. Book reviews: many.

1.2.8 *Currents in Biblical Research.* 1993–. Annual.

Formerly known as Currents in Research. Produced by Sheffield Academic Press in Sheffield, U.K. Articles written by prominent scholars describe and critically assess new and emerging facets or developments within biblical studies. Each article contains extensive bibliography. Language: English.

1.2.9 *Elenchus of Biblica.* 12 vols. Rome: Biblical Institute Press, 1985–. Annual.

The most complete listing (non-annotated) available on works in biblical studies, produced by the Pontifical Biblical Institute in Rome. It includes both articles and books (with select citations of book reviews) in all areas of biblical studies and in all languages. The volumes are slow to appear, usually about four years behind schedule.

1.2.10 *The Expository Times.* 1889–. Monthly.

British publication produced by T&T Clark, Edinburgh, Scotland, attends to all the theological and pastoral disciplines and often contains helpful articles in biblical studies, including treatments of biblical themes and issues as well as exposition of specific passages. Contributors are often of global reputation but are almost exclusively from the British Isles. Language: English. Book reviews: few, but lengthy.

1.2.11 *Interpretation: A Journal of Bible and Theology.* 1946–. Quarterly.

Published by Union Theological Seminary in Richmond, Virginia. From its inception has consistently emphasized the theological meaning of the text for the faith of the church. Articles model the ways in which theological and pastoral insights flow out of solid biblical exposition. Although the quality of the articles has in recent years become uneven, this journal seldom disappoints. Especially helpful are its "expository articles," in which scholars or gifted biblical preachers demonstrate how one might move from interpretation to proclamation of lectionary passages. Most highly recommended for those who regularly teach and preach in the context of the church or its institutions. Language: English. Book reviews: many.

1.2.12 *Journal of Biblical Literature*. 1881–. Quarterly.

Published by the Society of Biblical Literature in Atlanta, Georgia, arguably the world's foremost journal in biblical studies. Articles consistently reflect the highest academic standards, and are original contributions to the biblical guild. Although articles generally do not draw out the theological significance of passages treated, some of them do contribute to an interpretation of the text that is useful for preaching and teaching. Yet many of the articles are arcane and deal with matters that do not clearly illumine the text as the church's scripture. Language: mostly English, though with an occasional German or French article. Book reviews: many.

1.2.13 *Review of Biblical Literature*. 1996–. Annual.

Published by the Society of Biblical Literature in Atlanta, Georgia, offers the most comprehensive review of books (including monographs, reference works, commentaries, dictionaries, editions of the biblical text and related ancient texts, and biblical translations) available. Reviews works published in all languages. Frequently provides multiple contrasting reviews of the same volume. Reviews are written by prominent scholars, are relatively extensive, and include description, analysis, and evaluation. Language: primarily English, with some reviews in German or French.

1.2.14 *Semeia: An Experimental Journal for Biblical Criticism*. 1974–. Quarterly.

Published by the Society of Biblical Literature in Atlanta, Georgia. Articles represent new and emerging methods of interpretation, especially structuralism, poststructuralism, feminist interpretation, etc. Typically avoids theological reflection on the text in favor of illumining the new hermeneutical approaches on the one hand, and drawing out significance for contemporary cultural and political applications on the other. Of marginal value for teaching and preaching within the church. Language: English. Book reviews: none.

1.2.15 *Tyndale Bulletin* (formerly *Tyndale House Bulletin*). 1950–. Semiannual.

Produced by Tyndale House of Cambridge, England, an evangelical academic study center. Most articles pertain to biblical studies, though some represent other theological disciplines. The majority of contributors are younger scholars. Articles are consistently informed and innovative, with serious attention to theological issues. All conform to the evangelical confessional standards of Tyndale House but seek to engage seriously in the critical study of the text. Language: English. Book reviews: few to none, but with summaries of recent dissertations.

1.3 History of the Bible

H I G H L Y   R E C O M M E N D E D

1.3.1 Ackroyd, Peter R., and C. F. Evans, eds. *Cambridge History of the Bible.* 3 vols. Cambridge: Cambridge University Press, 1988. 649/566/590pp.

The most thorough and authoritative history of the Bible in existence. Articles produced by some of the world's most respected historians and biblical scholars deal with all relevant aspects of the history of the development of the biblical text as well as its translation, canonization, use, and influence from antiquity to the present. Should be in the library of every seminary student and pastor.

1.3.2 Bratton, F. Gladstone. *A History of the Bible.* London: Robert Hale, 1959. 287pp.

Something of a classic introduction to the history that surrounds the Bible. As such it deals with the history of the Hebrew people and the NT church as well as with the history of the text of the Bible itself, especially the canonization of the OT and NT, and the transmission of the Bible from the Greek manuscripts through the early versions to the English translations. Gives attention also to the history of exegesis. Designed for the general reader, but a helpful introduction or refresher for the seminary student or pastor.

1.3.3 Bruce, F. F. *The Books and Parchments: How We Got Our English Bible.* Rev. ed. Old Tappan, N.J.: Revell, 1984. 288pp.

Clearly written introduction to the history of the Bible in the form of brief treatments given to significant aspects of that history, including the Hebrew, Aramaic, and Greek languages, the significance of two testaments, the canon, the text of the OT, the Samaritan Pentateuch, the Targums, the Septuagint, the text of the NT, early versions of the NT, and the history of the English Bible. Produced by an unusually capable scholar who dealt confidently with each of these areas. Written for the general reader but may serve as a helpful survey for the seminary student or pastor.

1.3.4 Norton, David. *A History of the Bible as Literature*. 2 vols. Cambridge: Cambridge University Press, 1993. 375/493pp.

The only work in existence that thoroughly explores the relationship of the Bible, throughout its history, to the concept of literature. Addresses issues such as: In what sense have persons throughout history understood the Bible to be literature? How does the Bible relate to the various concepts of literature that have been operative over the past two millennia? Norton gives special attention to the reception of the King James Version as literature and to its role in the literary history of the English-speaking world. Informs understanding of the literary character of the Bible and the study of the Bible as literature, both of which have implications for several of the new and emerging interpretive methods, especially literary criticism.

1.3.5 Trebolle Barrera, Julio. *The Jewish Bible and the Christian Bible: An Introduction to the History of the Bible*. Grand Rapids: Eerdmans, 1998. 573pp.

Thorough, informed, and current overview of the history of the Bible, dealing with the formation of the collections of canonical and apocryphal books, the transmission and translation of the Bible, and biblical interpretation in Judaism and Christianity, all with an eye toward the ways in which the social and cultural context illumines each of these aspects of the Bible's history. Contains numerous bibliographies of the most current scholarly work. Highly recommended for serious study.

ALSO SIGNIFICANT

1.3.6 Cunningham, Philip J. *Exploring Scripture: How the Bible Came to Be*. New York: Paulist, 1992. 216pp.

1.3.7 Ewert, David. *A General Introduction to the Bible: From Ancient Tablets to Modern Translations*. Grand Rapids: Zondervan, 1990. 284pp.

1.3.8 Gilmore, Alec. *A Dictionary of the English Bible and Its Origins*. The Biblical Seminar 67. Sheffield: Sheffield Academic Press, 2000. 192pp.

1.3.9 Koch, Klaus. *The Book of Books: The Growth of the Bible*. Philadelphia: Westminster, 1968. 192pp.

1.3.10 Price, Ira M., William A. Irwin, and Allen P. Wikgren. *The Ancestry of Our English Bible: An Account of the Manuscripts, Texts, and Versions of the Bible*. 3d ed. New York: Harper & Row, 1956. 363pp.

1.3.11 Wegner, Paul D. *The Journey from Texts to Translations: The Origin and Development of the Bible.* Grand Rapids: Baker, 2000. 462pp.

1.4 History of the English Bible

H I G H L Y   R E C O M M E N D E D

1.4.1 Bailey, Lloyd R., ed. *The Word of God: A Guide to English Versions of the Bible.* Atlanta: John Knox, 1982. 228pp.

Noted biblical scholars (e.g., Bruce Metzger, James Smart, Eugene Nida) compare and contrast nine English versions (Revised Standard Version, New English Bible, New Jewish Version, Jerusalem Bible, New American Standard Bible, Good News Bible, Living Bible, New American Bible, New International Version), evaluating their relative worth on the basis of (1) quality of manuscripts employed, (2) basis of translation (etymology, context, cognate language, theological presuppositions), and (3) English usage (clarity, level, consistency). Concludes with annotated bibliography that lists book reviews and evaluative studies of each version discussed. Specific, informed, and very useful in evaluating the most popular contemporary versions.

1.4.2 Bruce, F. F. *History of the Bible in English.* New York: Oxford, 1978. 274pp.

Traces the history of the English Bible through its various translations from the very beginnings before Wycliffe through the Living Bible. Generally speaking, it is the most helpful survey of the history of the English Bible from the beginning through the 1970s, although its treatment of some of the major recent versions, especially the New American Standard Bible and the New International Version, is disappointing for its brevity.

1.4.3 Kerr, John Stevens. *Ancient Texts Alive Today: The Story of the English Bible.* Edited by Charles Houser. New York: American Bible Society, 1999. 229pp.

Concise description of the history of English translations from before William Tyndale through the Contemporary English Version. Replete with pictures and charts; presents a lively narrative that results not only in an understanding of the history and essential character of major translations, but also in a sense of the historical development of the task of English translation. Includes interesting biographical and historical details pertaining to the versions, especially the earlier ones, and concludes with a timeline of modern English Bibles.

1.4.4 Kubo, Sakae, and Walter Specht. *So Many Versions? Twentieth-Century English Versions of the Bible.* Rev. ed. Grand Rapids: Zondervan, 1983. 401pp.

Describes the aim, style, intended use, and target audience of each of the major twentieth-century translations through the Readers' Digest Bible, and provides a fair and trenchant evaluation of each. Concludes with an annotated list of all twentieth-century English translations, which provides essential information about those versions that were not treated more fully in the body of the book. Complements Bruce's volume (§1.4.2) in that it focuses on recent versions, whereas Bruce emphasizes the earlier translations.

1.4.5 Lewis, Jack P. *The English Bible from KJV to NIV: A History and Evaluation.* 2d ed. Grand Rapids: Baker, 1991. 512pp.

Similar in purpose and goal to the volume by Kubo and Specht (§1.4.4), it describes the history, character, and aims of the translations and critically evaluates each. It differs from the aforementioned volume in that it contains a chapter on the King James Version, and discusses only thirteen twentieth-century translations. Lewis is thereby able to provide more depth in both description and evaluation than Kubo-Specht.

1.4.6 Metzger, Bruce M. *The Bible in Translation: Ancient and English Versions.* Grand Rapids: Baker, 2001. 200pp.

In spite of the subtitle, "Ancient and English Versions," Metzger dedicates only 38 pages to ancient versions, thus giving by far the bulk of attention to English translations. Among the English translations, Metzger devotes the greatest attention to the Authorized Version, the Revised Standard Version and the New Revised Standard Version. Treatment of other contemporary English versions is extremely brief and tends to focus on details surrounding the emergence of the version. Whereas one might hope that Metzger would discuss the general character of each version, assessing its positive and negative qualities, one finds that Metzger typically cites the version's translation of one or two biblical passages with a view toward criticizing or applauding the translation of that limited unit. Useful as a historical chronicle of the various versions, but one should look to Bruce (§1.4.2) for more helpful assessment of strengths and weaknesses of each.

ALSO SIGNIFICANT

1.4.7 Chamberlin, William J. *Catalogue of English Bible Translations: A Classified Bibliography of Versions and Editions Including Books, Parts, and Old and New Testament Apocrypha and Apocryphal Books.* New York: Greenwood, 1991. 898pp.

1.4.8   Glassman, Eugene H. *The Translation Debate: What Makes a Bible Translation Good?* Downers Grove, Ill.: InterVarsity, 1981. 128pp.

1.4.9   Hargreaves, Cecil. *A Translator's Freedom: Modern English Bibles and Their Language.* The Biblical Seminar. Sheffield: JSOT, 1993. 206pp.

1.4.10 Kohlenberger, John R., III. *Words about the Word: A Guide to Choosing and Using Your Bible.* Regency Reference Library. Grand Rapids: Zondervan, 1987. 218pp.

1.4.11 Sheeley, Steven M., and Robert N. Nash Jr. *The Bible in English Translation: An Essential Guide.* Nashville: Abingdon, 1997. 116pp.

1.5   History of the Canon and History of Interpretation

See also EXEGETICAL METHOD/HERMENEUTICS (§1.12)

H I G H L Y   R E C O M M E N D E D

1.5.1   Abraham, William J. *Canon and Criterion in Christian Theology: From the Fathers to Feminism.* Oxford: Oxford University Press, 1998. 508pp.

A detailed and intellectually engaging study of the relationship between (biblical) canon and the criteria for determining doctrinal and ethical norms in the Christian faith. Written by a leading evangelical theologian, it traces the development of the canon in the early church and the subsequent functioning of the canon in the church in order to demonstrate the importance of distinguishing between the biblical canon itself and the church's complex and sophisticated use of that canon for its theological and moral life. Extremely helpful for probing the significance of the canon for the ongoing life of the church.

1.5.2   Barton, John. *Holy Writings, Sacred Text: The Canon in Early Christianity.* Louisville: Westminster John Knox, 1997. 210pp.

Presents a historical investigation into the development of the biblical canon in the church, addressing such issues as how the church came to accept as authoritative scripture these and only these 27 books that comprise the NT, and why the church placed the Hebrew scriptures alongside these books. An excellent book for exploring the theological and historical problems of canonization of the Christian scriptures.

1.5.3 Bruce, F. F. *The Canon of Scripture.* Downers Grove, Ill.: InterVarsity, 1988. 349pp.

Comprehensive survey of the history of the process of canonization of both the Old and New Testaments, with greater attention to the New. Especially illuminating are three final chapters that discuss canonical issues of continuing significance: criteria of canonicity, canon within the canon, and relationship of the canon to biblical criticism and interpretation (including "canonical criticism"). Highly recommended for general overview.

1.5.4 Campenhausen, Hans von. *The Formation of the Christian Bible.* Philadelphia: Fortress, 1972. 342pp.

A book that sets the standard in the study of the historical process of the formation of the canon. Campenhausen discusses the theological and historical problems of the Christian canon, and explores the pressures that led to the emergence of the canon, the forces that arose to challenge the formation of the canon, the outcome of the controversies surrounding the canon, and the theological significance of that outcome. Detailed, carefully documented, and original. The most authoritative treatment available.

1.5.5 Grant, Robert M., and David Tracy. *A Short History of the Interpretation of the Bible.* 2d ed. Philadelphia: Fortress, 1984. 213pp.

Offers a brief but solid history of interpretive method in the church from the NT itself (how Jesus and the NT writers treat the OT) through the 1970s, though gives bulk of attention to the early periods. Of special value are the final chapters, written by the noted Roman Catholic theologian David Tracy, which draw out the significance of this history for the theological interpretation of the Bible today.

1.5.6 Hayes, John H., ed. *Dictionary of Biblical Interpretation.* 2 vols. Nashville: Abingdon, 1999. 653/675pp.

By far the most comprehensive and current dictionary on biblical interpretation, it contains entries on the history of interpretation of the various biblical books (including apocryphal and deuterocanonical ones), on significant biblical interpreters throughout the history of the church, and on various interpretive methods and movements. Features almost four hundred contributors representing Jewish, Protestant, Orthodox, and Roman Catholic backgrounds. The range of essays is so broad that of necessity the individual articles tend to be quite brief; this drawback is somewhat mitigated by the bibliographies, which direct readers to additional research.

1.5.7 Margerie, Bertrand de. *An Introduction to the History of Exegesis.* 2 vols. Petersham, Mass.: St. Bede's, 1993, 1995. 277/154pp.

The first volume deals with the Greek fathers, while the second treats the Latin fathers. Analyzes the exegesis of the most significant fathers with a view toward calling the church to follow the model of the fathers, who sought to interpret the Bible within an avowedly confessional framework. Very selective in the number of fathers treated, especially in regard to the Latin fathers.

1.5.8 McDonald, Lee Martin, and James A. Sanders, eds. *The Canon Debate.* Peabody, Mass.: Hendrickson, 2002. 662pp.

This book includes contributions from 32 scholars of international repute, all of whom are recognized authorities on that aspect of the canon about which they write in this volume. Includes the most current thinking on the wide range of issues related to the canon (both OT and NT) to be found in a single volume. Contributors represent a variety of positions on canonical issues and a spectrum of theological traditions.

ALSO SIGNIFICANT

1.5.9 Barr, James. *Holy Scripture: Canon, Authority, Criticism.* Philadelphia: Westminster, 1983. 175pp.

1.5.10 Bray, Gerald. *Biblical Interpretation: Past and Present.* Downers Grove, Ill.: InterVarsity, 1996. 608pp.

1.5.11 Elwell, Walter A., and J. D. Weaver. *Bible Interpreters of the Twentieth Century: A Selection of Evangelical Voices.* Grand Rapids: Baker, 1999. 445pp.

1.5.12 Farrar, Frederick W. *History of Interpretation.* New York: Dutton, 1886. 553pp.

1.5.13 Frei, Hans. *The Eclipse of Biblical Narrative.* New Haven, Conn.: Yale, 1974. 355pp.

1.5.14 Froelich, Karlfried. *Biblical Interpretation in the Early Church.* Sources of Early Christian Thought. Philadelphia: Fortress, 1984. 135pp.

1.5.15 Hall, Christopher A. *Reading Scripture with the Church Fathers.* Downers Grove, Ill.: InterVarsity, 1998. 223pp.

1.5.16 Harrisville, Roy A., and Walter Sundberg. *The Bible in Modern Culture: Theology and Historical-Critical Method from Spinoza to Käsemann.* Grand Rapids: Eerdmans, 1995. 282pp.

1.5.17 Hauser, Alan J., and Duane F. Watson. *A History of Biblical Interpretation.* Vol. 1. *The Ancient Period.* Grand Rapids: Eerdmans, 2002. 512pp.

1.5.18 Kugel, James L., and Rowan A. Greer. *Early Biblical Interpretation.* Library of Earliest Christianity. Philadelphia: Westminster, 1986. 214pp.

1.5.19 Lubac, Henri de. *Medieval Exegesis: The Four Senses of Scripture.* 2 vols. Ressourcement: Retrieval and Renewal in Catholic Thought. Grand Rapids: Eerdmans, 1998, 2000. 466/430pp.

1.5.20 McDonald, Lee Martin. *The Formation of the Christian Biblical Canon.* Rev. ed. Peabody, Mass.: Hendrickson, 1995. 340pp.

1.5.21 McKim, Donald K. *Historical Handbook of Major Biblical Interpreters.* Downers Grove, Ill.: InterVarsity, 1998. 643pp.

1.5.22 Miller, John W. *The Origins of the Bible: Rethinking Canon History.* New York: Paulist, 1994.

1.5.23 Noll, Mark. *Between Faith and Criticism: Evangelicals, Scholarship, and the Bible in America.* Society of Biblical Literature Confessional Perspective Series. Grand Rapids: Baker, 1986. 271pp.

1.5.24 Sanders, James A. *From Sacred Story to Sacred Text: Canon as Paradigm.* Philadelphia: Fortress, 1986. 200pp.

1.5.25 Silva, Moisés. *Has the Church Misread the Bible? The History of Interpretation in the Light of Contemporary Issues.* Grand Rapids: Zondervan, 1987. 136pp.

1.5.26 Simonetti, Manlio. *Biblical Interpretation in the Early Church: An Historical Introduction to Patristic Exegesis.* Edited by Anders Bergquist and Markus Bockmuehl. Edinburgh: T&T Clark, 1994. 154pp.

1.5.27 Smalley, Beryl. *The Study of the Bible in the Middle Ages.* Notre Dame, Ind.: University of Notre Dame Press, 1964. 406pp.

1.5.28 Stokes, Mack B. *The Bible in the Wesleyan Heritage.* Nashville: Abingdon, 1979. 95pp.

1.5.29 Uffenheimer, Benjamin, and Henning Graf Reventlow, eds. *Creative Biblical Exegesis: Christian and Jewish Hermeneutics through the Centuries.* Journal for the Study of the Old Testament Supplement Series 59. Sheffield: JSOT Press, 1988. 225pp.

1.6 Biblical History and Geography

See also BIBLE ATLASES (§1.7)

H I G H L Y   R E C O M M E N D E D

1.6.1 Aharoni, Yohanan. *The Land of the Bible: A Historical Geography.* Edited by A. F. Rainey. Rev. ed. Philadelphia: Westminster, 1979. 481pp.

Produced by a leading Israeli archaeologist, describes the history of the land of Palestine in general as well as the various regions, and even cities, roads, and highways. Presents both an introductory survey of the geography of the Holy Land and a chronologically ordered history of Palestine in the OT period, with special attention to the role of specific geographical locations in the various stages of that history. Concludes with helpful indexes of biblical passages and of geographical names.

1.6.2 Coogan, Michael D., ed. *The Oxford History of the Biblical World.* New York: Oxford University Press, 1998. 643pp.

The most complete and authoritative history of the biblical world. In chronologically ordered chapters discusses the history, art, architecture, languages, culture, society, literature, and religion of the Bible, carefully synthesizing historical data and archaeological findings with the biblical text. Includes numerous prints, illustrations, and maps.

1.6.3 Finegan, Jack. *Myth and Mystery: An Introduction to the Pagan Religions of the Biblical World.* Grand Rapids: Baker, 1989. 335.

It is important to interpret biblical materials, which are theological texts, against the backdrop of the religious environment of the biblical world. This is the most authoritative examination of nine pagan religions influential during Old and New Testament times. Finegan discusses their beliefs, practices, writings, history, and relation to the biblical faith.

1.6.4 Kee, Howard Clark, Eric M. Meyers, John Rogerson, and Anthony Saldarini. *The Cambridge Companion to the Bible.* Cambridge: Cambridge University Press, 1997. 615pp.

Readable survey of the whole of the history of the Bible and its cultural environment from before the patriarchs through the first centuries of the church. Its breadth results in some lack of depth and detail in the discussions of the individual periods. Represents the general consensus of contemporary mainline critical scholarship in historical questions and reconstructions.

1.6.5   Turner, George Allen. *Historical Geography of the Holy Land.* Grand Rapids: Baker, 1973. 368pp.

A comprehensive synthesis of the history and geography of the Holy Land. Nowhere will one find clearer and more straightforward discussions of the regions and major specific geographical locations of Palestine and their significance for the biblical account. Geared toward seminary students and trained pastors.

1.6.6   Vos, Howard F. *New Illustrated Bible Manners and Customs: How the People of the Bible Really Lived.* Nashville: Thomas Nelson, 1999. 661pp.

Moves chapter by chapter through biblical history, discussing in readable fashion various aspects of the history of Bible times, emphasizing everyday life. Although geared to a popular audience, contains much information that is directly helpful for the interpretation of specific passages, presented in an accessible format. Represents a conservative historical perspective.

ALSO SIGNIFICANT

1.6.7   Baly, Denis. *Basic Biblical Geography.* Philadelphia: Fortress, 1987. 80pp.

1.6.8   Barton, John. *The Biblical World.* 2 vols. New York: Routledge, 2002. 1115pp.

1.6.9   Corswant, Willy, and Edouard Urech. *A Dictionary of Life in Bible Times.* New York: Oxford University Press, 1960. 308pp.

1.6.10 DeVries, LaMoine F. *Cities of the Biblical World.* Peabody, Mass.: Hendrickson, 1997. 398pp.

1.6.11 Gray, John. *A History of Jerusalem.* London: Robert Hall, 1969. 336pp.

1.6.12 Harris, Robert L. *The World of the Bible.* London: Thames and Hudson, 1995. 192pp.

1.6.13 Harrison, R. K., ed. *Major Cities of the Biblical World.* New York: Thomas Nelson, 1985. 292pp.

1.6.14 Matthews, Victor H. *Manners and Customs in the Bible.* Rev. ed. Peabody, Mass.: Hendrickson, 1991. 283pp.

1.6.15 Page, Charles R. II, and Carl A. Volz. *The Land and the Book: An Introduction to the World of the Bible.* Nashville: Abingdon, 1993. 285pp.

1.6.16 Pfeiffer, Charles F., and Howard F. Vos. *The Wycliffe Historical Geography of Bible Lands.* Chicago: Moody, 1967. 588pp.

1.6.17 Porter, J. R. *An Illustrated Guide to the Bible.* New York: Oxford University Press, 1995. 288pp.

1.6.18 Shanks, Hershel, ed. *Ancient Israel: A Short History from Abraham to the Roman Destruction of the Temple.* Washington, D.C.: Biblical Archaeology Society, 1988. 267pp.

1.6.19 Smith, George Adam. *The Historical Geography of the Holy Land.* 25th ed. London: Hodder & Stoughton, 1931. 512pp.

1.6.20 Thompson, J. A. *Handbook of Life in Bible Times.* Downers Grove, Ill.: InterVarsity, 1986. 384pp.

1.6.21 Yamauchi, Edwin M. *Persia and the Bible.* Grand Rapids: Baker, 1990. 580pp.

1.7 Bible Atlases

HIGHLY RECOMMENDED

1.7.1 Aharoni, Yohanan, and Michael Avi-Yonah. *The Carta Biblical Atlas.* 3d ed. New York: Macmillan, 1993. 215pp.

Perviously titled *The Macmillan Bible Atlas.* Completely revised from the second edition. Provides maps and illustrations covering 3000 B.C.E. to 200 C.E. and dealing with settlements and mass migrations of populations; conquests and battles described in the Bible; economic developments, trade routes, and natural resources; movements of biblical characters within districts and cities; archaeological excavation; and growth of the church through the second century. Brief but specific and useful historical narrative accompanies each map. Along with Harper's (§1.7.4), most comprehensive Bible atlas available.

1.7.2 Bahat, Dan, and Chaim T. Rubinstein. *The Illustrated Atlas of Jerusalem.* New York: Simon & Schuster, 1990. 152pp.

Most comprehensive and authoritative atlas of this most important biblical site. Makes use of the latest archaeological discoveries. Presents maps, drawings, isometric reconstructions, and detailed descriptions of specific features of Jerusalem and consistently relates these descriptions to biblical narrative and biblical history.

1.7.3 Briscoe, Thomas V. *The Holman Bible Atlas*. Nashville: Broadman & Holman, 1998. 298pp.

Well-formatted and informed synthesis of maps, illustration, and historical and geographical discussions. Less comprehensive or authoritative than *The Carta Biblical Atlas* (§1.7.1) or *The Harper Atlas* (§1.7.4) but represents a responsible conservative complement to them.

1.7.4 Pritchard, James B. *The Harper Atlas of the Bible*. San Francisco: Harper, 1987. 254pp.

Among the most complete, comprehensive, and authoritative available. Compiled by fifty archaeologists, linguists, epigraphers, archaeological illustrators, geographers, interpreters, geologists, and historians, and containing 450 illustrations, with visual reconstructions of historical sites, e.g., Jerusalem as Jesus saw it. Text pertaining to historical background treats customs, beliefs, practices, texts, crafts, industries, weaponry, everyday life, etc. Combines geography, history, culture, and archaeology in dynamic synthesis with the biblical text. Comparable in quality to *The Carta Biblical Atlas* (§1.7.1).

ALSO SIGNIFICANT

1.7.5 Baly, Denis, and A. D. Tushingham. *Atlas of the Biblical World*. Cleveland: World, 1971. 208pp.

1.7.6 Beitzel, Barry. *The Moody Atlas of Bible Lands*. Chicago: Moody, 1985. 234pp.

1.7.7 Bimson, J. J., et al., eds. *New Bible Atlas*. Downers Grove, Ill.: InterVarsity, 1985. 128pp.

1.7.8 Frank, Harry Thomas, ed. *Hammond's Atlas of the Bible Lands: An Illustrated Atlas of the Bible*. Rev. ed. Maplewood, N.J.: Hammond, 2000. 48pp.

1.7.9 Grollenberg, L. H. *Atlas of the Bible*. Edited by Joyce M. H. Reid and H. H. Rowley. London: Thomas Nelson, 1956. 165pp.

1.7.10 Kraeling, Emil Gottlieb Heinrich. *Rand McNally Bible Atlas*. Edited by Carl H. Kraeling. New York: Rand McNally, 1956. 485pp.

1.7.11 May, Herbert G. *Oxford Bible Atlas*. 3d ed. New York: Oxford University Press, 1984. 144pp.

1.7.12 Negenman, Jan H. *New Atlas of the Bible.* Edited by H. H. Rowley. New York: Doubleday, 1969. 208pp.

1.7.13 Pritchard, James B., ed. *The HarperCollins Concise Atlas of the Bible.* San Francisco: HarperSanFrancisco, 1997. 151pp.

1.7.14 Rasmussen, Carl. *The Zondervan NIV Atlas of the Bible.* Grand Rapids: Zondervan, 1989. 256pp.

1.7.15 Rogerson, John. *Atlas of the Bible.* New York: Facts on File Publications, 1985. 237pp.

1.7.16 Wright, G. Ernest, and Floyd V. Filson, eds. *The Westminster Historical Atlas to the Bible.* Rev. ed. Philadelphia: Westminster, 1956. 128pp.

1.8 Biblical Archaeology

See also EXEGETICAL METHOD/HERMENEUTICS (§1.12)

H I G H L Y   R E C O M M E N D E D

1.8.1 Bartlett, John R., ed. *Archaeology and Biblical Interpretation.* London: Routledge, 1997. 176pp.

The authors of the articles assembled here demonstrate how archaeology can illumine the social, political, and theological concerns of the biblical text, if used properly and with due caution. After an instructive introductory article by Bartlett ("What Has Archaeology to Do with the Bible—or Vice Versa?"), six scholars explore applications of archaeology to specific biblical texts or issues.

1.8.2 Blaiklock, E. M., and R. K. Harrison, eds. *The New Dictionary of Biblical Archaeology.* Grand Rapids: Zondervan, 1983. 514pp.

Readable yet scholarly entries on all significant aspects of the science of archaeology, on excavations, and on archaeological significance of sites, persons, and objects mentioned in the Bible. Each entry concludes with a select bibliography.

1.8.3 Charlesworth, James H., and Walter P. Weaver, eds. *What Has Archaeology to Do with Faith?* Faith and Scholarship Colloquies. Valley Forge, Pa.: Trinity Press International, 1992. 116pp.

Five prominent scholars explore the limits and potential of archaeology for interpreting the Bible and for faith. Probes the significance of archaeology for the study of Israelite history, the NT, and the historical Jesus, and argues for more intentionality in using archaeology to reconstruct ancient social history. Complements the volume edited by Bartlett (§1.8.1) in introducing readers to the relevance of archaeology for interpretation.

1.8.4   Hoppe, Leslie J. *What Are They Saying about Biblical Archaeology?* New York: Paulist, 1984. 107pp.

Concise but illuminating introduction to contemporary issues in biblical archaeology. The first chapter ("Archaeology—Use and Abuse") and the last ("The Future of Biblical Archaeology") discuss theoretical issues, while the intervening chapters describe the process of excavation and explore how four current digs clarify the theoretical issues.

1.8.5   Kenyon, Kathleen M. *Archaeology in the Holy Land.* 5th ed. New York: Norton, 1979. 359pp.

A classic, written by an innovative and towering figure in the history of archaeology, this book presents both a description of her discoveries in various sites and her brilliant interpretation of these discoveries. Although this fifth edition represents a complete revision completed shortly before Kenyon's death, it is now somewhat dated in parts and should be supplemented with accounts of newer discoveries.

1.8.6   Mazar, Amihai. *Archaeology of the Land of the Bible: 10,000–586 B.C.E.* Anchor Bible Reference Library. Garden City, N.Y.: Doubleday, 1990. 576pp.

Comprehensive, current, and informed description of archaeological research of Palestine relating to the OT and dealing with the period of 10,000 B.C.E. to the Babylonian Captivity. It is careful to represent differences of scholarly opinion. Gives some (secondary) consideration to the implications of the archaeological discoveries discussed for biblical history. A most helpful survey.

1.8.7   Morrey, P. R. S. *A Century of Biblical Archaeology.* Louisville: Westminster John Knox, 1991. 189pp.

A most comprehensive and accessible critical history of biblical archaeology. Explores especially the relationship between archaeologists and biblical scholars, made complex by their different views on the purpose of biblical archaeology. Provides valuable information on major schools, scholars, and excavations in archaeology since 1890.

1.8.8 Rousseau, John J., and Rami Arav (with Carol Meyers). *Jesus and His World: An Archaeological and Cultural Dictionary.* Philadelphia: Fortress, 1994. 189pp.

Entries arranged alphabetically treat various subjects (e.g., coins, magic, medicine), places, and persons that pertain to Jesus and the Gospels, in each case including scripture references, general information, archaeological data, and implications for Jesus research, concluding with a select bibliography. Very accessible, readable, and illuminating background material.

1.8.9 Stern, Ephraim. *The New Encyclopedia of Archaeological Excavations in the Holy Land.* 4 vols. New York: Simon & Schuster, 1993. 1551pp.

Most comprehensive, detailed, scholarly dictionary of archaeological excavations available. Discussions are highly technical, but contributors consistently relate archaeological discoveries to relevant biblical passages (and an index to biblical passages is included). Generously illustrated with charts, maps, and photographs.

PERIODICALS

1.8.10 *Archaeology in the Biblical World.* Shafter, Calif.: Near East Archaeological Society, 1991–.

1.8.11 *The Biblical Archaeological Review.* Washington, D.C.: Biblical Archaeology Society, 1975–.

1.8.12 *The Biblical Archaeologist.* Cambridge, Mass.: American Schools of Oriental Research, 1938–1997.

1.8.13 *The Bulletin of the American Schools of Oriental Research.* Ann Arbor, Mich.: American Schools of Oriental Research, 1919–.

ALSO SIGNIFICANT

1.8.14 Albright, William Foxwell. *The Archaeology of Palestine.* Rev. ed. Harmondsworth, U.K.: Penguin, 1960. 271pp.

1.8.15 Campbell, Edward F., and David Noel Freedman. *The Biblical Archaeologist Reader.* Vols. 2–3. New York: Doubleday, 1961–1970. 420/424pp.

1.8.16 ———. *Biblical Archaeologist Reader.* Vol. 4. Sheffield: Almond, 1983. 390pp.

1.8.17 Coogan, Michael D., Cheryl J. Exum, and Lawrence E. Stager, eds. *Scripture and Other Artifacts: Essays on the Bible and Archaeology in Honor of Philip J. King.* Louisville: Westminster John Knox, 1994. 452pp.

1.8.18 Currid, John D. *Doing Archaeology in the Land of the Bible: A Basic Guide.* Grand Rapids: Baker, 1999. 666pp.

1.8.19 Dever, William G. *What Did the Biblical Writers Know and When Did They Know It? What Archaeology Can Tell Us about the Reality of Ancient Israel.* Grand Rapids: Eerdmans, 2001. 275pp.

1.8.20 Finegan, Jack. *The Archaeology of the New Testament: The Life of Jesus and the Beginning of the Early Church.* Rev. ed. Princeton, N.J.: Princeton University Press, 1992. 409pp.

1.8.21 Fritz, Volkmar. *An Introduction to Biblical Archaeology.* Journal for the Study of the Old Testament Supplement Series 172. Sheffield: JSOT, 1994. 223pp.

1.8.22 Lance, H. Darrell. *The Old Testament and the Archaeologist.* Guides to Biblical Scholarship. Philadelphia: Fortress, 1981. 98pp.

1.8.23 Meyers, Eric M., ed. *The Oxford Encyclopedia of Archaeology in the Near East.* 5 vols. Oxford: Oxford University Press, 1997. 2592pp.

1.8.24 Negev, Avraham, ed. *Archaeological Encyclopedia of the Holy Land.* Revised by Shimon Gibson. New York: Continuum, 2001. 559pp.

1.8.25 Rast, Walter E. *Through the Ages in Palestinian Archaeology: An Introductory Handbook.* Philadelphia: Trinity Press International, 1992. 221pp.

1.8.26 Schoville, Keith. *Biblical Archaeology in Focus.* Grand Rapids: Baker, 1978. 511pp.

1.8.27 Stern, Ephraim. *Archaeology of the Land of the Bible.* Vol. 2. *The Assyrian, Babylonian, and Persian Periods (733–332 B.C.E.).* Anchor Bible Reference Library. New York: Doubleday, 2001. 592pp.

1.8.28 Thomas, D. Winton, ed. *Archaeology and Old Testament Study.* Oxford: Clarendon, 1967. 493pp.

1.8.29 Thompson, J. A. *The Bible and Archaeology.* Grand Rapids: Eerdmans, 1981. 474pp.

1.8.30 Wright, G. Ernest. *Biblical Archaeology.* Rev. ed. Philadelphia: Westminster, 1962. 291pp.

1.8.31 Wright, G. Ernest, and David Noel Freedman. *The Biblical Archaeologist Reader.* Vol. 1. New York: Doubleday, 1961–1970. 342pp.

1.9 Concordances to the English Bible

H I G H L Y   R E C O M M E N D E D

1.9.1 Goodrick, Edward W., and John R. Kohlenberger III. *Zondervan NIV Exhaustive Concordance.* 2d ed. Grand Rapids: Zondervan, 1999. 1647pp.

Only concordance based on the NIV that includes every occurrence of every word. Contains dictionary index that defines every Hebrew, Aramaic, and Greek words in the Bible, including frequency counts for each original language word and for each of its English translations. Uses numbering system developed by the authors (which seeks to replace the old Strong's numbering system), and indexes this new numbering system to Strong's.

1.9.2 Metzger, Bruce M. *New Revised Standard Version Exhaustive Concordance.* Nashville: Thomas Nelson, 1991. 1828pp. + indexes.

Compiled by chairman of the NRSV translation committee, contains every occurrence of every word in the NRSV. Includes topical index, referencing more than eight thousand biblical persons, places, things, concepts, events, and doctrines. Comparable to Kohlenberger's *NRSV Concordance* (§1.9.8), but the topical index in this volume is more complete. A deficiency in both Metzger and Kohlenberger is that neither employs a system whereby the reader can identify the Greek, Hebrew, or Aramaic word lying behind the NRSV translation.

1.9.3 Strong, James. *The New Strong's Exhaustive Concordance to the Bible.* Nashville: Thomas Nelson, 1996. 1908pp. + indexes.

For over a century the most widely used concordance to the King James Version. Contains the well-known Strong's numbering system, which assigns a number to each Greek, Hebrew, or Aramaic word used in the Bible, with the result that the reader can, by using the index provided, locate passages where individual Greek, Hebrew, or Aramaic words appear (although this index contains some gaps and errors). Since several significant original-language reference works are coded to the Strong's numbers, this concordance can serve as the basis for the use of these original-language resources by persons who do not know Greek or Hebrew. This edition is "new" only in format and contains no substantial revisions over against earlier editions.

1.9.4 Thomas, Robert L., and W. Don Wilkins. *New American Standard Exhaustive Concordance of the Bible.* Updated ed. Anaheim, Calif.: Lockman Foundation Publications, 1988. 1582pp.

Contains every occurrence of every word in the updated NASB, indexed to Greek, Hebrew, and Aramaic words lying behind the English translation, using Strong's numbering system. Includes Greek and Hebrew-Aramaic dictionary.

A L S O   S I G N I F I C A N T

1.9.5 Cruden, Alexander. *Cruden's Complete Concordance to the Old and New Testaments.* Peabody, Mass.: Hendrickson, 1988. 783pp. (Originally published in 1737.)

1.9.6 Ellison, John W. *Nelson's Complete Concordance of the Revised Standard Version of the Bible.* New York: Nelson, 1957. 2157pp.

1.9.7 Hazard, M. C. *A Complete Concordance to the American Standard Version of the Holy Bible.* New York: Thomas Nelson, 1922. 1234pp.

1.9.8 Kohlenberger, John R., III. *The NRSV Concordance: Unabridged.* Grand Rapids: Zondervan, 1991. 1483pp. + indexes.

1.9.9 Whitaker, Richard E. *RSV Analytical Concordance.* Grand Rapids: Eerdmans, 1988. 1548pp.

1.9.10 Young, Robert. *Analytical Concordance to the Bible.* Rev. ed. Nashville: Thomas Nelson, 1982. 1090pp. + indexes.

1.10 Topical Concordances

H I G H L Y   R E C O M M E N D E D

1.10.1 Day, A. Colin. *Roget's Thesaurus of the Bible.* San Francisco: Harper, 1992. 927pp.

Employs Roget's familiar category concept (known to most readers through *Roget's International Thesaurus*) that groups together related subjects (both similar and opposite). Readers can use subject categories to find relevant biblical references, or can use the scripture index to find appropriate subject categories. Not tied to one translation, but based on Day's own paraphrase, representing his eclectic examination of several versions (and of the Greek and Hebrew). Not as complete in either categories or citations as Kohlen-berger's *Nave's,* but since even Kohlenberger's volume is not absolutely com-plete it is well to supplement Kohlenberger's volume with this one.

1.10.2 Kohlenberger, John R., III. *Zondervan NIV Nave's Topical Bible.* Grand Rapids: Zondervan, 1992. 1152pp.

Kohlenberger's extensive revision and expansion of the classic produced by Orville J. Nave more than a century ago, it is the most complete topical con-cordance to the Bible in existence. Invaluable for locating all biblical passages pertaining to a given topic.

ALSO SIGNIFICANT

1.10.3 Hitchcock, Roswell D. *Baker's Topical Bible.* Rev. ed. Grand Rapids: Baker, 1975. 685pp.

1.10.4 Joy, Charles R. *Harper's Topical Concordance.* Rev. ed. New York: Harper & Row, 1962. 628pp.

1.10.5 Viening, Edward, ed. *The Zondervan Topical Bible.* Grand Rapids: Zondervan, 1969. 1114pp.

1.11 Bible Dictionaries

HIGHLY RECOMMENDED

1.11.1 Achtemeier, Paul J., ed. *The HarperCollins Bible Dictionary.* San Fran-cisco: HarperSanFrancisco, 1996. 1256pp.

Commissioned by the Society of Biblical Literature, and containing 3700 ar-ticles by leading Protestant, Catholic, and Jewish scholars, probably the most comprehensive and authoritative single-volume Bible dictionary. Never-theless, it shares with all one-volume dictionaries the significant limitations of breadth and detail over against the multivolume ones.

1.11.2 Bromiley, Geoffrey W., ed. *International Standard Bible Encyclopedia.* Rev. ed. 4 vols. Grand Rapids: Eerdmans, 1979–1988. 1005/1175/1060/1211pp.

First revision since 1929 of the classic encyclopedia that originally appeared in 1915. Although fully revised, it does include some of the monumental ar-ticles from earlier editions. Some entries include very selective bibliographies.

Along with the *Anchor Bible Dictionary* (§1.11.3), the most useful dictionary available. Generally more conservative and often more concise than the *Anchor.*

1.11.3 Freedman, David Noel, ed. *The Anchor Bible Dictionary.* 6 vols. New York: Doubleday, 1992. 1232/1100/1135/1162/1230/1176pp.

Almost universally considered the standard multivolume Bible dictionary in English. Contributors include the most recognized scholars in the world, and represent a broad theological spectrum. All articles of significant length include brief but helpful bibliographies. Although the most comprehensive dictionary in English, it evinces some notable omissions. It is therefore well to supplement this dictionary with others, especially the *International Standard Bible Encyclopedia* (§1.11.2).

1.11.4 Freedman, David Noel, ed. *Eerdmans Dictionary of the Bible.* Grand Rapids: Eerdmans, 2000. 1425pp.

Contains five thousand articles, written by approximately six hundred scholars, although contributors include many graduate students along with some of the world's most recognized authorities. Comparable to *HarperCollins* (§1.11.1), and along with the latter the most current, wide-ranging, and generally useful single-volume dictionary. The quality of the articles, however, is more uneven than is the case with *HarperCollins.*

1.11.5 Tenney, Merrill C. *The Zondervan Pictorial Encyclopedia of the Bible.* 5 vols. Grand Rapids: Zondervan, 1975. 1056/854/1015/964/1093pp.

Informative, comprehensive, and thoroughly evangelical. Gives particular emphasis to the key themes and doctrines of the Bible. Describes varying viewpoints on major theological and historical issues and seeks to evaluate these viewpoints fairly, doing so from a conservative Protestant perspective. Major articles include rather full bibliographies. Not revised since it first appeared in 1975; some articles should be supplemented with more recent treatments.

A L S O   S I G N I F I C A N T

1.11.6 Browning, W. R. F. *A Dictionary of the Bible.* New York: Oxford University Press, 1997. 423pp.

1.11.7 Butler, Trent C., ed. *Holman Bible Dictionary.* Nashville: Holman, 1991. 1450pp.

1.11.8 Buttrick, George Arthur, ed. *The Interpreter's Dictionary of the Bible.* 4 vols. plus *Supplementary Volume.* Nashville: Abingdon, 1962, 1976. 876/1030/878/964/998pp.

1.11.9   Douglas, J. D., and N. Hillyer, eds. *The Illustrated Bible Dictionary.* 3 vols. Downers Grove, Ill.: InterVarsity, 1986. 1726pp.

1.11.10 Elwell, Walter A., ed. *Baker Encyclopedia of the Bible.* 2 vols. Grand Rapids: Baker, 1988. 2210pp.

1.11.11 Hastings, James, ed. *Dictionary of the Bible.* 5 vols. Edinburgh: T&T Clark, 1898. 864/870/896/994/936pp.

1.11.12 Marshall, I. Howard, A. R. Millard, and J. I. Packer, eds. *New Bible Dictionary.* 3d ed. Downers Grove, Ill.: InterVarsity, 1996. 1298pp.

1.11.13 Mills, Watson E., ed. *Mercer Dictionary of the Bible.* Macon, Ga.: Mercer University Press, 1990. 993pp.

1.11.14 Pfeiffer, Charles F., Howard F. Vos, and John Rea, eds. *Wycliffe Bible Dictionary.* Peabody, Mass.: Hendrickson, 1998. 1851pp. Repr. of *Wycliffe Bible Encyclopedia.* Chicago: Moody, 1975.

1.12 Exegetical Method/Hermeneutics

H I G H L Y   R E C O M M E N D E D

1.12.1   Caird, G. B. *The Language and Imagery of the Bible.* Philadelphia Westminster, 1980. 280pp.

A classic exploration of the ways in which an understanding of the function of language informs the interpretation of Scripture. Unlike many current studies of biblical linguistics that are based on recent, and in some cases questionable, trends, this work moves out from established and solid linguistic research.

1.12.2   Carson, D. A. *Exegetical Fallacies.* 2d ed. Grand Rapids: Baker, 1996. 148pp.

Practical and eminently usable discussion of the most common exegetical mistakes in the form of word-study fallacies, grammatical fallacies, logical fallacies, and presuppositional and historical fallacies. Indispensable for every seminary student, pastor, and teacher.

1.12.3   Coggins, R. J., and J. L. Houlden, eds. *A Dictionary of Biblical Interpretation.* Philadelphia: Trinity Press International, 1990. 748pp.

Deals with the ways the Bible has been interpreted throughout history and today. The articles, written by distinguished biblical scholars from Europe and

North America and representing a cross-section of theological perspectives, are devoted to the history of interpretation of each book of the Bible, various interpretive methods and techniques, the main phases of biblical interpretation, major interpretive schools and movements, and significant interpreters of the Bible, both ancient and modern. Articles conclude with brief bibliographies.

1.12.4 Cotterell, Peter, and Max Turner. *Linguistics and Biblical Interpretation.* Downers Grove, Ill.: InterVarsity, 1989. 348pp.

Collaborative project by a linguist and an exegete, this book provides a solid introduction to the most current insights into the exegesis of Scripture from the perspective of contemporary linguistics. Deals with concept of meaning, and particularly meaning of words; significance to be assigned to author, text, and reader in pursuit of meaning of biblical passages; and significance of role of the broader discourse in the interpretation of a specific passage. By giving attention to newer developments in linguistics, it complements Caird's fine classic treatment (§1.12.1).

1.12.5 Hayes, John H., and Carl R. Holladay. *Biblical Exegesis: A Beginner's Handbook.* Rev. ed. Atlanta: John Knox, 1987. 159pp.

Written by leading Old Testament and New Testament scholars, probably the most recognized basic introduction to exegetical method of the Bible as a whole. Provides orientation to the major aspects of interpretation from a mainstream critical approach. Although the revised edition gives some attention to the emerging methods as of 1987—e.g., rhetorical criticism and canonical criticism—it focuses on the traditional grammatical- and historical-critical approaches.

1.12.6 McKenzie, Steven L., and Stephen R. Haynes, eds. *To Each Its Own Meaning: An Introduction to Biblical Criticisms and Their Application.* Louisville: Westminster John Knox, 1993. 251pp.

Informative introduction to the most significant methods of biblical criticism, giving attention to both historical and literary approaches. Each chapter is written by a leading practitioner of the method and addresses five issues: (1) description, history, and assumptions; (2) relation to other methods; (3) examples of the application of the method to specific passages; (4) drawbacks; (5) suggested further reading. Chapters suffer somewhat from brevity, but still the most useful introduction to the range of contemporary approaches.

1.12.7 Osborne, Grant R. *The Hermeneutical Spiral.* Downers Grove, Ill.: InterVarsity, 1992. 499pp.

The most comprehensive, informed, and readable introduction to biblical interpretation from an evangelical perspective. Insists that biblical hermeneutics involve a constant spiral from text to contemporary application with the result that the interpreter progressively comes closer to the intended meaning of the biblical author. Deals with all major aspects of hermeneutics but gives special attention to the role of genre and to applied hermeneutics (i.e., biblical, systematic, contextual, and homiletical theology). Two appendixes address contemporary philosophical challenges to the notion of "fixed meanings" in biblical texts.

1.12.8 Thiselton, Anthony C. *New Horizons in Hermeneutics: The Theory and Practice of Transforming Biblical Reading.* Grand Rapids: Zondervan, 1992. 703pp.

A philosophically and historically informed textbook in advanced hermeneutics, and yet one that is concerned with the use of the Bible in the church and with practical questions about how readers engage biblical texts. Describes and evaluates all the major theoretical models and approaches in contemporary hermeneutics and shows how these models find expression in specific approaches to biblical passages and issues in biblical interpretation. Indispensable for a thorough understanding of contemporary hermeneutics.

1.12.9 Traina, Robert A. *Methodical Bible Study: A New Approach to Hermeneutics.* New York: Ganis & Harris, 1952. 269pp.

The standard resource for the "inductive method" of biblical study that presents a practical, comprehensive, and holistic approach to the study of the Bible, and one that is methodologically rigorous in its attempt to allow the Bible to speak on its own terms. A thorough manual of Bible study that moves from observation through interpretation to the evaluation and application of passages. Concerned also with correlating the teaching of various passages into a broader biblical theology. Now fifty years old, the volume is somewhat dated, but still usable and very helpful.

ALSO SIGNIFICANT

1.12.10 Alter, Robert. *The World of Biblical Literature.* San Francisco: Harper, 1993. 225pp.

1.12.11 Barr, James. *The Semantics of Biblical Language.* London: SCM, 1961. 313pp.

1.12.12 Bartholomew, Colin, Colin Greene, and Karl Möller, eds. *Renewing Biblical Interpretation.* Grand Rapids: Zondervan, 2000. 366pp.

1.12.13 Barton, John, ed. *The Cambridge Companion to Biblical Interpretation.* Cambridge: Cambridge University Press, 1998. 338pp.

1.12.14 Dockery, David S. *Biblical Interpretation Then and Now: Contemporary Hermeneutics in the Light of the Early Church.* Grand Rapids: Baker, 1992. 247pp.

1.12.15 Dockery, David S., Kenneth A. Mathews, and Robert B. Sloan. *Foundations for Biblical Interpretation: A Complete Library for Tools and Resources.* Nashville: Broadman & Holman, 1994. 614pp.

1.12.16 Fee, Gordon D., and Douglas Stuart. *How to Read the Bible for All Its Worth.* 2d ed. Grand Rapids: Zondervan, 1993. 265pp.

1.12.17 Goldingay, John. *Models for the Interpretation of Scripture.* Grand Rapids: Eerdmans, 1994. 328pp.

1.12.18 Gorman, Michael J. *Elements of Biblical Exegesis: A Basic Guide for Students and Ministers.* Peabody, Mass.: Hendrickson, 2001. 239pp.

1.12.19 Kaiser, Otto, and Werner Georg Kümmel. *Exegetical Method: A Student's Handbook.* Rev. ed. New York: Seabury, 1981. 115pp.

1.12.20 Kaiser, Walter C., Jr. *Toward an Exegetical Theology: Biblical Exegesis for Preaching and Teaching.* Grand Rapids: Baker, 1981. 268pp.

1.12.21 Kaiser, Walter C., Jr., and Moisés Silva. *An Introduction to Biblical Hermeneutics: The Search for Meaning.* Grand Rapids: Zondervan, 1994. 298pp.

1.12.22 Klein, William W., Craig L. Blomberg, and Robert L. Hubbard. *Introduction to Biblical Interpretation.* Dallas: Word, 1993. 518pp.

1.12.23 Kuist, Howard T. *These Words upon Thy Heart: Scripture and the Christian Response.* Richmond, Va.: John Knox, 1947. 189pp.

1.12.24 Krentz, Edgar. *The Historical-Critical Method.* Guides to Biblical Scholarship. Philadelphia: Fortress, 1975. 88pp.

1.12.25 Longman, Tremper, III. *Literary Approaches to Biblical Interpretation.* Foundations of Contemporary Interpretation 3. Grand Rapids: Zondervan, 1987. 164pp.

1.12.26 McCown, Wayne, and James Massey, eds. *God's Word for Today: An Inquiry into Hermeneutics from a Biblical Theological Perspective.* Wesleyan Theological Perspectives 2. Anderson, Ind.: Warner, 1982. 264pp.

1.12.27 McKim, Donald K., ed. *A Guide to Contemporary Hermeneutics: Major Trends in Biblical Interpretation.* Grand Rapids: Eerdmans, 1986. 385pp.

1.12.28 McKnight, Edgar V. *The Bible and the Reader: An Introduction to Literary Criticism.* Philadelphia: Fortress, 1985. 147pp.

1.12.29 Mickelsen, A. Berkeley, and Alvera M. Mickelsen. *Understanding Scripture: How to Read and Study the Bible.* Peabody, Mass.: Hendrickson, 1992. 141pp.

1.12.30 Morgan, Robert, and John Barton. *Biblical Interpretation.* Oxford Bible Series. Oxford: Oxford University Press, 1988. 342pp.

1.12.31 Mulholland, M. Robert, Jr. *Shaped by the Word: The Power of Scripture in Spiritual Formation.* Rev. ed. Nashville: Upper Room, 2000. 176pp.

1.12.32 Ramm, Bernard L. *Protestant Biblical Interpretation: A Textbook of Hermeneutics for Conservative Protestants.* 3d ed. Grand Rapids: Baker, 1970. 298pp.

1.12.33 Ricoeur, Paul. *Essays on Biblical Interpretation.* Philadelphia: Fortress, 1980. 182pp.

1.12.34 Segovia, Fernando F., and Mary Ann Tolbert, eds. *Reading from This Place: Social Location and Biblical Interpretation in Global Perspective.* 2 vols. Minneapolis: Fortress, 1995. 321/365pp.

1.12.35 Silva, Moisés. *Biblical Words and Their Meaning: An Introduction to Lexical Semantics.* Grand Rapids: Zondervan, 1983. 201pp.

1.12.36 ———. *God, Language, and Scripture: Reading the Bible in Light of General Linguistics.* Foundations of Contemporary Hermeneutics. Grand Rapids: Zondervan, 1990. 160pp.

1.12.37 Soulen, Richard N. *Handbook of Biblical Criticism.* 3d ed. Louisville: Westminster John Knox, 2001. 264pp.

1.12.38 Sternberg, Meir. *The Poetics of Biblical Narrative: Ideological Literature and the Drama of Reading.* Bloomington: Indiana University Press, 1985. 580pp.

1.12.39 Stuhlmacher, Peter. *Historical Criticism and the Theological Interpretation of Scripture.* Philadelphia: Fortress, 1977. 93pp.

1.12.40 Tate, W. Randolph. *Biblical Interpretation: An Integrated Approach.* Rev. ed. Peabody, Mass.: Hendrickson, 1997. 276pp.

1.12.41 Terry, Milton S. *Biblical Hermeneutics.* New York: Eaton and Mains, 1911. 782pp.

1.12.42 Thompson, David L. *Bible Study That Works*. Rev. ed. Nappanee, Ind.: Evangel, 1994. 128pp.

1.12.43 Vanhoozer, Kevin J. *Is There a Meaning in This Text? The Bible, the Reader, and the Morality of Literary Knowledge*. Grand Rapids: Zondervan, 1998. 496pp.

1.12.44 Wink, Walter. *Transforming Bible Study: Completely Revised and Expanded*. Nashville: Abingdon, 1980. 176pp.

1.13 Biblical Theology

See also OLD TESTAMENT: EXEGETICAL METHOD/HERMENEUTICS (§2.13); NEW TESTAMENT: EXEGETICAL METHOD/HERMENEUTICS (§4.12)

H I G H L Y   R E C O M M E N D E D

1.13.1 Alexander, T. Desmond, Brian S. Rosner, D. A. Carson, and Graeme Goldsworthy, eds. *New Dictionary of Biblical Theology: Exploring the Unity and Diversity of Scripture*. Downers Grove, Ill.: InterVarsity, 2000. 866pp.

The most comprehensive current dictionary on biblical theology from an evangelical perspective. Part 1 includes twelve major articles dealing with key issues of biblical theology; part 2 contains articles on major sections of the Bible as well as on the theology of the individual biblical books; and part 3 consists of articles on major biblical themes. Emphasizes the unity of the Bible's theology over against the tendency in some circles to stress diversity and perceived disunity between the biblical witnesses. The breadth of issues treated requires that many of the articles be given brief and somewhat cursory treatment. Written with an eye toward teaching and preaching within the context of the church.

1.13.2 Barr, James. *The Concept of Biblical Theology: An Old Testament Perspective*. Minneapolis: Fortress, 1999. 715pp.

Offers a comprehensive overview of biblical theology by tracing the development of the discipline of biblical theology, describing and critiquing the major contributors (e.g., von Rad, Childs, Brueggemann), and providing his own analysis of such key issues as the typologies for doing biblical theology, the role of the apocrypha and pseudepigrapha, the relationship between the OT and NT, and the biblical theology movement. As its subtitle suggests, gives relatively greater attention to the OT than the NT. Moreover, Barr is stronger in critique than in offering his own compelling program. Nevertheless, the best critical description of the history of biblical theology.

1.13.3   Bauer, Johannes Baptist, ed. *Encyclopedia of Biblical Theology: The Complete Sacramentum Verbi.* Rev. ed. New York: Crossroad, 1981. 1141pp.

Articles discuss the theologically most significant biblical words, with the intention of revealing the modes of thought of the biblical writers themselves. Contributors are among the most prominent scholars in the German-speaking world. Comparable in quality and in purpose to the *New Dictionary of Biblical Theology* (§1.13.1) but contributors represent critical German scholarship rather than American and British evangelicalism. Moreover, since this volume contains articles dealing only with biblical concepts it is more focused than the *New Dictionary,* and its individual articles tend to be more comprehensive and detailed.

1.13.4   Bright, John. *The Kingdom of God.* Nashville: Abingdon, 1953. 288pp.

This prominent Old Testament scholar compellingly argues that the central and unifying theological concept in the whole of the Bible is the kingdom of God. He presents an articulate, cohesive, and insightful exposition of this concept. A model for the study of a biblical concept throughout the canon.

1.13.5   Childs, Brevard S. *Biblical Theology of the Old and New Testaments: Theological Reflection on the Christian Bible.* Minneapolis: Fortress, 1993. 745pp.

The first comprehensive biblical theology to appear in a generation. Argues that the fundamental issue in biblical theology is the relationship between the testaments, and that both testaments bear witness to Jesus Christ, but each in its distinctive way. Introductory chapters outline the history of biblical theology and set forth a new program for doing biblical theology. Then follow examples of exegesis done in the service of biblical theology and discussions of the major themes of the Christian Bible. The volume ends with discussion of what is involved in a holistic theological reading of the Christian scriptures. The most significant recent contribution to biblical theology.

1.13.6   Cullmann, Oscar. *Salvation in History.* New York: Harper & Row, 1967. 352pp.

Written by a prominent New Testament scholar who emphasized the role of "salvation history," i.e., that the history of God's redemptive acts on behalf of Israel coming to culmination in Jesus Christ is the central concern of the whole of biblical revelation. As such, the historical manifestation of Christ is the center and defining point of all history and of all human existence. This book offers the most compelling presentation of the salvation-history model of biblical theology, and is an excellent conceptual synthesis of the entire biblical revelation.

1.13.7 Watson, Francis. *Truth and Text: Redefining Biblical Theology.* Grand Rapids: Eerdmans, 1997. 344pp.

Rejects the tendency in recent times to divorce biblical studies from systematic theology, arguing that biblical theology must be an interdisciplinary approach that maintains the essential distinctives of the OT, the NT, and systematics, but at the same time relates them in a holistic process of ascertaining Christian truth. From this perspective, Watson discusses in the first part of the volume certain specific issues in hermeneutics from an explicitly theological perspective, and in the second part he explores the Christian theological use of the OT. Challenging, groundbreaking work pertaining to the way in which the Bible must function theologically in the church.

ALSO SIGNIFICANT

1.13.8 Achtemeier, Paul J., and Elizabeth Achtemeier. *The Old Testament Roots of Our Faith.* Rev. ed. Peabody, Mass.: Hendrickson, 1995. 142pp.

1.13.9 Burrows, Millar. *An Outline of Biblical Theology.* Philadelphia: Westminster, 1946. 380pp.

1.13.10 Childs, Brevard S. *Biblical Theology: A Proposal.* Facets. Minneapolis: Fortress, 2002. 96pp.

1.13.11 ———. *Biblical Theology in Crisis.* Philadelphia: Fortress, 1970. 255pp.

1.13.12 Gerhardsson, Birger. *The Ethos of the Bible.* Philadelphia: Fortress, 1981. 152pp.

1.13.13 Hafemann, Scott J., ed. *Biblical Theology: Retrospect and Prospect.* Downers Grove, Ill.: InterVarsity, 2002. 304pp.

1.13.14 Hanson, Paul D. *The Diversity of Scripture: A Theological Interpretation.* Overtures to Biblical Theology. Philadelphia: Fortress, 1982. 157pp.

1.13.15 ———. *Dynamic Transcendence: The Correlation of Confessional Heritage and Contemporary Experience in a Biblical Model of Divine Activity.* Philadelphia: Fortress, 1978. 109pp.

1.13.16 Kraftchick, Steven J., Charles D. Myers Jr., and Ben C. Ollenburger, eds. *Biblical Theology: Problems and Perspectives, in Honor of J. Christiaan Beker.* Nashville: Abingdon, 1995. 336pp.

1.13.17 Léon-Dufour, Xavier. *Dictionary of Biblical Theology.* 2d ed. New York: Seabury, 1973. 617pp.

1.13.18 O'Collins, Gerald, and Daniel Kendall. *The Bible for Theology: Ten Principles for the Theological Use of Scripture.* New York: Paulist, 1997. 208pp.

1.13.19 Reumann, John. *The Promise and Practice of Biblical Theology.* Philadelphia: Fortress, 1991. 214pp.

1.13.20 Reventlow, Henning Graf. *Problems of Biblical Theology in the Twentieth Century.* Philadelphia: Fortress, 1986. 188pp.

1.13.21 Smart, James D. *The Past, Present, and Future of Biblical Theology.* Philadelphia: Westminster, 1979. 162pp.

1.13.22 Stuhlmacher, Peter. *How to Do Biblical Theology.* Allison Park, Pa.: Pickwick, 1995. 95pp.

1.13.23 Terrien, Samuel. *The Elusive Presence: Toward a New Biblical Theology.* Religious Perspectives 26. San Francisco: Harper & Row, 1978. 511pp.

1.13.24 Turner, George Allen. *The Vision Which Transforms: Is Christian Perfection Scriptural?* Kansas City, Mo.: Beacon Hill, 1964. 348pp.

1.13.25 Vos, Geerhardus. *Biblical Theology: Old and New Testaments.* Grand Rapids: Eerdmans, 1948. 426pp.

1.13.26 Watson, Francis. *Text, Church, and World: Biblical Interpretation in Theological Perspective.* Grand Rapids: Eerdmans, 1994. 366pp.

1.14 Biblical Ethics

HIGHLY RECOMMENDED

1.14.1 Birch, Bruce C., and Larry L. Rasmussen. *Bible and Ethics in the Christian Life.* Rev. ed. Minneapolis: Augsburg, 1989. 239pp.

The result of collaboration between an ethicist (Rasmussen) and a biblical scholar (Birch), this volume attempts to bridge the gap between biblical studies and ethics by clarifying the major issues that are involved and by offering specific guidance for the church's use of the Bible for its ethical decisions. Deals with the task and process of using the Bible for ethics rather than discussing specific contemporary ethical issues. A most helpful, readable introduction.

1.14.2 McDonald, J. I. H. *Biblical Interpretation and Christian Ethics.* Cambridge: Cambridge University Press, 1993. 305pp.

Probes the issues involved in using the Bible for ethical decision making by tracing the history of the enterprise from the liberalism of the eighteenth and nineteenth centuries, through the emphasis on an eschatological ethic that was prominent at the beginning of the twentieth century, to the present stress on the ways in which the cultural and personal participation of the reader of the Bible fundamentally determines how one can and should use the Bible as a guide for ethics. Includes many examples that employ specific ethical issues. Assumes something of an evolutionary model according to which the earlier periods are judged in light of the most recent developments and these recent developments are given the greatest approval. Nevertheless, extremely helpful critical review of the history of the relation between biblical interpretation and ethics, and one that greatly illumines the task of deriving ethics from Scripture.

1.14.3 Siker, Jeffrey S. *Scripture and Ethics: Twentieth-Century Portraits.* New York: Oxford, 1997. 294pp.

Describes how the Bible has actually functioned in theological ethics in the twentieth century by exploring how eight of the century's most influential theologians have appropriated Scripture for ethics; these include Reinhold Niebuhr, H. Richard Niebuhr, Bernard Häring, Paul Ramsey, Stanley Hauerwas, Gustavo Gutierrez, James Cone, and Rosemary Radford Reuther. In each case Siker explores which biblical passages were used, the ways in which these texts were employed, the view of the Bible's authority, the hermeneutic employed, and the practical ethical results. Each chapter includes critical evaluation. Although one might quibble about the choice of theologians selected in this book, still it is helpful not only as historical review but as the basis for clarification of the issues and for the constructing of one's own approach. Might be supplemented by Spohn's volume (§1.14.9), which includes other prominent theologians (e.g., Bonhoeffer) but treats them more briefly and less critically than does Siker's approach.

ALSO SIGNIFICANT

1.14.4 Bretzke, James T. *Bibliography on Scripture and Christian Ethics.* Studies in Religion and Theology. Lewiston, Pa.: Mellen, 1997. 364pp.

1.14.5   Brown, William P. *The Ethos of the Cosmos: The Genesis of Moral Imagination in the Bible.* Grand Rapids: Eerdmans, 1999. 458pp.

1.14.6   Everding, H. Edward, Jr., and Dana W. Wilbanks. *Decision-Making and the Bible.* Valley Forge, Pa.: Judson, 1975. 160pp.

1.14.7   Ogletree, Thomas W. *The Use of the Bible in Christian Ethics.* Philadelphia: Westminster, 1983. 220pp.

1.14.8   Sleeper, C. Freeman. *The Bible and the Moral Life.* Louisville: Westminster John Knox, 1992. 181pp.

1.14.9   Spohn, William C. *What Are They Saying about Scripture and Ethics?* Rev. ed. New York: Paulist, 1995. 142pp.

1.14.10 Swartley, Willard M. *Slavery, Sabbath, War, and Women: Case Issues in Biblical Interpretation.* Scottsdale, Pa.: Herald, 1983. 366pp.

1.14.11 Webb, William J. *Slaves, Women, and Homosexuals: Exploring the Hermeneutics of Cultural Analysis.* Downers Grove, Ill.: InterVarsity, 2001. 320pp.

1.15 Bible Commentaries: One-Volume

H I G H L Y   R E C O M M E N D E D

1.15.1   Brown, Raymond E., Joseph A. Fitzmyer, and Roland E. Murphy, eds. *The New Jerome Biblical Commentary.* Englewood Cliffs, N.J.: Prentice-Hall, 1990. 1484pp.

The best single-volume commentary available from the Roman Catholic tradition, with articles written by leading Roman Catholic scholars. Includes introductory topical articles dealing with background issues. Interpretations employ critical approaches, especially source, form, redaction, and textual criticism, and give attention to the range of interpretations among Roman Catholic scholars. More technical and with less emphasis on theology and application than is the case with most single-volume commentaries, but the consistently high quality of the scholarship makes this a most impressive and, in respect to critical and historical issues, helpful volume.

1.15.2   Carpenter, Eugene, and Wayne McCown, eds. *Asbury Bible Commentary.* Grand Rapids: Zondervan, 1992. 1246pp.

Represents the best current biblical scholarship from the Wesleyan tradition. Although the articles are somewhat uneven in quality, most of them are (given the limits of space) remarkably insightful in their exposition of the theological message of the text and are useful even to students outside of the Wesleyan tradition. The general articles stress theological and hermeneutical issues rather than historical or cultural ones; especially helpful is the discussion on the place and functions of Scripture (in the Wesleyan tradition).

1.15.3 Mays, James Luther, ed. *HarperCollins Bible Commentary*. Rev. ed. San Francisco: HarperSanFrancisco, 2000. 1203pp.

Commissioned by the Society of Biblical Literature, this volume is probably the most authoritative single-volume commentary in existence. Includes commentary on the Old Testament Apocrypha. Contains helpful background articles on the literary, cultural, and historical context of the Bible. Somewhat less technical and more concerned to ascertain the essential meaning and function of passages than is *The New Jerome Biblical Commentary* (§1.15.1), but not necessarily more theological than the latter.

ALSO SIGNIFICANT

1.15.4 Bruce, F. F. *The International Bible Commentary with the New International Version*. Grand Rapids: Zondervan, 1986. 1269pp.

1.15.5 Carson, D. A., R. T. France, Gordon J. Wenham, J. A. Motyer, eds. *New Bible Commentary: 21st Century Edition*. Downers Grove, Ill.: InterVarsity, 1994. 1455pp.

1.15.6 Elwell, Walter A., ed. *Evangelical Commentary on the Bible*. Grand Rapids: Baker, 1989. 1229pp.

1.15.7 Farmer, William R., ed. *International Bible Commentary: A Catholic and Ecumenical Commentary for the Twenty-first Century*. Collegeville, Minn.: Liturgical Press, 1998. 1918pp.

1.15.8 Laymon, Charles M., ed. *The Interpreter's One-Volume Commentary on the Bible*. Nashville: Abingdon, 1971. 1386pp.

1.15.9 Mills, Watson E., and Richard F. Wilson, eds. *Mercer Commentary on the Bible*. Macon, Ga.: Mercer University Press, 1995. 1347pp.

1.15.10 Peake, Arthur S., ed. *A Commentary on the Bible*. New York: Thomas Nelson, 1920. 1014pp.

1.15.11 Radmacher, Earl D., ed. *Nelson's New Illustrated Bible Commentary.* Nashville: Thomas Nelson, 1999. 1804pp.

1.16 Bible Commentaries: Multivolume

H I G H L Y   R E C O M M E N D E D

1.16.1 Calvin, John. *Calvin's Commentaries.* 45 vols. in 22. Grand Rapids: Baker, 1979. (Originally published in Latin and French, ca. 1550–1555.) Volumes average 500pp.

Bible students should consult commentaries from a variety of periods of the church, and Calvin was the most authoritative, comprehensive, informed, and insightful commentator of the Reformation period. Calvin is uniformly clear and concise, with a keen theological interest and a pastoral concern.

1.16.2 Gaebelein, Frank E., and J. D. Douglas, eds. *The Expositor's Bible Commentary.* 12 vols. Grand Rapids: Zondervan, 1979. Volumes average 600pp.

The most comprehensive and academically solid multivolume commentary from a thoroughly conservative evangelical perspective. Contributors represent both the Reformed and Wesleyan-Arminian traditions. The commentary stresses the basic meaning of passages by focusing on the significance of the original language (primarily in terms of lexicography, but also with some concern for grammatical structure and syntax), historical background, and relation to other biblical passages. Brief "notes" discuss more technical text-critical, terminological, hermeneutical, and theological issues. Little explicit attention given to theological implications or application.

1.16.3 Keck, Leander E., et al., eds. *The New Interpreter's Bible.* 12 vols. Nashville: Abingdon, 1994–2002. Volumes average 1000pp.

The most comprehensive and respected of the multivolume commentaries. Written by leading biblical scholars, contributions are readable and accessible to pastors and professional academicians alike. Includes comment on the apocryphal/deuterocanonical books. On each passage, provides "commentary" (exegetical "close reading" employing various methods, e.g., historical-critical, literary, sociological) and "reflection" (significance for contemporary faith and life). In contrast to the original edition of *The Interpreter's Bible* (§1.16.4), the reflection here grows directly out of what is said in the commentary. Contributors represent a broad spectrum of Christian traditions (including evangelical).

A L S O   S I G N I F I C A N T

1.16.4 Buttrick, George Arthur, ed. *The Interpreter's Bible (IB).* 12 vols. Nashville: Abingdon, 1952. Volumes average 1000pp. (Replaced by *The New Interpreter's Bible* [§1.16.3].)

1.16.5 Carter, Charles W., ed. *The Wesleyan Bible Commentary.* 7 vols. Grand Rapids: Eerdmans, 1964–1969. Volumes average 650pp.

1.16.6 Clarke, Adam. *Clarke's Commentary.* 8 vols. London: Butterworth, 1810–1825. Volumes average 1000pp.

1.16.7 Lange, John Peter, et al. *A Commentary on the Holy Scriptures: Critical, Doctrinal, and Homiletical.* Translated from the German, and edited, with additions, by Philip Schaff et al. 24 vols. New York: Scribners, 1865–1879. Volumes average 800pp.

1.16.8 Purkiser, W. T., Ralph Earle, and A. F. Harper, eds. *Beacon Bible Commentary.* 10 vols. Kansas City, Mo.: Beacon Hill, 1969. Volumes average 600pp.

1.17 Bible Commentaries: Series

H I G H L Y   R E C O M M E N D E D

1.17.1 Ancient Christian Commentary on Scripture (ACCS). Edited by Thomas C. Oden. 13 vols. presently available. Downers Grove, Ill.: InterVarsity, 1998–. Volumes average 225pp.

Recently scholars have recognized the value of ancient commentary, especially from the Fathers. Much of this material that has been unavailable or hard to find has now become accessible through this series. Each passage receives one or more brief quotations from the Fathers, with selection on the basis of depth of insight, value for theological instruction, "rhetorical power," representation of "consensual exegesis" of the early church, enrichment for preaching and teaching, and inclusion of commentators from various early Eastern, Western, and African churches. Each quote is referenced so that readers can examine it in its context. Volumes are appearing in rapid succession.

1.17.2 The Expositor's Bible. Edited by W. Robertson Nicoll. 25 vols. New York: Armstrong, 1903. Volumes average 400pp.

A classic work written by the most prominent British biblical scholars at the turn of the twentieth century. Combines the most solid exegetical insights with theological and pastoral concerns. Excellent for exposure to aspects of the text that might be missed by persons whose focus is determined almost exclusively by the framework of the twenty-first century.

1.17.3   International Theological Commentary (ITC). Edited by Fredrick Carlson Holmgren and George A. F. Knight. 28 vols. Grand Rapids: Eerdmans, 1983–1998. Volumes average 185pp.

Contributors represent critical scholars from twenty countries. After brief introduction to the biblical book with discussion of authorship, date, etc., commentary moves section by section, setting forth basic meaning of passage in its literary context, noting most significant exegetical and historical issues, but giving primary attention to theological meaning and contemporary significance. Responsible and reliable, but also brief and therefore tends toward either superficial or highly selective treatment.

1.17.4   The New American Commentary: An Exegetical and Theological Exposition of Holy Scripture (NAC). Edited by David S. Dockery. 31 vols. presently available. Nashville: Broadman, 1991–. Volumes average 450pp.

Contributors represent some of the most significant conservative biblical scholars from the Baptist tradition in America. Assumes inerrancy of Scripture. Emphasizes most important exegetical issues involving theological meaning of the text, which in turn leads to contemporary application and suggestions for preaching and teaching. Written primarily for pastors and interested laypersons. Footnotes reference major current works in biblical studies.

1.17.5   New International Biblical Commentary. Edited by Robert L. Hubbard Jr. and Robert K. Johnston. 28 vols. presently available (including all of New Testament). Peabody, Mass.: Hendrickson, 1988–. Volumes average 400pp.

Written by prominent biblical scholars who respect the text as the church's scripture and are concerned with preaching and teaching within the church. Directed primarily at general readers, with section-by-section comments discussing the basic meaning of the text in its literary, historical, and canonical contexts. Includes few brief technical notes on text-critical issues and language. Contains select bibliography.

1.17.6   The NIV Application Commentary. Edited by Terry Muck. 30 vols. presently available. Grand Rapids: Zondervan, 1994–. Volumes average 325pp.

Represents evangelical perspective, with many leading evangelical biblical scholars among the contributors. Attempts to assist readers in moving from original meaning to contemporary application in informed and responsible ways. Treats each passage in terms of "original significance" (original meaning derived from language, historical background, context, etc.), "bridging contexts" (which reflects on the process of applying the ancient passage to today's world), and "contemporary significance" (which identifies contemporary situations that are comparable to those encountered in the text and explores various possible applications). Generally very useful for teaching and preaching, though quality of both interpretation and application varies from volume to volume. Clearly written, accessible to nonspecialists.

A L S O   S I G N I F I C A N T

1.17.7   The Anchor Bible: A New Translation with Introduction and Commentary (AB). Edited by William Foxwell Albright and David Noel Freedman. Garden City, N.Y.: Doubleday, 1964–.

1.17.8   The Cambridge Bible Commentary: New English Bible (CBC). Edited by Peter R. Ackroyd, A. R. C. Leaney, and J. W. Packer. Cambridge: Cambridge University Press, 1963–1979.

1.17.9   Hermeneia: A Critical and Historical Commentary on the Bible. Edited by Frank Moore Cross and Helmut Koester. Minneapolis: Fortress, 1971–.

1.17.10 The International Critical Commentary (ICC). Original series edited by S. R. Driver, Alfred Plummer, and Charles A. Briggs, 1895–1951. New series edited by J. A. Emerton, C. E. B. Cranfield, and Graham N. Stanton. Edinburgh: T&T Clark, 1975–.

1.17.11 Interpretation: A Bible Commentary for Teaching and Preaching (IBC). Edited by James Luther Mays. Louisville: Westminster John Knox, 1983–.

1.17.12 New Century Bible (NCB). Edited by Ronald E. Clements and Matthew Black. Grand Rapids: Eerdmans, 1967–.

1.17.13 Word Biblical Commentaries (WBC). Edited by Bruce M. Metzger. Nashville: Thomas Nelson, 1982–.

With commentary series, it is generally advisable to select individual volumes rather than purchase the whole set; individual volumes tend to vary in terms of quality and usefulness.

1.17.14 Extended commentary by select church fathers (e.g., St. Augustine and St. John Chrysostom) is available in The Nicene and Post-Nicene Fathers. Series 1, 14 vols., edited by Philip Schaff. Series 2, 14 vols., edited by Philip Schaff and Henry Wace. Peabody, Mass.: Hendrickson, 1994.

THE OLD TESTAMENT

2.1 Bibliographic Helps

See also PERIODICALS (§2.2); HISTORY OF INTERPRETATION (§2.3); INTRODUCTIONS (§2.14)

H I G H L Y   R E C O M M E N D E D

2.1.1 Brooke, George J., ed. *Society for Old Testament Study Booklist, 2002.* Sheffield: JSOT, 2002. 240pp.

Published annually by the Society of Old Testament Studies, includes annotations of various books pertaining to OT study, including archaeology, history, geography, sociology, texts and versions, exegesis, literary criticism, introductions, life and thought of surrounding peoples, apocrypha and postbiblical studies, philosophy and grammar. Annotations written by leading OT scholars (mostly British). Annotations are concise but descriptive and evaluative.

2.1.2 Childs, Brevard S. *Old Testament Books for Pastor and Teacher.* Philadelphia: Westminster, 1977. 120pp.

Select annotated bibliography dealing with various types of resources for OT study, but with emphasis on commentaries. Provides practical assistance for pastors in the building of their libraries, but is of value for scholars as well. Prioritizes and critically evaluates works on the basis of their usefulness for preaching and teaching in the church. Gives attention to older works (including ancient ones) as well as modern. Although somewhat dated, it remains indispensable.

2.1.3 Longman, Tremper, III. *Old Testament Commentary Survey.* Grand Rapids: Baker, 1995. 160pp.

Highly selective annotated bibliography of works pertaining to various aspects of OT study, including introductions, surveys, theologies, dictionaries, translations, and computer software, but focuses especially on commentaries. Annotations include description of purpose, audience, and use, and critically evaluate the work on the basis of value for pastor's library, grading each work according to a five-star system. Written from conservative evangelical stance, but includes works from various theological perspectives. Annotations are fair, balanced, and very useful.

A L S O   S I G N I F I C A N T

2.1.4 Barker, Kenneth L., Bruce K. Waltke, and Roy B. Zuck. *Bibliography for Old Testament Exegesis and Exposition.* 4th ed. Dallas: Dallas Theological Seminary, 1979. 66pp.

2.1.5 Hostetter, Edwin C. *Old Testament Introduction.* IBR Bibliographies 11. Grand Rapids: Baker, 1995. 106pp.

2.1.6 Zannoni, Arthur E. *The Old Testament: A Bibliography.* Collegeville, Minn.: Michael Glazier, 1992. 277pp.

2.2 Periodicals

2.2.1 *Journal for the Study of the Old Testament.* 1976–. Quarterly.

Published by the Department of Biblical Studies at the University of Sheffield. Contributors employ various approaches, including the older, established ones (e.g., redaction criticism), but especially the emerging methods (e.g., literary criticism). Serious academic explorations of the meaning of the text. Gives little to no attention to historical background, archaeology, or surrounding cultures. Also gives little specific attention to theological issues. Contributors largely from the British Isles. Language: English. Book reviews: none.

2.2.2 *Old Testament Abstracts.* 1978–. 3 issues/year.

Published by the Catholic Biblical Association in Washington, D.C., contains abstracts of articles and books pertaining to the OT and related fields. Each issue lists more than three hundred journal articles (from approximately three hundred journals) and about fifty books. Annotations are brief, but helpful, and are descriptive rather than evaluative.

2.2.3 *Vetus Testamentum.* 1951–. Quarterly.

Published by Brill Academic Publishers at Leiden, the Netherlands; academic, technical, and authoritative. Employs a variety of critical methods in the study of the biblical text and other matters pertinent to OT study. Little explicit attention given to theological issues. Languages: English, French, German, and Dutch. Book reviews: few.

2.3　History of the Canon and History of Interpretation

See also INTRODUCTIONS (§2.14)

H I G H L Y　　R E C O M M E N D E D

2.3.1　Beckwith, Roger T. *The Old Testament Canon of the New Testament Church and Its Background in Early Judaism.* Grand Rapids: Eerdmans, 1985. 529pp.

The most comprehensive and informed study available on the several issues involved in the church's canon of OT scriptures. Treats in the process the notion of the canon and the process of canonization in early Judaism. Deals with the historical development of the debate on the canon, the concept of canon, the structure of the canon, and the disputes pertaining to included and excluded books. Indispensable for any study of these issues.

2.3.2　Clements, Ronald E. *One Hundred Years of Old Testament Interpretation.* Philadelphia: Westminster, 1976. 152pp.

Readable narrative history of scholarship from Wellhausen to 1976 pertaining to major areas of OT study (Pentateuch, historical books, prophets, psalms, wisdom literature, and OT theology), giving approximately equal attention to each of these areas. Emphasizes the interdependence of critical methods, and argues that these critical methods were intended to be instruments of faith and can be used to shed light on the nature of biblical faith. Mostly descriptive, but with some modest evaluation. Should be supplemented with *The Hebrew Bible and Its Modern Interpreters* (§2.3.3) for more recent work.

2.3.3　Knight, Douglas A., and Gene M. Tucker, eds. *The Hebrew Bible and Its Modern Interpreters.* The Bible and Its Modern Interpreters. Chico, Calif.: Scholars, 1985. 516pp.

Commissioned by the Society of Biblical Literature and containing contributions from leading (primarily North American) OT scholars representing the mainline critical consensus, this volume charts developments in major aspects of critical OT study since 1945. Its chapters are arranged topically, and each chapter concludes with a fairly extensive bibliography. More emphasis on historical and literary than theological features. Must reading for recent developments in OT studies.

2.3.4 Saebo, Magne, ed. *Hebrew Bible/Old Testament: The History of Its Interpretation.* 3 vols. (Vols. 1–2 presently available.) Göttingen: Vandenhoeck & Ruprecht, 1996–. 847pp.

By far the most complete and authoritative study of the history of the interpretation of the OT within the OT itself, in Judaism, and in Christianity (including the use of the OT within the NT). Written by leaders in their respective fields, these articles are original contributions based on painstaking study of the primary sources. Includes extensive bibliographies, listing works in Latin, German, French, and English. Essential for any complete study of this area.

ALSO SIGNIFICANT

2.3.5 Chapman, Stephen B. *The Law and the Prophets: A Study in Old Testament Canon Formation.* Forschungen zum Alten Testament 27. Tübingen: Mohr Siebeck, 2000. 356pp.

2.3.6 Davies, Philip R. *Scribes and Schools: The Canonization of the Hebrew Scriptures.* Library of Ancient Israel. Louisville: Westminster John Knox, 1998. 219pp.

2.3.7 Evans, Craig A., and James A. Sanders, eds. *The Function of Scripture in Early Jewish and Christian Tradition.* Journal for the Study of the New Testament Supplement Series 154; Studies in Scripture in Early Judaism and Christianity 6. Sheffield: Sheffield Academic Press, 1998. 350pp.

2.3.8 Exum, J. Cheryl, and David J. A. Clines, eds. *The New Literary Criticism and the Hebrew Bible.* Valley Forge, Pa.: Trinity Press International, 1993. 276pp.

2.3.9 Fishbane, Michael. *Biblical Interpretation in Ancient Israel.* Oxford: Clarendon, 1985. 617pp.

2.3.10 Freedman, David Noel. *The Unity of the Hebrew Bible.* Ann Arbor: University of Michigan Press, 1991. 125pp.

2.3.11 Halbertal, Moshe. *People of the Book: Canon, Meaning, and Authority.* Cambridge, Mass.: Harvard University Press, 1997. 185pp.

2.3.12 Kraeling, Emil G. *The Old Testament Since the Reformation.* New York: Harper, 1955. 320pp.

2.3.13 Levenson, Jon D. *The Hebrew Bible, the Old Testament, and Historical Criticism: Jews and Christians in Biblical Studies.* Philadelphia: Westminster, 1993. 192pp.

2.3.14 Rogerson, John. *Old Testament Criticism in the Nineteenth Century.* Philadelphia: Fortress, 1985. 320pp.

2.3.15 Rowley, H. H. *Growth of the Old Testament.* 3d ed. London: Hutchinson's University, 1967. 192pp.

2.3.16 Saebo, Magne. *On the Way to Canon: Creative Tradition History in the Old Testament.* Journal for the Study of the Old Testament Supplement Series 191. Sheffield: Sheffield Academic Press, 1998. 401pp.

2.3.17 Sanders, James A. *Torah and Canon.* Philadelphia: Fortress, 1972. 121pp.

2.3.18 Sarna, Nahum. *Studies in Biblical Interpretation.* JPS Scholar of Distinction Series. Philadelphia: Jewish Publication Society, 2000. 452pp.

2.3.19 Vasholz, Robert I. *The Old Testament Canon in the Old Testament Church: The Internal Rationale for Old Testament Canonicity.* Ancient Near Eastern Texts and Studies 7. Lewiston, N.Y.: Edwin Mellen, 1990. 105pp.

2.4 History and Geography

H I G H L Y   R E C O M M E N D E D

2.4.1 Ahlström, Gösta W. *The History of Ancient Palestine.* Edited by Diana Edelman. Minneapolis: Fortress, 1993. 990pp.

Learned, massive, and detailed history of the peoples of Palestine from earliest times to the conquest of Alexander. Employs all available source material (textual, epigraphic, archaeological) to reconstruct the major epochs and events so as to analyze the social, political, military, and economic conditions of Palestine as contextual background for the history of Israel. Ahlström belonged to the "Uppsala" or "Scandinavian" school of OT historical criticism, with its unique and (in the judgment of some) eccentric positions, yet was an independent thinker who moved beyond the accepted positions of any specific school. His historical reconstruction will often appear at odds with the OT text, since he attempts to be "free from the bias of the biblical writers." Nevertheless, a very helpful resource for interpreting the OT in its environment.

2.4.2 Albertz, Rainer. *A History of Israelite Religion in the Old Testament Period.* 2 vols. Old Testament Library. Louisville: Westminster John Knox, 1994. 738pp.

Combines general history of Israel and Judah with the history specifically of Israel's religion in an attempt to explore the interaction between historical events, religious experiences, and theological responses as various groups within Israel and Judah gave religious expression to historical and social situations. Adopts a thoroughly critical approach, sometimes following the more established critical lines of (for example) Noth, and sometimes more recent critical movements, but affirms the early dating of many texts over against the view that we have virtually nothing from the preexilic period. Readers will sometimes be disappointed that he seeks to explain religious phenomena almost entirely in terms of historical events and social realities without giving place to the transcendent activity of God. But insofar as even the OT writers assume the importance of social and historical context, this work will be helpful in understanding the faith of the OT in that light.

2.4.3 Bright, John. *A History of Israel.* 4th ed. Philadelphia: Westminster, 2000. 533pp.

Revised with a helpful appendix by William P. Brown, this is the most authoritative and accessible history of Israel from the "Albright school," which engaged in critical historical reconstruction but was more inclined to identify substantive connections between the archaeological and historical evidence and the perspectives of the OT texts than certain other schools. The result is a history that is at once both critical and relatively conservative. Perhaps the best overall introduction to the history of Israel for the interpreter of the OT.

2.4.4 Matthews, Victor H., and Don C. Benjamin. *Social World of Ancient Israel: 1250–587 B.C.E.* Peabody, Mass.: Hendrickson, 1993. 832pp.

Historical/cultural background information is obviously essential for biblical interpretation, and interpreters often find it difficult to locate the most relevant background information for specific passages. This volume offers a readable, nontechnical presentation of such data for each passage of the OT. The fact that the whole of OT background is treated in a single-volume commentary results in the information being highly selective. Moreover, it sometimes presents only general background information derived from other OT passages rather than specific cultural insights from archaeological or cultural studies. Nevertheless it is usually quite helpful and the only resource of its kind available.

2.4.5 Miller, Patrick D., Jr. *The Religion of Ancient Israel.* Library of Ancient Israel. Louisville: Westminster John Knox, 2000. 335pp.

Readable, informed, and current discussion of the history of Israel's religion according to major themes and institutions: deity and the divine world; types of religion; sacrifice and offering; holiness and purity; and leadership. Written with a view toward informing the actual interpretation of the OT text.

2.4.6 Vaux, Roland de. *Ancient Israel: Its Life and Institutions*. 2 vols. New York: McGraw-Hill, 1965. 592pp.

From a leading Roman Catholic biblical historian and archaeologist associated with the famous École Biblique in Jerusalem, this work is something of a classic treatment of the social and religious life of ancient Israel, focusing on the principal institutions that provided the framework for Israel's life. Draws heavily on data from the OT itself, which he tends to treat as historically reliable, and relates these data to archaeological evidence and the history of Israel's neighbors. Readable, reliable, and useful resource for deeper understanding of specific passages as well as of the OT as a whole.

2.4.7 Wellhausen, Julius. *Prolegomena to the History of Israel: With a Reprint of the Article "Israel" from the Encylopaedia Britannica*. Edinburgh: A. & C. Black, 1885; reprint, Gloucester, Mass.: Peter Smith, 1973. 552pp.

Probably the most influential work ever written on the history of Israel. Responsible for establishing the basic direction of OT study until the present, although some of its specific positions have been modified or largely abandoned. Important not so much for the assistance it can give in the interpretation of the final form of the text, for in fact its value for preaching and teaching in the church is extremely limited. Rather, its significance is in its role in the development of the discipline of OT study.

ALSO SIGNIFICANT

2.4.8 Ackroyd, Peter R. *Exile and Restoration: A Study of Hebrew Thought of the Sixth Century B.C.* The Old Testament Library. Philadelphia: Westminster, 1975. 286pp.

2.4.9 Clements, Ronald E., ed. *The World of Ancient Israel: Sociological, Anthropological, and Political Perspectives*. Cambridge: Cambridge University Press, 1991. 436pp.

2.4.10 Fohrer, Georg. *A History of Israelite Religion*. Nashville: Abingdon, 1972. 416pp.

2.4.11 Hayes, John H., and J. Maxwell Miller, eds. *Israelite and Judaean History*. Old Testament Library. Philadelphia: Westminster, 1977. 736pp.

2.4.12 Herrmann, Siegfried. *A History of Israel in Old Testament Times*. 2d ed. Philadelphia: Fortress, 1981. 440pp.

2.4.13 Kaufmann, Yehezkel. *The Religion of Israel: From Its Beginnings to the Babylonian Exile.* New York: Schocken, 1960. 486pp.

2.4.14 King, Philip J., and Lawrence E. Stager. *Life in Biblical Israel.* Library of Ancient Israel. Louisville: Westminster John Knox, 2001. 440pp.

2.4.15 Long, V. Philips, David W. Baker, and Gordon J. Wenham, eds. *Windows into Old Testament History: Evidence, Argument, and the Crisis of Biblical Israel.* Grand Rapids: Eerdmans, 2002. 200pp.

2.4.16 McDermott, John J. *What Are They Saying About the Formation of Israel?* New York: Paulist, 1998. 113pp.

2.4.17 Noth, Martin. *The History of Israel.* 2d ed. New York: Harper & Row, 1960. 487pp.

2.4.18 Schmidt, Werner H. *The Faith of the Old Testament: A History.* Philadelphia: Westminster, 1983. 302pp.

2.4.19 Westermann, Claus. *A Thousand Years and a Day: Our Time in the Old Testament.* Philadelphia: Muhlenberg, 1962. 280pp.

2.4.20 Wiseman, D. J., ed. *Peoples of Old Testament Times.* Oxford: Oxford University Press, 1973. 402pp.

2.4.21 Wood, Leon. *A Survey of Israel's History.* Revised by D. McBride. Grand Rapids: Zondervan, 1986. 416pp.

2.5 Ancient Near Eastern Literature and Art

HIGHLY RECOMMENDED

2.5.1 Hallo, William W., and K. Lawson Younger Jr., eds. *The Context of Scripture.* 3 vols. Leiden: Brill, 1997–. (Volumes 1 and 2 presently available.) 599/433pp.

A work that promises to be the authoritative standard in this area well into the twenty-first century. The first volume includes Ancient Near Eastern texts that pertain to the OT. The selection is broad, balanced, and representative, and includes the most recent discoveries and fresh translations of long-familiar texts. The second volume deals with monumental inscriptions from the biblical world. In both of these volumes there are cross-references to OT passages, but little specific discussion of the relationship to the OT. Includes critical footnotes and extensive bibliographies of works in English, German, and French. The third (forthcoming) volume will include indexes and develop connections between these materials and the OT.

2.5.2 Matthews, Victor H., and Don C. Benjamin. *Old Testament Parallels: Laws and Stories from the Ancient Near East.* 2d ed. New York: Paulist, 1997. 384pp.

Probably the most readable, accessible, and current anthology of Near Eastern parallels to OT passages. The translations are fresh and understandable to contemporary English speakers (indeed, they border on paraphrase). The book moves through the OT canonically, presenting parallels according to their relationship to specific biblical passages. In addition to the citation of the ANE text itself, each entry includes a brief discussion of the ANE passage and an explanation of its relationship to the biblical passage; the authors identify similarities and differences between the ANE passage and the biblical text so as to note the distinctive features of the biblical perspective. Excellent introduction to the most significant ANE parallels.

2.5.3 Pritchard, James B., ed. *Ancient Near Eastern Texts Relating to the Old Testament.* 3d ed. with supplement. Princeton, N.J.: Princeton University Press, 1969. 710pp.

Complete, authoritative, meticulously accurate translation of ANE texts pertaining to the OT. Very little introduction to the texts or discussion regarding their relationship to and significance for OT passages. The text and translations are technically accurate, but not as reader-friendly or understandable as those presented by Matthews and Benjamin (§2.5.2). Excellent for the scholar and others trained in the field, but not as useful for nonspecialists.

2.5.4 Walton, John H. *Ancient Israelite Literature in Its Cultural Context: A Survey of Parallels between Biblical and Ancient Near Eastern Texts.* Library of Biblical Interpretation. Grand Rapids: Zondervan, 1990. 256pp.

Not so much an anthology of ANE parallels as a survey of texts that have typically been identified as parallels to OT passages, and a discussion of the considerations involved in deciding whether such a text is truly parallel, and if so, how it should be used to interpret the OT and to understand Israel's faith. Written from a consciously conservative perspective, but fair, balanced, and judicious. Notes common elements between Israel and its neighbors but emphasizes the distinctiveness of Israel's faith.

Note also the series Society of Biblical Literature Writings from the Ancient World (edited by Burke O. Long; Atlanta: Scholars Press, 1990–), which presents current, readable translations of a variety of texts from ANE cultures from Sumerian civilization to the age of Alexander. Each volume deals with a specific type of text from a particular area (e.g., letters from ancient Egypt) and contains an introduction describing the texts presented, but there is little explicit attention given to the relationship to the biblical material. Now the standard comprehensive reference work for ANE texts. Thus far, nine volumes have appeared.

ALSO SIGNIFICANT

2.5.5 Arnold, Bill T., and Bryan E. Beyer. *Readings from the Ancient Near East: Primary Sources for Old Testament Study.* Encountering Biblical Studies. Grand Rapids: Baker, 2001. 256pp.

2.5.6 Beyerlin, Walter, ed. *Near Eastern Religious Texts Relating to the Old Testament.* Old Testament Library. Philadelphia: Westminster, 1978. 288pp.

2.5.7 Pritchard, James B., ed. *The Ancient Near East: An Anthology of Texts and Pictures.* 2 vols. Princeton, N.J.: Princeton University Press, 1958, 1976. 280/ 249pp.

2.5.8 Pritchard, James B. *The Ancient Near East in Pictures Relating to the Old Testament.* 2d ed. Princeton, N.J.: Princeton University Press, 1969. 396pp.

2.6 Editions of the Old Testament

HIGHLY RECOMMENDED

2.6.1 Dotan, Aron, ed. *Biblia Hebraica Leningradensia: Prepared According to the Vocalization, Accents, and Masora of Aaron ben Moses ben Asher in the Leningrad Codex.* Edited by Aron Dotan. Peabody, Mass.: Hendrickson, 2001.

This printed edition of the Leningrad Codex (L), an important eleventh-century manuscript of the Masoretic Text, has no Masora (a traditional apparatus devised by medieval Hebrew scribes) and no critical apparatus but follows L with a high degree of accuracy and clearly indicates when it departs from L for certain specified reasons.

2.6.2 Elliger, K., and W. Rudolph, eds. *Biblia Hebraica Stuttgartensia.* 2d ed., edited by W. Rudolph and H. P. Rüger. Stuttgart: Deutsche Bibelgesellschaft, 1977.

The edition of the Hebrew Bible most widely used by scholars and students. Based on earlier editions by R. Kittel and others, its text is an edition of the Leningrad Codex (L), an important eleventh-century manuscript of the Masoretic Text. Also included are an edition of L's version of the Masora and a modern critical apparatus.

2.6.3 Rahlfs, Alfred. *Septuaginta*. Stuttgart: Deutsche Bibelgesellschaft, 1935. 941pp.

The most commonly used edition of the Septuagint. Based primarily on the three major uncials Vaticanus, Sinaiticus, Alexandrinus. Contains brief and basic text-critical apparatus.

2.6.4 Ziegler, Joseph, et al., eds. *Septuaginta: Vetus Testamentum Graecum*. 16 vols. Göttingen: Vandenhoeck & Ruprecht, 1930–1999. Volumes vary greatly in size, averaging around 300pp.

Often called the "Göttingen Septuagint," this is the standard critical edition of those books that have been published. When complete, it will contain 16 "volumes" comprising half again as many physical volumes. Ziegler edited the earliest volumes, but the subsequent volumes were edited by various scholars. Each volume contains an introduction (in German), the text of the Septuagint, and a much more complete and detailed textual apparatus than that which appears in Rahlfs.

A L S O   S I G N I F I C A N T

2.6.5 Brenton, Lancelot C. L. *The Septuagint with Apocrypha: Greek and English*. Peabody, Mass.: Hendrickson, 1986.

2.7 Hebrew Grammars

H I G H L Y   R E C O M M E N D E D

2.7.1 Joüon, Paul, and T. Muraoka. *A Grammar of Biblical Hebrew*. 2 vols. Subsidia Biblica 14.1–2. Rome: Biblical Institute Press, 1991. 779pp.

Current and comprehensive reference grammar for intermediate-level Hebrew, though on the detailed and technical end of the range of intermediate Hebrew texts. Comparable to Waltke-O'Connor (§2.7.3), though treats all branches of Hebrew grammar, including phonetics/phonology and morphology, whereas Waltke-O'Connor deals almost exclusively with syntax. Consequently does not deal as fully with syntax as Waltke-O'Connor, and the latter should be used to complement this volume. Footnotes interact with current scholarly discussions on major issues. Includes a fairly extensive bibliography.

2.7.2   Kautzsch, E., ed. *Gesenius' Hebrew Grammar*. 2d ed. Rev. by A. E. Cowley. Oxford: Clarendon, 1909. 598pp.

The classic and still most authoritative standard grammar of biblical Hebrew, although portions are becoming dated, and therefore it should be used in connection with more recent works, especially Waltke-O'Connor (§2.7.3). Indispensable for thorough, serious study of Hebrew grammar.

2.7.3   Waltke, Bruce K., and M. O'Connor. *An Introduction to Biblical Hebrew Syntax*. Winona Lake, Ind.: Eisenbrauns, 1990. 765pp.

Overall the most complete and useful intermediate grammar. It focuses almost entirely on syntax, and its discussions of syntactical issues are consistently clear, with numerous helpful examples from the OT. Its introductory discussions on the history of the study of Hebrew grammar and on basic methodological issues are also very helpful. At a few points its explanation of syntax can be usefully supplemented by Joüon (§2.7.1).

2.7.4   Williams, Ronald J. *Hebrew Syntax: An Outline*. 2d ed. Toronto: University of Toronto Press, 1976. 122pp.

Extremely practical general guide to intermediate-level Hebrew syntax. Intended as an "outline," it is skeletal in relation to works like Waltke-O'Connor (§2.7.3) but very useful to have at hand as one reads through the Hebrew text and wishes to identify the grammatical functions and exegetical significance of various forms or parts of speech or clauses.

ALSO   SIGNIFICANT

2.7.5   Bodine, Walter R., ed. *Linguistics and Biblical Hebrew*. Winona Lake, Ind.: Eisenbrauns, 1992. 323pp.

2.7.6   Chisholm, Robert B. *From Exegesis to Exposition: A Practical Guide to Using Biblical Hebrew*. Grand Rapids: Baker, 1998. 304pp.

2.7.7   Davidson, A. B. *Hebrew Syntax*. 3d ed. Edinburgh: T&T Clark, 1924. 233pp.

2.7.8   Driver, S. R. *A Treatise on the Use of the Tenses in Hebrew*. 3d ed. Oxford: Clarendon, 1892. 306pp.

2.7.9   Gogel, Sandra Landis. *A Grammar of Epigraphic Hebrew.* Atlanta: Scholars, 1998. 522pp.

2.7.10   Horsnell, Malcolm J. A. *A Review and Reference Grammar for Biblical Hebrew.* Rev. ed. Hamilton, Ont.: McMaster University Press, 1999. 463pp.

2.7.11   Waldman, Nahum M. *The Recent Study of Hebrew: A Survey of the Literature with Selected Bibliography.* Winona Lake, Ind.: Eisenbrauns, 1989. 464pp.

P O P U L A R   B E G I N N I N G   G R A M M A R S

2.7.12   Kelley, Page H. *Biblical Hebrew: An Introductory Grammar.* Grand Rapids: Eerdmans, 1992. 453pp.

2.7.13   Lambdin, T. O. *Introduction to Biblical Hebrew.* New York: Scribners, 1971. 345pp.

2.7.14   LaSor, William Sanford. *Handbook of Biblical Hebrew.* 2 vols. Grand Rapids: Eerdmans, 1988. 189/249pp.

2.7.15   Marks, John H., and Virgil Rogers. *A Beginner's Handbook to Biblical Hebrew.* Nashville: Abingdon, 1958. 174pp.

2.7.16   Martin, James D. *Davidson's Introductory Hebrew Grammar,* 27th ed. Edinburgh: T&T Clark, 1993. 225pp.

2.7.17   Seow, C. L. *A Grammar for Biblical Hebrew.* Rev. ed. Nashville: Abingdon, 1995. 366pp.

2.7.18   Weingreen, J. *A Practical Grammar for Classical Hebrew.* 2d ed. Oxford: Clarendon, 1959. 316pp.

2.8 Hebrew Lexicons

H I G H L Y   R E C O M M E N D E D

2.8.1   Armstrong, Terry A., Douglas L. Busby, and Cyril F. Carr. *A Reader's Hebrew-English Lexicon of the Old Testament.* 4 vols. in 3. Grand Rapids: Zondervan, 1982–1988. 230/220/296pp.

> Companion volume to Kubo's *Reader's Greek-English Lexicon of the New Testament* (§4.8.2). Designed for the student or pastor, offers assistance in rapid

reading of the Hebrew Bible by listing, according to passage, words that occur fifty times or fewer in the OT. Definitions are brief, and are based on Brown-Driver-Briggs (§2.8.2). Each entry indicates also the page number in BDB where the definition can be found, and frequencies of the word both in the biblical book and in the OT as a whole. Contains many errors, but still a most helpful resource.

2.8.2 Brown, Francis, S. R. Driver, and Charles A. Briggs. *A Hebrew and English Lexicon of the Old Testament.* Oxford: Oxford University Press, 1907. Reprint, Peabody, Mass.: Hendrickson, 1979 (indexed to Strong's). 1185pp.

A classic work, and among the most authoritative, based on Gesenius's dictionary. Now somewhat dated, and rather difficult to use given the arrangement, system of abbreviations, and even print format. An index, available separately (§2.8.7), helps greatly. Still an indispensable resource for serious study of the Hebrew Bible.

2.8.3 Davidson, Benjamin. *The Analytical Hebrew and Chaldee Lexicon.* 2d ed. Peabody, Mass.: Hendrickson, 1990. 784pp.

Originally published in 1850, lists, parses, and identifies the root of every word in the Hebrew Bible. Gives basic definitions of each root. Regularly alludes to relevant morphological and grammatical discussions found at the beginning of the volume. Somewhat dated insofar as it is based on a less reliable edition of the Hebrew text than more recent works, but remains extremely helpful as a parsing guide, especially for unusual or irregular forms.

2.8.4 Holladay, William L. *A Concise Hebrew and Aramaic Lexicon of the Old Testament.* Grand Rapids: Eerdmans, 1971. 425pp.

Probably the most reader-friendly and accessible of the more recent, up-to-date lexicons. Based on Koehler-Barmgartner (§2.8.5) and produced for English-speaking audiences before Koehler-Barmgartner had been fully published in English in revised form, this abridgment retains its value for reliable, quick-reference definition. Recognizing that most students are less familiar with Aramaic than with Hebrew, it offers fuller treatment of Aramaic words, including identification of number, person, and gender of verbs.

2.8.5 Koehler, Ludwig, and Walter Baumgartner. *The Hebrew and Aramaic Lexicon of the Old Testament.* Revised by Walter Baumgartner and Johann Jakob Stamm. Translated and edited under the supervision of M. E. J. Richardson. 3d ed. 5 vols. Leiden: Brill, 1994–2000. 2094pp.

Now the standard dictionary for the OT and related literature in Hebrew and Aramaic. In contrast to older works, like Brown-Driver-Briggs (§2.8.2), it lists entries in alphabetical order rather than according to verbal roots, thus making this lexicon easier to use and saving much time. It incorporates data and insights from recent discoveries and the most recent research into these languages.

ALSO   SIGNIFICANT

2.8.6 Clines, David J. A., ed. *The Dictionary of Classical Hebrew.* 8 vols. Sheffield: Sheffield Academic Press, 1993–. (Volumes 1 through 5 are presently available.) Volumes average 500pp.

2.8.7 Einspahr, Bruce. *Index to Brown, Driver & Briggs Hebrew Lexicon.* Chicago: Moody, 1980. 456pp.

2.8.8 Fohrer, Georg, ed. *Hebrew and Aramaic Dictionary of the Old Testament.* Berlin: Walter De Gruyter, 1973. 332pp.

2.8.9 Girdlestone, Robert B. *Synonyms of the Old Testament: Their Bearing on Christian Doctrine.* 3d ed. Revised and edited by Donald R. White. Grand Rapids: Baker, 1983. 388pp.

2.8.10 Klein, Ernest. *A Comprehensive Etymological Dictionary of the Hebrew Language for Readers of English.* New York: Macmillan, 1987. 721pp.

2.9 Theological Dictionaries (Wordbooks)

HIGHLY   RECOMMENDED

2.9.1 Botterweck, G. Johannes, Helmer Ringgren, and Heinz-Josef Fabry, eds. *Theological Dictionary of the Old Testament.* Grand Rapids: Eerdmans, 1974. (Vols. 1–12 are presently available.)

Companion to *Theological Dictionary of the New Testament* (§4.9.3), this magisterial work offers in-depth discussions of key Hebrew and Aramaic terms in the OT. Each entry focuses on meaning, moving from general, everyday senses to full understanding of theological significance. Each key word is related to its larger linguistic and semantic fields, and attention is given to cognate terms and concepts in surrounding Ancient Near Eastern cultures. Attention is given also to use in Qumran and the Septuagint. Contributors represent a wide range of nations and religious traditions, though most are European and North American, and virtually all assume the general critical consensus of the historical and textual development of the OT and thus make use of form-

and tradition-critical insights. Contains extensive bibliographies. The standard work in this category.

2.9.2 Jenni, Ernst, and Claus Westermann, eds. *Theological Lexicon of the Old Testament*. 3 vols. Peabody, Mass.: Hendrickson, 1997. 1638pp.

Mainline critical alternative to conservative-evangelical theological dictionaries such as those edited by VanGemeren (§2.9.3) and Harris-Archer-Waltke (§2.9.4), etc. Articles produced by some of most prominent OT scholars from the German-speaking world. Includes significant interaction with history of interpretation, and includes fairly extensive bibliographies (most works cited are in German, though some in English or French). Emphasizes insights from form- and tradition-criticism, and therefore discussions sometimes focus on the function of the word in sources or traditions that lie behind the OT text rather than in the final form of the text. For those who do not know Hebrew, or do not know it well, words are numerically coded to Strong's numbers.

2.9.3 VanGemeren, Willem A., ed. *New International Dictionary of Old Testament Theology and Exegesis*. 5 vols. Grand Rapids: Zondervan, 1997. Volumes average 1100pp.

This counterpart to *New International Dictionary of New Testament Theology* (§4.9.2) is designed to provide both scholars and nonspecialists understanding of the basic meaning of key OT terms as well as their fuller theological significance. Briefer and more basic than *Theological Dictionary of the Old Testament* (§2.9.1) and representing a conservative-evangelical perspective over against *TDOT* and *Theological Lexicon of the Old Testament* (§2.9.2), although contributors represent a spectrum that includes both Wesleyan and Reformed scholars. Contains brief bibliographies. Solid, informed, and reliable.

See also the discussions of Old Testament terms found in Gerhard Kittel and Gerhard Friedrich, eds., *Theological Dictionary of the New Testament* (§4.9.3), and the discussions of Old Testament passages and concepts found in Karl Barth, *Church Dogmatics* (14 vols.; Edinburgh: T&T Clark, 1975–1977).

A L S O   S I G N I F I C A N T

2.9.4 Harris, R. Laird, G. L. Archer, and Bruce K. Waltke, eds. *Theological Wordbook of the Old Testament*. 2 vols. Chicago: Moody, 1980. 1124pp.

2.9.5 Unger, Merrill F., and William White, eds. *Nelson's Expository Dictionary of the Old Testament*. Nashville: Thomas Nelson, 1980. 509pp.

2.10 Concordances to the Hebrew Bible

2.10.1 Even-Shoshan, Abraham. *A New Concordance of the Old Testament.* Jerusalem: Kiryat Sepher; Grand Rapids: Baker, 1984. 1242pp.

Most complete, current, and accessible Hebrew concordance among those that employ the Hebrew exclusively and make no use of English translation. Includes several features that make it simpler to use than Lisowsky or Mandelkern. Entries cite synonyms and related words. Includes not just single words, but also collocations (phrases). Employs certain "space-saving" devices for high-frequency words, and these can cause confusion. For this reason, the user should consult the introduction by John Sailhamer (§2.10.7).

2.10.2 Kohlenberger, John R., III. *The Hebrew-English Concordance to the Old Testament: with the New International Version.* Grand Rapids: Zondervan, 1998. 2192pp.

Lists all occurrences of a Hebrew word (even where there is no English equivalent in the NIV or other standard translations). Uses Goodrick-Kohlenberger numbering system, which is keyed to major lexicons, e.g., Brown, Driver, Briggs; Koehler-Barmgartner; and Holladay. Also includes cross-references to Strong's numbers. Each entry gives the various ways the Hebrew word is translated by the NIV, transliteration, part of speech, frequency count, related words, context lines, textual variants, and (in verbs) identification of stem. Contains also concise Hebrew-English and Aramaic-English dictionary. Reliable, current, full of helpful information, and user-friendly.

2.10.3 Wigram, George V. *The Englishman's Hebrew Concordance of the Old Testament.* Peabody, Mass.: Hendrickson, 1996. 1680pp.

First published in the middle of the nineteenth century, now somewhat dated in terms of the quality of the Hebrew text employed and suffers from some omissions. Still, accessible and user-friendly and generally reliable. Numerically coded to Strong's.

2.10.4 Andersen, Francis I. *The Vocabulary of the Old Testament.* Rome: Pontifical Biblical Institute Press, 1989. 721pp.

2.10.5 Lisowsky, Gerhard. *Konkordanz zum Hebräaischen Alten Testament.* 2d ed. Stuttgart: Wurttembergische Bibelanstalt, 1958. 1672pp.

2.10.6 Mandelkern, Solomon. *Veteris Testamenti Concordantiae: Hebraica atqua Chaldaicae.* Tel Aviv: Sumptibus Schocken Hierosolymis, 1971. 1532pp.

2.10.7 Sailhamer, John. *Introduction to* A New Concordance of the Old Testament. Grand Rapids: Baker, 1987. 37pp.

2.11 Textual Criticism

H I G H L Y   R E C O M M E N D E D

2.11.1 Brotzman, Ellis R. *Old Testament Textual Criticism: A Practical Intro-duction.* Grand Rapids: Baker, 1994. 208pp.

Most readable and accessible introduction to all the major aspects of OT tex-tual criticism, including a history of the transmission of the OT in Hebrew, a description of the ancient versions of the OT, guidance for the use of *Biblia Hebraica Stuttgartensia* (§2.6.2), a discussion of the role of the Dead Sea Scrolls, an explanation of scribal errors, a study of the principles and practice of textual criticism, and an illustrative application of textual criticism directed at the Book of Ruth. Includes a select bibliography.

2.11.2 McCarter, P. Kyle. *Textual Criticism: Recovering the Text of the Hebrew Bible.* Guides to Biblical Scholarship. Philadelphia: Fortress, 1986. 94pp.

Like Brotzman (§2.11.1), an introduction to the discipline of textual criticism, but more narrow in focus, emphasizing the types of textual corruption and the main considerations in adjudicating between variant readings. Also some-what more theoretical, less concerned to lead the reader through the actual process of doing textual criticism. Yet contains many illuminating examples. A useful supplement to Brotzman.

2.11.3 Tov, Emanuel. *Textual Criticism of the Hebrew Bible.* Philadelphia: Fortress, 1993. 456pp.

An introduction to OT textual criticism, but more thorough and technical than Brotzman (§2.11.1) or McCarter (§2.11.2), and indeed more than an in-troduction in that its discussions on specific issues often pertain to current scholarly debate and carry that debate forward. Especially valuable for its descriptions of texts and versions. Probably the most authoritative treatment of OT textual criticism, but the reader should be aware that some of Tov's specific perspectives and conclusions are debatable and are not universally shared by scholars in the field.

2.11.4 Wurthwein, E. *The Text of the Old Testament: An Introduction to the Biblia Hebraica.* Rev. ed. Grand Rapids: Eerdmans, 1994. 293pp.

Probably the most readable introduction to the major texts of the OT, with special attention to the Masoretic text, the Septuagint, the Peshitta, and the Dead Sea Scrolls. Also helpful is the chapter that discusses the theological significance of textual criticism.

A L S O   S I G N I F I C A N T

2.11.5 Kelley, Page H., Daniel S. Mynatt, and Timothy G. Crawford, eds. *The Masorah of Biblia Hebraica Stuttgartensia: Introduction and Annotated Glossary.* Grand Rapids: Eerdmans, 1998. 241pp.

2.11.6 Klein, Ralph W. *Textual Criticism of the Old Testament: The Septuagint after Qumran.* Guides to Biblical Scholarship. Philadelphia: Fortress, 1974. 84pp.

2.11.7 Tov, Emanuel. *The Text-Critical Use of the Septuagint in Biblical Research.* 2d ed. Jerusalem Biblical Studies 8. Jerusalem: Simor, 1997. 289pp.

2.11.8 Weingreen, J. *Introduction to the Critical Study of the Text of the Hebrew Bible.* Oxford: Clarendon, 1982. 103pp.

2.11.9 Wonneberger, Reinhard. *Understanding BHS: A Manual for Users of Biblica Hebraica Stuttgartensia.* 2d ed. Subsidia Biblica 8. Rome: Biblical Institute Press, 1990. 104pp.

2.12 Septuagint

See also TEXTUAL CRITICISM (§2.11); EDITIONS OF THE OLD TESTAMENT (§2.6)

H I G H L Y   R E C O M M E N D E D

2.12.1 Conybeare, F. C., and St. George Stock. *Grammar of Septuagint Greek: With Selected Readings, Vocabularies, and Updated Indexes.* Peabody, Mass.: Hendrickson, 1988. 382pp.

This reprint of the original 1905 volume adds indexes of ancient sources (including biblical passages) and Greek words, and glossaries. Although an older work, still indispensable for translation and study of the Greek of the Septuagint. Contains discussion (somewhat dated) of origin, inspiration, date, and Greek of the Septuagint; analysis of accidence and syntax of Septuagintal grammar, with numerous examples; and selected readings from the Septuagint with introductions and textual and grammatical notes.

2.12.2 Fernandez Marcos, Natalio. *The Septuagint in Context: Introduction to the Greek Versions of the Bible.* Leiden: Brill, 2001. 394pp.

A more technical introduction to the Septuagint than Jobes and Silva (§2.12.5), and one that focuses on the various contexts of the Septuagint, e.g., the linguistic, cultural, and historical contexts of its emergence and the relation of the Septuagint to the Hebrew Bible and to the Christian tradition. Actually deals not exclusively with the Septuagint, but with all the major Greek translations of the OT through Origen's Hexapla and the Lucianic Recension, and even deals with secondary versions such as the Old Latin and the Coptic versions, these secondary versions being useful for reconstructing the old Greek translations. Each chapter concludes with a brief and current bibliography.

2.12.3 Hatch, Edwin, and Henry A. Redpath. *A Concordance to the Septuagint and the Other Greek Versions of the Old Testament.* 2 vols. Oxford: Clarendon, 1897–1906. 1504pp. + supp.

This work, now a century old, continues to be the most reliable and comprehensive concordance to the Septuagint. Includes complete listing of every word appearing in the three major manuscripts of the Septuagint (Alexandrinus, Vaticanus, and Sinaiticus) and Sixtine edition of 1587, identifies in every instance the Hebrew word standing behind it, and includes the most significant textual variants. The citations are long enough to show the grammatical construction of the word and the words with which it is usually associated. In the absence of Bible software programs that will conduct exhaustive searches, this is an indispensable work.

2.12.4 Jellicoe, Sidney. *The Septuagint and Modern Study.* Oxford: Oxford University Press, 1968. 423pp.

Generally regarded as something of a classic in Septuagintal studies. Attempts to consolidate in one volume the significant amount of scholarship in the study of the Septuagint since the magisterial works of Swete and Ottley (§2.12.17, not "highly recommended" because of its age). The value of this volume is its comprehensive and at points detailed description of the recent history of Septuagintal studies, a value that is, of course, somewhat mitigated by the fact that this volume appeared in 1968.

2.12.5 Jobes, Karen H., and Moisés Silva. *Invitation to the Septuagint*. Grand Rapids: Baker, 2000. 351pp.

Readable introduction to the Septuagint designed for the nonspecialist yet containing current discussions of interest also to the scholar. Explores the importance of the Septuagint for the interpretation of both the OT and NT, describes the various Greek versions of the OT, evaluates the current printed editions, discusses textual criticism of the Septuagint, explores the use of the Septuagint for OT textual criticism, examines its relationship to the Dead Sea Scrolls, and gives examples of the interpretation of specific Septuagint passages (these examples require basic knowledge of Greek and Hebrew). Includes extremely brief bibliography.

2.12.6 Lust, J., E. Eynikel, and K. Hauspie (with the collaboration of G. Chamberlain), eds. *A Greek-English Lexicon of the Septuagint*. 2 vols. Stuttgart: Deutsche Bibelgesellschaft, 1992, 1996. 528pp.

The only lexicon of the Septuagint available in English. Lists every word that appears in Rahlfs's edition of the Septuagint, giving brief definitions, identifying up to five references to biblical texts in which the word occurs, and providing brief bibliography. The second volume contains an extensive bibliography on the Septuagint.

2.12.7 Taylor, Bernard A. *The Analytical Lexicon to the Septuagint: A Complete Parsing Guide*. Grand Rapids: Zondervan, 1994. 460pp.

Designed to assist beginning students in reading the Septuagint in the original Greek, but helpful also for more advanced students who might need assistance with rare or irregular forms. Parses every Greek word found in Rahlfs's edition of the Septuagint. The word "lexicon" in the title is somewhat misleading, since this volume gives no definition of terms. One should consult Lust's lexicon (§2.12.6) for definitions.

ALSO SIGNIFICANT

2.12.8 Brock, Sebastian P., Charles T. Fritzsch, and Sidney Jellicoe. *A Classified Bibliography of the LXX*. Philadelphia: Fortress, 1974. 217pp.

2.12.9 Dogniez, Cécile. *Bibliography of the Septuagint: 1970–1993*. Vetus Testamentum Supplemental Series 60. Leiden: Brill, 1995. 325pp.

2.12.10 Hatch, Edwin. *Essays in Biblical Greek*. Oxford: Oxford University Press, 1889. 293pp.

2.12.11 Hengel, Martin. *The Septuagint and Christian Scripture in Prehistory and the Problem of Its Canon.* Old Testament Studies. Edinburgh: T&T Clark, 2001. 256pp.

2.12.12 Morrish, George. *A Concordance to the Septuagint.* Grand Rapids: Zondervan, 1976. 284pp.

2.12.13 Müller, Mogens. *The First Bible of the Church: A Plea for the Septuagint.* Copenhagen International Seminar 1; Journal for the Study of the Old Testament Supplement Series 206. Sheffield: Sheffield Academic Press, 1996. 163pp.

2.12.14 Olofsson, Staffan. *God Is My Rock: A Study of Translation Technique and Theological Exegesis in the Septuagint.* Stockholm: Almqvist & Wiksell, 1990. 208pp.

2.12.15 Orlinsky, Harry M., ed. *Studies in the Septuagint: Origins, Recension, and Interpretations: Selected Essays with a Prolegomena by Sidney Jellicoe.* New York: Ktav, 1974. 609pp.

2.12.16 Ottley, R. R. *Handbook to the Septuagint.* London: Methuen, 1920. 296pp.

2.12.17 Swete, Henry Barclay. *An Introduction to the Old Testament in Greek.* Revised by R. R. Ottley. Cambridge: Cambridge University Press, 1914. 626pp.

2.12.18 Thackeray, H. St. J. *A Grammar of the Old Testament in Greek: According to the Septuagint.* Cambridge: Cambridge University Press, 1909. 325pp.

2.12.19 Walters, Peter, and D. W. Gooding. *The Text of the Septuagint: Its Corruptions and Their Emendation.* Cambridge: Cambridge University Press, 1973. 418pp.

2.13 Exegetical Method/Hermeneutics

H I G H L Y   R E C O M M E N D E D

2.13.1 Achtemeier, Elizabeth. *Preaching from the Old Testament.* Louisville: Westminster John Knox, 1989. 187pp.

Written by a prominent authority on both the OT and preaching, this book presents solid theoretical foundation, practical guidelines, and engaging and illuminating examples of the Christian use of the OT. Emphasizes that the continuity between the testaments is based on the continuous activity of God's salvation-historical activity coming to fulfillment in Christ. Especially helpful are her discussions pertaining to Christian preaching from various types of OT material: narrative, law, prophets, psalms, wisdom.

2.13.2 Alter, Robert. *The Art of Biblical Narrative.* San Francisco: Harper, 1983. 195pp.

The pioneering work in the literary approach (now often called "narrative-critical") to the study of the OT. Employs engaging examples to demonstrate the value of and, to some extent, the techniques for making use of insights from the literary study of narrative for the interpretation of the OT.

2.13.3 Armerding, Carl. E. *The Old Testament and Criticism.* Grand Rapids: Eerdmans, 1983. 134pp.

Though now somewhat dated in its discussion of various types of OT criticism, and though quite brief, this book is a thoughtful, lucid appeal from a conservative biblical scholar for an evangelical appreciation for and use of OT criticism. Armerding also offers a critique of the use of criticism by certain mainstream scholars.

2.13.4 Barton, John. *Reading the Old Testament: Method in Biblical Study.* Rev. ed. Louisville: Westminster John Knox, 1996. 294pp.

Lucid introduction to the various methods currently employed in OT study. It probes the purpose of the various methods, their interrelationship, and critiques each one. Special attention is given to the emerging literary approaches, and their relationship to the more traditional methods of source, form, and redaction criticism. Contains extremely brief bibliography at the end of each chapter, and a selective bibliography at the conclusion of the book.

2.13.5 Goldingay, John. *Models for Interpretation of Scripture.* Grand Rapids: Eerdmans, 1995. 328pp.

An insightful and practical examination of what is involved in interpreting the several types of OT material, taking into account the various methods that have been and continue to be employed, and demonstrating how the concerns of these various methods can be brought together in a holistic approach. Gives attention both to foundational theoretical issues and to the demands of Christian proclamation.

2.13.6 Stuart, Douglas. *Old Testament Exegesis: A Primer for Students and Pastors.* 3d ed. Louisville: Westminster John Knox, 2001. 168pp.

An introduction to the task of OT exegesis for the seminary student and pastor. Assumes very little regarding biblical and hermeneutical background. Clearly written and eminently practical guide for the basic steps involved in the interpretation of the text with a view toward preaching and teaching.

A L S O   S I G N I F I C A N T

2.13.7 Achtemeier, Elizabeth. *The Old Testament and the Proclamation of the Gospel.* Philadelphia: Westminster, 1973. 224pp.

2.13.8 Alter, Robert. *The Art of Biblical Poetry.* San Francisco: Harper, 1987. 228pp.

2.13.9 Bar-Efrat, Shimon. *Narrative Art in the Bible.* Journal for the Study of the Old Testament Supplemental Series 70; Bible and Literature Series 17. Sheffield: Sheffield Academic Press, 1997. 295pp.

2.13.10 Broyles, Craig C., ed. *Interpreting the Old Testament: A Guide for Exegesis.* Grand Rapids: Baker, 2001. 272pp.

2.13.11 Brueggemann, Walter. *Interpretation and Obedience: From Faithful Reading to Faithful Living.* Minneapolis: Fortress, 1991. 325pp.

2.13.12 Exum, J. Cheryl, and David J. A. Clines, eds. *The New Literary Criticism and the Hebrew Bible.* Sheffield: JSOT, 1993. 276pp.

2.13.13 Goldingay, John. *Approaches to Old Testament Interpretation.* Rev. ed. Downers Grove, Ill.: InterVarsity, 1990. 207pp.

2.13.14 Gowan, Donald E. *Reclaiming the Old Testament for the Christian Pulpit.* Atlanta: John Knox, 1980. 163pp.

2.13.15 Greidanus, Sidney. *Preaching Christ from the Old Testament: A Contemporary Hermeneutical Method.* Grand Rapids: Eerdmans, 1999. 373pp.

2.13.16 Gunn, David M., and Danna Nolan Fewell. *Narrative in the Hebrew Bible.* Oxford Bible Series. Oxford: Oxford University Press, 1993. 263pp.

2.13.17 Gunneweg, A. H. S. *Understanding the Old Testament.* Philadelphia: Westminster, 1978. 265pp.

2.13.18 Hayes, John H., ed. *Old Testament Form Criticism.* San Antonio, Tex.: Trinity University Press, 1974. 289pp.

2.13.19 Holmgren, Fredrick C. *The Old Testament and the Significance of Jesus: Embracing Change, Maintaining Christian Identity.* Sources for Biblical and Theological Study 2. Grand Rapids: Eerdmans, 1999. 204pp.

2.13.20 House, Paul R., ed. *Beyond Form Criticism: Essays in Old Testament Literary Criticism*. Winona Lake, Ind.: Eisenbrauns, 1992. 446pp.

2.13.21 Koch, Klaus. *The Growth of the Biblical Tradition: The Form-Critical Method*. New York: Scribner's, 1969. 233pp.

2.13.22 Kugel, James L. *The Idea of Biblical Poetry: Parallelism and Its History*. New Haven, Conn.: Yale University Press, 1981. 339pp.

2.13.23 McCurley, Foster R. *Wrestling with the Word: Christian Preaching from the Hebrew Bible*. Valley Forge, Pa.: Trinity Press International, 1996. 243pp.

2.13.24 Rad, Gerhard von. *Biblical Interpretations in Preaching*. Nashville: Abingdon, 1977. 125pp.

2.13.25 Smith, George Adam. *Modern Criticism and the Preaching of the Old Testament*. 3d ed. New York: Armstrong, 1902. 325pp.

2.13.26 Steck, Odil Hannes. *Old Testament Exegesis: A Guide to Methodology*. Society of Biblical Literature Resources for Biblical Study 33. Atlanta: Scholars, 1995. 208pp.

2.13.27 Westermann, Claus, ed. *Essays on Old Testament Hermeneutics*. Atlanta: John Knox, 1963. 363pp.

The following volumes in the Guides to Biblical Scholarship series are relevant:

2.13.28 Habel, Norman C. *Literary Criticism of the Old Testament*. Philadelphia: Fortress, 1971. 86pp.

2.13.29 Hens-Piazza, Gina. *The New Historicism*. Minneapolis: Fortress, 2002. 94pp.

2.13.30 Kille, D. Andrew. *Psychological Biblical Criticism*. Minneapolis: Fortress, 2001. 161pp.

2.13.31 Miller, J. Maxwell. *The Old Testament and the Historian*. Philadelphia: Fortress, 1976. 87pp.

2.13.32 Niditch, Susan. *Folklore and the Hebrew Bible*. Minneapolis: Fortress, 1983. 117pp.

2.13.33 Overholt, Thomas W. *Cultural Anthropology and the Old Testament*. Minneapolis: Fortress, 1996. 116pp.

2.13.34 Petersen, David L., and Kent Harold Richards. *Interpreting Hebrew Poetry*. Minneapolis: Fortress, 1992. 117pp.

2.13.35 Rast, Walter E. *Tradition History and the Old Testament*. Philadelphia: Fortress, 1972. 82pp.

2.13.36 Robertson, David. *The Old Testament and the Literary Critic*. Philadelphia: Fortress, 1977. 87pp.

2.13.37 Sanders, James A. *Canon and Community: A Guide to Canonical Criticism*. Philadelphia: Fortress, 1984. 78pp.

2.13.38 Trible, Phyllis. *Rhetorical Criticism: Context, Method, and the Book of Jonah*. Minneapolis: Fortress, 1994. 264pp.

2.13.39 Tucker, Gene M. *Form Criticism of the Old Testament*. Philadelphia: Fortress, 1971. 84pp.

2.13.40 Wilson, Robert R. *Sociological Approaches to the Old Testament*. Philadelphia: Fortress, 1984. 83pp.

2.14 Old Testament Introductions

H I G H L Y   R E C O M M E N D E D

2.14.1 Anderson, Bernhard W. *Understanding the Old Testament*. 4th ed. Upper Saddle River, N.J.: Prentice-Hall, 1998. 635pp.

This basic introduction to the OT moves in the direction of a "survey" of the OT, but contains more technical historical, hermeneutical, and literary discussion than typically found in surveys. Moves chronologically from the beginnings of Israel's existence as a people to the threshold to the NT period. Employs a narrative style that weaves together in a lively and readable fashion historical, literary, and theological concerns. Generally assumes conclusions of mainline critical scholarship, but is critically and theologically moderate in comparison with much recent OT study.

2.14.2 Childs, Brevard S. *Introduction to the Old Testament as Scripture*. Philadelphia: Fortress, 1979. 688pp.

A classic work and extremely significant in the history of twentieth century OT scholarship both for the cogent description at the beginning of this volume of the "canonical approach" to OT study for which Childs is famous and for the fact that this volume, written from the perspective of the canonical approach, is a new type of OT introduction. There is virtually no attention here to many issues that are normally addressed in introductions, e.g., historical development of Israel, archaeology. Rather, the emphasis is on the "canonical form" of the text (essentially the final form), and the ways in which the history of the tradition that lies behind the final form and the history of OT interpretation can illumine the canonical form and the church's theological and pastoral appropriation of that canonical text.

2.14.3 Dillard, Raymond B., and Tremper Longman III. *An Introduction to the Old Testament*. Grand Rapids: Zondervan, 1994. 473pp.

Lucid, basic introduction that concentrates on the final form of the text as the church's scripture, and consequently gives relatively little attention to source analysis or the history of the development of individual books. Emphasizes "special introduction" (study of individual books) rather than "general introduction" (topics pertaining to the OT as a whole, e.g., textual criticism or the canon). In the process, concentrates on three issues: (1) historical background, (2) literary analysis, (3) theological message. Written from a conservative perspective, but offering fair and open interaction with less conservative historical criticism.

2.14.4 Eissfeldt, Otto. *The Old Testament: An Introduction.* New York: Harper & Row, 1965. 861pp.

Most thorough, detailed, authoritative introduction representing the results of German critical scholarship (which had definitive global influence) in the latter half of the twentieth century. Also discusses the Apocrypha, Pseudepigrapha, and the Dead Sea Scrolls. Now somewhat dated; it should be supplemented with more recent critical studies (e.g., Schmidt [§2.14.6]). Complemented by Harrison (§2.14.5), which presents the conservative rejoinder to many of the conclusions found here.

2.14.5 Harrison, R. K. *Introduction to the Old Testament.* Grand Rapids: Eerdmans, 1969. 1325pp.

In many ways a conservative corollary to Eissfeldt (§2.14.4). Written by perhaps the most prominent conservative OT scholar of his generation, a massive, learned, and detailed introduction that discusses virtually every major aspect of OT. Includes the Apocrypha. Employs a type of historical-critical study, but consistently arrives at conservative positions. Now dated; it should be supplemented by more recent treatments (e.g., Dillard and Longman [§2.14.3]).

2.14.6 Schmidt, Werner H. *Old Testament Introduction.* 2d ed. Louisville: Westminster John Knox, 1995. 452pp.

Lucid presentation of contemporary critical perspectives on major issues of OT history, source analysis, origin and development of OT books, and theology and hermeneutics. Schmidt offers the "consensus" view on the various questions, and thus puts forth little of his own original thinking. Discussions tend to be quite brief, but still a helpful basic orientation.

A L S O   S I G N I F I C A N T

2.14.7   Birch, Bruce C., Walter Brueggemann, Terence E. Fretheim, and David L. Peterson. *A Theological Introduction to the Old Testament.* Nashville: Abingdon, 1999. 475pp.

2.14.8   Coggins, Richard. *Introducing the Old Testament.* Oxford Bible Series. 2d ed. Oxford: Oxford University Press, 2001. 192pp.

2.14.9   Craigie, Peter C. *The Old Testament: Its Background, Growth, and Content.* Nashville: Abingdon, 1986. 351pp.

2.14.10 Crenshaw, James L. *Old Testament Story and Faith: A Literary and Theological Introduction.* Peabody, Mass.: Hendrickson, 1992. 472pp.

2.14.11 Drane, John. *Introducing the Old Testament.* New ed. Oxford: Lion, 2000. 368pp.

2.14.12 Gottwald, Norman K. *The Hebrew Bible: A Socio-Literary Introduction.* Philadelphia: Fortress, 1985. 702pp.

2.14.13 Hayes, John H. *An Introduction to Old Testament Study.* Nashville: Abingdon, 1979. 400pp.

2.14.14 Kaiser, Otto. *Introduction to the Old Testament.* Oxford: Blackwell, 1975. 420pp.

2.14.15 Orr, James. *The Problem of the Old Testament Considered with Reference to Recent Criticism.* New York: Scribners, 1906. 562pp.

2.14.16 Peckham, Brian. *History and Prophecy: Its Development of Late Judean Literary Traditions.* New York: Doubleday, 1993. 880pp.

2.14.17 Rendtorff, Rolf. *The Old Testament: An Introduction.* Philadelphia: Fortress, 1985. 308pp.

2.14.18 Sandmel, Samuel. *The Hebrew Scriptures: An Introduction to Their Literature and Religious Ideas.* Oxford: Oxford University Press, 1978. 546pp.

2.14.19   Schultz, Samuel, *The Old Testament Speaks*. 4th ed. New York: Harper, 1990. 440pp.

2.14.20   Sellin, Ernst, and Georg Fohrer. *Introduction to the Old Testament*. Rev. ed. Nashville: Abingdon, 1968. 540pp.

2.14.21   Smith, W. Robertson. *The Old Testament in the Jewish Church*. 3d ed. London: A. & C. Black, 1926. 458pp.

2.14.22   Soggin, J. Alberto. *Introduction to the Old Testament*. 3d ed. Old Testament Library. Louisville: Westminster John Knox, 1989. 604pp.

2.14.23   Young, Edward J. *An Introduction to the Old Testament*. Revised ed. Grand Rapids: Eerdmans, 1964. 432pp.

2.15 Old Testament Theology

HIGHLY   RECOMMENDED

2.15.1   Bright, John. *The Authority of the Old Testament*. Nashville: Abingdon, 1967.

Probably the most definitive treatment of the theological and practical issues of the authority of the OT for the Christian church. Deals especially with the use of the OT in Christian preaching, and includes illuminating examples of Christian preaching from some of the most difficult and problematic OT passages.

2.15.2   Brueggemann, Walter. *Theology of the Old Testament: Testimony, Dispute, Advocacy*. Minneapolis: Fortress, 1997. 777pp.

Massive, learned, and creative, attempts to move OT theology beyond the ruling paradigms of preceding generations into the new era of postmodernism. As such, emphasizes the pluralistic testimonies to Yahweh in the OT and interaction between those testimonies. Understands the object of the study of OT theology to be the dynamic process of theological dispute between competing visions of God found within the OT rather than the content of the theological claims of the OT themselves. Helpful for considering how the contemporary cultural environment affects the doing of OT theology, but less helpful for understanding that theology itself.

2.15.3   Childs, Brevard S. *Old Testament Theology in a Canonical Context*. Philadelphia: Fortress, 1985. 255pp.

Here Childs applies his canonical approach to OT study (as set forth para-digmatically at the beginning of his *Introduction to the Old Testament as Scrip-ture* [§2.14.2]) to the writing of an OT theology. Thus it focuses on the canonical writings rather than events or experiences behind them. Understands the OT specifically as part of Christian theology, and thus engages in a distinctively Christian reading of the OT, and one that is at times implicitly informed by Child's own Reformed tradition. Extremely relevant and practical for Christian reflection on the various major themes and aspects of OT theology.

2.15.4 Eichrodt, Walther. *Theology of the Old Testament.* 2 vols. Old Testa-ment Library. Philadelphia: Westminster, 1967. 542/ 573pp.

Produced by one of the most prominent OT scholars in the twentieth century, a classic and standard work that emphasizes that Israel's faith was essentially unique among its neighbors and was self-consistent (over against the pluralistic view of Brueggemann [§2.15.2]). Finds the unity of OT theology in the concept of "covenant." Deals with OT theology on the basis of the final form of the text, and treats it synchronically, i.e., as it stands in the OT with little regard to historical development. If one were to buy just one OT theology, this might be the best.

2.15.5 Hasel, Gerhard F. *Old Testament Theology: Basic Issues in the Current Debate.* 4th ed. Grand Rapids: Eerdmans, 1991. 262pp.

Surveys the various approaches to OT theology pursued especially in recent works, and critically examines them in order to identify both positive and negative aspects. As a result of this study, Hasel presents his own method, em-phasizing the nature of the biblical materials themselves without depending on external categories. Contains extensive bibliography.

2.15.6 Hayes, John H., and Frederick Prussner. *Old Testament Theology: Its History and Development.* Atlanta: John Knox, 1985. 290pp.

Similar in purpose and character to the volume by Hasel [§2.15.5], but more concerned with the major figures and historical development of the discipline of OT theology, with relatively less attention to OT theology's major issues or methods. Contains rather extensive bibliographies for each section. Most comprehensive and current history of OT theology available.

2.15.7 Rad, Gerhard von. *Old Testament Theology.* 2 vols. New York: Harper & Row, 1962. 483/470pp.

A monumental work by arguably the greatest OT scholar of the twentieth century. Argues that the theology of the OT reflects Israel's experience of God's acts of salvation, and that OT theology moves progressively forward to full realization in Christ according to a process in which Israel constantly re-interpreted ("re-actualization") earlier traditions in light of contemporary concerns. As such, he depends much on tradition-critical reconstruction. Rich in profound insight even for those who do not accept his critical conclusions or his specific method.

A L S O   S I G N I F I C A N T

2.15.8 Anderson, Bernhard W. *From Creation to New Creation: Old Testament Perspectives.* Overtures to Biblical Theology. Minneapolis: Fortress, 1994. 256pp.

2.15.9 ———. *Contours of Old Testament Theology.* Minneapolis: Fortress, 1999. 358pp.

2.15.10 Barth, Christoph. *God with Us: A Theological Introduction to the Old Testament.* Grand Rapids: Eerdmans, 1991. 403pp.

2.15.11 Becker, Joachim. *Messianic Expectation in the Old Testament.* Edinburgh: T&T Clark, 1977. 96pp.

2.15.12 Brueggemann, Walter. *Old Testament Theology: Essays on Structure, Theme, and Text.* Edited by Patrick D. Miller Jr. Minneapolis: Fortress, 1991. 318pp.

2.15.13 Davidson, A. B. *The Theology of the Old Testament.* International Theological Library. Edinburgh: T&T Clark, 1904. 553pp.

2.15.14 Gerstenberger, Erhard S. *Theologies in the Old Testament.* Minneapolis: Fortress, 2002. 384pp.

2.15.15 Goldingay, John. *Theological Diversity and the Authority of the Old Testament.* Grand Rapids: Eerdmans, 1987. 308pp.

2.15.16 Holladay, William L. *Long Ago God Spoke: How Christians May Hear the Old Testament Today.* Minneapolis: Fortress, 1995. 355pp.

2.15.17 Kaiser, Walter C., Jr. *Toward an Old Testament Theology.* Grand Rapids: Zondervan, 1978. 303pp.

2.15.18 Knierim, Rolf P. *The Task of Old Testament Theology: Substance, Method, and Cases.* Grand Rapids: Eerdmans, 1995. 390pp.

2.15.19 Martens, Elmer A. *Old Testament Theology.* IBR Bibliographies 13. Grand Rapids: Baker, 1997. 138pp.

2.15.20 Nicholson, Ernest W. *God and His People: Covenant and Theology in the Old Testament.* Oxford: Clarendon, 1986. 244pp.

2.15.21 Ollenburger, Ben C., Elmer A. Martens, and Gerhard F. Hasel, eds. *The Flowering of Old Testament Theology*. Sources for Biblical and Theological Study 1. Winona Lake, Ind.: Eisenbrauns, 1992. 547pp.

2.15.22 Perdue, Leo G. *The Collapse of History: Reconstructing Old Testament Theology*. Overtures to Biblical Theology. Minneapolis: Fortress, 1994. 317pp.

2.15.23 Preuss, Horst Dietrich. *Old Testament Theology*. 2 vols. Louisville: Westminster John Knox, 1995. 372/438pp.

2.15.24 Rendtorff, Rolf. *Canon and Theology: Overtures to an Old Testament Theology*. Overtures to Biblical Theology. Minneapolis: Fortress, 1993. 235pp.

2.15.25 Reventlow, Henning Graf. *Problems of Old Testament Theology in the Twentieth Century*. Philadelphia: Fortress, 1985. 194pp.

2.15.26 Sailhamer, John H. *Introduction to Old Testament Theology: A Canonical Approach*. Grand Rapids: Zondervan, 1995. 327pp.

2.15.27 Satterthwaite, Philip E., Richard S. Hess, and Gordon J. Wenham, eds. *The Lord's Anointed: Interpretation of Old Testament Messianic Texts*. Grand Rapids: Baker, 1995. 320pp.

2.15.28 Schmidt, Werner H. *The Faith of the Old Testament: A History*. Philadelphia: Westminster, 1983. 302pp.

2.15.29 Seitz, Christopher R. *Word without End: The Old Testament as Abiding Theological Witness*. Grand Rapids: Eerdmans, 1998. 355pp.

2.15.30 Snaith, Norman H. *The Distinctive Ideas of the Old Testament*. New York: Schocken, 1964. 193pp.

2.15.31 Vriezen, Theodorus Christiaan. *An Outline of Old Testament Theology*. 2d ed. Newton, Mass.: Branford, 1970. 479pp.

2.15.32 Westermann, Claus. *Elements of Old Testament Theology*. Atlanta: John Knox, 1982. 261pp.

2.15.33 Wright, Christopher J. H. *Knowing Jesus through the Old Testament*. Downers Grove, Ill.: InterVarsity, 1992. 256pp.

2.15.34 Wright, G. Ernest. *God Who Acts: Biblical Theology as Recital*. Studies in Biblical Theology 8. London: SCM, 1952. 132pp.

2.15.35 Zimmerli, Walther. *Old Testament Theology in Outline*. Atlanta: John Knox, 1978. 258pp.

2.16 Old Testament Ethics

H I G H L Y   R E C O M M E N D E D

2.16.1 Birch, Bruce C. *Let Justice Roll Down: The Old Testament, Ethics, and the Christian Life*. Louisville: Westminster John Knox, 1991. 383pp.

Written by a leading authority in biblical (and especially OT) ethics, this volume is not a description of ethical thinking or systems within the OT itself, but rather a hermeneutical exploration of the use of the OT for contemporary Christian ethics. Its emphasis is therefore methodological. Although Birch makes serious use of exegesis employing the historical-critical method, he focuses on the canonical shape of the text (and in the process reads the OT in light of the NT). He moves through the OT, discussing the issues involved in the ethical use of its various parts.

2.16.2 Janzen, Waldemar. *Old Testament Ethics: A Paradigmatic Approach*. Louisville: Westminster John Knox, 1994. 236pp.

Identifies five models of the good life in the OT (priestly, wisdom, royal, prophetic, familial) and argues that each of these includes stories that are paradigmatic for OT ethics in general, and that each of these models comes to full expression in the portrait of Jesus in the NT. These models reflect various genres of the OT and thus support Janzen's major claim that the whole of the OT, and not just certain genres (e.g., law), is relevant for ethics. Suggestive and engaging, although more dependent on Janzen's unique construal of passages and his distinctive hermeneutical perspective than is Birch's work (§2.16.1).

2.16.3 Wright, Christopher J. H. *Walking in the Ways of the Lord: The Ethical Authority of the Old Testament*. Downers Grove, Ill.: InterVarsity, 1995. 319pp.

Wright here develops his own model for doing OT ethics, which he set forth originally in *An Eye for an Eye* (§2.16.9). Moves from a brief but helpful discussion of the issues, to the ways in which the church has appropriated the OT ethically, including a survey of contemporary approaches, to the final section in which he presents his own method by examining issues of the land, the jubilee, the state, human rights, and struggles against corruption, dishonesty, and injustice. Lucid, engaging, and practical. Best overall introduction to the study of OT ethics.

ALSO   SIGNIFICANT

2.16.4 Barton, John. *Ethics and the Old Testament*. Harrisburg, Pa.: Trinity Press International, 1998. 100pp.

2.16.5 Birch, Bruce C. *What Does the Lord Require? The Old Testament Call to Social Witness*. Louisville: Westminster John Knox, 1985. 116pp.

2.16.6 Crenshaw, James L., and John T. Willis, eds. *Essays in Old Testament Ethics*. New York: Ktav, 1974. 284pp.

2.16.7 Kaiser, Walter C., Jr. *Toward Old Testament Ethics*. Grand Rapids: Zondervan, 1983. 345pp.

2.16.8 Rodd, Cyril S. *Glimpses of a Strange Land: Studies in Old Testament Ethics*. Old Testament Studies. Edinburgh: T&T Clark, 2000. 384pp.

2.16.9 Wright, Christopher J. H. *An Eye for an Eye: The Place of Old Testament Ethics Today*. Downers Grove, Ill.: InterVarsity, 1983. 224pp.

2.17 Old Testament Commentaries: Multivolume

2.17.1 Keil, Carl Friedrich, and Franz Delitzsch. *Commentary on the Old Testament*. 10 vols. Peabody, Mass.: Hendrickson, 1996. Reprinted from the English edition originally published by T&T Clark, Edinburgh, 1860–1891. Volumes average 800pp.

Learned commentary on every passage of the OT from two of the most prominent nineteenth-century German OT scholars, representing an evangelical and generally conservative position. Gives serious attention to details of the Hebrew text, but equally concerned with historical and literary context and theological significance. Especially useful in providing solid exposition for parts of the OT for which there are relatively few helpful commentaries. Now dated, and should be used in combination with more recent contributions. This retypeset edition corrects typographical errors, uses current abbreviations, and incorporates other changes to improve readability.

2.17.2 Wesley, John. *Explanatory Notes upon the Old Testament*. 3 vols. Bristol, U.K.: William Pine, 1765–1766. 2613pp.

Comparable to Wesley's better-known *Explanatory Notes upon the New Testament* (§4.18.5), the founder of Methodism offers terse commentary for the "unlettered" reader of the Bible. Very basic comment, with frequent insights pertaining to the relation of the text to other biblical passages, fulfillment in

Christ, and significance for Christian living. More helpful for exposure to eigh-
teenth-century British commentary and to Wesley's interpretive methods and
conclusions than for its critical interpretation of the details of the text in their
historical and literary contexts.

2.18 Old Testament Commentaries: Series

2.18.1 Daily Study Bible: Old Testament. Edited by John C. L. Gibson. Louisville:
Westminster John Knox, 1981–1987.

2.18.2 Historical Commentary on the Old Testament. Edited by Cornelius Houtman,
Willem S. Prinsloo, Wilfred G. E. Watson, and Al Wolters. Leuven: Peeters,
1993–.

2.18.3 New International Commentary on the Old Testament (NICOT). Edited by
R. K. Harrison and Robert L. Hubbard Jr. Grand Rapids: Eerdmans, 1976–.

2.18.4 Old Testament Library (OTL). Edited by Peter R. Ackroyd, Bernhard Anderson,
James Barr, James Luther Mays, and G. Ernest Wright. Original series. Louisville:
Westminster John Knox, 1962–1988; James Luther Mays, Carol A. Newsome,
and David L. Petersen. New Series. Louisville: Westminster John Knox, 1991–.

2.18.5 Proclamation Commentaries: The Old Testament Witnesses for Preaching.
Edited by Foster R. McCurley. Minneapolis: Fortress, 1977–1995.

2.18.6 Tyndale Old Testament Commentaries (TOTC). Edited by D. J. Wiseman.
Grand Rapids: Eerdmans, 1968–1996.

2.19 The Pentateuch: General Works

HIGHLY RECOMMENDED

2.19.1 Blenkinsopp, Joseph. *The Pentateuch: An Introduction to the First Five
Books of the Bible.* Anchor Bible Reference Library. New York:
Doubleday, 1992. 273pp.

Readable, comprehensive study from a leading OT scholar. Describes and
evaluates recent developments in the source-critical analysis of the Pentateuch, and argues for a modified form of the documentary hypothesis. Employs source analysis, historical background, and a close reading of the final
form of the text to arrive at a holistic interpretation, presented passage by passage through the Pentateuch. Probably the best overall introduction to the
Pentateuch. Includes extensive bibliography.

2.19.2 Brueggemann, Walter, and Hans Walter Wolff. *The Vitality of Old Testament Traditions.* 2d ed. Atlanta: John Knox, 1982. 180pp.

Two prominent OT scholars address the theology of the major sources (according to the general critical consensus) of the Pentateuch: Yahwist, Elohist, Deuteronomist, and Priestly. The discussions are lucid and engaging, and provide insight also into the theology of the final form of the text, and thus are useful even to those who are skeptical regarding these sources.

2.19.3 Clines, David J. A. *The Theme of the Pentateuch.* 2d ed. Journal for the Study of the Old Testament Supplemental Series 10. Sheffield: JSOT, 1997. 176pp.

The brevity of this book belies its value as an illuminating study of the identification and exposition of the unifying theme of the Pentateuch, which Clines takes to be the partial fulfillment (and therefore also partial nonfulfillment) of the promise of blessing to the patriarchs. Includes a sustained reading of the Pentateuch from the perspective of this central theme. Clines focuses on the final form of the text, while relating his method and conclusions to the dominant theories of the history of tradition that lies behind the final text.

2.19.4 Crüsemann, Frank. *The Torah: Theology and Social History of Old Testament Law.* Minneapolis: Fortress, 1996. 460pp.

Most comprehensive treatment available of OT law. Traces the development of the commandments of the Pentateuch from their earliest formulation to their inclusion in oral and written sources to their role in the final form of the Pentateuch. Attends to historical background, social context, and theological significance.

2.19.5 Livingston, G. Herbert. *The Pentateuch in Its Cultural Environment.* 2d ed. Grand Rapids: Baker, 1987. 322pp.

A most comprehensive, learned, and balanced treatment of the various aspects of the Pentateuch (historical, literary, theological) from a conservative perspective. Offers informed and lucid discussions, replete with illustrations, photos, and maps. Each section concludes with select bibliography. Very useful as an introduction to the study of the Pentateuch, valuable even to those who do not share its conservative orientation.

2.19.6 Sailhamer, John H. *The Pentateuch as Narrative: A Biblical-Theological Commentary.* Grand Rapids: Zondervan, 1992. 522pp.

Solid commentary on the final form of the Pentateuch from a conservative perspective. Treats the Pentateuch as a continuous narrative, and thus makes very little of the distinction between the five books and gives no attention to the sources that might lie behind the final text. Argues that the author of the Pentateuch (possibly Moses) had lived under the Law of the Covenant given at Sinai and had come to recognize that it could not produce true faith in Yahweh and thus looked forward to the hope of the new covenant that would be established entirely on God's faithfulness. Despite its avowedly narrative approach, draws very little on current narrative-critical theory and suffers somewhat from its general lack of attention to historical background. Still, offers helpful theological insights into the final form of the text.

A L S O   S I G N I F I C A N T

2.19.7 Alexander, T. Desmond. *From Paradise to the Promised Land: An Introduction to the Main Themes of the Pentateuch.* Carlisle, U.K.: Paternoster, 1995. 227pp.

2.19.8 Bailey, Lloyd R. *The Pentateuch.* Interpreting Biblical Texts. Nashville: Abingdon, 1981. 160pp.

2.19.9 Buber, Martin. *Moses: The Revelation and the Covenant.* New York: Harper, 1958. 226pp.

2.19.10 Campbell, Antony F., and Mark A. O'Brien. *Sources of the Pentateuch: Texts, Introductions, Annotations.* Minneapolis: Fortress, 1993. 266pp.

2.19.11 Coats, George W. *Moses: Heroic Man, Man of God.* Journal for the Study of the Old Testament Supplement Series 57. Sheffield: JSOT, 1988. 250pp.

2.19.12 Fretheim, Terence E. *The Pentateuch.* Interpreting Biblical Texts. Nashville: Abingdon, 1996. 183pp.

2.19.13 Hamilton, Victor P. *Handbook on the Pentateuch.* Grand Rapids: Baker, 1982. 496pp.

2.19.14 Lohfink, Norbert. *Theology of the Pentateuch: Themes of the Priestly Narrative and Deuteronomy.* Minneapolis: Fortress, 1994. 314pp.

2.19.15 McCarthy, D. J. *Old Testament Covenant: A Survey of Current Opinions.* Growing Points in Theology. Atlanta: John Knox, 1972. 112pp.

2.19.16 Nicholson, Ernest. *The Pentateuch in the Twentieth Century: The Legacy of Julius Wellhausen.* Oxford: Clarendon, 1998. 294pp.

2.19.17 Noth, Martin. *A History of Pentateuchal Traditions.* Atlanta: Scholars, 1981. 296pp.

2.19.18 ———. *Laws in the Pentateuch and Other Studies.* London: SCM, 1966. 289pp.

2.19.19 Patrick, Dale. *Old Testament Law.* Atlanta: John Knox, 1985. 278pp.

2.19.20 Rad, Gerhard von. *The Problem of the Hexateuch and Other Essays.* London: SCM, 1966. 340pp.

2.19.21 Rofé, Alexander. *Introduction to the Composition of the Pentateuch.* Sheffield: Sheffield Academic Press, 1999. 152pp.

2.19.22 Sherwood, Stephen K. *Leviticus, Numbers, and Deuteronomy.* Sacra Pagina. Collegeville, Minn.: Michael Glazier, 2002. 320pp.

2.19.23 Sparks, Kenton L. *The Pentateuch: An Annotated Bibliography.* IBR Bibliographies 1. Grand Rapids: Baker, 2002. 160pp.

2.19.24 Suelzer, A. *The Pentateuch: A Study in Salvation History.* New York: Herder & Herder, 1964. 224pp.

2.19.25 Whybray, R. N. *Introduction to the Pentateuch.* Grand Rapids: Eerdmans, 1995. 146pp.

2.20 Genesis

HIGHLY RECOMMENDED

2.20.1 Brueggemann, Walter. *Genesis.* Interpretation: A Bible Commentary for Teaching and Preaching. Atlanta: John Knox, 1982. 384pp.

One of the best in the Interpretation series, this volume focuses on the theological witness of the final form of the text. Sets forth engaging, profound, and practical theological insights based on careful exegesis. Elegantly written, and almost poetic in places.

2.20.2 Hamilton, Victor P. *The Book of Genesis.* 2 vols. New International Commentary on the Old Testament. Grand Rapids: Eerdmans, 1990, 1995. 522/774pp.

Thorough, current commentary from an evangelical perspective by a prominent OT scholar in the Wesleyan tradition. Affirms literary and theological unity of the book, and thus does not deal with multiple layers of tradition. Emphasizes the development throughout Genesis of the book's main theme:

God's gracious promise of blessing and reconciliation in the face of sin and evil. Each section concludes with discussion of the use of that portion of Genesis in the NT.

2.20.3 Rad, Gerhard von. *Genesis: A Commentary.* Rev. ed. Old Testament Library. Philadelphia: Westminster, 1972. 440pp.

One of the finest commentaries ever written on any biblical book, this is a masterpiece of brilliant literary analysis that leads to engaging theological insight. Although at a few points the commentary depends on von Rad's critical reconstruction of sources, generally the focus is on the final form of the text.

2.20.4 Wenham, Gordon J. *Genesis.* 2 vols. Word Biblical Commentary. Waco, Tex.: Word, 1987, 1994. 352/517pp.

Employs lucid, terse style to communicate a wealth of information pertaining to text-critical analysis, compositional sources, and theological significance. Engages in broad interaction with current research, and consistently reaches conclusions that are well informed and judicious. Draws insights from historical background and tradition history, but in the service of an interpretation of the final text that takes its compositional artistry seriously. Represents the best of British evangelical scholarship.

2.20.5 Westermann, Claus. *Genesis: A Commentary.* 3 vols. Continental Commentary. Minneapolis: Augsburg, 1984–1986. 636/604/269pp.

Most complete, comprehensive, and erudite commentary on Genesis ever produced. Encyclopedic in treatment of text-critical issues, historical and archaeological background, linguistic matters, and history of interpretation. Technical in content, but readable in form. Makes use of source-critical insights, but focuses on final shape of the text. Gives serious attention to theological significance. Westermann's "Practical Commentary" (§2.20.18) is an abridgment of this work.

A L S O   S I G N I F I C A N T

2.20.6 Cassuto, Umberto. *Commentary on the Book of Genesis.* 2 vols. Jerusalem: Magnes, 1961–1964. 323/386pp.

2.20.7 Coats, George W. *Genesis: With an Introduction to Narrative Literature.* Forms of Old Testament Literature 1. Grand Rapids: Eerdmans, 1983. 322pp.

2.20.8 Delitzsch, Franz. *A New Commentary on Genesis.* 2 vols. 5th ed. Edinburgh: T&T Clark, 1899. 412/408pp.

2.20.9   Driver, S. R. *The Book of Genesis.* Westminster Commentaries. London: Methuen, 1904. 420pp.

2.20.10 Fokkelman, J. P. *Narrative Art in Genesis: Specimens of Stylistic and Structural Analysis.* 2d ed. Sheffield: JSOT, 1991. 244pp.

2.20.11 Gunkel, Hermann. *Genesis.* Mercer Library of Biblical Studies. Macon, Ga.: Mercer University Press, 1997. (Original German edition, 1910.) 477pp.

2.20.12 Kidner, Derek. *Genesis: An Introduction and Commentary.* Tyndale Kidner Old Testament Commentaries. Downers Grove, Ill.: InterVarsity, 1967. 244pp.

2.20.13 Mills, Watson E. *Genesis.* Bibliographies for Biblical Research: Old Testament 1. Lewiston, N.Y.: Mellen Biblical Press, 2000. 265pp.

2.20.14 Sarna, Nahum. *Understanding Genesis.* New York: McGraw-Hill, 1966. 267pp.

2.20.15 Skinner, John. *A Critical and Exegetical Commentary on the Book of Genesis.* 2d ed. International Critical Commentary. Edinburgh: T&T Clark, 1930. 551pp.

2.20.16 Speiser, Ephraim A. *Genesis.* 3d ed. Anchor Bible. Garden City, N.Y.: Doubleday, 1964. 378pp.

2.20.17 Waltke, Bruce K., and Cathi J. Fredricks. *Genesis: A Commentary.* Grand Rapids: Zondervan, 2001. 656pp.

2.20.18 Westermann, Claus. *Genesis.* Text and Interpretation: A Practical Commentary. Grand Rapids: Eerdmans, 1987. 338pp

2.21 Exodus

HIGHLY RECOMMENDED

2.21.1   Childs, Brevard S. *The Book of Exodus: A Critical, Theological Commentary.* Old Testament Library. Philadelphia: Westminster, 1974. 659pp.

A new type of commentary, one that puts into practice Childs's "canonical approach," as set forth at the beginning of his *Introduction to the Old Testament as Scripture* (§2.14.2). Childs employs insights from a philological examination of the language of the text, the growth of the tradition through its various stages to the final (canonical) shape, the function of the passage in its literary context, its role in the canon of the OT, and the history of Jewish and Christian exegesis in order to interpret the theological significance of the text as scripture for the church. Probably the most authoritative commentary on Exodus, and the most helpful for teaching and preaching.

2.21.2 Durham, John I. *Exodus.* Word Biblical Commentary. Waco, Tex.: Word, 1987. 516pp.

Emphasizes the theological unity of Exodus in its canonical form, and finds the book's unity in its central theme, viz., Yahweh as present in the midst of his people Israel. Interpretation focuses on language and literary context, with little attention given to growth of the tradition, historical background or archaeological discoveries, since Durham regards most attempts to reconstruct actual historical events or earlier traditions to be hopelessly speculative. Deals seriously with theological issues as they are encountered in the text, but gives little explicit attention to theological implications or contemporary application.

2.21.3 Fretheim, Terence E. *Exodus.* Interpretation: A Bible Commentary for Teaching and Preaching. Louisville: Westminster John Knox, 1991. 321pp.

Outstanding example of engaging and profound theological reflection on issues of contemporary concern based on careful exegesis of the text. Deals especially with issues of the relationship between history and faith, theology of creation, the knowledge of God, images of God, Exodus as a paradigm for liberation, theology of worship, and the role of law and covenant for Israel's identity. Complements the more "traditional" commentaries that are heavy on technical matters, but give little attention to contemporary theological significance.

2.21.4 Gowan, Donald E. *Theology in Exodus: Biblical Theology in the Form of a Commentary.* Philadelphia: Westminster, 1994. 297pp.

Like Childs's commentary (§2.21.1), this book is intended to chart new methodological paths. Whereas Childs attempted to write a new kind of commentary, Gowan attempted a new type of biblical theology, viz., one that emerges out of a careful reading of the text in its literary (i.e., book) and canonical contexts. Organized like a commentary, but asks a single question: What does this book say about God? Traces the major affirmations about God through the rest of Scripture and into Judaism and Christianity. Somewhat restrictive, in that the theology of the book is broader than the doctrine of God, yet certainly God is the primary concern, and this restriction establishes and maintains focus.

A L S O   S I G N I F I C A N T

2.21.5 Cassuto, Umberto. *A Commentary on the Book of Exodus.* Jerusalem: Magnes, 1967. 509pp.

2.21.6 Clements, Ronald E. *Exodus*. Cambridge Bible Commentary. Cambridge: University Press, 1972. 248pp.

2.21.7 Cole, Robert A. *Exodus*. Tyndale Old Testament Commentaries. Downers Grove, Ill.: InterVarsity, 1973. 239pp.

2.21.8 Driver, S. R. *The Book of Exodus*. Cambridge Bible for Schools and Colleges. Cambridge: Cambridge University Press, 1911. 443pp.

2.21.9 Houtman, Cornelius. *Exodus*. 3 vols. Historical Commentary on the Old Testament. Kampen: Kok, 1993–2000. 554/466/737pp.

2.21.10 Knight, George A. F. *Theology as Narration: A Commentary on the Book of Exodus*. Edinburgh: Handsel, 1976. 209pp.

2.21.11 Larsson, Gören. *Bound for Freedom: The Book of Exodus in Jewish and Christian Traditions*. Peabody, Mass.: Hendrickson, 1999. 334pp.

2.21.12 Meyer, Lester. *The Message of Exodus: A Theological Commentary*. Minneapolis: Augsburg, 1983. 171pp.

2.21.13 Mills, Watson E. *Exodus*. Bibliographies for Biblical Research: Old Testament Series 2. Lewiston, N.Y.: Mellen Biblical Press, 2001. 167pp.

2.21.14 Noth, Martin. *Exodus*. Old Testament Library. Philadelphia: Westminster, 1962. 283pp.

2.21.15 Propp, William H. C. *Exodus 1–18*. Anchor Bible. New York: Doubleday, 1998. 680pp.

2.21.16 Sarna, Nahum. *Exploring Exodus: The Heritage of Biblical Israel*. New York: Schocken, 1986. 277pp.

2.22 Leviticus

HIGHLY RECOMMENDED

2.22.1 Hartley, John E. *Leviticus*. Word Biblical Commentary. Dallas: Word, 1992. 496pp.

Careful attention by this evangelical scholar to exegetical detail combined with emphasis on theological issues and implications make this volume extremely helpful for preaching and teaching on a portion of the canon that resists easy or immediate application to contemporary concerns. Identifies the central issue of Leviticus as the significance of pure worship and holy living, with a subordinate (though still important) issue pertaining to leadership and the relationship between priest and laity. Contends that the book contains a core of laws originating with Moses that has been supplemented by applications of these laws pertinent to later generations of Israelites.

2.22.2 Milgrom, Jacob. *Leviticus.* 2 vols. Anchor Bible. New York: Doubleday, 1991, 2000. 1892pp.

Technical, detailed, and encyclopedic treatment of text-critical, source-critical, linguistic, and historical considerations, with serious interaction with the history of interpretation, especially ancient interpretation (e.g., rabbis and interpretation implicit in the Septuagint versions). Written by a Jewish scholar, these volumes offer exposure to critical Jewish scholarship, but of course do not relate Leviticus to the NT or Christian fulfillment. Finds the center of the book in the presence of Yahweh dwelling in the midst of camp and congregation as the basis of the unique privilege and responsibility of Israel, a people thus called to worship and service. Excellent for serious study of the development of traditions and the original meaning and function of the text, but less helpful for theological implications and discussion of contemporary application.

2.22.3 Wenham, Gordon J. *The Book of Leviticus.* New International Commentary on the Old Testament. Grand Rapids: Eerdmans, 1979. 362pp.

Like Hartley (§2.22.1), Wenham gives careful attention to the language of the text and to issues of historical background, with a view toward development of theological issues and suggestions regarding contemporary Christian application. Refuses to take a position on critical issues of the book's origins, and thus remains independent of any specific theory of authorship, sources, and date. Briefer, less technical, with less bibliography than Hartley's, but still quite helpful for both serious academic work and tasks of preaching and teaching.

A L S O   S I G N I F I C A N T

2.22.4 Bonar, A. A. *A Commentary on the Book of Leviticus: Expository and Practical.* 2d ed. London: Nisbet, 1863. 513pp.

2.22.5 Budd, Philip J. *Leviticus.* New Century Bible. Grand Rapids: Eerdmans, 1996. 395pp.

2.22.6 Douglas, Mary. *Leviticus as Literature*. Oxford: Oxford University Press, 1999. 280pp.

2.22.7 Gerstenberger, Erhard S. *Leviticus: A Commentary*. Old Testament Library. Louisville: Westminster John Knox, 1996. 450pp.

2.22.8 Harrison, R. K. *Leviticus*. Tyndale Old Testament Commentaries. Downers Grove, Ill.: InterVarsity, 1980. 252pp.

2.22.9 Kellogg, S. H. *The Book of Leviticus*. 3d ed. New York: A. C. Armstrong, 1899. Repr., Minneapolis: Klock & Klock, 1978. 566pp.

2.22.10 Noth, Martin. *Leviticus: A Commentary*. Rev. ed. Old Testament Library. Philadelphia: Westminster, 1977. 208pp.

2.22.11 Warning, Wilfried. *Literary Artistry in Leviticus*. Leiden: Brill, 1999. 256pp.

2.23 Numbers

H I G H L Y   R E C O M M E N D E D

2.23.1 Ashley, Timothy R. *The Book of Numbers*. New International Commentary on the Old Testament. Grand Rapids: Eerdmans, 1993. 667pp.

Careful attention to the details of the text, especially linguistic details. This commentary from an evangelical scholar grants the reality of a long process of transmission of tradition toward the final form, but asserts that because this process is unrecoverable with any degree of certainty we should focus on the final form of the text. Identifies the overall theological and pastoral purpose as a call to exact obedience to God. Helpful for dealing with technical matters essential for interpretation, but offers relatively little explicit comment on theological significance of passages.

2.23.2 Budd, Philip J. *Numbers*. Word Biblical Commentary. Waco, Tex.: Word, 1984. 409pp.

Informed and current, lucid in style though with a focus on technical linguistic and tradition-critical issues. Treats Numbers as composed in its final form by priestly writers in the early postexilic period as part of the priestly redaction of the whole Pentateuch, yet argues that Numbers has its own unity and distinct themes and theology, one that concerns especially the Levitical order and the tent of meeting. Commentary focuses on the ways the priestly writers edited received tradition in order to address concerns that Israel faced in the sixth century B.C.E. This emphasis might mitigate somewhat the value of commentary for those who disagree with this historical or methodological perspective. Gives serious attention to the theology of the text.

2.23.3   Levine, Baruch A. *Numbers*. 2 vols. Anchor Bible. New York: Doubleday, 1993, 2000. 528/613pp.

Meticulous, detailed commentary by a leading Jewish Pentateuchal scholar. Focuses on technical linguistic and historical issues. Like Budd (§2.23.2), emphasizes the role of priestly traditions and priestly editorial activity in the sixth century B.C.E., but without the concern for theological issues found in Budd's volume. Helpful for serious exploration of technical matters pertaining to interpretation, less so for theological reflection.

2.23.4   Olson, Dennis T. *Numbers*. Interpretation: A Bible Commentary for Teaching and Preaching. Louisville: Westminster John Knox, 1996. 196pp.

Readable, reliable exposition of the meaning of the text in its final form, with engaging and creative connections to the NT and contemporary issues facing the church. Important complement to the majority of commentaries on Numbers, which give little attention to theology and virtually no attention to contemporary application. Does suffer some from brevity.

ALSO SIGNIFICANT

2.23.5   Gray, George Buchanan. *A Critical and Exegetical Commentary on Numbers*. International Critical Commentary. Edinburgh: T&T Clark, 1903. 489pp.

2.23.6   Harrison, R. K. *Numbers: An Exegetical Commentary*. Grand Rapids: Baker, 1992. 542pp.

2.23.7   Ibn Ezra, with annotations by H. Norman Strickman and Arthur M. Silver. *Commentary on the Pentateuch: Numbers*. New York: Menorah, 1999. 270pp.

2.23.8   Maarsingh, B. *Numbers*. Text and Interpretation: A Practical Commentary. Grand Rapids: Eerdmans, 1987. 122pp.

2.23.9   Olson, Dennis T. *The Death of the Old and the Birth of the New: The Framework of the Book of Numbers and the Pentateuch*. Brown Judaic Studies 71. Chico, Calif.: Scholars, 1985. 253pp.

2.23.10 Riggans, Walter. *Numbers*. Daily Study Bible. Philadelphia: Westminster, 1983. 251pp.

2.23.11 Wenham, Gordon J. *Numbers*. Tyndale Old Testament Commentaries. Downers Grove, Ill.: InterVarsity, 1981. 240pp.

2.24 Deuteronomy

See also FORMER PROPHETS (§2.25)

H I G H L Y   R E C O M M E N D E D

2.24.1 Christensen, Duane. *Deuteronomy*. 2d ed. 2 vols. Word Biblical Commentary. Nashville: Thomas Nelson, 2001, 2002. 915pp.

Argues the unusual thesis that Deuteronomy is a didactic poem, intended to be recited publicly to music within a liturgical setting, and thus emphasizes the artistic and literary structures of Deuteronomy, comparing them to modern epic poetry and music. While acknowledging the role of Moses in the traditions found in this book, focuses on the post-Mosaic formation and liturgical use of the book. Many readers will find Christensen's thesis unpersuasive, but all readers will find its theological reflections and probes into contemporary relevance and application useful.

2.24.2 Clements, Ronald E. *God's Chosen People: A Theological Interpretation of the Book of Deuteronomy*. London: SCM, 1968. 126pp.

Brief but solid and illuminating discussion of the major theological themes in Deuteronomy, within the context of the historical production of the book (reforms under Josiah) and its place in OT theology. Useful as an introduction to Deuteronomy's theology.

2.24.3 Craigie, Peter C. *The Book of Deuteronomy*. New International Commentary on the Old Testament. Grand Rapids: Eerdmans, 1976. 424pp.

Clear and solid commentary espousing a conservative position regarding date and unity: Deuteronomy is a record of the words of Moses as Israel gathered for a ceremonial renewal of the Sinai covenant before entering Canaan. Craigie grants it might have been edited in Joshua's time. Finds the theme to be the covenant, and this theme forms the basis for the book's contemporary significance to the people of the new covenant. Gives careful attention to the language of the text, book context, and historical background.

2.24.4 Miller, Patrick D., Jr. *Deuteronomy*. Interpretation: A Bible Commentary for Teaching and Preaching. Louisville: Westminster John Knox, 1990. 253pp.

The best commentary available for the theological meaning of Deuteronomy. Deals with the original significance of the text at the time of its production (sixth century B.C.E.), and uses this discussion as the basis for canonical reflection on its relation to other OT and NT passages, and for creative and compelling theological reflection that has practical ramifications for contemporary Christian life.

2.24.5 Nelson, Richard D. *Deuteronomy: A Commentary*. Old Testament Library. Louisville: Westminster John Knox, 2002. 424pp.

Informed and judicious commentary, attending to historical background, linguistic analysis, literary structure and other rhetorical features pertaining to the final form of the text, the history of composition (i.e., the stages of the book's development), and the significance of the book for the original audience (who lived during the reigns of Manasseh and Josiah). Is concerned to present the distinctive theology of Deuteronomy, especially the call to reform, the centralization of sacrifice, the repudiation of competing religions, election, and covenant. Commentary is thus ambitious in scope. This ambitious scope is both a strength and a weakness, for Nelson struggles in a commentary of this length to treat each of these concerns thoroughly and to relate them in significant ways to one another.

2.24.6 Rad, Gerhard von. *Deuteronomy*. Old Testament Library. Philadelphia: Westminster, 1966. 210pp.

Authoritative and learned; argues that the central concern of the book is loyalty to the one God and worship at one place. Maintains that the book was composed of a vast array of traditions connected with the holy war and that it emerged at the end of eighth century B.C.E. in response to an unparalleled threat to the existence of Israel and its worship. The commentary carefully explains the text within this framework. Provides many helpful insights, yet somewhat constrained by its brevity and by the narrow (and by no means universally accepted) view of the book's origin. Offers less theological reflection than does his commentary on Genesis (§2.20.3).

ALSO SIGNIFICANT

2.24.7 Driver, S. R. *A Critical and Exegetical Commentary on Deuteronomy*. International Critical Commentary. Edinburgh: T&T Clark, 1895. 434pp.

2.24.8 McConville, J. Gordon. *Deuteronomy*. Apollos Old Testament Commentary. Downers Grove, Ill.: InterVarsity, 2002. 448pp.

2.24.9 Millar, J. Gary. *Now Choose Life: Theology and Ethics in Deuteronomy*. New Studies in Biblical Theology. Grand Rapids: Eerdmans, 1998. 216pp.

2.24.10 Nicholson, E. W. *Deuteronomy and Tradition*. Oxford: Oxford University Press, 1967. 145pp.

2.24.11 Olson, Dennis T. *Deuteronomy and the Death of Moses*. Overtures to Biblical Theology. Philadelphia: Fortress, 1994. 191pp.

2.24.12 Rad, Gerhard von. *Studies in Deuteronomy*. Studies in Biblical Theology. London: SCM, 1953. 96pp.

2.24.13 Rofé, Alexander. *Deuteronomy: Issues and Interpretation*. Old Testament Studies. Edinburgh: T&T Clark, 2001. 224pp.

2.24.14 Smith, George Adam. *The Book of Deuteronomy*. Cambridge Bible for Schools and Colleges. Cambridge: Cambridge University Press, 1918. 396pp.

2.24.15 Thompson, J. A. *Deuteronomy*. Tyndale Old Testament Commentaries. Downers Grove, Ill.: InterVarsity, 1974. 320pp.

2.24.16 Tigay, Jeffrey. *Deuteronomy*. JPS Torah Commentary. Philadelphia: Jewish Publication Society, 1996. 538pp.

2.24.17 Weinfeld, Moshe. *Deuteronomy 1–11*. Anchor Bible. New York: Doubleday, 1991. 455pp.

2.24.18 Welch, Adam C. *Deuteronomy: The Framework to the Code*. London: Oxford University Press, 1932. 215pp.

2.25 The Former Prophets: General Works

See also PENTATEUCH: GENERAL WORKS (§2.19)

H I G H L Y   R E C O M M E N D E D

2.25.1 Bendavid, Abba. *Maqbilot baMiqra [Parallels in the Bible]*. Jerusalem: Carta, 1972. 219pp.

Reliable and accessible synopsis between the Books of Chronicles and Samuel/Kings as well as other relevant biblical parallels. Less extensive than

Vanuttelli (§2.25.7), especially in the area of textual criticism and the Septuagint. Useable for those who have a firm basic knowledge of Hebrew.

2.25.2   Endres, John C., William R. Millar, and John Barclay Burns, eds. *Chronicles and Its Synoptic Parallels in Samuel, Kings, and Related Biblical Texts.* Collegeville, Minn.: Liturgical Press, 1998. 356pp.

Probably the most current and accessible synopsis of the historical books. Includes a helpful introduction to the history of synopses or harmonies of the historical books and the use of these resources, followed by the synopsis proper, in which the text from Chronicles appears on the left column with parallels on the right. Includes a new "synoptic" translation that seeks to reflect points of similarity in the original Hebrew between Chronicles and parallel passages that might be missed by the standard versions.

2.25.3   Fretheim, Terence E. *Deuteronomic History.* Interpreting Biblical Texts. Nashville: Abingdon, 1983. 160pp.

Engaging and practical guide for theological interpretation and contemporary application of the Deuteronomic History, which Fretheim believes was produced for exiles in Babylonian captivity. After dealing briefly but specifically with the most relevant introductory matters (e.g., historicity and the overall theology of the Deuteronomic History), Fretheim presents models of interpretation and application of four key passages, one each from Joshua, Judges, Samuel, and Kings.

2.25.4   McConville, J. Gordon. *Grace in the End: A Study in Deuteronomic Theology.* Studies in Old Testament Biblical Theology. Grand Rapids: Zondervan, 1993. 176pp.

Illuminating review of recent scholarly contributions to both the critical issues and theology of the Book of Deuteronomy and the Deuteronomic History. McConville includes his own conclusions regarding the theological message of this corpus, which asserts God's continuing grace to Israel in spite of Israel's constant sin and rebellion.

2.25.5   Nelson, Richard D. *The Historical Books.* Interpreting Biblical Texts. Nashville: Abingdon, 1998. 190pp.

Basic introduction to the study of the Historical Books (including both the Deuteronomic and Chronistic histories), dealing with the concept of history and historical writing in the ancient, and especially biblical, world, and major interpretive methods employed in the study of these books. Moves from meaning of individual books to their role in the overall theological program of the Deuteronomic History and/or the Chronicler's History. Emphasizes theological meaning of the final form of the text.

2.25.6 Polzin, Robert. *Moses and the Deuteronomist: A Literary Study of the Deuteronomic History.* New York: Seabury, 1980. 226pp.

The first volume of a proposed four-part study of the Deuteronomic History (two others are available, §2.29.5; §2.29.6) that employs contemporary reader-response theory to grasp the meaning of the narrative in its final form. Recognizes the existence of earlier sources and a complex process of redaction lying behind the extant text, but argues that the final form is a coherent narrative and should be read as such. Provides many illuminating insights, but should be supplemented with more traditional verse-by-verse commentaries on the specific books that offer fuller and more sustained treatment of individual passages. This commentary covers Deuteronomy through Judges.

2.25.7 Vannutelli, Primus. *Libri Synoptici Veteris Testamenti seu Librorum Regum et Chronicorum Loci Paralleli.* Rome: Pontifical Biblical Institute Press, 1931–1934. 701pp.

Most complete and authoritative synoptic parallel between Chronicles and Samuel/Kings (and other parallel biblical material) available. Includes both Hebrew and Greek (Septuagint) texts, and contains extensive text-critical apparatus. But it is accessible only to those who read the biblical languages, and is somewhat difficult to find, since it has been long out of print. Students who wish to consult a Hebrew synopsis that is more accessible and less expensive (though also less extensive) might consider Abba Bendavid (2.25.1).

A L S O   S I G N I F I C A N T

2.25.8 Auld, A. Graeme. *Kings without Privilege: David and Moses in The Story of the Bible's Kings.* Edinburgh: T&T Clark, 1994. 203pp.

2.25.9 Gerbrandt, Gerald Eddie. *Kingship according to the Deuteronomistic History.* Society of Biblical Literature Dissertation Series 87. Atlanta: Scholars, 1986. 229pp.

2.25.10 Hamilton, Victor P. *Handbook on the Historical Books.* Grand Rapids: Baker, 2001. 560pp.

2.25.11 Mayes, A. D. H. *The Story of Israel between Settlement and Exile: A Redactional Study of the Deuteronomistic History.* London: SCM, 1983. 202pp.

2.25.12 Newsome, James. *A Synoptic Harmony of Samuel, Kings, and Chronicles with Related Passages from Psalms, Isaiah, Jeremiah and Ezra.* Grand Rapids: Baker, 1986. 275pp.

2.25.13   Noth, Martin. *The Deuteronomistic History.* Journal for the Study of the Old Testament Supplement Series 15. Sheffield: JSOT, 1981. 153pp.

2.25.14   Rast, Walter E. *Joshua, Judges, Samuel, Kings.* Proclamation Commentaries. Philadelphia: Fortress, 1978. 124pp.

2.25.15   Weinfeld, Moshe. *Deuteronomy and the Deuteronomistic School.* Oxford: Clarendon, 1972. 467pp.

2.26 Joshua

H I G H L Y   R E C O M M E N D E D

2.26.1   Auld, A. Graeme. *Joshua, Judges, and Ruth.* Daily Study Bible. Philadelphia: Westminster, 1984. 282pp.

A remarkably perceptive and helpful volume, in spite of its brevity and the amount of biblical material it attempts to cover. Written by a leading authority in this part of the canon, this volume is based on solid and informed exegesis but emphasizes the continuing theological, and indeed, pastoral significance of the final form of the text for Christian thought and life.

2.26.2   Butler, Trent C. *Joshua.* Word Biblical Commentary. Waco, Tex.: Word, 1983. 304pp.

An informed and judicious commentary focusing on the technical issues surrounding this biblical book, including text-critical issues, the oral stages of tradition lying behind the extant text, and the theological purposes of the final compiler. Butler deals with these issues separately and together in a holistic interpretation of passages that focus on their final form. Technical, but richly suggestive in issues of theological significance.

2.26.3   Hawk, L. Daniel. *Joshua.* Berit Olam: Studies in Hebrew Narrative and Poetry. Collegeville, Minn.: Liturgical Press, 2000. 303pp.

A careful, sensitive interpretation of the final form of Joshua, employing with sophistication the principles of the emerging literary methods of OT interpretation. Insists that the book is in fact unified and intentional in its literary design, but that the book's theological program is complex, concerned to present Israel's identity not in terms of racial or ethnic realities or the possession of the land or cultic practices, but rather in terms of a people constantly living at the point of decision in the face of the gracious (though also judgmental) word of God.

2.26.4 Nelson, Richard D. *Joshua*. Old Testament Library. Louisville: Westminster John Knox, 1997. 310pp.

Informed, current commentary dealing with all the major issues of this biblical book, including the significant text-critical differences between the Hebrew and Greek (Septuagint) forms of the text, tradition-critical considerations, and the Deuteronomic redactions that pertain to the final composition. Emphasizes especially the meaning of passages within the context of Deuteronomy and the whole Deuteronomic History.

2.26.5 Woudstra, M. H. *The Book of Joshua*. New International Commentary on the Old Testament. Grand Rapids: Eerdmans, 1981. 396pp.

Solid and theologically illuminating commentary from a conservative perspective that avers that the book was written close to the events recorded. Considers the central theological theme to be the fulfillment of God's promises to the patriarchs regarding the land, and identifies how other subordinate themes contribute to this main one. Thus, emphasizes both historical accuracy and theological coherence. Theological insights frequently reflect an evangelical Reformed perspective, but are helpful even for those who belong to other theological traditions.

ALSO SIGNIFICANT

2.26.6 Auld, A. Graeme. *Joshua Retold: Synoptic Perspectives*. Old Testament Studies. Edinburgh: T&T Clark, 1998. 179pp.

2.26.7 Boling, Robert G., and G. Ernest Wright. *Joshua*. Anchor Bible. Garden City, N.Y.: Doubleday, 1982. 580pp.

2.26.8 Gray, John. *Joshua, Judges, and Ruth*. Rev. ed. New Century Bible. Grand Rapids: Eerdmans, 1986. 325pp.

2.26.9 Hawk, L. Daniel. *Every Promise Fulfilled: Contesting Plots in Joshua*. Literary Currents in Biblical Interpretation. Louisville: Westminster John Knox, 1991. 172pp.

2.26.10 Hess, Richard S. *Joshua: An Introduction and Commentary*. Tyndale Old Testament Commentaries. Downers Grove, Ill.: InterVarsity, 1996. 320pp.

2.26.11 Mitchell, Gordon. *Together in the Land: A Reading of the Book of Joshua*. Journal for the Study of the Old Testament Supplemental Series 134. Sheffield: JSOT, 1993. 219pp.

2.26.12 Soggin, J. Alberto. *Joshua*. Old Testament Library. Philadelphia: Westminster, 1972. 245pp.

2.27 Judges

See also JOSHUA (2.26)

H I G H L Y   R E C O M M E N D E D

2.27.1 Buber, Martin. *The Kingship of God*. New York: Harper & Row, 1967. 228pp.

Brilliant theological discussions of major issues in the book of Judges from one of the twentieth century's foremost Jewish philosophers and theologians. Discusses textual and historical problems in the book, but always in the context of the book's broader theological concern, which emphasizes the establishment of God's people as those who are in dialogue with God through their various experiences, and who are called and empowered through this dialogue to live under God's kingship.

2.27.2 Burney, C. F. *Judges and Kings*. 2d ed. London: Rivingtons, 1919. 384pp.

Represents the first serious and sustained attempt to interpret the text of Judges according to insights from the history of the Ancient Near East. Although some of Burney's conclusions are now dated, this volume remains rich and authoritative in its discussion of the Hebrew text, archaeological evidence, and historical background. Should be supplemented with more recent critical studies. Since it offers little explicit theological reflection, should be supplemented by volumes that deal more intentionally with enduring religious significance.

2.27.3 Cundall, Arthur E., and Leon Morris. *Judges and Ruth: An Introduction and Commentary*. Tyndale Old Testament Commentaries. Downers Grove, Ill.: InterVarsity, 1968. 318pp.

Written from a conservative perspective. Dates the final composition of Judges to the period of the early monarchy, and insists on the historical accuracy of the record. Attends to theological and pastoral significance and to the relation of passages to other biblical texts and motifs. Sometimes uncritically mixes historical reconstruction of events with the witness of the canonical text according to its own narrative world. Since, however, there are few commentaries on Judges that deal seriously at all with theological issues, this volume is generally recommended.

2.27.4 McCann, J. Clinton. *Judges*. Interpretation: A Bible Commentary for Teaching and Preaching. Louisville: Westminster John Knox, 2002. 146pp.

This commentary, along with the volume by Webb (§2.27.5), is the most useful work available for the theological interpretation of Judges. Focuses on the final form of the text, but Introduction provides brief yet helpful discussion of critical issues and historical background, as well as Judges' role in the canon and its major theological motifs. McCann employs insights from the Introduction in his comments throughout. Commentary consistently draws out significance for the contemporary church and world in a way that is not at all forced, but entirely natural. A longer commentary than this on the Book of Judges would have been justified and would have allowed McCann to develop his fine treatment in an even more satisfying way.

2.27.5 Webb, Barry G. *The Book of Judges: An Integrated Reading*. Journal for the Study of the Old Testament Supplement Series 46. Sheffield: JSOT, 1987. 280pp.

Although not a commentary in the strict sense of the term, but rather a monograph that examines the meaning of the narrative of the Book of Judges, this volume does move through the book passage by passage and discusses the meaning of these passages especially in terms of their role in the flow of the narrative. Assumes the literary unity of the book in its final form, and adopts a narrative-critical approach that seeks to identify how the reader is intended to construe the narrative through a close reading of the Hebrew text. Fully interactive with the history of interpretation and richly conversant with the nuances of the Hebrew, this volume offers the most satisfying interpretation of Judges currently available in English.

ALSO SIGNIFICANT

2.27.6 Boling, Robert G. *Judges*. Anchor Bible. Garden City, N.Y.: Doubleday, 1975. 338pp.

2.27.7 Klein, Lillian R. *The Triumph of Irony in the Book of Judges*. Journal for the Study of the Old Testament Supplement Series 68. Sheffield: Almond, 1988. 280pp.

2.27.8 Lindars, Barnabas. *Judges 1–5: A New Translation and Commentary*. Edited by A. D. H. Mays. Edinburgh: T&T Clark, 1995. 302pp.

2.27.9 Moore, George Foot. *A Critical and Exegetical Commentary on Judges*. International Critical Commentary. Edinburgh: T&T Clark, 1895. 476pp.

2.27.10 O'Connell, Robert H. *The Rhetoric of the Book of Judges*. Leiden: Brill, 1996. 541pp.

2.27.11 Schneider, Tammi J. *Judges*. Berit Olam: Studies in Hebrew Narrative and Poetry. Collegeville, Minn.: Liturgical Press, 2000. 317pp.

2.27.12 Soggin, J. Alberto. *Judges: A Commentary*. Old Testament Library. Louisville: Westminster John Knox, 1981. 305pp.

2.27.13 Yee, Gale A., ed. *Judges and Method: New Approaches in Biblical Studies*. Minneapolis: Fortress, 1995. 186pp.

2.28 Ruth

See also JOSHUA (§2.26); JUDGES (§2.27)

H I G H L Y   R E C O M M E N D E D

2.28.1 Bush, Frederic. *Ruth and Esther*. Word Biblical Commentary. Dallas: Word, 1996. 514pp.

Drawing heavily on recent work on genre studies and discourse analysis as well as narrative poetics, explores the theme, purpose, theology, and dates of these books and interprets their individual passages in great depth. It is the most detailed, complete, and technical of the major commentaries on these books, and is probably the best overall commentary on Esther, although it could be more explicit in theological reflection and more intentional in presenting possibilities for contemporary application.

2.28.2 Campbell, Edward F. *Ruth*. Anchor Bible. Garden City, N.Y.: Doubleday, 1975. 188pp.

Probably the best commentary on Ruth, and one of the best volumes in the Anchor Bible series. Combines sensitive and profound narrative analysis, discussion of ancient customs, and insights from word origins and the nuances to produce a holistic and engaging interpretation, rich in theological reflection. Emphasizes the hidden and subtle, yet determinative, role of God in the book, which Campbell considers a historical novelette composed around the time of Solomon. Accessible to students but also invaluable to scholars.

2.28.3 Hals, Ronald M. *The Theology of the Book of Ruth*. Facet Books. Philadelphia: Fortress, 1966. 81pp.

Lucid, careful, and insightful study of the theology (i.e., specifically the doctrine of *God*) in Ruth, comparing it with similar stories in the OT, and concluding that both form and content suggest that Ruth was written during the "Solomonic enlightenment." A must for preaching or teaching on Ruth.

2.28.4 Hubbard, Robert L., Jr. *The Book of Ruth*. New International Commentary on the Old Testament. Grand Rapids: Eerdmans, 1988. 317pp.

Gives attention to historical background and linguistic analysis, but focuses especially on the author's use of literary artistry to develop significant theological themes and to draw the reader into the story and effect changes in the reader at the affective as well as cognitive levels. Argues that Ruth was composed to counter opposition to the Davidic monarchy during Solomon's reign. Gives relatively less attention than does Bush (§2.28.1) to technical matters (e.g., careful analysis of the Hebrew), but more attention to the tracing of major theological themes through the narrative and to contemporary application.

ALSO SIGNIFICANT

2.28.5 Beattie, D. R. G. *Jewish Exegesis of the Book of Ruth*. Journal or the Study of the Old Testament Supplement Series 2. Sheffield: JSOT, 197 . 251pp.

2.28.6 Caspi, Mishael. *The Book of Ruth: An Annotated Bibliography*. I ew York: Garland, 1994. 133pp.

2.28.7 Fewell, Danna Nolan, and David Miller Gunn. *Compromising Redemption: Relating Characters in the Book of Ruth*. Literary Currents in Bil ical Interpretation. Louisville: Westminster John Knox, 1990. 141pp.

2.28.8 Gowan, Murray D. *The Book of Ruth: Its Structure, Theme, nd Purpose*. Leicester, U.K.: Apollos, 1992. 240pp.

2.28.9 Linafelt, Tod, and Timothy K. Beal. *Ruth and Esther*. Berit Olam. Collegeville, Minn.: Liturgical Press, 1999. 130pp.

2.28.10 Nielsen, Kirsten. *Ruth*. Old Testament Library. Louisville: Westm inster John Knox, 1997. 103pp.

2.28.11 Sakenfeld, Katherine Doob. *Ruth*. Interpretation: A Bible Comr entary for Teaching and Preaching. Louisville: Westminster John Knox, 1999. 91pp.

2.28.12 Sasson, Jack M. *Ruth: A New Translation with a Philological Commentary and a Formalist-Folklorist Interpretation*. 2d ed. Sheffield: Sheffield Academic Press, 1995. 292pp.

2.29 Books of Samuel

2.29.1 Fokkelman, J. P. *Narrative Art and Poetry in the Books of Samuel: A Full Interpretation Based on Stylistic and Structural Analyses.* 4 vols. Studia Semitica Neerlandica. Winona Lake, Ind.: Eisenbrauns, 1981–1993. 517/796/441/651pp.

Massive, detailed attempt to combine modern literary study and OT exegesis, focusing on the final form of the text as an integrated narrative. Treats the text at three levels, each building upon the preceding: (1) literary analysis exploring the narrative artistry of the passage; (2) psychological analysis exploring the narrator's probing of the deep dimensions of human life; and (3) "psychagogical" analysis exploring the ways in which contemporary readers engage the text spiritually or existentially. The first of these levels receives the most attention. Methodological perspective biases the interpretation toward a human-centered over against God-centered reading, but volumes offer (perhaps inadvertently) much theological insight, since they deal seriously with narratives that are concerned primarily with God.

2.29.2 Hertzberg, Hans Wilhelm. *I and II Samuel: A Commentary.* Old Testament Library. Philadelphia: Westminster, 1964. 416pp.

Overall the best commentary on these books. Elegant, compelling, engaging interpretation focusing on the theological message of the text, while giving some brief attention to the structure of passages and the history of the formation of passages from earlier sources. A must for those interested in rich and profound theological treatment in the service of preaching and teaching.

2.29.3 McCarter, P. Kyle. *1 Samuel.* Anchor Bible. Garden City, N.Y.: Doubleday, 1980. 474pp.

This volume, like McCarter's commentary on 2 Samuel (§2.29.4), offers a most complete and detailed examination of text-critical (significant especially for the Books of Samuel), historical, source-critical, archaeological, and linguistic matters, all essential for ascertaining the meaning of the text. Tends to deal with the text as an amalgam of traditions and redactional processes rather than as an integrated narrative that functions within the canon of the church, and therefore does relatively little with theological reflection.

2.29.4 McCarter, P. Kyle. *2 Samuel.* Anchor Bible. Garden City, N.Y.: Doubleday, 1984. 553pp.

See comments under McCarter's *1 Samuel* (§2.29.3).

2.29.5 Polzin, Robert. *Samuel and the Deuteronomist: A Literary Study of the Deuteronomic History: 1 Samuel.* San Francisco: Harper & Row, 1989. 296pp.

Sequel to Polzin's *Moses and the Deuteronomist.* See description of the series presented under that title (§2.25.6) in the Former Prophets.

2.29.6 Polzin, Robert. *David and the Deuteronomist: 2 Samuel.* Indiana Studies in Biblical Literature. Bloomington: University of Indiana Press, 1993. 245pp.

Sequel to Polzin's *Moses and the Deuteronomist.* See description of the series presented under that title (§2.25.6).

2.29.7 Welch, Adam C. *Kings and Prophets of Israel.* London: Lutterworth, 1952. 264pp.

Presents biographical sketches of Saul and David as well as Hosea, Amos, and Isaiah. Mentioned here because Welch's treatment of Saul and David is rich in expositional insight from the Books of Samuel. In spite of its age, remains an eminently rewarding study of the Saul and David narratives.

ALSO SIGNIFICANT

2.29.8 Ackroyd, Peter R. *The First Book of Samuel.* Cambridge Bible Commentary on the New English Bible. Cambridge: Cambridge University Press, 1971. 237pp.

2.29.9 ———. *The Second Book of Samuel.* Cambridge Bible Commentary on the New English Bible. Cambridge: Cambridge University Press, 1977. 247pp.

2.29.10 Anderson, Arnold. *2 Samuel.* Word Biblical Commentary. Waco, Tex.: Word, 1989. 301pp.

2.29.11 Baldwin, Joyce G. *1 and 2 Samuel.* Tyndale Old Testament Commentaries. Downers Grove, Ill.: InterVarsity, 1988. 299pp.

2.29.12 Brueggemann, Walter. *First and Second Samuel.* Interpretation: A Bible Commentary for Teaching and Preaching. Louisville: Westminster John Knox, 1990. 362pp.

2.29.13 ———. *David's Truth in Israel's Imagination and Memory.* 2d ed. Minneapolis: Fortress, 2002. 144pp.

2.29.14 Cartledge, Tony W. *1 and 2 Samuel.* Smyth & Helwys Bible Commentary. Macon, Ga.: Smyth & Helwys, 2001. 748pp.

2.29.15 Driver, S. R. *Notes on the Hebrew Text of the Books of Samuel.* Oxford: Clarendon, 1890. 296pp.

2.29.16 Edelman, Diana Vikander. *King Saul in the Historiography of Judah.* Journal for the Study of the Old Testament Supplement Series 121. Sheffield: JSOT, 1991. 347pp.

2.29.17 Gordon, Robert P. *I and II Samuel: A Commentary.* Grand Rapids: Zondervan, 1988. 375pp.

2.29.18 Gunn, David M. *The Fate of King Saul: An Interpretation of a Biblical Story.* Journal for the Study of the Old Testament Supplemental Series 14. Sheffield: JSOT, 1980. 181pp.

2.29.19 ———. *The Story of King David: Genre and Interpretation.* Journal for the Study of the Old Testament Supplement Series 6. Sheffield: JSOT, 1978. 164pp.

2.29.20 Jobling, David. *1 Samuel.* Berit Olam: Studies in Hebrew Narrative and Poetry. Collegeville, Minn.: Liturgical Press, 1998. 330pp.

2.29.21 Klein, Ralph W. *1 Samuel.* Word Biblical Commentary. Waco, Tex.: Word, 1983. 307pp.

2.29.22 Long, V. Philips. *The Reign and Rejection of King Saul: A Case for Literary and Theological Coherence.* Society of Biblical Literature Dissertation Series 118. Atlanta: Scholars, 1989. 276pp.

2.29.23 Miscall, Peter D. *1 Samuel: A Literary Reading.* Indiana Studies in Biblical Literature. Bloomington: Indiana University Press, 1986. 198pp.

2.29.24 Payne, David F. *I and II Samuel.* Daily Study Bible. Philadelphia: Westminster, 1982. 277pp.

2.29.25 Smith, Henry Preserved. *A Critical and Exegetical Commentary on the Books of Samuel.* International Critical Commentary. Edinburgh: T&T Clark, 1899. 421pp.

2.30 Books of Kings

See also BOOKS OF SAMUEL (§2.29)

2.30.1 Brueggemann, Walter. *1 and 2 Kings*. Smith & Helwys Bible Commentary. Macon, Ga.: Smyth & Helwys, 2000. 645pp.

Primarily for theological students and pastors, but useful for a broad audience, from interested laypersons to scholars. Format is user friendly, with sidebars providing additional historical, theological, bibliographic, and homiletical discussions. Commentary focuses on the theological meaning of the final form of the text, which emerges from careful attention to narrative artistry, but without excessively technical language. Proceeds passage by passage, focusing on Solomon, Elijah, Elisha, and Josiah as models of faith. Each section of commentary is followed by "connections," comprising applications to contemporary personal, church, and national life. Brueggemann is interested in dynamics of (political) power, and that issue (which is certainly significant in these books) is emphasized. This tendency to focus on the human characters tends to de-emphasize the actions of Yahweh, which are arguably the primary concern of these books.

2.30.2 Cohn, Robert L. *2 Kings*. Berit Olam: Studies in Hebrew Narrative and Poetry. Collegeville, Minn.: Liturgical Press, 2000. 186pp.

Like the companion volume on 1 Kings by Walsh (§2.30.7), probes the literary impact of the text in its final form. Cohn recognizes the existence of sources and employs some insights from source and redaction criticism to illumine the final narrative, but the emphasis is almost exclusively on the extant text. Perhaps even more than Walsh, Cohn is careful to interpret individual passages in light of the book's overall narrative and purpose, yet gives less attention to the structure of specific passages and their linguistic nuances than does Walsh. Both Cohn and Walsh give little explicit attention to theological significance and virtually none to contemporary appropriation. Suffers somewhat from its brevity, but still extremely helpful for the interpretation of the text in its final form.

2.30.3 Ellul, Jacques. *The Politics of God and the Politics of Man*. Grand Rapids: Eerdmans, 1972. 198pp.

Written by one of the most perceptive theological thinkers of the twentieth century, this volume is not a commentary in the accepted sense of the term, but rather a series of profound and probing theological reflections pertaining to the contemporary appropriation of selected narratives from the Book of Kings. Focuses on matters such as the relationship between God's work and political action, the appropriateness of God's people to be involved in social action, the nature of prophetic activity, the concept of success, and the acceptance of a utilitarian perspective. A model for rich and original theologizing and application of the Bible, and particularly Kings.

2.30.4   Gray, John. *I and II Kings: A Commentary*. 3d ed. Old Testament Library. Louisville: Westminster John Knox, 1985. 813pp.

Definitive treatment of the range of technical issues pertaining to these books, especially text-critical considerations, analysis of Hebrew terms and constructions, matters of historical background, and redaction of earlier sources. Gives serious attention to narrative development and to the theology of the text. Especially helpful in its interaction with the history of interpretation, particularly critical scholarship.

2.30.5   Hobbs, T. R. *2 Kings*. Word Biblical Commentary. Waco, Tex.: Word, 1985. 387pp.

Argues that 2 Kings was written by a single author who composed a carefully crafted literary product that evinces a pastoral concern to give to the exilic community of Judah a new understanding of their past and hope for their future under the sovereign faithfulness of God. Emphasizes the role of the prophet, the power of the word of God, and the divine demand for obedience to the law as the condition for the continuation of the Davidic covenant. Carefully considers the author's selectivity and editing of his sources, the nuance of Hebrew terms and constructions, historical background, intercanonical connections (including NT passages and themes), and theological significance.

2.30.6   Nelson, Richard D. *First and Second Kings*. Interpretation: A Bible Commentary for Teaching and Preaching. Atlanta: John Knox, 1987. 273pp.

Lucid and engaging examination of the literary impact of the final form of Kings leading to a discovery of its theological message for the community of faith. Attends to the role of the theological claims of the text of Kings within the biblical canon as a whole. Concerned also to probe the significance of these passages for contemporary Christian existence. One of the most solid, original, and compelling volumes in the *Interpretation* series, and the most helpful commentary available for teaching and preaching the Books of Kings.

2.30.7   Walsh, Jerome T. *1 Kings*. Berit Olam: Studies in Hebrew Narrative and Poetry. Collegeville, Minn.: Liturgical Press, 1996. 393pp.

Employing the literary approach known as "narrative criticism," focuses on the meaning of the narrative itself in its final form over against a concern for historical events or the identification of sources or the history of the development of the traditions. Attends to the structure of passages, verbal techniques employed (uses Hebrew, but does not require a knowledge of Hebrew on the part of the reader), narrator, plot, point of view, and characterization. This careful reading of the text is most useful for an understanding of the impact of the text in its final form and hence for teaching and preaching, even though Walsh does little with canonical connections or reflections on theological significance.

ALSO SIGNIFICANT

2.30.8 Auld, A. Graeme. *I and II Kings*. Daily Study Bible. Philadelphia: Westminster, 1986. 258pp.

2.30.9 Burney, C. F. *Notes on the Hebrew Text of the Books of Kings*. Oxford: Clarendon, 1903. 384pp.

2.30.10 Cogan, Mordechai. *I Kings*. Anchor Bible. New York: Doubleday, 2001. 336pp.

2.30.11 Cogan, Mordechai, and Hayim Tadmor. *II Kings*. Anchor Bible. New York: Doubleday, 1988. 371pp.

2.30.12 DeVries, Simon J. *1 Kings*. Word Biblical Commentary. Waco, Tex.: Word, 1985. 286pp.

2.30.13 Jones, G. H. *1 and 2 Kings*. 2 vols. New Century Bible Commentary. Grand Rapids: Eerdmans, 1984. 666pp.

2.30.14 Knoppers, Gary N. *Two Nations under God: The Deuteronomistic History of Solomon and the Dual Monarchies*. 2 vols. Harvard Semitic Museum Monographs 52–53. Atlanta: Scholars, 1993. 302/348pp.

2.30.15 Linville, James Richard. *Israel in the Book of Kings: The Past as a Project of Social Identity*. Journal for the Study of the Old Testament Supplement Series 272. Sheffield: Sheffield Academic Press, 1998. 331pp.

2.30.16 Long, Burke O. *1 Kings: With an Introduction to Historical Literature*. Forms of the Old Testament Literature 9. Grand Rapids: Eerdmans, 1984. 265pp.

2.30.17 ———. *2 Kings*. Forms of the Old Testament Literature 10. Grand Rapids: Eerdmans, 1991. 324pp.

2.30.18 McKenzie, Steven L. *The Trouble with Kings: The Composition of the Book of Kings in the Deuteronomistic History*. Leiden: Brill, 1991. 186pp.

2.30.19 Montgomery, James A., and Henry Snyder Gehman. *A Critical and Exegetical Commentary on the Books of Kings*. International Critical Commentary. Edinburgh: T&T Clark, 1951. 575pp.

2.30.20 Skinner, John. *Kings*. New Century Bible. New York: Henry Frowde, 1904. 459pp.

2.30.21 Wiseman, Donald J. *1 and 2 Kings*. Tyndale Old Testament Commentaries. Downers Grove, Ill.: InterVarsity, 1993. 318pp.

2.31 Books of Chronicles

H I G H L Y   R E C O M M E N D E D

2.31.1 Ackroyd, Peter R. *The Chronicler in His Age*. Journal for the Study of the Old Testament Supplement Series 101. Sheffield: JSOT, 1991. 397pp.

Comprehensive, informed, and judicious study of the Books of Chronicles, dealing with all major issues, especially the social and religious environment in which these books were composed. Relates this historical background to the theology of the Chronicler. Considers the Chronicler as a redactor of earlier traditions and as an exegete. Extremely helpful for the theological interpretation of these books.

2.31.2 Braun, Roddy. *1 Chronicles*. Word Biblical Commentary. Waco, Tex.: Word, 1986. 311pp.

Solid and reliable, though not particularly original or imaginative. Gives significant attention to historical background, the role of passages within their book context, and relation to parallel passages in Samuel/Kings. Gives also some attention to the Chronicler's unique contributions to an understanding of Israel's history and to OT theology. Relates theological concerns of the Chronicler to issues of contemporary Christian existence, but tends to do so briefly and generally.

2.31.3 Dillard, Raymond B. *2 Chronicles*. Word Biblical Commentary. Waco, Tex.: Word, 1987. 323pp.

Lucid and somewhat more engaging in terms of probing the theological significance of the text than is Braun's commentary on 1 Chronicles. Especially strong in showing the ways in which the Chronicler interacted with other canonical materials, and in demonstrating the work of the Chronicler as both historian and theologian. Uses the "Explanation" section to relate the theology of Chronicles to the rest of the canon and especially its development in the NT. Contains virtually no introduction; depends on the introductory material in Braun (§2.31.2).

2.31.4 Japhet, Sara. *1 and 2 Chronicles: A Commentary*. Old Testament Library. Louisville: Westminster John Knox, 1993. 1077pp.

Massive, detailed, and probably the most authoritative commentary on these books. Argues for the unity of the work composed by a single author with a definite literary method and theological purpose. Emphasizes the structure, form, and linguistic aspects of passages as well as the author's redaction of earlier sources. Gives relatively little attention to theological claims in the commentary proper, but does briefly discuss the theology of Chronicles in the introduction.

2.31.5 Japhet, Sara. *The Ideology of the Book of Chronicles and Its Place in Biblical Thought*. Beiträge zur Erforschung des Alten Testaments und des Antiken Judentums 9. 2d ed. Frankfurt: Peter Lang, 1997. 553pp.

Helpful supplement to Japhet's fine commentary, which gives little treatment to theological matters. Probes in an informed, balanced, and judicious fashion every major aspect of the theology of the Books of Chronicles. This prominent Jewish scholar gives special attention to the relationship of the theology of Chronicles to that of Samuel/Kings and to roughly contemporary biblical materials (e.g., Jeremiah or Ezra/Nehemiah).

2.31.6 Selman, Martin J. *1 and 2 Chronicles: An Introduction and Commentary*. 2 vols. Tyndale Old Testament Commentaries. Downers Grove, Ill.: InterVarsity, 1994. 551pp.

Lucid and engaging commentary that emphasizes the Chronicler as a pastoral theologian who expounded the Bible as he knew it so as to communicate a divine word of healing and reaffirm hope of restoration and of the fulfillment of God's promises. Not as technically oriented as Japheth's commentary or the Word volumes, but more focused on core interpretive issues and matters of concern to most contemporary expositors.

2.31.7 Tuell, Steven S. *First and Second Chronicles*. Interpretation: A Bible Commentary for Teaching and Preaching. Louisville: John Knox, 2001. 252pp.

Focusing on the final form of the text, Tuell argues that the Books of Chronicles represented an attempt to read scripture (especially the Deuteronomic History) in such a way that it would speak anew to the generation of the Chronicler. This new reading of scripture involved especially a fuller appreciation of God's plan and purposes through the history of Israel, with special reference to David and his line. All of this was intended to lead the postexilic readers of Chronicles to recognize that God was now at work among them as ordinary people in ordinary ways in their own ordinary times. Tuell concludes that Chronicles was written as part of a larger historical work that included Ezra and Nehemiah, and he thus interprets Chronicles in light of those books. But Tuell gives primary attention to the ways the Chronicler adapts earlier biblical tradition to fulfill his own theological purpose. This volume gives much less attention than do most in this series to theological implications for Christians or to contemporary appropriation.

2.31.8 Williamson, H. G. M. *I and II Chronicles*. New Century Bible. Grand Rapids: Eerdmans, 1982. 428pp.

Comparable to Selman (§2.31.6) for accessibility and straightforward discussion of crucial matters for the meaning of the text. Especially helpful are Williamson's introductions to each passage, in which he discusses the history of interpretation and gives judicious conclusions regarding history and theology. Interacts more with other interpreters than does Selman, but does less than Selman to relate passages in Chronicles to other parts of the canon, especially the NT.

A L S O   S I G N I F I C A N T

2.31.9 Ackroyd, Peter R. *I and II Chronicles, Ezra, Nehemiah*. Torch Bible Commentaries. London: SCM, 1973. 320pp.

2.31.10 Curtis, Edward Lewis, and Albert Alonzo Madsen. *A Critical and Exegetical Commentary on the Books of Chronicles*. International Critical Commentary. Edinburgh: T&T Clark, 1910. 534pp.

2.31.11 Dyck, Jonathan E. *The Theocratic Ideology of the Chronicler*. Biblical Interpretation Series. Leiden: Brill, 1998. 256pp.

2.31.12 Graham, M. Patrick, and Steven L. McKenzie, eds. *The Chronicler as Author: Studies in Text and Texture*. Journal for the Study of the Old Testament Supplemental Series 263. Sheffield: Sheffield Academic Press, 1999. 422pp.

2.31.13 Johnstone, William. *1 and 2 Chronicles*. 2 vols. Journal for the Study of the Old Testament Supplemental Series 253. Sheffield: Sheffield Academic Press, 1997. 411/300pp.

2.31.14 McKenzie, Steven L. *The Chronicler's Use of the Deuteronomistic History*. Harvard Semitic Monographs 33. Atlanta: Scholars, 1985. 219pp.

2.31.15 Myers, Jacob M. *I Chronicles*. 2d ed. Anchor Bible. Garden City, N.Y.: Doubleday, 1973. 239pp.

2.31.16 ———. *2 Chronicles*. Anchor Bible. 2d ed. Garden City, N.Y.: Doubleday, 1973. 268pp.

2.31.17 Noth, Martin. *The Chronicler's History*. Journal for the Study of the Old Testament Supplement Series 50. Sheffield: JSOT Press, 1987. 200pp.

2.31.18 Welch, Adam C. *The Work of the Chronicler: Its Purpose and Date*. London: British Academy, 1939. 163pp.

2.32 Ezra and Nehemiah

H I G H L Y   R E C O M M E N D E D

2.32.1 Blenkinsopp, Joseph. *Ezra-Nehemiah: A Commentary*. Old Testament Library. Louisville: Westminster John Knox, 1988. 366pp.

Perhaps the most authoritative commentary on these books. Gives careful attention to historical background, development of traditions, and relationship to other biblical books and passages from the same period. Uses these data to probe the beginnings of emergent Judaism. Argues strongly (against the tide of recent scholarship) for a close connection between these books and Chronicles. Helpful for basic understanding of the text, but gives relatively little attention to theological issues.

2.32.2 Davis, Gordon F. *Ezra and Nehemiah*. Berit Olam: Studies in Hebrew Narrative and Poetry. Collegeville, Minn.: Liturgical Press, 1999. 148pp.

Employs "rhetorical criticism," i.e., a careful analysis of the literary strategies of the final form of the text on ten key passages in order to ascertain the theological goal of this literary strategy and how the book accomplishes that goal. This approach illumines both the original intention of these books and their continuing significance to readers in every age, including our own. Concerned especially to draw out the theological application of faithfulness on the part of the community of God and of leadership and preaching in the church today. A more sophisticated and intentional employment of current rhetorical-critical methods than Throntveit (§2.32.4).

2.32.3 Fensham, F. Charles. *The Books of Ezra and Nehemiah*. New International Commentary on the Old Testament. Grand Rapids: Eerdmans, 1982. 288pp.

Lucid and engaging commentary from a conservative perspective, arguing for the historical accuracy of these books, which Fensham takes to have been written by the Chronicler. Emphasizes Ancient Near Eastern context, historical and

religious background, and the development of postexilic Judaism. Less technical and comprehensive than Blenkinsopp (§2.32.1), but gives greater attention
to religious concerns of the text in ways that help the reader identify points of
contemporary significance.

2.32.4   Throntveit, Mark A. *Ezra-Nehemiah*. Interpretation: A Bible Commen-
          tary for Teaching and Preaching. Louisville: Westminster John Knox,
          1992. 127pp.

Although Throntveit discusses historical issues in the introduction, the commentary itself focuses on the ways in which the reader construes meaning
from the story in its final narrative form so as to derive theological insight from
the text. The commentary emphasizes the structure of passages and narrative
development. Theological insights grow out of these literary probes, but
Throntveit gives little explicit attention to contemporary theological significance or the relation of religious ideas in these passages to other parts of the
biblical canon. Still, a helpful complement to most other commentaries on
Ezra-Nehemiah, which deal almost entirely with historical questions.

2.32.5   Williamson, H. G. M. *Ezra, Nehemiah*. Word Biblical Commentary.
          Waco, Tex.: Word, 1985. 417pp.

Careful and erudite, focusing on technical issues of historical reconstruction,
literary sources, literary forms, and nuances of Hebrew terms and constructions. Argues that these books were not written by the Chronicler but arose
from the same community. Traces three stages of development: (1) primary
sources contemporaneous with events described (fifth century B.C.E.); (2) Ezra
memoir and Nehemiah memoir (400 B.C.E.); and (3) final redaction (300
B.C.E.). Probes the theological purpose of each of these levels, especially the
Ezra and Nehemiah memoirs. Especially helpful for historical, linguistic, and
literary aspects of the text, with some value for theological reflection. But usefulness of commentary is somewhat mitigated by dependence on very specific (and somewhat speculative) reconstructions.

ALSO SIGNIFICANT

2.32.6   Batten, Loring W. *A Critical and Exegetical Commentary on the Books of Ezra
          and Nehemiah*. International Critical Commentary. Edinburgh: T&T Clark,
          1913. 384pp.

2.32.7   Clines, David J. A. *Ezra, Nehemiah, Esther*. New Century Bible. Grand Rapids:
          Eerdmans, 1984. 342pp.

2.32.8   Kidner, Derek. *Ezra and Nehemiah*. Tyndale Old Testament Commentaries.
          Downers Grove, Ill.: InterVarsity, 1979. 174pp.

2.32.9 McConville, J. G. *Ezra, Nehemiah, and Esther.* Daily Study Bible. Philadelphia: Westminster, 1985. 197pp.

2.32.10 Myers, Jacob M. *Ezra, Nehemiah.* Anchor Bible. Garden City, N.Y.: Doubleday, 1965. 268pp.

2.33 Esther

See also EZRA AND NEHEMIAH (§2.32); RUTH (§2.28)

H I G H L Y   R E C O M M E N D E D

2.33.1 Baldwin, Joyce G. *Esther.* Tyndale Old Testament Commentaries. Downers Grove, Ill.: InterVarsity, 1984. 126pp.

Complement to the other volumes listed in that it interprets Esther as part of the Christian canon and discusses its significance for a Christian audience. Adopts a conservative position that espouses the historicity of the story. Contains a helpful and quite lengthy introduction, while the commentary itself is brief and laconic.

2.33.2 Bechtel, Carol M. *Esther.* Interpretation: A Bible Commentary for Teaching and Preaching. Louisville: John Knox, 2002. 101pp.

Introduction deals with historical setting, literary structure, and theology, especially the theological motifs of proportion and balance in life, living faithfully in the midst of a faithless culture, and significance of the written word (the last an emphasis often missed, but certainly present in view of its prominence in the summary of Esther 9). Although Introduction contains discussion of the Christian use of Esther in preaching and teaching, the commentary itself gives little attention to these matters, but offers almost exclusively a sensitive literary examination of the flow of the narrative. Suffers slightly from extreme brevity.

2.33.3 Berlin, Adele. *Esther.* JPS Bible Commentary. Philadelphia: Jewish Publication Society, 2001. 110pp.

Offers a coherent and largely compelling interpretation, emphasizing how literary features point to the book's distinctive character and message. Understands Esther to belong to the literary form of comedy, and argues that the author drew heavily on literary motifs associated with Persia. Thus, commentary examines motifs about Persia especially from the Greek writings of the period with a view to the connotations their appearance in Esther would have for the ancient reader. But emphasizes also that it is a Jewish book, and part of the Jewish canon, and thus commentary is concerned to read Esther in the light of earlier canonical materials and later Jewish interpretation, especially the rabbis.

2.33.4 Fox, Michael V. *Character and Ideology in the Book of Esther.* 2d ed. Grand Rapids: Eerdmans, 2001. 352pp.

Engaging and illuminating study that focuses on the ways in which the presentation of characters in Esther reveals the assumptions, ideas, values, and teachings of the author. Insists that Esther is presented as a model for life in the Diaspora. Commentary proper is followed by discussions on historicity and dating, genres, structures, each of the major characters, God, the world, and the three textual versions of Esther. Fox's treatment of God (in this book that does not explicitly mention God) is especially helpful.

2.33.5 Levenson, Jon D. *Esther.* Old Testament Library. Louisville: Westminster John Knox, 1997. 142pp.

Methodologically comprehensive treatment in that this prominent Jewish scholar examines the interplay between the longer Greek version of Esther and the shorter Hebrew one, tracks the narrative development of the story, draws heavily on historical and linguistic background, relates passages in Esther to other OT material, extensively cites ancient Jewish interpretation of the book, and interacts vigorously with more recent history of interpretation. Remarkably, Levenson brings these diverse data together into a coherent and illuminating interpretation.

ALSO SIGNIFICANT

2.33.6 Berg, Sandra Beth. *The Book of Esther: Motifs, Themes, and Structure.* Society of Biblical Literature Dissertation Series 44. Missoula, Mont.: Scholars, 1979. 219pp.

2.33.7 Clines, David J. A. *The Esther Scroll: The Story of the Story.* Journal for the Study of the Old Testament Supplement Series 30. Sheffield: JSOT, 1984. 260pp.

2.33.8 Craig, Kenneth. *Reading Esther: A Case for the Literary Carnivalesque.* Literary Currents in Biblical Interpretation. Louisville: Westminster John Knox, 1995. 192pp.

2.33.9 Day, Linda. *Three Faces of a Queen: Characterization in the Books of Esther.* Journal for the Study of the Old Testament Supplement Series 186. Sheffield: Sheffield Academic Press, 1995. 254pp.

2.33.10 Moore, Carey. *Esther.* Anchor Bible. Garden City, N.Y.: Doubleday, 1971. 117pp.

2.33.11 Paton, Lewis B. *Critical and Exegetical Commentary on the Book of Esther.* International Critical Commentary. Edinburgh: T&T Clark, 1908. 339pp.

2.34 Wisdom Literature: General Works

H I G H L Y   R E C O M M E N D E D

2.34.1 Blenkinsopp, Joseph. *Wisdom and Law in the Old Testament: The Ordering of Life in Israel and Early Judaism.* Rev. ed. Oxford Bible Series. Oxford: Oxford University Press, 1995. 197pp.

Comprehensive and original study of two major streams of tradition, law and wisdom, in terms of their respective origins, their points of connection, their role in the ordering of life within the Jewish people, and their eventual synthesis in the latest OT writings and in the intertestamental period. Emphasizes continuity between Jewish thought and NT theology. Gives special attention to literary genres and social settings as key interpretive contexts for understanding wisdom (and law).

2.34.2 Crenshaw, James L. *Old Testament Wisdom: An Introduction.* Rev. ed. Louisville: Westminster John Knox, 1998. 255pp.

Produced by a leading authority on OT wisdom, this introductory textbook is accessible to beginning students but its acute insights and wealth of current information make it valuable also for the scholar. Remarkably comprehensive, it covers the world of wisdom (language and literary forms) and the self-understanding of the wisdom teachers, the development of wisdom traditions (with special emphasis on role of Solomon), each wisdom book in the OT and intertestamental writings (identifying the central themes of each), and the continuing significance of the wisdom tradition for contemporary life. A final chapter treats the relationship between OT wisdom and wisdom texts from Egypt and Mesopotamia.

2.34.3 Murphy, Roland E. *The Tree of Life: An Exploration of Biblical Wisdom Literature.* 2d ed. Grand Rapids: Eerdmans, 1996. 233pp.

Traces the quest for wisdom within the OT and deuterocanonical writings. After a general introduction, devotes a separate chapter each to Proverbs, Job, Ecclesiastes, Ben Sira, and Wisdom of Solomon. Concludes with a series of chapters synthesizing the major aspects of the presentation of wisdom within these materials, including a fine discussion on wisdom and theology. Supplement contains significant interaction with recent interpreters.

2.34.4 Perdue, Leo G. *Wisdom and Creation: The Theology of the Wisdom Literature.* Nashville: Abingdon, 1994. 420pp.

Most comprehensive and insightful study available on the theology of the wisdom tradition. Probes the theology of wisdom literature in the OT and deuterocanonical materials around the theme of creation, emphasizing the relationship between two sets of creation images: creation of the world and creation of humanity. Employs the theme of creation as basis of coherence in wisdom theology without forcing all wisdom texts into a creation "straightjacket." Emphasis on creation is important for biblical theology especially within the Christian tradition, which often minimizes the role of creation in favor of a spiritual redemption of the individual and so fails to do full justice to God's work in and purposes for the cosmos.

ALSO SIGNIFICANT

2.34.5 Bergant, Dianne. *What Are They Saying about Wisdom Literature?* New York: Paulist, 1984. 96pp.

2.34.6 Berry, Donald K. *An Introduction to Wisdom and Poetry in the Old Testament.* Nashville: Broadman & Holman, 1995. 463pp.

2.34.7 Brown, William P. *Character in Crisis: A Fresh Approach to the Wisdom Literature of the Old Testament.* Grand Rapids: Eerdmans, 1996. 179pp.

2.34.8 Brueggemann, Walter. *In Man We Trust: The Neglected Side of Biblical Faith.* Richmond, Va.: John Knox, 1972. 144pp.

2.34.9 Clements, Ronald E. *Wisdom for a Changing World: Wisdom in Old Testament Theology.* Berkeley, Calif.: BIBAL, 1990. 77pp.

2.34.10 ———. *Wisdom in Theology.* Grand Rapids: Eerdmans, 1992. 188pp.

2.34.11 Enns, Peter. *Poetry and Wisdom.* IBR Bibliographies 3. Grand Rapids: Baker, 1997. 171pp.

2.34.12 Murphy, Roland E. *Wisdom Literature: Job, Proverbs, Ruth, Canticles, Ecclesiastes, and Esther.* Forms of Old Testament Literature 13. Grand Rapids: Eerdmans, 185pp.

2.34.13 Noth, Martin, and D. Winton Thomas, eds. *Wisdom in Israel and in the Ancient Near East.* Supplement to Vetus Testamentum 3. Leiden: Brill, 1953. 301pp.

2.34.14 Rad, Gerhard von. *Wisdom in Israel.* Nashville: Abingdon, 1972. 330pp.

2.34.15 Scott, R. B. Y. *The Way of Wisdom in the Old Testament.* New York: Macmillan, 1971. 238pp.

2.34.16 Westermann, Claus. *Roots of Wisdom: The Oldest Proverbs of Israel and Other Peoples.* Louisville: Westminster John Knox, 1994.

2.35 Job

HIGHLY RECOMMENDED

2.35.1 Andersen, Francis I. *Job.* Tyndale Old Testament Commentaries. Downers Grove, Ill.: InterVarsity, 1976. 294pp.

Among the most substantive and authoritative volumes in the Tyndale series, written by a scholar who would in subsequent years become a leading commentator on various OT books. The 70-page introduction presents readable and informed discussion of all major aspects of Job. Commentary itself emphasizes Ancient Near Eastern historical background and insights from other OT material. Interacts significantly with the history of interpretation, and seriously engages theological meaning. Remarkable for the amount of relevant information packed into a small volume.

2.35.2 Clines, David J. A. *Job.* 2 vols. Word Biblical Commentary. Nashville: Thomas Nelson, 1990, 2002. 501/532pp.

By far the most detailed and meticulous commentary on Job, and yet consistently concerned to demonstrate how each detail plays an essential role in the complex argument of the whole book. Comprehensive in treatment, dealing with textual, linguistic, historical, and theological issues. Emphasizes especially the interplay of the distinct viewpoints of major speakers in Job. Contains massive bibliographies.

2.35.3 Habel, Norman C. *The Book of Job: A Commentary.* Old Testament Library. Louisville: Westminster John Knox, 1985. 586pp.

Comprehensive commentary that engages in a careful, close reading of the text that emphasizes the interplay of literary artistry and theological issues. Rejects stages of development in the book's history in favor of understanding Job as a literary whole that masterfully interweaves prose and poetry in such a way as to express theological truth creatively. Focuses more on literary matters, e.g., narrative plot and literary structures, than does Clines. Original and insightful, of much value for preaching and teaching.

2.35.4 Hartley, John E. *Job.* New International Commentary on the Old Testament. Grand Rapids: Eerdmans, 1988. 591pp.

Solid, readable commentary that gives attention to text-critical and technical linguistic matters, but focuses especially on salient issues that are at the heart of the interpretation of the text itself. Emphasizes the role of passages within broader-book context and the connection of passages in Job to other OT and Jewish writings so as to explore the place of these passages and of the entire book within the witness of the whole Bible (especially the OT, but with some attention to significance for the NT as well).

2.35.5 Janzen, J. Gerald. *Job.* Interpretation: A Bible Commentary for Teaching and Preaching. Louisville: Westminster John Knox, 1985. 273pp.

Treats the final form of the text as a complex literary entity that requires the reader to track carefully the literary dynamics of the book in order thereby to confront both theological and existential issues. Is concerned to relate Job to the history of Israel's religion, and to psychological, spiritual, and existential realities that persons in all periods and in all places continue to confront. By giving attention to both of these aspects, Janzen points to contemporary application of the text both for the community of faith as a corporate body and for individual believers. Readers should be aware, however, of the potential for allowing contemporary existential concerns to be read back into the text.

A L S O   S I G N I F I C A N T

2.35.6 Dailey, Thomas F. *Job.* Bibliographies for Biblical Research: Old Testament Series 13. Lewiston, N.Y.: Mellen Biblical Press, 1997. 148pp.

2.35.7 Dhorme, Edouard Paul. *A Commentary on the Book of Job.* London: Thomas Nelson, 1967. 675pp.

2.35.8 Driver, S. R., and George Buchanan Gray. *A Critical and Exegetical Commentary on the Book of Job.* International Critical Commentary. Edinburgh: T&T Clark, 1921. 360pp.

2.35.9 Gordis, Robert. *The Book of Job.* New York: Jewish Theological Seminary of America, 1978. 602pp.

2.35.10 Hoffman, Yair. *A Blemished Perfection: The Book of Job in Context.* Journal for the Study of the Old Testament Supplement Series 213. Sheffield: JSOT, 1996. 360pp.

2.35.11 Perdue, Leo G. *Wisdom in Revolt: Metaphorical Theology in the Book of Job.* Journal for the Study of the Old Testament Supplement Series 112. Sheffield: Almond, 1991. 296pp.

2.35.12 Perdue, Leo G., and W. Clark Gilpin, eds. *The Voice from the Whirlwind: Interpreting the Book of Job.* Nashville: Abingdon, 1992. 264pp.

2.35.13 Pope, Marvin H. *Job.* Anchor Bible. 3d ed. Garden City, N.Y.: Doubleday, 1973. 405pp.

2.35.14 Rowley, H. H. *Job.* Rev. ed. New Century Bible Commentary. Grand Rapids: Eerdmans, 1980. 281pp.

2.35.15 Simundson, Daniel J. *The Message of Job: A Theological Commentary.* Augsburg Old Testament Studies. Minneapolis: Augsburg, 1985. 159pp.

2.35.16 Westermann, Claus. *The Structure of the Book of Job: A Form-Critical Analysis.* Philadelphia: Fortress, 1981. 148pp.

2.36 Psalms

HIGHLY RECOMMENDED

2.36.1 Allen, Leslie C. *Psalms 101–150.* Rev. ed. Word Biblical Commentary. Nashville: Thomas Nelson, 2002. 384pp.

This commentary, along with the two companion volumes on the Psalms in the Word Biblical Commentary (see Craigie [§2.36.2] and Tate [§2.36.8]), is a detailed treatment of each psalm, dealing with technical textual and linguistic matters, but giving primary attention to the form, structure, and original liturgical setting or devotional function of the psalm in Israel. Gives little attention to the role of individual psalms within the final canonical Book of Psalms, but does attend to theological significance, the use of the psalm elsewhere in the canon, connections of thought between the psalm and other biblical passages (including NT ones), and contemporary Christian application. This volume contains an introduction to the Psalms that is assumed in the volumes by Tate and Allen. Although written by three separate scholars, these volumes are remarkably consistent in purpose and perspective.

2.36.2 Craigie, Peter C. *Psalms 1–50.* Word Biblical Commentary. Waco, Tex.: Word, 1983. 375pp.

See Allen (§2.36.1).

2.36.3 Kirkpatrick, A. F. *The Book of Psalms*. Cambridge: Cambridge University Press, 1910. 852pp.

Erudite classic commentary of enduring worth despite its age. Discusses background, structure, and significance of each psalm, and provides trenchant comment on each phrase of the psalm. Adopts a conservative critical position, arguing that David was largely responsible for the origin of the psalter. Interprets the psalms in terms of the original significance for psalmist and intended audience, but relates that original significance to the rest of the canon, to NT teachings, and to Christian application.

2.36.4 Kraus, Hans-Joachim. *Psalms: A Commentary*. 2 vols. Minneapolis: Augsburg, 1988, 1989. 559/587pp.

Represents the best of contemporary critical German scholarship on the Psalms. After a lengthy and comprehensive introduction, deals with each psalm by providing a select bibliography (mostly German and French titles), original translation, linguistic notes, identification of the psalm according to form-critical categories and discussion of significance of form, commentary on each verse (emphasizing linguistic, literary, and historical elements), and the theological thrust of the psalm (from a Christian, and more specifically Lutheran, perspective). Emphasizes the original setting of the psalm and gives no serious attention to the role of a psalm within the Book of Psalms. Requires basic knowledge of Hebrew for full use.

2.36.5 Kraus, Hans-Joachim. *Theology of the Psalms*. Minneapolis: Augsburg, 1986. 235pp.

Draws on Kraus's interpretation of the psalter presented in his commentaries (§2.36.4), but can be used without reference to the commentaries. Argues that the theological thrust of the psalms is "Israel in the presence of God," and analyzes how the major issues in the psalms (e.g., God of Israel, worship, suffering and joy, king and temple, response to hostility) develop this central thrust. Involves somewhat technical discussions of the origin and development of each theological concept in ancient Israel in relation to the religious environment of the Ancient Near East. Of special value is the discussion of the use of the Psalms in the NT.

2.36.6 Mays, James Luther. *Psalms*. Interpretation: A Bible Commentary for Teaching and Preaching. Louisville: Westminster John Knox, 1994. 457pp.

Insightful and original commentary from a recognized authority on the psalter. Adopts a two-track approach: (a) provides a concise description of certain psalms, and (b) offers fuller exposition of those psalms that are prominent in worship, used in the NT, significant for the church's theology, or play an important role in the psalter as a whole. In this way Mays can give detailed treatment to the more important psalms, while giving at least a broad interpretation of each of the others. For those treated more fully, Mays employs literary structure, original setting, and role within the psalter as a basis for a robust Christian reading, probing the theological and religious aspects of most concern to contemporary Christians.

2.36.7 Mays, James Luther. *The Lord Reigns: A Theological Handbook to the Psalms*. Philadelphia: Westminster, 1994. 159pp.

A most helpful discussion of the theological value of the psalms for the Christian church. Insists that the theological foundation for all the psalms is the confession that "the Lord reigns," and thus the psalter provides the framework for life within the kingdom of God. Mays employs insights from the history of original composition and the history of the use of the psalms to shed light on practical issues that pertain especially to the devotional, liturgical, and confessional lives of Christians.

2.36.8 Tate, Marvin. *Psalms 51–100*. Word Biblical Commentary. Dallas: Word, 1990. 578pp.

See Allen (§2.36.1).

A L S O   S I G N I F I C A N T

2.36.9 Anderson, Bernhard W. *Out of the Depths: The Psalms Speak for Us Today*. 3d ed. Philadelphia: Westminster, 2000. 249pp.

2.36.10 Bellinger, William H. *Psalms: Reading and Studying the Book of Praises*. Peabody, Mass.: Hendrickson, 1990. 166pp.

2.36.11 Briggs, Charles Augustus, and Emilie Grace Briggs. *A Critical and Exegetical Commentary on the Book of Psalms*. International Critical Commentary. 2 vols. Edinburgh: T&T Clark, 1906–1907.

2.36.12 Brueggemann, Walter. *The Message of the Psalms: A Theological Commentary*. Augsburg Old Testament Studies. Minneapolis: Augsburg, 1984. 206pp.

2.36.13 Bullock, C. Hassell. *Encountering the Book of Psalms: A Literary and Theological Introduction*. Encountering Biblical Studies. Grand Rapids: Baker, 2001. 256pp.

2.36.14 Crenshaw, James L. *The Psalms: An Introduction*. Grand Rapids: Eerdmans, 2001. 187pp.

2.36.15 Dahood, Mitchell. *Psalms*. 3 vols. Anchor Bible. Garden City, N.Y.: Double-day, 1965–1970. 329/399/490pp.

2.36.16 Gerstenberger, Erhard S. *Psalms, Part 1: With an Introduction to Cultic Poetry.* Forms of Old Testament Literature 14. Grand Rapids: Eerdmans, 1988. 275pp.

2.36.17 ———. *Psalms, Part 2, and Lamentations.* Forms of Old Testament Literature 15. Grand Rapids: Eerdmans, 2001. 565pp.

2.36.18 Gunkel, Hermann. *The Psalms: A Form-Critical Introduction.* Facet Books Biblical Series 19. Philadelphia: Fortress, 1967. 52pp.

2.36.19 Holladay, William L. *The Psalms through Three Thousand Years: Prayerbook of a Cloud of Witnesses.* Philadelphia: Fortress, 1993. 395pp.

2.36.20 Kidner, Derek. *Psalms: An Introduction and Commentary.* 2 vols. Tyndale Old Testament Commentaries. Downers Grove, Ill.: InterVarsity, 1975. 492pp.

2.36.21 McCann, J. Clinton, Jr. *A Theological Introduction to the Book of Psalms.* Nashville: Abingdon, 1994. 204pp.

2.36.22 McCann, J. Clinton, Jr., ed. *The Shape and Shaping of the Psalter.* Journal for the Study of the Old Testament Supplement Series 159. Sheffield: JSOT, 1993. 130pp.

2.36.23 Miller, Patrick D., Jr. *Interpreting the Psalms.* Philadelphia: Fortress, 1986. 165pp.

2.36.24 Mowinkel, Sigmund. *The Psalms in Israel's Worship.* 2 vols. Nashville: Abingdon, 1963. 303pp.

2.36.25 Perowne, John. *The Book of Psalms.* London: D. Ball, 1878–1879. 523pp.

2.36.26 Schaefer, Konrad. *Psalms.* Berit Olam: Studies in Hebrew Narrative and Poetry. Collegeville, Minn.: Liturgical Press, 2001. 448pp.

2.36.27 Weiser, Artur. *The Psalms.* Old Testament Library. Philadelphia: Westminster, 1962. 841pp.

2.36.28 Westermann, Claus. *The Psalms: Structure, Content, and Message.* Minneapolis: Augsburg, 1990. 128pp.

2.36.29 Zenger, Erich. *A God of Vengeance?: Understanding the Psalms of Divine Wrath.* Louisville: Westminster John Knox, 1996. 104pp.

2.37 Proverbs

H I G H L Y   R E C O M M E N D E D

2.37.1 Boström, Lennart. *The God of the Sages: The Portrayal of God in the Book of Proverbs*. Coniectanea Biblica: Old Testament Series 29. Stockholm: Almqvist & Wiksell, 1990. 260pp.

Insofar as commentaries on Proverbs generally give inadequate attention to the book's theology, this volume is a welcome contribution. While focusing on the doctrine of God, Boström discusses also such theological issues as creation, order of the world, retribution, and theodicy. Recognizes the complexity of Proverbs' portrait of God as both transcendent sovereign Lord and an imminent God who relates intimately to humans and is seriously involved in the world. Explores both continuity and discontinuity between theology of Proverbs and that of the wisdom traditions of Israel's neighbors.

2.37.2 Clifford, Richard J. *Proverbs*. Old Testament Library. Louisville: Westminster John Knox, 1999. 286pp.

While attending to such matters as philology, textual criticism, and comparison with wisdom material from Israel's neighbors, the focus and distinctive value of this commentary is its attention to the rhetoric of Proverbs, i.e., ways in which the language, structure, and literary features engage the reader to encourage and guide the quest for wisdom (which is taken to be the purpose and main theme of the book). This commentary is more engaging to the modern reader than most others, since it focuses on matters that the text invites the reader to ponder. Yet insofar as it emphasizes Proverbs' relationship to the secular wisdom tradition of the Ancient Near East, it gives no serious consideration to its role within the OT canon or to its witness specifically to the creator God of Israel, or to its contribution to Jewish and Christian theology.

2.37.3 Fox, Michael V. *Proverbs 1–9*. Anchor Bible. New York: Doubleday, 2000. 474pp.

This leading Jewish authority on OT wisdom presents a thorough verse-by-verse commentary, with emphasis on the meaning of key terms, connections with other OT passages, Ancient Near Eastern parallels, interaction with the history of interpretation, and the stages of tradition leading to the final text. Especially helpful excurses on the most significant issues encountered in the text. The second volume, dealing with the remainder of Proverbs and including a more comprehensive discussion of historical and ideological issues, is awaited.

2.37.4 McKane, William. *Proverbs*. Old Testament Library. Philadelphia: Westminster, 1970. 670pp.

Interprets Proverbs by examining especially (a) its relation to Egyptian and Babylonian-Assyrian wisdom literature; (b) a careful and original reclassification of literary forms employed in Proverbs (a reclassification not universally accepted by scholars); and (c) ancient Palestinian background. This threefold emphasis is a strength but also a weakness, since it results in little attention to other interpretive evidence, to the function of Proverbs within the canon, or to theological significance.

2.37.5 Perdue, Leo G. *Proverbs*. Interpretation: A Bible Commentary for Teaching and Preaching. Louisville: Westminster John Knox, 2000. 289pp.

Divides Proverbs into eight collections, composed at different times by a variety of sages. Emphasizes especially the role of social setting, and (unlike most commentaries) the literary structure of smaller units as well as the entire book in the interpretation of individual passages. The introduction gives an exceptionally clear and accessible presentation of the history of wisdom tradition, the sages responsible for the proverbs, the development of the wisdom collections toward the formation of the final book, the role of Proverbs within the canon, and its contribution to Christian theology and life. The commentary itself, however, treats the theology of the text according to its religious significance specifically for the original audience and gives little attention to possible theological appropriation by contemporary Christians.

A L S O   S I G N I F I C A N T

2.37.6 Kidner, Derek. *Proverbs*. Tyndale Old Testament Commentaries. Downers Grove, Ill.: InterVarsity, 1964. 192pp.

2.37.7 Oesterley, William O. E. *The Book of Proverbs*. Westminster Commentaries. London: Methuen, 1929. 294pp.

2.37.8 Philip, Johannes Nel. *The Structure and Ethos of the Wisdom Admonitions in Proverbs*. Berlin: Walter De Gruyter, 1982. 142pp.

2.37.9 Scott, R. B. Y. *Proverbs and Ecclesiastes*. Anchor Bible. Garden City, N.Y.: Doubleday, 1965. 255pp.

2.37.10 Toy, C. H. *A Critical and Exegetical Commentary on the Book of Proverbs*. International Critical Commentary. Edinburgh: T&T Clark, 1899. 554pp.

2.37.11 Weeks, Stuart. *Early Israelite Wisdom*. Oxford Theological Monographs. Oxford: Oxford University Press, 1994. 212pp.

2.37.12 Westermann, Claus. *Roots of Wisdom: The Oldest Proverbs of Israel and Other Peoples*. Philadelphia: Westminster, 1995. 178pp.

2.37.13 Whybray, R. N. *The Book of Proverbs: A Survey of Modern Study*. History of Biblical Interpretation Series 1. Leiden: Brill, 1995. 184pp.

2.37.14 ———. *Proverbs*. New Century Bible Commentary. Grand Rapids: Eerdmans, 1994. 446pp.

2.37.15 ———. *Wealth and Poverty in the Book of Proverbs*. Journal for the Study of the Old Testament Supplement Series 99. Sheffield: JSOT, 1990. 132pp.

2.38 Ecclesiastes (Qohelet)

See also PROVERBS (§2.37); SONG OF SOLOMON (§2.39)

H I G H L Y   R E C O M M E N D E D

2.38.1 Brown, William P. *Ecclesiastes*. Interpretation: A Bible Commentary for Teaching and Preaching. Louisville: Westminster John Knox, 2000. 143pp.

Creative, lucid, and engaging. Rather than attempting to press a kind of logical and theological coherence that Brown believes is absent from Ecclesiastes, he shows how the ambivalence of the text witnesses to enduring spiritual and theological truth. Gives attention to Ecclesiastes' distinctive thought, but helps the reader discern the place of this book within the larger witness of Scripture. Engages as a Christian believer in constant dialogue with the strange and challenging perspective of Ecclesiastes. The epilogue, "Qoheleth's Place in Christian Faith and Life," is itself worth the prices of the volume.

2.38.2 Crenshaw, James L. *Ecclesiastes: A Commentary*. Old Testament Library. Louisville: Westminster John Knox, 1987. 192pp.

Crenshaw brings his comprehensive knowledge of OT wisdom to bear on the language and historical background of the book (the two emphases of his commentary). The commentary is thus illuminating of technical matters, but does little to engage the reader who desires to probe theological and existential issues. The introduction offers a lucid and enlightening orientation to the book's most significant aspects, including its teachings (from which Crenshaw excludes the "secondary addition" of 12:8–14).

2.38.3 Longman, Tremper, III. *The Book of Ecclesiastes*. New International Commentary on the Old Testament. Grand Rapids: Eerdmans, 1998. 306pp.

Writes from a conservative perspective, but rejects Solomonic authorship. Posits a later writer who adopts the persona of Solomon and is responsible for 1:12–12:7, and a second unnamed wisdom teacher who provides a frame to the book (1:1–11 and 12:8–14) and qualifies and clarifies the intervening material. Thus, in contrast to most commentators, insists that 12:8–14 is not merely a secondary addition, but critical for understanding the book's message. Longman's major contribution is to show how Qohelet's claim that everything is meaningless fits into the rest of biblical revelation. Excellent in moving from original significance of the text to Christian theological reflection and contemporary application.

2.38.4 Murphy, Roland E. *Ecclesiastes*. Word Biblical Commentary. Dallas: Word, 1992. 165pp.

Prominent Roman Catholic OT scholar offers a serious examination of the book's most vexing problems and passages by careful analysis of the text in conversation with the history of interpretation, leading to judicious and informed conclusions. Concise and accessible discussion of textual, linguistic, and historical issues, always in the service of understanding as precisely as possible the author's thought. Attempts to identify the specific theological meaning of larger passages in the book, often moving on to discuss concerns of contemporary (Christian) readers. Sees more fundamental coherence in the book than most modern commentators, who make much of inconsistencies in Ecclesiastes.

2.38.5 Seow, C. L. *Ecclesiastes*. Anchor Bible. New York: Doubleday, 1997. 419pp.

Arguably the most current and comprehensive treatment presently available. Offers detailed technical discussion in the "Notes," while providing fresh and persuasive interpretation accessible to the general reader in the "Comments." Presents a helpful description of Ecclesiastes' theology in the introduction, but the commentary itself generally avoids theological issues, and does nothing to probe the ideological and existential struggle readers (including modern ones) have with the apparently fatalistic perspective of Ecclesiastes. Gives little attention to potential for Christian application.

2.38.6 Whybray, R. N. *Ecclesiastes*. New Century Bible Commentary. Grand Rapids: Eerdmans, 1989. 179pp.

In spite of its brevity, packs in a great deal of useful information and provides clear and compelling interpretation of the most salient features of theological claims of passages within Ecclesiastes. Emphasizes the role of individual passages in the development of themes of the entire book.

A L S O   S I G N I F I C A N T

2.38.7   Bartholomew, Craig G. *Reading Ecclesiastes: Old Testament Exegesis and Hermeneutical Theory.* Rome: Editrice Pontificio Instituto, 1998. 319pp.

2.38.8   Barton, George A. *A Critical and Exegetical Commentary on the Book of Ecclesiastes.* International Critical Commentary. Edinburgh: T&T Clark, 1908. 212pp.

2.38.9   Christianson, Eric S. *A Time to Tell: Narrative Strategies in Ecclesiastes.* Journal for the Study of the Old Testament Supplement Series 280. Sheffield: Sheffield Academic Press, 1998. 299pp.

2.38.10 Eaton, Michael A. *Ecclesiastes: An Introduction and Commentary.* Tyndale Old Testament Commentaries. Downers Grove, Ill.: InterVarsity, 1983. 159pp.

2.38.11 Ellul, Jacques. *Reason for Being: A Meditation on Ecclesiastes.* Grand Rapids: Eerdmans, 1990. 306pp.

2.38.12 Fox, Michael V. *A Time to Tear Down and a Time to Build Up: A Rereading of Ecclesiastes.* Grand Rapids: Eerdmans, 1999. 421pp.

2.38.13 Gordis, Robert. *Koheleth: The Man and His World.* 3d ed. New York: Block, 1968. 421pp.

2.38.14 Plumptre, E. H. *Ecclesiastes, or, The Preacher.* Cambridge Bible for Schools and Colleges. Cambridge: Cambridge University Press, 1888. 271pp.

2.38.15 Whitley, Charles F. *Koheleth: His Language and Thought.* Beiheft zur Zeitschrift für die alttestamentliche Wissenschaft 148. Berlin: Walter De Gruyter, 1979. 199pp.

2.38.16 Williams, Arthur Lukyn. *Ecclesiastes.* Cambridge Bible for Schools and Colleges. Cambridge: Cambridge University Press, 1922. 184pp.

2.39 Song of Solomon

See also ECCLESIASTES (§2.38)

H I G H L Y   R E C O M M E N D E D

2.39.1 Carr, G. Lloyd. *The Song of Solomon: An Introduction and Commentary.* Tyndale Old Testament Commentaries. Downers Grove, Ill.: InterVarsity, 1983. 175pp.

Because of the problem of vocabulary and syntax in the Song of Solomon, this volume gives greater attention to technical matters than is typical for this series. But all technical discussion is pursued explicitly for the purpose of explicating the most salient issues for the text's meaning. According to Carr, the book celebrates and gives guidance to human love, especially in its emotional and sexual aspects. Carr traces this theme throughout his commentary, and thus the commentary tends to be more consistently theologically oriented than most other Song of Solomon commentaries. Considers that the poem was essentially completed at the time of Solomon (and is thus one of the very few modern commentators who link it to Solomon), but revised during the time of the divided monarchy.

2.39.2 Keel, Othmar. *The Song of Songs.* Continental Commentary. Philadelphia: Fortress, 1994. 308pp.

A careful analysis of the meaning of the language of this book, drawing especially on literary forms employed, the significance of metaphorical and symbolic language, and parallels from Palestine, Egypt, and Mesopotamia. Gives special attention to iconographic parallels, and thus is replete with illustrations from the Ancient Near East. Introduction contains helpful discussion of theological significance, but commentary proper offers little theological reflection.

2.39.3 Longman, Tremper, III. *Song of Songs.* New International Commentary on the Old Testament. Grand Rapids: Eerdmans, 2001. 238pp.

This prominent evangelical OT scholar, known especially for his work on literary aspects of biblical interpretation, offers a comprehensive and careful examination of this book, which Longman takes to be an anthology of several originally independent poems, most of which are post-Solomonic. In spite of its varied origins, the Song of Songs coheres in its final form, and Longman focuses almost exclusively on this final form, finding here a celebration of the love between husband and wife and thus a celebration of male-female relationship that is analogous to God's love for his people. Contains critical discussion of the history of interpretation and a helpful section on the theology of the book, where Longman explores its relation to the rest of the OT and (to a limited extent) to the NT. Commentary itself emphasizes examination of the Hebrew (gives more attention to lexical than to syntactical matters), literary forms, and Ancient Near Eastern parallels. In spite of its attention to technical matters, is accessible to non-specialists.

2.39.4 Murphy, Roland E. *The Song of Songs*. Hermeneia: A Critical and Historical Commentary on the Bible. Philadelphia: Fortress, 1990. 237pp.

Informed, careful, and judicious examination of the language and background of the text. Lengthy introduction deals with significant aspects of the
book, including the history of interpretation and major possibilities for its
theological use. Murphy sees the Song, understood within the framework of
the biblical canon, as expressing a theology of human sexuality, with emphasis
on the emotional experiences of love. All of this contributes to Scripture's affirmation that human love, and particularly sexual love, is part of God's gracious design for his human creation.

2.39.5 Pope, Marvin H. *Song of Songs*. Anchor Bible. Garden City, N.Y.:
Doubleday, 1977. 743pp.

Massive, learned, detailed, and technical commentary focusing on the text,
language, historical background, and history of interpretation. Considers the
poem to be a celebration of sexual love, which in its depth reveals the nature
of all human love and in its transcendence points to divine love. Finds the
bases for this poem to be in fertility religions of the Ancient Near East, the sacred marriage rite, and the funeral feast. Rejects allegorical interpretations,
but recognizes that these interpretations sometimes contain helpful theological insight and therefore cites traditional Jewish and Christian allegorical interpretations for each passage.

A L S O   S I G N I F I C A N T

2.39.6 Bergant, Dianne. *The Song of Songs*. Berit Olam: Studies in Hebrew Narrative
and Poetry. Collegeville, Minn.: Liturgical Press, 2001. 138pp.

2.39.7 Ginsburg, Christian David. *The Song of Songs*. London: Longman, Brown,
Green, Longmans, and Roberts, 1857. 191pp.

2.39.8 Gordis, Robert. *The Song of Songs and Lamentations*. New York: Ktav, 1974.
203pp.

2.39.9 Harper, Andrew. *The Song of Songs*. Cambridge Bible for Schools and Colleges. Cambridge: Cambridge University Press, 1912. 96pp.

2.39.10 LaCocque, André. *Romance She Wrote: A Hermeneutical Essay on Song of
Songs*. Harrisburg, Pa.: Trinity Press International, 1998. 240pp.

2.39.11 Stadelmann, Luis I. J. *Love and Politics: A New Commentary on the Song of
Songs*. New York: Paulist, 1992. 243pp.

2.40 Prophetic Literature: General Works

H I G H L Y   R E C O M M E N D E D

2.40.1 Blenkinsopp, Joseph. *A History of Prophecy in Israel: From the Settlement in the Land to the Hellenistic Period.* Rev. ed. Louisville: Westminster John Knox, 1993. 291pp.

A critical history of the phenomenon of prophecy in Israel, from the settlement through early Judaism. Treats the origin and development of Israelite prophecy against the background of the political, social, and religious environment of the Ancient Near East and the role of the prophetic materials in the OT canon. Emphasizes lines of continuity, but considers also distinctive character of each prophet and diverging courses of development. Accepts generally held critical views regarding sources and dates.

2.40.2 Gowan, Donald E. *Theology of the Prophetic Books: The Death and Resurrection of Israel.* Louisville: Westminster John Knox, 1998. 250pp.

Clearly written and illuminating study of the theology of each of the prophetic books, taking seriously the way the prophet's own historical context influenced his message and how later prophets built on earlier ones. Insists that the individual prophetic messages are all variations of the overarching prophetic theme of the death and resurrection of Israel, which can serve as the bridge to Christian appropriation.

2.40.3 Heschel, Abraham. *The Prophets.* 2 vols. New York: Harper, 1969. 235/287pp.

Something of a modern classic, this work by a prominent Jewish scholar of an earlier generation is an elegant, insightful, and sympathetic exploration into the phenomenon of Israel's prophecy, including presuppositions, character of prophetic inspiration, prophetic consciousness, and the major theological concerns of the prophets. Treats all of these matters with religious and spiritual sensitivity. Emphasizes the uniqueness of prophecy in Israel over against prophetic phenomena among Israel's neighbors.

2.40.4 Koch, Klaus. *The Prophets.* 2 vols. Philadelphia: Fortress, 1982, 1983. 182/216pp.

Lucid and comprehensive description of Israelite prophecy in general and of each of the prophetic books in particular (the latter receiving the bulk of attention). Discusses each of the literary prophets in terms of historical, religious, and social background, and the method and forms of his prophecy so as to illumine the prophet's message. Emphasizes lines of development between the prophets. Provides depth, clarification, and perspective to the theological message of the prophets. Accepts generally held critical views regarding sources and dates, but recognizes the speculative character of much literary reconstruction and is therefore generally reluctant to dismiss large passages as later additions or interpolations.

2.40.5   VanGemeren, Willem A. *Interpreting the Prophetic Word: An Introduction to the Prophetic Literature of the Old Testament.* Grand Rapids: Zondervan, 1990. 545pp.

Written by a leading evangelical scholar, this volume provides a conservative alternative to many of the critical conclusions regarding dates and sources assumed by most other scholars listed here. Emphasizes historical background, literary form and structure, and theological message of each prophetic book. Notes how each book contributes to biblical revelation as a whole, and constantly draws connections between these books and NT fulfillment.

A L S O   S I G N I F I C A N T

2.40.6   Brueggemann, Walter. *The Prophetic Imagination.* Minneapolis: Fortress, 1978. 127pp.

2.40.7   Clements, Ronald E. *Old Testament Prophecy: From Oracles to Canon.* Louisville: Westminster John Knox, 1996. 278pp.

2.40.8   Gordon, Robert P., ed. *The Place Is Too Small for Us: The Israelite Prophets in Recent Scholarship.* Sources for Biblical and Theological Study 5. Winona Lake, Ind.: Eisenbrauns, 1995. 638pp.

2.40.9   Lindblom, Johannes. *Prophecy in Ancient Israel.* Oxford: Blackwell, 1962. 472pp.

2.40.10   Matthews, Victor H. *Social World of the Hebrew Prophets.* Peabody, Mass.: Hendrickson, 2001. 217pp.

2.40.11   Mays, James Luther, and Paul J. Achtemeier, eds. *Interpreting the Prophets.* Philadelphia: Fortress, 1987. 287pp.

2.40.12   Nissinen, Martti, ed. *Prophecy in Its Ancient Near Eastern Context: Mesopotamian, Biblical, and Arabian Perspectives.* Society of Biblical Literature Symposium Series 15. Atlanta: Scholars, 2000. 160pp.

2.40.13 Petersen, David L., ed. *Prophecy in Israel.* Issues in Religion and Theology 10. Philadelphia: Fortress, 1987. 178pp.

2.40.14 ———. *The Prophetic Literature: An Introduction.* Louisville: Westminster John Knox, 2002. 260pp.

2.40.15 Rad, Gerhard von. *The Message of the Prophets.* London: SCM, 1968. 289pp.

2.40.16 Robinson, T. H. *Prophecy and Prophets in Ancient Israel.* 2d ed. London: Duckworth, 1953. 231pp.

2.40.17 Sawyer, John F. A. *Prophecy and the Biblical Prophets.* Rev. ed. Oxford Biblical Series. Oxford: Oxford University Press, 1993. 180pp.

2.40.18 Scott, R. B. Y. *The Relevance of the Prophets.* Rev. ed. New York: Macmillan, 1968. 248pp.

2.40.19 Steck, Odil Hannes. *The Prophetic Books and Their Theological Witness.* St. Louis, Mo.: Chalice, 2000. 246pp.

2.40.20 Ward, James M. *Thus Says the Lord: The Message of the Prophets.* Nashville: Abingdon, 1991. 282pp.

2.40.21 Westermann, Claus. *Basic Forms of Prophetic Speech.* Philadelphia: Westminster, 1991. 222pp.

2.40.22 Wilson, Robert R. *Prophecy and Society in Ancient Israel.* Philadelphia: Fortress, 1980. 322pp.

2.40.23 Young, Edward J. *My Servants the Prophets.* Grand Rapids: Eerdmans, 1952. 231pp.

2.41 Isaiah

H I G H L Y   R E C O M M E N D E D

2.41.1 Blenkinsopp, Joseph. *Isaiah.* 3 vols. Anchor Bible. New York: Doubleday, 2000, 2002. 524/528pp.

The first two of three volumes by this formidable OT scholar have thus far appeared. The most current and judicious example of a type of commentary on Isaiah (represented also in the massive commentaries by Kaiser (§2.41.15, 16), Westermann (§2.41.22), and Wildberger [§2.41.8]) that carefully identifies earlier traditions and probes the centuries-long editorial process that led to the composition of First (chs. 1–39), Second (chs. 40–55), and Third (chs. 56–66) Isaiah. Rich in linguistic analysis, historical background, and Ancient Near Eastern parallels, but little concerned with theological issues of the text. Helpful for full discussion of technical matters, but should be supplemented with commentaries that give greater attention to the final form of the text and adopt a more intentional theological perspective.

2.41.2 Childs, Brevard S. *Isaiah*. Old Testament Library. Louisville: Westminster John Knox, 2001. 555pp.

Argues for theological unity of the book, resulting from a redactional process according to which the influence of Second Isaiah (chs. 40–55) was responsible for reshaping First Isaiah (chs. 1–39) and largely determined Third Isaiah (chs. 56–66). Childs insists that a recognition of this compositional growth enriches the theological witness of the book in its final canonical shape. Thus he argues against a "synchronic" reading that simply takes the text as it stands without any concern for the stages of tradition, but argues also against a focus on the stages of tradition or redactional processes as ends in themselves. Consistently presses for his approach over against these two alternatives throughout the commentary. Commentary also attends to development of thought within the book, and offers acute theological insights. Focuses on Isaiah's own discrete theological witness, but in a few instances relates Isaiah to other OT materials and probes significance for NT faith.

2.41.3 Hanson, Paul D. *Isaiah 40–66*. Interpretation: A Bible Commentary for Teaching and Preaching. Louisville: Westminster John Knox, 1995. 255pp.

In contrast to the companion volume on chs. 1–39 by Seitz, this commentary isolates Second (chs. 40–55) and Third (chs. 56–66) Isaiah from chs. 1–39, and emphasizes the historical setting of these materials for their interpretation rather than their literary structure or their role within the final form of the entire book. Yet this commentary emphasizes the theological concerns of the writers, and frequently makes explicit connections with moral, religious, and spiritual challenges that face contemporary readers.

2.41.4 Oswalt, John N. *The Book of Isaiah*. 2 vols. New International Commentary on the Old Testament. Grand Rapids: Eerdmans, 1986, 1998. 746/755pp.

Argues strongly for the traditional position that the entire book represents the prophecy of Isaiah of Jerusalem. Chapters 1–39 were written for Isaiah's contemporaries in the eighth century B.C.E.; chs. 40–55 presuppose the exile of the sixth century; and ch. 56–66 presuppose the eventual return from exile.

Chapters 40–66 thus contain predictive prophecy from Isaiah. Introduction contains comprehensive and illuminating discussion of the book's theology and its function within the canon. Commentary deals extensively with textual, linguistic, literary, and historical matters, but emphasizes structure of passages, their function within the broader book, and their relation to other biblical materials, including the NT. Probes theological significance from an evangelical Christian perspective. Most helpful for preaching and teaching.

2.41.5 Seitz, Christopher R. *Isaiah 1–39*. Interpretation: A Bible Commentary for Teaching and Preaching. Louisville: Westminster John Knox, 1993. 271pp.

Limited to chs. 1–39, but Seitz interprets these chapters in terms of the final form of the entire book and focuses on the structure of passages and their function within the book as the basis for their theological meaning. Constantly reflects on hermeneutical issues facing Christian interpreters of Isaiah, and deftly models the movement from the theological claims of the original compilers of the book to contemporary Christian appropriation.

2.41.6 Seitz, Christopher R., ed. *Reading and Preaching the Book of Isaiah*. Philadelphia: Fortress, 1988. 126pp.

Several leading OT scholars probe the character, original meaning, and theological significance of the various portions of Isaiah with a view toward exploring the issues involved in Christian proclamation of these passages. Contains two essays on chs.1–39, two essays on chs. 40–55, and one essay on chs. 56–66. Concludes with a final chapter on reading the entire book as a holistic theological unity.

2.41.7 Watts, John D. W. *Isaiah*. 2 vols. Word Biblical Commentary. Waco, Tex.: Word, 1985, 1987. 449/385pp.

Maintains that the overall concern of Isaiah is God's inauguration of a new age for his people, when servanthood rather than authoritarian domination will be the mark of election. Israel's rejection of Isaiah's message is the basis for Isaiah's vision of the realization of this divine purpose in the future. Understands the book to be, in form, an example of "vision genre," and hence argues that its dramatic presentation is similar to a play, with scenes, stage direction, and twelve acts. The prophecy of Isaiah of Jerusalem forms the core of the book, but was supplemented by extensive additions until the book reached its final composition in the Persian period. Even those who do not accept Watts's literary and historical hypotheses will benefit from his detailed discussion of text and language, his informed and judicious interpretations, and his attention to the text's theological claims. Especially helpful are his excurses (in-depth discussions) of significant issues.

2.41.8 Wildberger, Hans. *Isaiah: A Commentary.* 3 volumes. Continental Commentary. Minneapolis: Fortress, 1991, 1997, 2002. 524/624/781pp.

Extremely thorough (indeed, encyclopedic), erudite, and technical commentary on "First Isaiah," representing the German critical tradition. Interpretation informed by Ancient Near Eastern background, text-critical issues, analysis of the Hebrew, considerations of the formation of the book of Isaiah from Isaiah himself through post-Isaianic redaction, and the history of interpretation. Commentary on each passage concludes with "Purpose and Thrust," which offers brief theological reflections of the text as Christian scripture. Introductory matters, including a fine discussion of the book of Isaiah, are treated at the end of the third volume. Wildberger died in 1986, well before this English translation was published, but the extensive bibliography in the third volume was updated through 2001.

ALSO SIGNIFICANT

2.41.9 Achtemeier, Elizabeth. *The Community and Message of Isaiah 55–66: A Theological Commentary.* Minneapolis: Augsburg, 1982. 157pp.

2.41.10 Baltzer, Klaus. *Deutero-Isaiah.* Hermeneia: A Critical and Historical Commentary on the Bible. Minneapolis: Fortress, 2001. 400pp.

2.41.11 Clements, Ronald E. *Isaiah 1–39.* New Century Bible Commentary. Grand Rapids: Eerdmans, 1981. 301pp.

2.41.12 Conrad, Edgar W. *Reading Isaiah.* Overtures to Biblical Theology. Philadelphia: Fortress, 1991. 185pp.

2.41.13 Gray, George Buchanan. *A Critical and Exegetical Commentary on the Book of Isaiah: I-XXXIX.* International Critical Commentary. Edinburgh: T&T Clark, 1912. 472pp.

2.41.14 Hayes, John H. *Isaiah, the Eighth Century Prophet: His Times and His Preaching.* Nashville: Abingdon, 1987. 416pp.

2.41.15 Kaiser, Otto. *Isaiah 1–12: A Commentary.* 2d ed. Old Testament Library. Philadelphia: Westminster, 1983. 272pp.

2.41.16 ———. *Isaiah 13–39: A Commentary.* Old Testament Library. Philadelphia: Westminster, 1974. 412pp.

2.41.17 Kissane, Edward J. *The Book of Isaiah.* 2 vols. Dublin: Brown & Nolan, 1941. 413/328pp.

2.41.18 Motyer, J. Alec. *The Prophecy of Isaiah: An Introduction and Commentary.*
         Downers Grove, Ill.: InterVarsity, 1993. 544pp.

2.41.19 North, Christopher R. *The Suffering Servant in Deutero-Isaiah: An Historical
         and Critical Study.* 2d ed. London: Oxford University Press, 1948. 264pp.

2.41.20 Sawyer, John F. A. *The Fifth Gospel: Isaiah in the History of Christianity.* Cam-
         bridge: Cambridge University Press, 1996. 281pp.

2.41.21 Schmitt, John J. *Isaiah and His Interpreters.* New York: Paulist, 1986. 137pp.

2.41.22 Westermann, Claus. *Isaiah 40–66.* Old Testament Library. Philadelphia: West-
         minster, 1969. 429pp.

2.41.23 Whybray, R. N. *Isaiah 40–66.* New Century Bible. London: Oliphants, 1975.
         301pp.

2.42 Jeremiah

H I G H L Y   R E C O M M E N D E D

2.42.1 Brueggemann, Walter. *A Commentary on Jeremiah: Exile and Home-
        coming.* Grand Rapids: Eerdmans, 1998. 502pp.

Stimulating and engaging study. Breaks new ground in interpretive method.
Rejects concern to reconstruct history of Jeremiah's prophetic ministry in
favor of understanding the book as an ideological appeal to accept its new
and daring framework of reality, i.e., to live and think differently in relation to
God. By combining sociological insights, literary analysis, and perspectives
from other OT passages with playful imagination, Brueggemann helps the
reader to experience the power of this ideological transformation. Because
his imagination sometimes leaps beyond the data of the text, the reader
should critically evaluate Brueggemann's interpretations in light of pertinent
evidence. But the reader will consistently find this volume richly suggestive of
meaning for contemporary life.

2.42.2 Carroll, Robert P. *Jeremiah: A Commentary.* Old Testament Library.
        Philadelphia: Westminster, 1986. 874pp.

Massive commentary that has significantly influenced recent Jeremiah studies. Argues that the book is composed of a variety of responses to the fall of Jerusalem emerging from different groups in different settings throughout an
extended period well into postexilic times. Each of these responses is con-

cerned to press its own ideology. Carroll concludes that the book tells us little about the historical Jeremiah and that it lacks an overarching scheme and a coherent theology. The commentary focuses on the ideological appeal of these various voices, and as such it gives attention to the theological meaning of individual passages. Carroll relies on (reconstructed) historical background and close attention to the language of the text (especially meaning of metaphor and symbolic language) rather than broader-book context for interpretation. Although commentary is closely joined to Carroll's critical theories, its attention to language and its ideological analysis can illuminate the meaning of passages even for those who do not share Carroll's critical perspective.

2.42.3 Clements, Ronald E. *Jeremiah.* Interpretation: A Bible Commentary for Teaching and Preaching. Atlanta: John Knox, 1988. 276pp.

Focuses on the audience of the book rather than the audience of Jeremiah's own prophetic ministry. Probes how those who compiled this book in its final form addressed concerns of its original readers who needed a message of hope against a background of political disaster and tremendous suffering. Commentary consistently draws connections between this proclamation to the original audience and the ways it can speak to contemporary persons who experience much the same type of personal anxiety and challenge. Tends to speak to the existence of persons in general, with relatively little explicit mention of how the text witnesses to Jesus Christ and Christian faith.

2.42.4 Holladay, William L. *Jeremiah.* 2 vols. Hermeneia: A Critical and Historical Commentary on the Bible. Philadelphia: Fortress, 1986, 1989. 682/543pp.

Most complete and detailed commentary on Jeremiah. Addresses two crucial matters: chronology of Jeremiah's career, and the literary history of the book's formation. Tends toward historical reliability of the book and the view that Jeremiah had much to do with its production. Gives special consideration to the structure of passages, linguistic analysis, historical background, and illumination from other OT texts. In spite of its technical interests, it is written in a lively style and attends to theological issues, at points reflecting briefly on matters of abiding theological significance for Christians.

2.42.5 McKane, William. *A Critical and Exegetical Commentary on the Book of Jeremiah.* 2 vols. International Critical Commentary. Edinburgh: T&T Clark, 1986, 1996. 1396pp.

On the basis of text-critical considerations concludes that the book developed as a "rolling corpus," i.e., an original core of Jeremiah traditions generated haphazard expansions from a variety of groups over a long period of time. McKane's purpose is not to reconstruct the life or words of Jeremiah, but to trace the history of the traditions around Jeremiah that found their way into this book. Gives meticulous attention to linguistic analysis and comparison of ancient versions, and engages in vigorous interaction with the history of interpretation. In the process, offers helpful and at times insightful illumination of the meaning of the final form of the text, with occasional profound theological insights.

2.42.6   Thompson, J. A. *The Book of Jeremiah.* New International Commentary on the Old Testament. Grand Rapids: Eerdmans, 1980. 819pp.

Writes from an evangelical perspective, and argues for the essential historical accuracy of the book. Largely ignores the significance of the final form of the book for the original intended readers in favor of focusing interpretive attention on the historical ministry of Jeremiah. Gives attention to language and historical background, including insights from other OT passages, so as to arrive at biographical reflections on Jeremiah's experience, historical reflections on Israel's moral and spiritual failure, and theological reflections on God's relationship with and actions toward his people, all with a view toward noting ongoing significance for the people of God, the church.

ALSO SIGNIFICANT

2.42.7   Bright, John. *Jeremiah.* Anchor Bible. Garden City, N.Y.: Doubleday, 1965. 372pp.

2.42.8   Craigie, Peter C., Page H. Kelly, and Joel F. Drinkard Jr. *Jeremiah 1–25.* Word Biblical Commentary. Waco, Tex.: Word, 1991. 388pp.

2.42.9   Curtis, A. H. W., and T. Römer, eds. *The Book of Jeremiah and Its Reception.* Louvain: Louvain University Press, 1997. 331pp.

2.42.10 Harrison, R. K. *Jeremiah and Lamentations.* Tyndale Old Testament Commentaries. Downers Grove, Ill.: InterVarsity, 1973. 240pp.

2.42.11 Jones, Douglas Rawlinson. *Jeremiah.* New Century Bible Commentary. Grand Rapids: Eerdmans, 1992. 557pp.

2.42.12 Keown, Gerald L., Pamela J. Sclaise, and Thomas G. Smothers. *Jeremiah 26–52.* Word Biblical Commentary. Dallas: Word, 1995. 402pp.

2.42.13 King, Philip J. *Jeremiah: An Archaeological Companion.* Philadelphia: Westminster, 1993. 204pp.

2.42.14 Lundbom, Jack R. *Jeremiah 1–20*. Anchor Bible. New York: Doubleday, 1999. 934pp.

2.42.15 McConville, J. G. *Judgment and Promise: An Interpretation of the Book of Jeremiah*. Winona Lake, Ind.: Eisenbrauns, 1994. 208pp.

2.42.16 Nicholson, E. W. *Preaching to the Exiles*. Oxford: Oxford University Press, 1970. 154pp.

2.42.17 Overholt, Thomas W. *The Threat of Falsehood: A Study in the Theology of the Book of Jeremiah*. Studies in Biblical Theology, Second Series 16. Naperville, Ill.: Allenson, 1970. 110pp.

2.42.18 Skinner, John. *Prophecy and Religion*. Cambridge: Cambridge University Press, 1948. 360pp.

2.42.19 Thompson, Henry O. *The Book of Jeremiah: An Annotated Bibliography*. ATLA Bibliography Series. Lanham, Md.: Scarecrow, 1996. 745pp.

2.42.20 Welch, Adam C. *Jeremiah: His Time and His Work*. Oxford: Basil Blackwell, 1951. 263pp.

2.43 Lamentations

See also JEREMIAH (§2.42)

HIGHLY RECOMMENDED

2.43.1 Berlin, Adele. *Lamentations*. Old Testament Library. Louisville: Westminster John Knox, 2002. 135pp.

Fills a significant gap in the study of Lamentations by approaching Lamentations as a literary product, examining its images, metaphors, and poetic discourse. Berlin pursues the meaning of these literary features in order to identify and understand the religious worldview that gave rise to them. In this worldview she focuses on such concepts as purity, mourning, repentance, and the Davidic covenant. In the process she engages in constant comparison with other biblical and Ancient Near Eastern materials. She considers the historical-critical reconstruction of events referenced in Lamentations or sources lying behind the final form to be speculative and, in any case, not necessary to experience the literary impact of the book. Draws heavily on the Hebrew Masoretic text, but one can easily use this volume without knowledge of Hebrew. Although Berlin constantly references religious ideas and themes that lie behind the language of Lamentations, she does little to provide a constructive presentation of the book's theology or its contribution to the theological vision of the OT.

2.43.2 Dobbs-Allsopp, F. W. *Lamentations*. Interpretation: A Bible Commentary for Teaching and Preaching. Louisville: John Knox, 2002. 159pp.

An incisive analysis of the thought of Lamentations that masterfully relates the original message of the book to the theology of the OT as a whole and to contemporary reflection on the perduring problems broached by Lamentations, e.g., suffering, violence, the hidden/mysterious plan of God, and hope. Gives some (limited) attention to significance of Lamentations for Christian theology and faith. Dobbs-Allsopp's ideological emphasis nicely complements Berlin's (§2.43.1) literary study and Renkema's (§2.43.4) historical examination.

2.43.3 Hillers, Delbert R. *Lamentations*. Rev. ed. Anchor Bible. New York: Doubleday, 1992. 116pp.

Argues that Lamentations was not written by Jeremiah but is a unity produced by an eyewitness to the events described. Gives special attention to the writer's adoption of biblical language, motifs, and rhythmic patterns so as to bind the laments together, to give voice to feelings of deep despair, and to communicate theological questions and affirmations. Depth of treatment is compromised somewhat by commentary's brevity. Contains no specific discussion of the book's theology, and thus should be supplemented with Westermann (§2.43.5).

2.43.4 Renkema, Johan. *Lamentations*. Historical Commentary on the Old Testament. Leuven: Peeters, 1998. 641pp.

Recently translated from the Dutch, the most comprehensive commentary on Lamentations presently available in English. Introduction addresses literary structure, authorship, date, provenance, and theology. Insists on the unity of the book, and holds that it was produced by temple singers left behind after the fall of Jerusalem. Exhaustive commentary provides technical but relevant discussions of structural and linguistic analysis, historical background, and history of interpretation.

2.43.5 Westermann, Claus. *Lamentations: Issues and Interpretation.* Minneapolis: Fortress, 1994. 252pp.

Carefully surveys history of research into Lamentations and concludes that the book's message has been largely missed because of certain invalid presuppositions, chiefly that laments have no theological significance. Sets Lamentations within the broader context of laments in the Ancient Near East, presents an overview of the book as a whole, pursues a close reading of each of the five lamentations in the book, paying special attention to literary structure and meaning of key elements in each, and concludes with an insightful summary of the theology of Lamentations.

A L S O   S I G N I F I C A N T

2.43.6 Baumgartner, Walter. *Jeremiah's Poems of Lament.* Historic Texts and Interpreters 7. Sheffield: Almond, 1988.

2.43.7 Gottwald, Norman K. *Studies in the Book of Lamentations.* Rev. ed. London: SCM, 1962. 126pp.

2.43.8 Neusner, Jacob. *Israel after Calamity: The Book of Lamentations.* The Bible of Judaism Library. Valley Forge, Pa.: Trinity Press International, 1995. 117pp.

2.43.9 Provan, Iain. *Lamentations.* New Century Bible Commentary. Grand Rapids: Eerdmans, 1991. 142pp.

2.44 Ezekiel

See also HOSEA (§2.47)

H I G H L Y   R E C O M M E N D E D

2.44.1 Allen, Leslie C. *Ezekiel.* 2 vols. Word Biblical Commentary. Dallas: Word, 1994, 1990. 306/301pp.

This evangelical scholar adopts a moderating position that affirms authentic Ezekiel tradition in the book, but gives full weight to the redactional process that led to the production of the final form of the book. Insists that Ezekiel himself initiated the literary production of the book soon after the conclusion of his ministry, and that his disciples, who knew Ezekiel well and shared his aims, completed the editorial process. Allen focuses on the final canonical text, but explores how the redactional process as he reconstructs it illumines the final form. He attends to the theological meaning for the original exilic audience and relates passages to other biblical texts (including NT ones), but gives no direct attention to contemporary appropriation. A significant contribution is the original and detailed discussion of text-critical matters.

2.44.2 Blenkinsopp, Joseph. *Ezekiel.* Interpretation: A Bible Commentary for Teaching and Preaching. Louisville: Westminster John Knox, 1990. 242pp.

Lucid and engaging interpretation of this difficult book according to a twofold focus: (1) meaning of the ministry and oracles of the prophet Ezekiel in relation to his original audience; and (2) meaning intended by the later compilers of this book to the generation of Jews they wished to address. As such, Blenkinsopp interprets Ezekiel by examining both the historical background of Ezekiel's ministry and the literary structure and method of composition of the book itself. In the course of commenting on original meaning, Blenkinsopp deftly weaves in suggestions pertaining to continuing relevance.

2.44.3 Block, Daniel I. *The Book of Ezekiel.* New International Commentary on the Old Testament. Grand Rapids: Eerdmans, 1997, 1998. 887/826pp.

Detailed, yet readable and engaging commentary by prominent evangelical OT scholar. Commentary on each passage is clearly organized around textual notes, structure of passage, verse-by-verse interpretation, and theological significance (where Block lists theological lessons derived from the passage). Considers it most likely that Ezekiel was responsible for the book. Commentary emphasizes structure, linguistic analysis, historical background, and broader-book context, but contains little interaction with history of interpretation.

2.44.4 Eichrodt, Walther. *Ezekiel.* Old Testament Library. Philadelphia: Westminster, 1970. 594pp.

This great OT scholar maintains that Ezekiel himself was the basic compiler of the book, though it was revised by editors who expanded or modified his message. The introduction, treating the "Prophet Ezekiel and His Book," is the most authoritative, lucid, and succinct description of Ezekiel to be found anywhere. The commentary attempts to capture the perspective of the prophet, employing careful exegesis based on language and literary and historical context to probe the thinking, emotions, and experience of Ezekiel. In the process, Eichrodt deftly shows how theological insights pertaining to NT faith arise out of this close, prophet-oriented reading of the text.

2.44.5 Zimmerli, Walther. *Ezekiel.* 2 vols. Hermeneia: A Critical and Historical Commentary on the Bible. Philadelphia: Fortress, 1979, 1983. 509/606pp.

Highly technical, detailed, and authoritative. Maintains that the present book was not produced by Ezekiel, but by a "school" that edited the prophet's oracles, with some additions and modifications. Commentary emphasizes text-critical considerations, form-critical analysis (probing how the form of the passage points to original setting, function, and significance), and tradition-critical analysis (evaluating the historicity of passages and their relationship to other OT traditions). Interacts extensively with other interpreters. Contains brief, but profound reflection on theological significance, with some suggestions as to how the theological message of Ezekiel bears witness to Jesus Christ.

ALSO   SIGNIFICANT

2.44.6   Brownlee, William H. *Ezekiel 1–19*. Word Biblical Commentary. Waco, Tex.: Word, 1986. 321pp.

2.44.7   Cooke, George A. *A Critical and Exegetical Commentary on the Book of Ezekiel*. International Critical Commentary. Edinburgh: T&T Clark, 1936. 558pp.

2.44.8   Davidson, A. B. *The Book of the Prophet Ezekiel*. Cambridge Bible for Schools and Colleges. Cambridge: Cambridge University Press, 1916. 368pp.

2.44.9   Fairbairn, Patrick. *Ezekiel and the Book of His Prophecy*. Edinburgh: T&T Clark, 1851. 504pp.

2.44.10 Greenberg, Moshe. *Ezekiel*. 2 vols. Anchor Bible. New York: Doubleday, 1983, 1997. 760pp.

2.44.11 Hals, Ronald M. *Ezekiel*. Forms of the Old Testament Literature 19. Grand Rapids: Eerdmans, 1989. 363pp.

2.44.12 Kutsko, John F. *Between Heaven and Earth: Divine Presence and Absence in the Book of Ezekiel*. Biblical and Judaic Studies 7. Winona Lake, Ind.: Eisenbrauns, 2000. 185pp.

2.44.13 Odell, Margaret S., and John T. Strong, eds. *The Book of Ezekiel: Theological and Anthropological Perspectives*. Society of Biblical Literature Symposium Series 9. Atlanta: Society of Biblical Literature, 2000. 270pp.

2.44.14 Renz, Thomas. *The Rhetorical Function of the Book of Ezekiel*. Supplements to Vetus Testamentum 76. Leiden: Brill, 1999. 298pp.

2.44.15 Taylor, John B. *Ezekiel: An Introduction and Commentary*. Tyndale Old Testament Commentaries. Downers Grove, Ill.: InterVarsity, 1969. 285pp.

2.45 Daniel

HIGHLY   RECOMMENDED

2.45.1   Baldwin, Joyce G. *Daniel*. Tyndale Old Testament Commentaries. Downers Grove, Ill.: InterVarsity, 1979. 210pp.

Unlike most other modern interpreters, this prominent British evangelical scholar argues that the book was likely composed around the turn of the fifth century B.C.E. Yet the commentary does not focus on historical reconstruction but on the development of the story and visions throughout the book and on details of the story and visions with a view toward ascertaining their theological significance. Gives some attention to historical background and evidence from other OT passages

2.45.2   Collins, John J. *Daniel*. Hermeneia: A Critical and Historical Commentary on the Bible. Minneapolis: Fortress, 1993. 499pp.

The most complete and detailed commentary available in English. Considers the stories of the book to be legendary, and maintains that Daniel never existed. Thus, the book is a work of religious fiction that has no historical value in relation to events described. The extensive introduction provides a wealth of information; most helpful is a discussion by Adela Yarbro Collins on the influence of Daniel on the NT. The commentary itself (a) discusses the literary structure of the passage; (b) gives a verse-by-verse interpretation that is rich in linguistic analysis, historical background, and the author's use of traditional material; (c) identifies the passage's genre and discusses significance of form for the construal of the passage; and (d) treats the setting and function of the passage, summarizing the religious and social significance for the original readers (with some suggestions regarding theology), and discussing its function within the book.

2.45.3   Goldingay, John E. *Daniel*. Word Biblical Commentary. Waco, Tex.: Word, 1989. 351pp.

Like Collins (§2.45.2), offers a detailed interpretation of Daniel, emphasizing text-critical, form-critical, linguistic, and historical analysis. Introduction is briefer and more general than Collins, and Goldingay insists on the possibility of some historical value to the book's stories, although maintains that the purpose is not historiography but religious instruction to Jews in the late Persian period. Emphasizes dynamic interplay between stories (chs. 1–6) and visions (chs. 7–12). Discusses at length the theological significance of passages for original readers and explicitly explores continuing theological and religious significance for Christians. Overall the most useful commentary on Daniel for preaching and teaching.

2.45.4   Porteous, Norman W. *Daniel: A Commentary*. 2d ed. Old Testament Library. Philadelphia: Westminster, 1979. 196pp.

Dates the book just before 164 B.C.E. Virtually ignores text-critical or linguistic matters so as to concentrate on the meaning of the book for the religious experience of Jews during the Maccabean period and to explore the book's theological witness. Interprets passages primarily in terms of (a) their function within the book and (b) significance of historical setting of Israel during the Maccabean period. Focuses on the theological witness of the Book of Daniel itself, but does discuss how passages in the book were used subsequently, including their use in the NT.

ALSO SIGNIFICANT

2.45.5 Buber, Martin. *Daniel: Dialogues on Realization.* New York: Holt, Rinehart, and Winston, 1964. 144pp.

2.45.6 Collins, John J. *The Apocalyptic Vision of the Book of Daniel.* Harvard Semitic Monographs. Missoula, Mont.: Scholars, 1977. 239pp.

2.45.7 ———. *Daniel: With an Introduction to Apocalyptic Literature.* Forms of the Old Testament Literature 20. Grand Rapids: Eerdmans, 1984. 120pp.

2.45.8 Collins, John J., and Peter W. Flint, eds. *The Book of Daniel: Composition and Reception.* 2 vols. Supplements to Vetus Testamentum 83. Leiden: Brill, 2001. 292/482pp.

2.45.9 Driver, S. R. *The Book of Daniel.* Cambridge Bible for Schools and Colleges. Cambridge: Cambridge University Press, 1900. 215pp.

2.45.10 Heaton, Eric W. *The Book of Daniel.* Torch Bible Commentaries. London: SCM, 1956. 251pp.

2.45.11 Lucas, Ernest C. *Daniel.* Apollos Old Testament Commentary. Downers Grove, Ill.: InterVarsity, 2002. 320pp.

2.45.12 Montgomery, James A. *A Critical and Exegetical Commentary on the Book of Daniel.* International Critical Commentary. Edinburgh: T&T Clark, 1927. 488pp.

2.45.13 Redditt, Paul L. *Daniel.* New Century Bible Commentary. Sheffield: Sheffield Academic Press, 1999. 211pp.

2.45.14 Russell, D. S. *Daniel.* Daily Study Bible. Philadelphia: Westminster, 1981. 234pp.

2.45.15 Thompson, Henry O. *The Book of Daniel: An Annotated Bibliography.* Garland Reference Library of the Humanities: Books of the Bible 1. New York: Garland, 1992. 547pp.

2.45.16 Towner, W. Sibley. *Daniel.* Interpretation: A Bible Commentary for Teaching and Preaching. Atlanta: John Knox, 1984. 186pp.

2.45.17 Wiseman, D. J., et al. *Notes on Some Problems in the Book of Daniel.* London: Tyndale, 1965. 79pp.

2.45.18 Woude, A. S. van der, ed. *The Book of Daniel in the Light of New Findings.* Bibliotheca Ephemeridum Theologicarum Lovaniensium 106. Leuven: Leuven University Press, 1993. 574pp.

2.46 The Twelve (Minor) Prophets: General Works

H I G H L Y   R E C O M M E N D E D

2.46.1 Achtemeier, Elizabeth. *Nahum-Malachi.* Interpretation: A Bible Commentary for Teaching and Preaching. Atlanta: John Knox, 1986. 201pp.

Solid discussion of the message of the text for the original audience based on careful but concise treatment of historical background, genre, literary structure, and the meaning of key words, leading to insightful reflections on the theology of the passage and its contribution to biblical revelation as a whole. Theological reflection leads in turn to helpful suggestions for present Christian application. Gives some attention to relation between the various Minor Prophets discussed, but for the most part deals with them as distinct and separate books.

2.46.2 Achtemeier, Elizabeth. *Preaching from the Minor Prophets: Texts and Sermon Suggestions.* Grand Rapids: Eerdmans, 1998. 143pp.

Eminently practical guide to assist ministers in preaching from the Minor Prophets. Treatment of each of the Minor Prophets includes recommended commentaries, historical context, theological context, and studies of selected passages, which provides a discussion of linguistic and literary features, sermon possibilities, and homiletical exposition. These studies of selected passages serve as models that can be applied to other portions of the Minor Prophets.

2.46.3 Limburg, James. *Hosea-Micah.* Interpretation: A Bible Commentary for Teaching and Preaching. Atlanta: John Knox, 1988. 201pp.

Like the companion volume by Achtemeier (§2.46.1), moves from careful examination of the message of passage based on solid interpretive work to theological significance and contemporary Christian application. Tends to present theology of passages in terms of major themes, to trace these themes throughout the whole of Scripture (including the NT), and to show how these themes can be used as the basis for Christian proclamation.

2.46.4 McComiskey, Thomas Edward, ed. *The Minor Prophets: An Exegetical and Expository Commentary.* 3 vols. Grand Rapids: Baker, 1998. 1412pp.

Consistently evangelical commentary, with contributions by Douglas Stuart, J. Alec Motyer, Joyce Baldwin, F. F. Bruce, and Raymond Dillard, among others. Notes on the Hebrew text (lexical, syntactical, and text-critical) appear at the top of each page (typically occupying about forty percent of the page), with exposition below, where there is virtually no reference to technical matters pertaining to the Hebrew. Exposition focuses on historical background, connections with other OT passages, theological reflection, and appropriation to contemporary Christian life. Solid and reliable, but rarely groundbreaking or original.

2.46.5 Smith, Ralph L. *Micah-Malachi.* Word Biblical Commentary. Waco, Tex.: Word, 1984. 358pp.

Adopts generally conservative conclusions on questions of the unity and authorship of the various books considered. Emphasizes ways in which the different audiences and circumstances addressed by the prophets determine the message of the several books discussed, while affirming also a fundamental unity lying behind all these books, viz., judgment and hope based on an understanding of the character of Yahweh. Somewhat less technical than most of the volumes in this series, but a major strength is Smith's practice of presenting clearly the major interpretive options from the history of exegesis, giving arguments for and against each. Employs principal of analogy in moving from original meaning to contemporary Christian application, noting how contemporary Christians experience the same kinds of questions, struggles, and challenges as the original audiences of the prophets.

2.46.6 Stuart, Douglas. *Hosea-Jonah.* Word Biblical Commentary. Waco, Tex.: Word, 1987. 537pp.

Like Smith, adopts conservative perspective on questions such as unity, authorship, and date of the various books. Emphasizes prophets' dependence on earlier biblical tradition, and argues that all of these prophets attempted to call the people back to obedience to the Mosaic covenant. Commentary is more technical than the volume by Smith (§2.46.5), but gives less attention to the history of interpretation. Concentrates on meaning of significant theological issues in the text, and attends to the ways in which contemporary Christians can apply the prophet's insights to these issues.

2.46.7 Sweeney, Marvin A. *The Twelve Prophets.* Berit Olam: Studies in Hebrew Narrative and Poetry. Collegeville, Minn.: Liturgical Press, 2000. 802pp.

Adopts a twofold interpretive perspective: Treats the Minor Prophets as a coherent literary work with its own structures, themes, and theology ("The Book of the Twelve"), but also deals with each of these books as a distinct literary work. Thus, commentary is concerned to identify the message of each book, and also to note how the message of that book is informed by its relationship to the other Minor Prophets and contributes to the overall impact of the Book of the Twelve. Concentrates on the canonical text, with little attention to the history of traditions or the process of editing lying behind the final form. Attends to literary structure, linguistic analysis, and historical, social, religious, and cultural background. Since his emphasis is on the final text, Sweeney attends to theological meaning, but provides no explicit reflection on broad theological implications or significance for contemporary Christians.

A L S O   S I G N I F I C A N T

2.46.8 Allen, Leslie C. *The Books of Joel, Obadiah, Jonah and Micah*. New International Commentary on the Old Testament. Grand Rapids: Eerdmans, 1976. 427pp.

2.46.9 Craigie, Peter C. *Twelve Prophets*. 2 vols. Daily Study Bible. Philadelphia: Westminster, 1984, 1985. 239/248pp.

2.46.10 Driver, S. R. *The Minor Prophets*. New York: Oxford University Press, 1904. 337pp.

2.46.11 Floyd, Michael H. *Minor Prophets: Part 2*. Forms of the Old Testament Literature 22. Grand Rapids: Eerdmans, 2000. 651pp.

2.46.12 House, Paul R. *The Unity of the Twelve*. Journal for the Study of the Old Testament Supplement Series 97. Sheffield: Almond, 1990. 262pp.

2.46.13 King, Philip J. *Amos, Hosea, Micah: An Archaeological Commentary*. Philadelphia: Westminster, 1988. 176pp.

2.46.14 Mitchell, Hinckley G., John Merlin Powis Smith, and Julius A. Bewer. *A Critical and Exegetical Commentary on Haggai, Zechariah, Malachi, and Jonah*. International Critical Commentary. Edinburgh: T&T Clark, 1912. 362 + 88 + 65pp.

2.46.15 Nogalski, James D., and Marvin A. Sweeney, eds. *Reading and Hearing the Book of the Twelve*. Society of Biblical Literature Symposium Series 15. Atlanta: Society of Biblical Literature, 2000. 235pp.

2.46.16 Orelli, Conrad von. *The Twelve Minor Prophets*. Edinburgh: T&T Clark, 1897. 405pp.

2.46.17 Smith, John Merlin Powis, William Hayes Ward, and Julius A. Bewer. *A Critical and Exegetical Commentary on Micah, Zephaniah, Nahum, Habakkuk, Obadiah, and Joel.* International Critical Commentary. Edinburgh: T&T Clark, 1911. 360 + 28 + 146pp.

2.47 Hosea

H I G H L Y   R E C O M M E N D E D

2.47.1 Andersen, Francis I., and David Noel Freedman. *Hosea.* Anchor Bible. Garden City, N.Y.: Doubleday, 1980. 699pp.

Massive, detailed commentary that emphasizes cultural background, linguistic analysis (especially Hebrew vocabulary, syntax, and poetic language), and literary structure in its careful interpretation of virtually every word of Hosea. Focuses on technical matters of language and history, and gives little specific attention to theological issues. Considers it likely that the book was compiled in the seventh century B.C.E. by reformers in Judah during the reign of Manasseh, and thus gives attention both to the significance of passages for audience of the historical Hosea and to the impact of the book on the later seventh-century audience.

2.47.2 Macintosh, A. A. *A Critical and Exegetical Commentary on Hosea.* International Critical Commentary. Edinburgh: T&T Clark, 1997. 600pp.

Focuses on ways in which Hosea's personal experience of his cultural, religious, and political environment shaped his message. Includes both comments accessible to the general reader and more technical discussions of linguistic and text-critical issues of interest to the specialist. Maintains that Hosea was himself responsible for the compilation of the book; the emphasis is therefore on the impact of this book as a literary product on Hosea's audience. Of special value are the constant allusions to the history of interpretation, and especially to ancient rabbinic interpreters. Introduction contains helpful discussion of the essence of Hosea's thought, and commentary necessarily deals with theological issues raised in the text; but Macintosh gives little explicit attention to theological reflection, and (as one would expect in the ICC) no attention to contemporary appropriation.

2.47.3 Mays, James Luther. *Hosea: A Commentary.* Old Testament Library. Philadelphia: Westminster, 1969. 190pp.

Produced by a most perceptive interpreter and lucid writer, this brief commentary focuses on the most significant interpretive issues of passages in

Hosea and their theological meaning. Deals primarily with the distinctive theological witness of Hosea, and therefore does not attempt to relate Hosea's theology to other parts of the OT canon or explicitly to the Christian faith.

2.47.4 Wolff, Hans Walter. *Hosea: A Commentary on the Book of the Prophet Hosea.* Hermeneia: A Critical and Historical Commentary on the Bible. Philadelphia: Fortress, 1974. 259pp.

Authoritative, judicious commentary by one of the most prominent German OT scholars. Argues that the original prophecy of Hosea forms the core of the book, which was subsequently compiled over a long process, reaching its present stage in the postexilic period. Deals with each passage in terms of its form (genre and literary structure), its setting (historical examination as to whether it belongs to the ministry of the historical Hosea or to a later editorial stage and function within the final book), its interpretation (careful exploration of technical linguistic and historical issues), and the theological aim of the passage, in which Wolff typically relates the message to NT faith.

ALSO SIGNIFICANT

2.47.5 Brueggemann, Walter. *Tradition for Crisis: A Study in Hosea.* Richmond, Va.: John Knox, 1968. 164pp.

2.47.6 Davies, Graham I. *Hosea.* New Century Bible Commentary. Grand Rapids: Eerdmans, 1992. 315pp.

2.47.7 Doorly, William J. *Prophet of Love: Understanding the Book of Hosea.* New York: Paulist, 1991. 138pp.

2.47.8 Emmerson, Grace I. *Hosea: An Israelite Prophet in Judean Perspective.* Journal for the Study of the Old Testament Supplement Series 28. Sheffield: JSOT, 1984. 224pp.

2.47.9 Hubbard, David A. *With Bands of Love: Lessons from the Book of Hosea.* Grand Rapids: Eerdmans, 1968. 114pp.

2.47.10 ———. *Hosea: An Introduction and Commentary.* Tyndale Old Testament Commentaries. Downers Grove, Ill.: InterVarsity, 1990. 234pp.

2.47.11 Robinson, H. Wheeler. *Two Hebrew Prophets: Studies in Hosea and Ezekiel.* London: Lutterworth, 1948. 125pp.

2.47.12 Ward, James M. *Hosea: A Theological Commentary.* New York: Harper & Row, 1966. 264pp.

2.48 Joel

H I G H L Y   R E C O M M E N D E D

2.48.1 Barton, John. *Joel and Obadiah*. Old Testament Library. Louisville: Westminster John Knox, 2001. 168pp.

Although produced at beginning of the twenty-first century, this solid commentary stands closer in method (and to some extent in conclusions) to those written at end of the nineteenth. Identifies sources lying behind the text, and insists on the literary disunity of both Joel and Obadiah. Accepts Duhm's theory that Joel is composed of two originally separate prophecies, and argues similarly that the end of Obadiah is a later addition. While emphasizing the interpretation of earlier stages of tradition, Barton gives some attention to the theological meaning of the final composition of the book. Employs linguistic analysis of the Hebrew, history of (modern) interpretation, and insights from other OT prophecies, an important consideration given significant role of earlier prophecies in both Joel and Obadiah. Develops theological meaning and contemporary relevance.

2.48.2 Crenshaw, James L. *Joel*. Anchor Bible. New York: Doubleday, 1995. 251pp.

Careful, sensitive interpretation, with original and compelling insights. Interpretation focuses on historical background, literary structure, and especially linguistic analysis (Hebrew terms and syntax), but commentary is accessible to those who do not know Hebrew. Maintains that the prophet Joel was "a learned scribe, a teacher of preserved religious tradition" around the turn of the fifth century B.C.E., and thus emphasizes the ways in which Joel has adopted and reinterpreted earlier prophetic material. Gives serious attention to Joel's religious views, but does little to address theological significance for NT faith.

2.48.3 Wolff, Hans Walter. *A Commentary on the Books of the Prophets Joel and Amos*. Hermeneia: A Critical and Historical Commentary on the Bible. Philadelphia: Fortress, 1977. 392pp.

Similar in quality and approach to Wolff's commentary on Hosea (§2.47.4). Seriously considers the setting of the passage in the ministry of the prophet and in the book, the genre and literary structure of the passage, the language and historical background, and theological claims. In Joel, Wolff gives somewhat more attention to the way in which the structure of the whole book affects meaning than he does in most of his other commentaries. In Amos, he posits an extended process of the growth of the book and emphasizes not only the final text but the interpretive significance of the history of tradition lying behind it. The theological discussions reflect a Lutheran perspective. This volume represents two commentaries, originally published separately, with an interval of several years between.

2.48.4 Coggins, Richard James. *Joel and Amos*. New Century Bible Commentary. Sheffield: Sheffield Academic Press, 2000. 170pp.

2.48.5 Driver, S. R. *The Books of Joel and Amos*. Cambridge Bible for Schools and Colleges. Cambridge: Cambridge University Press, 1915. 251pp.

2.48.6 Hubbard, David A. *Joel and Amos*. Tyndale Old Testament Commentaries. Downers Grove, Ill.: InterVarsity, 1989. 245pp.

2.48.7 Kapelrud, Arvid Schou. *Joel Studies*. Uppsala: Lundequistska, 1948. 211pp.

2.48.8 Prinsloo, Willem S. *The Theology of the Book of Joel*. Berlin: Walter De Gruyter, 1985. 136pp.

2.49 Amos

See also JOEL (§2.48)

2.49.1 Andersen, Francis I., and David Noel Freedman. *Amos*. Anchor Bible. New York: Doubleday, 1989. 979pp.

Massive, encyclopedic commentary. Introduction alone is almost two hundred pages in length. Considers that Amos, or someone close to the prophet, is responsible for the book's composition. Interprets the book as it stands over against concern with earlier traditions or forms, and emphasizes the role of book context for meaning of individual passages. Employs historical background, archaeological insights, analysis of literary structure and rhetorical devices, linguistic analysis of the Hebrew, comparative philology of cognate Semitic languages, relationship to other prophets, and history of interpretation. Gives attention to Amos's message, but the commentary tends not to develop the theological aspects of passages.

2.49.2 Hasel, Gerhard F. *Understanding the Book of Amos: Basic Issues in the Current Interpretations*. Grand Rapids: Baker, 1991. 171pp.

An introduction to the Book of Amos in the form of a survey of scholarly work on Amos between 1960 and 1990. Describes the development of modern interpretation of the book and devotes a separate chapter to each of the major issues of Amos. Review of literature is informed, balanced (with opposing views represented), and given with little of the author's own evaluations, but Hasel does discuss questions and issues derived from the review. Includes a bibliography of more than eight hundred works.

2.49.3 Jeremias, Jörg. *The Book of Amos*. Old Testament Library. Louisville: Westminster John Knox, 1998. 177pp.

Contends that the Book of Amos can tell us little about the ministry or oracles of Amos himself, since it is the product of an extended process of compilation that reached its final form in the postexilic period. Thus, Jeremias employs redaction criticism to identify the various stages of compilation and to interpret individual passages in terms of the intention of the editors responsible for their inclusion. Yet Jeremias gives primary attention to the message of the book in its final form, carefully interpreting passages in terms of their function within the book and their impact on the intended reader. Hence the commentary offers insights helpful even to students who do not share the author's critical views.

2.49.4 Mays, James Luther. *Amos: A Commentary*. Old Testament Library. Philadelphia: Westminster, 1969. 169pp.

Like Mays's commentary on Hosea (§2.47.3), this volume offers a concise and clearly written interpretation focusing on the theological message of the text. Asserts that the book contains authentic material from Amos but also includes later additions, and owes its arrangement to the intentions of later editors. Commentary deals with the meaning of passages both in the context of Amos's ministry and in the role they play within the setting of the book. Gives special attention to the interpretive significance of various forms of prophetic speech. Offers rich theological reflection from Christian perspective.

2.49.5 Paul, Shalom. *Amos*. Hermeneia: A Critical and Historical Commentary on the Bible. Minneapolis: Fortress, 1991. 409pp.

Learned, technical commentary by prominent Jewish scholar carefully differentiates elements that belong to the ministry of the historical Amos (and where they fit in his ministry) and those that were introduced by later editors, in an effort to identify as precisely as possible the meaning of passages in their original contexts. Employs historical background and especially meticulous linguistic analysis (including the meaning and background of Hebrew terms, syntactical analysis, and comparison with cognates from other Semitic languages). Interacts significantly with the history of interpretation, especially on higher-critical questions. Excellent for serious grappling with technical issues, but gives little attention to theological matters.

A L S O   S I G N I F I C A N T

2.49.6   Coote, Robert B. *Amos Among the Prophets: Composition and Theology.* Philadelphia: Fortress, 1981. 138pp.

2.49.7   Harper, William Rainey. *A Critical and Exegetical Commentary on Amos and Hosea.* International Critical Commentary. Edinburgh: T&T Clark, 1905. 424pp.

2.49.8   Hayes, John H. *Amos, the Eighth Century Prophet: His Times and His Preaching.* Nashville: Abingdon, 1988. 240pp.

2.49.9   Kapelrud, Arvid Schou. *Central Ideas in Amos.* Oslo: Universitets-forlaget, 1971. 86pp.

2.49.10 Polley, Max E. *Amos and the Davidic Empire: A Socio-Historical Approach.* New York: Oxford University Press, 1989. 243pp.

2.49.11 Smith, Gary V. *Amos: A Commentary.* Library of Biblical Interpretation. Grand Rapids: Zondervan, 1989. 307pp.

2.49.12 Watts, John D. W. *Vision and Prophecy in Amos.* Expanded ed. Macon, Ga.: Mercer University Press, 1997. 144pp.

2.50 Obadiah

H I G H L Y   R E C O M M E N D E D

2.50.1   Rabbe, Paul R. *Obadiah.* Anchor Bible. New York: Doubleday, 1996. 310pp.

Most current and complete commentary on Obadiah presently available. Engages in a sympathetic interpretation, attempting to read the book on its own terms and according to the concerns of its original writer and readers. To this end gives careful attention to grammatical and lexical issues, poetic forms, rhetorical strategies and goals, historical background pertaining to Edom, allusions to the Jacob-Esau narratives of Genesis, and theological claims. Claims that Obadiah summarizes many of the great prophetic themes, and thus explores Obadiah's contribution to the OT understanding of divine judgment against Israel's enemies, the day of Yahweh, the principle of retaliation, Zion theology, Israel's possession of the land, and the kingship of Yahweh.

2.50.2 Watts, John D. W. *Obadiah: A Critical and Exegetical Commentary.* Grand Rapids: Eerdmans, 1967. 78pp.

Packs a remarkable amount of relevant and helpful information in a very small compass. Includes discussion of history of interpretation, history of Edom, Obadiah's position in biblical prophecy, Obadiah's role in Israel's worship, theological background, and theology of the book itself, along with commentary that gives attention to text-critical, grammatical, and historical issues. Especially valuable for moving from careful historical and grammatical analysis to insightful theological reflection.

2.50.3 Wolff, Hans Walter. *Obadiah and Jonah: A Commentary.* Minneapolis: Augsburg, 1986. 191pp.

Employs technical linguistic and literary analysis and careful attention to historical background to ascertain the theological message of the text and to explore its contemporary significance. Asserts that both Obadiah and Jonah explore God's intention toward Gentiles and the relationship between Israel and the Gentile world, but answer these questions in quite different ways; this leads the Christian reader to draw insights regarding the relationship between the church as the people of God and the wider world of humanity. Stresses Obadiah's role as a "cult prophet" who reinterprets earlier traditions for his own day. Emphasizes the role of "comedy" in the Book of Jonah, and the ways in which that book employs various literary forms to achieve its intended didactic impact on the reader.

ALSO SIGNIFICANT

2.50.4 Baker, David W. *Obadiah, Jonah, Micah.* Tyndale Old Testament Commentaries. Downers Grove, Ill.: InterVarsity, 1989. 207pp.

2.50.5 Ben Zvi, Ehud. *A Historical-Critical Study of the Book of Obadiah.* Beihefte zur Zeitschrift für die alttestamentliche Wissenschaft 242. Berlin: Walter De Gruyter, 1996. 309pp.

2.50.6 Lanchester, H. C. O. *Obadiah and Jonah.* Rev. ed. Cambridge: Cambridge University Press, 1918. 76pp.

2.51 Jonah

See also OBADIAH (§2.50)

2.51.1 Fretheim, Terence E.. *The Message of Jonah: A Theological Commentary*. Minneapolis: Augsburg, 1977. 142pp.

Highly illuminating and engaging close reading of Jonah, emphasizing especially literary features of the book, leading to acute theological insights and suggestions regarding contemporary Christian appropriation. The most helpful volume available for preaching and teaching on Jonah.

2.51.2 Limburg, James. *Jonah: A Commentary*. Old Testament Library. Louisville: Westminster John Knox, 1993. 123pp.

Solid, reliable commentary dealing with the origin of the story, its place and function within the Bible, the theological claims of the text, and possibilities for contemporary (Christian) application. Interpretation gives primary attention to structure of the book, historical background, meaning of the Hebrew, and relation to other OT texts. A unique feature is insight from the use of Jonah by artists, musicians, painters, and sculptors to illuminate the meaning of the text. Includes extensive appendix dealing with the understanding of Jonah in Judaism, Islam, and Christianity.

2.51.3 Sasson, Jack M. *Jonah*. Anchor Bible. New York: Doubleday, 1990. 368pp.

Most comprehensive and detailed commentary on Jonah available. Involves a meticulous interpretation of each verse, with particular attention to Hebrew grammar and vocabulary, comparative analysis with other Semitic languages, literary forms and structures, historical background, and illumination from other OT passages. Although technical, commentary is readable and largely accessible to those who do not know Hebrew. Gives less explicit attention to theological matters than does Fretheim (§2.51.1) or Limburg (§2.51.2).

2.51.4 Bolin, Thomas M. *Freedom Beyond Forgiveness: The Book of Jonah Re-Examined*. Journal for the Study of the Old Testament Supplement Series 236; Copenhagen International Seminar 3. Sheffield: Sheffield Academic Press, 1997. 217pp.

2.51.5 Ellul, Jacques. *The Judgment of Jonah*. Grand Rapids: Eerdmans, 1971. 103pp.

2.51.6 Fairbairn, Patrick. *Jonah: His Life, Character, and Mission*. Edinburgh: John Johnstone, 1849. 237pp.

2.51.7 Hasel, Gerhard F. *Jonah: Messenger of the Eleventh Hour.* Mt. View, Calif.: Pacific, 1976. 112pp.

2.51.8 Magonet, Jonathan. *Form and Meaning: Studies in the Literary Techniques in the Book of Jonah.* Bible and Literature Series 8. Sheffield: Almond, 1983. 184pp.

2.51.9 Simon, Uriel. *Jonah.* JPS Bible Commentary. Philadelphia: Jewish Publication Society, 1999. 52pp.

See also Phyllis Trible's *Rhetorical Criticism: Context, Method, and the Book of Jonah* (§2.13.38).

2.52 Micah

See also OBADIAH (§2.50)

H I G H L Y   R E C O M M E N D E D

2.52.1 Andersen, Francis I., and David Noel Freedman. *Micah.* Anchor Bible. New York: Doubleday, 2000. 637pp.

Considers reconstruction of stages of the book's compilation hopelessly speculative and therefore treats the book in its final form as a literary unity, thus giving almost exclusive attention to literary and linguistic analysis. Emphasizes the structure of passages, their role within the broader book context, employment of poetic artistry and literary devices, and careful analysis of poetic Hebrew (which they consider to be decisively distinct from prose). Gives little attention to historical or theological matters.

2.52.2 Mays, James Luther. *Micah: A Commentary.* Old Testament Library. Philadelphia: Westminster, 1976. 169pp.

Argues that the book exhibits an extended process of transmission, from the prophet Micah himself to its final form in the postexilic period. Interprets individual sayings according to their literary form, historical setting, and function in the ministry of the prophets from whom they derived, as they were understood and used in the developing composition, and as they function in the final canonical book. Mays draws out the theological meaning of passages at each of these stages. Concerned only with the theological witness of this book; gives no serious attention to its contribution to OT theology or to NT faith.

2.52.3 McKane, William. *Micah: Introduction and Commentary.* Edinburgh: T&T Clark, 1998. 242pp.

Argues that chs. 1–3 contain the prophecy of Micah himself, but that the book was developed after the fall of Jerusalem by a "school" that adapted Micah's message to later contexts, at times underscoring Micah's proclamation of judgment and at other times emphasizing hope. Contains detailed textual and linguistic analysis, extended discussion of ancient versions, and careful description of history of interpretation (medieval and modern). Excellent for full discussion of technical matters of text and language, but gives little attention to the meaning of the final form of passages, to the message of the book, or to theological implications.

2.52.4 Wolff, Hans Walter. *Micah: A Commentary.* Minneapolis: Augsburg, 1990. 258pp.

Like Mays (§2.52.2), argues for an extended process of development from the prophet Micah to the early Persian period, and examines with more precision than Mays how each passage fits within this long process. Quite technical in his linguistic analysis and discussion of literary forms and historical background. Gives relatively little attention to the meaning of passages within the final canonical book, but does consider the theological message of passages and briefly discusses Christian appropriation. Contains extensive bibliographies of works in German, French, and English.

ALSO SIGNIFICANT

2.52.5 Ben Zvi, Ehud. *Micah.* Forms of the Old Testament Literature 21B. Grand Rapids: Eerdmans, 2000. 189pp.

2.52.6 Cheyne, T. K. *Micah.* Cambridge Bible for Schools and Colleges. Cambridge: Cambridge University Press, 1902. 64pp.

2.52.7 Copass, B. A., and E. L. Carlson. *A Study of the Prophet Micah.* Grand Rapids: Baker, 1950. 169pp.

2.52.8 Hagstrom, David Gerald. *The Coherence of the Book of Micah: A Literary Analysis.* Society of Biblical Literature Dissertation Series 89. Atlanta: Scholars, 1988. 152pp.

2.52.9 Hillers, Delbert R. *Micah.* Hermeneia: A Critical and Historical Commentary on the Bible. Philadelphia: Fortress, 1984. 116pp.

2.52.10 Jacobs, Mignon R. *The Conceptual Coherence of the Book of Micah*. Journal for the Study of the Old Testament Supplement Series 322. Sheffield: JSOT, 2001. 288pp.

2.52.11 Margolis, M. L. *The Holy Scripture with Commentary: Micah*. Philadelphia: Jewish Publication Society of America, 1908. 104pp.

2.52.12 Wal, Adri van der. *Micah: A Classified Bibliography*. Applicatio 8. Amsterdam: Free University Press, 1990. 207pp.

2.52.13 Wolff, Hans Walter. *Micah the Prophet*. Philadelphia: Fortress, 1981. 223pp.

2.53 Nahum, Habakkuk, and Zephaniah

HIGHLY RECOMMENDED

2.53.1 Andersen, Francis I. *Habakkuk*. Anchor Bible. New York: Doubleday, 2001. 387pp.

Most comprehensive and authoritative commentary on Habakkuk presently available in English. Attends seriously to literary structure of entire book and interprets individual passages in relation to the whole. Emphasizes, in addition, linguistic phenomena of the Hebrew (with special attention to the history of development of the Hebrew language), historical background (especially social, economic, religious, and political issues), Ancient Near Eastern culture, connections with other OT passages, and personal/existential experience of the prophet himself. All of this Andersen pursues in order to grasp fully the theological meaning of the final form of the text.

2.53.2 Berlin, Adele. *Zephaniah*. Anchor Bible. New York: Doubleday, 1994. 165pp.

Adopts a literary approach, but gives attention also to historical setting and relationship to other OT passages. Attends to rhetorical features, literary forms, structure of passage, and role within whole book. A valuable feature is repeated reference to traditional Jewish exegesis, especially medieval and early modern. Makes no attempt to be exhaustive, but focuses on issues significant for understanding the message of the prophet and aspects of the text of foremost concern to readers. Little explicit attention to theological significance.

2.53.3 Gowan, Donald E. *The Triumph of Faith in Habakkuk.* Atlanta: John Knox, 1976. 94pp.

A most informative and stimulating book. Explores the original meaning of Habakkuk by attending to issues of text, literary form, structure, and historical setting, but all for the sake of theological reflection surrounding the perennial issues of human life and suffering as addressed by Habakkuk. Carries on a successful dialogue between original meaning and specific contemporary concerns. Extremely helpful for preaching and teaching.

2.53.4 Maier, Walter A. *The Book of Nahum: A Commentary.* St. Louis, Mo.: Concordia, 1959. 386pp.

Serious, informed commentary from a conservative perspective. Examines historical background, relationship to other OT passages, Hebrew language, and literary structure in an attempt to ascertain the original message of Nahum and to probe its continuing relevance for Christians. Sees contemporary significance in the thrust of Nahum's message, which Maier takes to be Yahweh's active concern in the face of a powerful nation's abuse of its power by promoting its own selfish aims to oppress weak nations.

2.53.5 Roberts, J. J. M. *Nahum, Habakkuk, and Zephaniah: A Commentary.* Old Testament Library. Louisville: Westminster John Knox, 1990. 223pp.

Technical yet readable commentary employing textual criticism, philology, historical background, Ancient Near Eastern parallels, and literary conventions employed by prophets. Focuses on individual prophetic oracles in an attempt to interpret them in their original setting; correspondingly, has little interest in the overall scheme of the final canonical book or the role of individual oracles within the book as a whole. An exception is Habakkuk, which Roberts considers to be (unlike most prophetic books) a coherent literary unity. Concerned to relate the message of passages to other OT and even NT passages, and to develop briefly the theological meaning, with some suggestions regarding contemporary significance.

2.53.6 Robertson, O. Palmer. *The Books of Nahum, Habakkuk, and Zephaniah.* New International Commentary on the Old Testament. Grand Rapids: Eerdmans, 1990. 357pp.

Written from a conservative perspective. Emphasizes historical context, literary structure, role within the canon of OT and NT (with little concern for technical textual and linguistic issues), all in the pursuit of the theological message. Moves quickly from original message to specific contemporary Christian application. Suggestive for preaching and teaching, but should be used critically, since there is a tendency to interpret passages in light of Christian theological categories and the concerns of modern American evangelicals.

2.53.7 Spronk, Klaas. *Nahum*. Historical Commentary on the Old Testament. Kampen: Kok Pharos, 1997. 153pp.

Maintains that Nahum was written in Jerusalem around 660 B.C.E. by a royal scribe, using Nahum as a pseudonym pointing to his purpose: to encourage people of Judah living under Assyrian oppression. This purpose he accomplished by adapting earlier traditions from Isaiah and the Psalms, and by borrowing from the motifs of Assyrian literature, which he used against Assyria. Interprets final form of text by emphasizing its relationship to other OT passages, examining ancient versions and texts, linguistic analysis, discussion of literary forms and structure, and interaction with history of interpretation. Somewhat technical, but accessible to the nonspecialist while also illuminating for the scholar. Gives little explicit attention to theological reflection.

2.53.8 Vlaardingerbroek, Johannes. *Zephaniah*. Historical Commentary on the Old Testament. Leuven: Peeters, 1999. 222pp.

Interprets Zephaniah in its historical setting in relation to the Josianic Reform and thus emphasizes its relationship to Deuteronomic theology. Attends to linguistic analysis, ancient versions, history of interpretation, and the role of passages in the arrangement of the final form of book. Offers significant theological discussion of the original message of Zephaniah, with particular attention to the theology of the Day of Yahweh.

ALSO SIGNIFICANT

2.53.9 Baker, David W. *Nahum, Habakkuk, Zephaniah*. Tyndale Old Testament Commentaries. Downers Grove, Ill.: InterVarsity, 1989. 121pp.

2.53.10 Ben Zvi, Ehud. *A Historical-Critical Study of the Book of Zephaniah*. Beihefte zur Zeitschrift für die Alttestamentliche Wissenschaft 198. Berlin: Walter De Gruyter, 1991. 390pp.

2.53.11 Bennett, T. Miles. *The Books of Nahum and Zephaniah*. Grand Rapids: Baker, 1968. 102pp.

2.53.12 Davidson, A. B., and H. C. O. Lanchester. *Nahum, Habakkuk, and Zephaniah*. Rev. ed. Cambridge Bible for Schools and Colleges. Cambridge: Cambridge University Press, 1896. 156pp.

2.53.13 Eaton, John H. *Obadiah, Nahum, Habakkuk and Zephaniah*. Torch Bible Commentaries. London: SCM, 1961. 159pp.

2.53.14 Haak, Robert D. *Habakkuk.* Supplements to Vetus Testamentum 44. Leiden: Brill, 1992. 180pp.

2.53.15 House, Paul R. *Zephaniah: A Prophetic Drama.* Bible and Literature Series 16. Sheffield: Almond, 1988. 146pp.

2.53.16 Kapelrud, Arvid S. *The Message of the Prophet Zephaniah: Morphology and Ideas.* Oslo: Universitatesfolaget, 1975. 116pp.

2.53.17 Patterson, Richard D. *Nahum, Habakkuk, Zephaniah.* Wycliffe Exegetical Commentary. Chicago: Moody, 1991. 416pp.

2.53.18 Wal, Adri van der. *Nahum, Habakkuk: A Classified Bibliography.* Applicatio 6. Amsterdam: Free University Press, 1988. 208pp.

2.54 Haggai, Zechariah, and Malachi

H I G H L Y   R E C O M M E N D E D

2.54.1 Hill, Andrew E. *Malachi.* Anchor Bible. New York: Doubleday, 1998. 436pp.

Most thorough and current commentary on Malachi available in English. This evangelical scholar assumes the Masoretic text, avoids speculation regarding redactions and interpolations, and favors the authenticity and unity of Malachi. Emphasizes historical and sociopolitical background, language (lexical, philological, syntactic), history of interpretation (ancient and modern, Jewish and Christian), and literary structure. Analyzes Malachi's message within context of OT (and often NT) canon. Technical and detailed, treating every phrase or clause exhaustively. Gives relatively little attention to theological issues.

2.54.2 Meyers, Carol L., and Eric M. Meyers. *Haggai, Zechariah 1–8.* Anchor Bible. New York: Doubleday, 1987. 478pp.

Probably the most complete and detailed commentary on this material in English. Argues that Haggai and Zechariah 1–8 form a composite work, the product probably of redaction by Zechariah himself shortly after the conclusion of his and Haggai's prophetic activity around 518 B.C.E. Thus the authors see little difference between the work of the historical Haggai and Zechariah and the witness of the final book. Considers the literary impact of the book, emphasizing how the message is conveyed through literary artistry. Attends especially to sociopolitical issues and to the religious message, but (as is the case with most volumes in this series) does little with theological implications.

2.54.3 Meyers, Carol L., and Eric M. Meyers. *Zechariah 9–14*. Anchor Bible. New York: Doubleday, 1993. 552pp.

Similar in scope and method to their volume on Haggai and Zechariah 1–8 (§2.54.2). Argues that Zechariah 9–14 postdates Haggai and Zechariah 1–8 by more than fifty years, and thus has a distinct sociopolitical and religious setting. Views the period not as one of religious and political decline, but as a creative and dynamic time in which the people maintained their identity in the midst of a changing world. Attends also to the canonical process according to which this material was combined with Zechariah 1–8, and considers the significance of this process for both the formation of the canon and transmission of tradition. Emphasizes ways this material adopts and adapts earlier scriptures so as to communicate its own religious message.

2.54.4 Petersen, David L. *Haggai and Zechariah 1–8: A Commentary*. Old Testament Library. Philadelphia: Westminster, 1984. 320pp.

In contrast to Meyers and Meyers (§2.54.2), emphasizes differences between Haggai and Zechariah. Sees Haggai as an activist and Zechariah as a contemplative theologian, a difference that points to a kind of "prophetic pluralism" that exists in the OT as a whole. Employs linguistic analysis, historical criticism, historical background, and literary analysis selectively so as to illuminate the most significant interpretive issues. Concentrates on the historical ministry and oracles of Haggai and Zechariah over against the literary impact of the final form of the text. Discusses in detail the religious issues of the text, but does not address contemporary Christian appropriation.

2.54.5 Petersen, David L. *Zechariah 9–14 and Malachi*. Old Testament Library. Louisville: Westminster John Knox, 1995. 233pp.

Similar in scope and method to Petersen's volume on Haggai and Zechariah 1–8 (§2.54.4). Treats Zechariah 9–11, Zechariah 12–14, and Malachi as three separate collections that were bound together in the process of compiling the canonical Minor Prophets. Emphasizes the historical, political, social, and religious background of the Persian period in the interpretation of this material, with a view to how this material presents Israel's God in relation to the Persian Empire on the one hand and the community of faith on the other.

2.54.6 Verhoff, Pieter A. *The Books of Haggai and Malachi*. New International Commentary on the Old Testament. Grand Rapids: Eerdmans, 1987. 364pp.

Argues from a conservative evangelical perspective for the historical authenticity and authorial and literary unity of both books. Employs insights from the Ancient Near East, other OT passages and traditions, linguistic considerations (analysis of Hebrew and of comparative Semitic languages), and literary

structure of passages and of entire books for an interpretation that is fully informed and useful for the specialist, but readable and accessible to the nonspecialist. Concentrates on the theological message and relates it critically to
NT faith, noting both points of continuity and discontinuity. Extremely useful
for preaching and teaching.

2.54.7 **Wolff, Hans Walter.** *Haggai.* Minneapolis: Augsburg, 1988. 128pp.

Insists on the importance of Haggai as one of the most influential figures in
postexilic community. Considers the book a "model of effective proclamation," leading the audience from "soreness of failure to hope of glory" in five
scenes, based on Haggai's oracles, but developed and expanded to address
the book's own readership. Commentary thus adopts twofold concern: (1) to
reconstruct the ministry and oracles of Haggai and to consider their significance for his original hearers, and (2) to explore the function of passages in
the final book context. Includes technical discussions of text, form-critical categories, redaction, linguistic analysis, and historical background, but with
concern for the theological message and to some extent the relevance of this
theology for Christian fulfillment.

ALSO SIGNIFICANT

2.54.8 Baldwin, Joyce G. *Haggai, Zechariah, Malachi: An Introduction and Commentary.* Tyndale Old Testament Commentaries. Downers Grove, Ill.: InterVarsity,
1972. 253pp.

2.54.9 Baron, David. *The Visions and Prophecies of Zechariah: An Exposition.* London: Marshall, Morgan & Scott, 1919. 554pp.

2.54.10 Kaiser, Walter C., Jr. *God's Unchanging Love.* Grand Rapids: Baker, 1984.
171pp.

2.54.11 Mason, R. A. *The Books of Haggai, Zechariah and Malachi.* Cambridge Bible
Commentary. Cambridge: Cambridge University Press, 1977. 168pp.

2.54.12 McDonald, Beth Glazier. *Malachi: The Divine Messenger.* Society of Biblical
Literature Dissertation Series 98. Atlanta: Scholars, 1987. 288pp.

2.54.13 Oswalt, John N. *Where Are You, God?* Wheaton, Ill.: Victor, 1982. 156pp.

2.54.14 Perowne, T. T. *Haggai and Zechariah.* Cambridge Bible for Schools and Colleges. Cambridge: Cambridge University Press, 1886. 159pp.

2.54.15 Redditt, Paul L. *Haggai, Zechariah, Malachi.* New Century Bible Commentary.
Grand Rapids: Eerdmans, 1995. 196pp.

3

EARLY JUDAISM

3.1 Judaism and Jewish Culture: Primary Sources

See also APOCRYPHA AND PSEUDEPIGRAPHA OF THE OLD TESTAMENT
(§3.3)

HIGHLY RECOMMENDED

3.1.1 Cathcart, Kevin, Michael Maher, and Martin McNamara, eds. *The Aramaic Bible: The Targums.* Collegeville, Minn.: Liturgical Press, 1987–. Volumes average 270pp. (19 vols. out of 22 available).

The only readily accessible English edition of these Aramaic translations of the Hebrew Bible from the early Christian era. Includes all traditionally known targums, translated into modern English idiom. Produced by a variety of scholars, but with consistent quality and generally uniform translation style. Translators consulted both critical editions and manuscripts. Includes textual apparatus and notes, which primarily clarify the translation. Begins each targum with an introduction containing necessary background information. Each volume concludes with select bibliography and index of biblical, Qumranic, rabbinic, early Jewish, and early Christian (including NT) references.

3.1.2 Danby, Herbert. *The Mishnah: Translated from the Hebrew with Introduction and Brief Explanatory Notes.* London: Oxford University Press, 1933. 844pp.

Offers a translation of the entire Mishnah that is literal and easily accessible to the average reader. Contains brief annotations that explain allusions and clarify difficulties, but no commentary. Follows traditional Jewish interpretation in translation and notes. Includes full index of biblical passages, persons, and subjects.

3.1.3 Epstein, Isidore, ed. *The Babylonian Talmud.* 18 vols. London: Soncino, 1961. Volumes average 700pp.

The most complete and current translation of this material until Neusner (§3.1.11). Translations were produced by various scholars, and thus style or mode of translations vary somewhat. Yet translations are consistently accurate and readable. Includes brief annotations consisting of basic explanations and cross-references to other Talmudic and biblical passages. Epstein revised and supplemented these translations and interpretations, and added footnotes in brackets containing alternative explanations and discussions of matters pertaining to history and geography. Each volume contains a glossary and index of persons, subjects, and biblical passages. Final volume consists of general index.

3.1.4 Epstein, Isidore, ed. *The Midrash Rabbah.* 10 vols. London: Soncino, 1977. Volumes average 500pp.

Similar in approach to Epstein's *Talmud* (§3.1.3). The midrashim are translated by a variety of scholars, with a generally high level of accuracy and readability. Contains brief notes, mostly explaining meaning or clarifying the translation. Text includes frequent citation of terms from original language (in transliteration). Final volume contains index of persons, subjects, and biblical passages.

3.1.5 Whiston, William. *The Works of Josephus: Complete and Unabridged.* New updated ed. Peabody, Mass.: Hendrickson, 1985. 782pp.

Although produced in the eighteenth century, probably still the standard translation of the works of this significant Jewish historian. Includes only the English (as opposed to the Loeb edition, which includes the original Greek). Offers a new numbering system that corresponds to the one used in the Loeb edition, as well as citations, cross-references, and indexes to biblical passages, persons, and subjects. Contains a few very brief explanatory annotations.

3.1.6 Yonge, C. D. *The Works of Philo: Complete and Unabridged.* New updated ed. Peabody, Mass.: Hendrickson, 1993. 918pp.

Produced by C. D. Yonge, an eminent classicist of the mid-nineteenth century, this volume is virtually the only affordable and easily accessible translation of Philo presently available. Yonge's translation was based on Mangey's text, which is different in sequence and completeness from the superior Cohn-Wendland text that appeared about forty years after Yonge. This edition updates Yonge's work: it conforms to the sequence of the Cohn-Wendland text and contains newly translated passages from Cohn-Wendland. Includes informative foreword by David M. Scholer, describing the life and significance of Philo and the editions of his writings, and offering a select bibliography. Unlike the Loeb edition, contains only English translation.

A L S O   S I G N I F I C A N T

3.1.7 Blackman, Philip. *Mishnayot: Pointed Hebrew Text: English Translation, Introductions.* 7 vols. Rev. ed. New York: Judaica, 1963–1964.

3.1.8 Colson, F. H., G. H. Whitaker, J. W. Earp, and Ralph Marcus. *Philo.* 12 vols. Loeb Classical Library. Cambridge: Harvard University Press, 1929–1953.

3.1.9 Gianotti, Charles R. *The New Testament and the Mishnah: A Cross-Reference Index.* Grand Rapids: Baker, 1983. 63pp.

3.1.10 Glatzer, Norman, ed. *The Essential Philo.* New York: Schocken, 1971. 360pp.

3.1.11 Neusner, Jacob. *The Talmud of Babylonia: An American Translation.* 31 vols. Brown Judaic Studies. Chico, Calif.: Scholars, 1984.

3.1.12 ———. *The Talmud of the Land of Israel: Preliminary Translation and Explanation.* 35 vols. Chicago: University of Chicago Press, 1982–1993.

3.1.13 ———. *The Tosefta: Translated from the Hebrew with a New Introduction.* 6 vols. in 2. Peabody, Mass.: Hendrickson, 2002.

3.1.14 Nickelsburg, George W. E., and Michael E. Stone. *Faith and Piety in Early Judaism: Texts and Documents.* Philadelphia: Fortress, 1983. 243pp.

3.1.15 Thackeray, H. St. J., Ralph Marcus, Allen Wikgren, and L. H. Feldman. *Josephus.* 10 vols. Loeb Classical Library. Cambridge: Harvard University Press, 1926–1965.

3.2 Judaism and Jewish Culture: Secondary Sources

See also NEW TESTAMENT: HISTORY AND GEOGRAPHY (§4.5)

H I G H L Y   R E C O M M E N D E D

3.2.1 Boccaccini, Gabriele. *Middle Judaism: Jewish Thought, 300 B.C.E.– 200 C.E.* Minneapolis: Fortress, 1991. 289pp.

Seeks to establish a "non-biased" reconstruction of Jewish thought (primarily religious, but also philosophical and social), employing a method that is free from the confessional constraints of either Judaism or Christianity. This method involves a commitment to examine all relevant material and to recognize not only unity but also diversity between various Judaisms. Explores how the different Judaic systems related to each other. Most complete, current, and authoritative account of the intellectual history of the period. Includes extensive bibliography.

3.2.2 Davies, W. D., Louis Finkelstein, William Horbury, and John Sturdy, eds. *The Cambridge History of Judaism*. 4 vols. Cambridge: Cambridge University Press, 1984. 1254pp.

Articles by most prominent Jewish and Gentile scholars on both sides of the Atlantic deal with every major issue pertaining to the history of the Jews from the exile in 587 B.C.E. to the codification of the Mishnah around 250 C.E., with special attention to interaction with Persian, Hellenistic, and Roman cultures. Articles consider all relevant literary and archaeological evidence. Volumes deal in succession with the Persian, Hellenistic, and Roman periods. The final and forthcoming volume will deal with the period between 70 and 250 C.E. Authoritative, complete, and extremely helpful in providing historical background for biblical interpretation.

3.2.3 Grabbe, Lester L. *Judaism from Cyrus to Hadrian: Sources, History, Synthesis*. 2 vols. Philadelphia: Fortress, 1992. 792pp.

The most complete guide to early Judaism, from the latter stages of the OT into the time of the NT. Grabbe divides his study into historical segments; in each he moves from critical evaluation of primary extant sources to a survey of major interpretive issues, where he presents a range of scholarly opinions, to a synthesis of that historical period. He concludes each segment with a bibliography of modern works.

3.2.4 Kraft, Robert A., and George W. E. Nickelsburg, eds. *Early Judaism and Its Modern Interpreters*. The Bible and Its Modern Interpreters. Atlanta: Scholars, 1986. 494pp.

Describes major developments in the study of "early Judaism" (330 B.C.E. to 138 C.E.) from about 1945 through 1980, when most of the essays in this volume were written. Includes a lengthy and helpful introductory chapter discussing the field, new tools and methods, major issues, and prospects for the future. Deals with the major approaches to the political, social, and religious history of the period, recent discoveries pertaining to early Judaism, and discussions of different types of literature, primarily the Apocrypha, Pseudepigrapha, Philo, and Josephus. Each article contains critical survey of scholarship, with focus on trends, emphases, and prospects for future study, and includes a bibliography.

3.2.5 Neusner, Jacob. *Introduction to Rabbinic Literature*. Anchor Bible Reference Library. New York: Doubleday, 1994. 720pp.

Written for the nonspecialist, this is a fine introduction to Neusner's views on rabbinic literature, which are developed in the several books he has produced on more specific aspects of this literature. Here he describes the major writings, where they can be found, how they should be read, and how they bear on the OT and Christianity.

3.2.6 Neusner, Jacob, and William Scott Green, eds. *Dictionary of Judaism in the Biblical Period.* Peabody, Mass.: Hendrickson, 1996. 693pp.

This dictionary seeks to define concepts, religious practices, theological terms, persons, places, and vocabulary that are found in the writings of Judaism or in those that are related to Judaism (including Jewish elements in early Christianity) from 450 B.C.E. through C.E. 600. Is in fact a dictionary, not an encyclopedia, in that it gives lexical definitions and basic descriptions rather than full-length discussions. Contains more than thirty-three hundred entries written by seventy scholars of global recognition. Most current and reliable repository of essential information concerning Judaism in this period to be found in a single volume.

3.2.7 Sanders, E. P. *Judaism: Practice and Belief, 63 B.C.E.–66 C.E.* Philadelphia: Trinity Press International, 1992. 580pp.

This lucid, comprehensive, and groundbreaking work argues that the dominant portrait of Palestinian Judaism derived from such classic works as Schürer's *History of the Jewish People in the Age of Jesus Christ* (§4.5.6) or Jeremias's *Jerusalem in the Time of Jesus* (§4.5.20) is seriously skewed in that the Pharisees are presented as determinative for Judaism prior to the destruction of the temple and the Mishnah is assumed to describe general practice. Sanders insists on a recovery of "common Judaism," the daily observance of the people as a whole, and argues that early rabbinic material should be understood as reflecting debates within the context of the life of the people. Offers detailed examination of various common aspects of religious life of the people.

A L S O   S I G N I F I C A N T

3.2.8 Bickerman, E. *From Ezra to the Last of the Maccabees.* New York: Schocken, 1962. 186pp. Reprint of *The Jews: Their History, Culture, and Religion* (New York: Harper & Bros., 1949) and *The Maccabees: Their History from the Beginnings to the Fall of the House of the Hasmoneans* (New York: Schocken, 1947).

3.2.9 Collins, John J. *Between Athens and Jerusalem: Jewish Identity in the Hellenistic Diaspora.* 2d ed. Biblical Resource Series. Grand Rapids: Eerdmans, 2000. 327pp.

3.2.10 Elliott, Mark Adam. *The Survivors of Judaism: A Reconsideration of the Theology of Pre-Christian Judaism.* Grand Rapids: Eerdmans, 2000. 760pp.

3.2.11 Foerster, Werner. *From the Exile to Christ: Historical Introduction to Palestinian Judaism.* Philadelphia: Fortress, 1964. 247pp.

3.2.12 Hayes, John H., and Sara R. Mandell. *The Jewish People in Classical Antiquity: From Alexander to Bar Kochba.* Louisville: Westminster John Knox, 1998. 246pp.

3.2.13 Hengel, Martin. *Judaism and Hellenism: Studies in Their Encounter in Palestine during the Early Hellenistic Period.* 2 vols. in 1. Philadelphia: Fortress, 1974. 314/335pp.

3.2.14 ———. *Jews, Greeks and Barbarians.* Philadelphia: Fortress, 1980. 174pp.

3.2.15 Murphy, Frederick. *Early Judaism: The Exile to the Time of Jesus.* Peabody, Mass.: Hendrickson, 2002. 474pp.

3.2.16 Neusner, Jacob. *The Mishnah: Introduction and Reader.* Philadelphia: Trinity Press International, 1992. 226pp.

3.2.17 ———. *The Talmud: Introduction and Reader.* South Florida Studies in the History of Judaism. Atlanta: Scholars, 1995. 155pp.

3.2.18 ———. *The Tosefta: Translated from the Hebrew, with a New Introduction.* 2 vols. Peabody, Mass.: Hendrickson, 2002. 1984pp.

3.2.19 ———. *What Is Midrash?* Guides to Biblical Scholarship. Philadelphia: Fortress, 1987. 114pp.

3.2.20 Nickelsburg, George W. E. *Jewish Literature between the Bible and the Mishnah: A Historical and Literary Introduction.* Philadelphia: Fortress, 1981. 332pp.

3.2.21 Peters, F. E. *The Harvest of Hellenism: A History of the Near East from Alexander the Great to the Triumph of Christianity.* New York: Simon & Schuster, 1970. 800pp.

3.2.22 Russell, D. S. *The Jews from Alexander to Herod.* London: Oxford, 1967. 329pp.

3.2.23 Schechter, Solomon. *Aspects of Rabbinic Theology: Major Concepts of the Talmud.* New York: Macmillan, 1909. Repr. Peabody, Mass.: Hendrickson, 1998. 384pp.

3.2.24 Strack, Hermann L., and Gunter Stemberger. *Introduction to the Talmud and Midrash.* Minneapolis: Fortress, 1992. 472pp.

3.2.25 Tcherikover, Victor. *Hellenistic Civilization and the Jews*. New York: Atheneum, 1975. 563pp.

3.2.26 VanderKam, James C. *An Introduction to Early Judaism*. Grand Rapids: Eerdmans, 2001. 234pp.

Note also the series Compendia Rerum Iudaicarum ad Novum Testamentum (CRINT). Section 2 is titled The Literature of the Jewish People in the Period of the Second Temple and the Talmud. Section 3 is titled Jewish Traditions in Early Christian Literature.

3.2.27 Mulder, Martin Jan, ed. *Mikra: Text, Translation, Reading and Interpretation of the Hebrew Bible in Ancient Judaism and Early Christianity*. CRINT 2.1. Philadelphia: Fortress, 1988. 327pp.

3.2.28 Runia, David T., ed. *Philo in Early Christian Literature: A Survey*. CRINT 3.3. Minneapolis: Fortress, 1993. 418pp.

3.2.29 Safrai, Shemuel. *The Literature of the Sages: Oral Tora, Halakha, Mishna, Tosefta, Talmud, External Tractates*. CRINT 2.3A. Philadelphia: Fortress, 1988. 418pp.

3.2.30 Schreckenberg, Heinz, and Kurt Schubert. *Jewish Historiography and Iconography in Early and Medieval Christianity*. CRINT 3.2. Philadelphia: Fortress, 1991. 307pp.

3.2.31 Stone, Michael E. *Jewish Writings of the Second Temple Period: Apocrypha, Pseudepigrapha, Qumran, Sectarian Writings, Philo, Josephus*. CRINT 2.2. Philadelphia: Fortress, 1984. 307pp.

3.2.32 Tomson, Peter J. *Paul and the Jewish Law: Halakha in the Letters of the Apostle to the Gentiles*. CRINT 3.1. Philadelphia: Fortress, 1990. 327pp.

3.3 Apocrypha and Pseudepigrapha of the Old Testament

H I G H L Y   R E C O M M E N D E D

3.3.1 Charles, R. H., ed. *The Apocrypha and Pseudepigrapha of the Old Testament in English: With Introductions and Critical and Explanatory Notes*. 2 vols. Oxford: Clarendon, 1913. 657/871pp.

Edited by arguably the foremost authority on this material in his generation, and including introductions and explanatory notes by the most prominent authorities of Jewish intertestamental literature, this work is a solid and reliable classic. Each contribution includes an introduction (discussing the book's contents, title, manuscripts, versions, date, unity, authorship, influence on later Jewish or Christian literature, and theology, with bibliography). The notes are brief but technical, and assume a significant amount of linguistic and historical background. Should be supplemented at points by more recent treatments, especially the two volumes edited by Charlesworth (§3.3.2 and 3.3.3§).

3.3.2 Charlesworth, James H., ed. *The Old Testament Pseudepigrapha.* 2 vols. Garden City, N.J.: Doubleday, 1983, 1985. 996/1006pp.

Similar to Charles's second volume (§3.3.1), dealing with the Pseudepigrapha, which it attempts to replace. Differs from Charles in that it gives no consideration to the Apocrypha, but includes under Pseudepigrapha a number of later works and fragments not found in Charles. Naturally, it also brings to bear more recent discoveries and scholarly discussion. Each contribution was written by a recognized authority on the book, and includes a synopsis of the book's contents, and discussion of text, original language, date, provenance, historical background, theology, relationship to canonical material, relationship to apocryphal material, and cultural importance. The translations are literal, and the brief interpretive notes are informed and technical.

3.3.3 Charlesworth, James H. *The Old Testament Pseudepigrapha and the New Testament: Prolegomena for the Study of Christian Origins.* New ed. Cambridge: Cambridge University Press, 1998. 145pp.

This clearly written volume deals with the study of the Pseudepigrapha as a whole; there is no attempt here to treat introductory matters pertaining to the individual books (for such treatment one should consult Charlesworth's *The Old Testament Pseudepigrapha* [§3.3.2]). Argues here for the significance of the Pseudepigrapha for understanding early Judaism and especially the NT. In the process, explores history of research into the Pseudepigrapha and shows how social history and ideology of scholars influenced that research, demonstrates sophistication and erudition of this literature, polemicizes against easy dismissal of religious value of these writings, provides historical context in which the writings can be appreciated and assessed, demonstrates the wide range of accepted views in early Judaism, and discusses proper method for studying these documents and comparing them with Christian and other Jewish materials.

3.3.4 Kohlenberger, John R., III, ed. *The Parallel Apocrypha.* New York: Oxford University Press, 1997. 1188pp.

Only parallel Apocrypha readily available. Contains Greek, KJV, Douay, Ronald Knox, NRSV, NAB, and NJB. Includes also six introductory essays dealing with the significance of the Apocrypha for Jewish, Orthodox, Anglican,

Protestant, and evangelical communities, written by leading representatives of these groups.

3.3.5 Metzger, Bruce M. *An Introduction to the Apocrypha: Based on the Revised Standard Version.* New York: Oxford University Press, 1957. 274pp.

Although written more than forty years ago, this volume remains a most reliable and comprehensive introduction to the Apocrypha. Contends that the Apocrypha is a necessary link between the testaments, and that an understanding of these books is essential for interpreting the NT. Having discussed the exclusion of these books in the development of the Hebrew canon, Metzger analyzes briefly each of the individual books according to their date, historical background, content, religious ideas, and significance for later literature and events. Especially helpful is a series of final thematic chapters dealing with the influence of the Apocrypha in the NT, in the history of the church, and in Western culture.

P E R I O D I C A L

3.3.6 *Journal for the Study of the Pseudepigrapha.* Sheffield: Sheffield Academic Press, 1987–.

A L S O   S I G N I F I C A N T

3.3.7 DeSilva, David A. *Introducing the Apocrypha: Message, Context, and Significance.* Grand Rapids: Baker, 2002. 384pp.

3.3.8 DiTommoso, Lorenzo. *A Bibliography of Pseudepigrapha Research 1850–1999.* Journal for the Study of the Pseudepigrapha Supplement Series 39. Sheffield: Sheffield Academic Press, 2001. 650pp.

3.3.9 Lightfoot, J. B., et al., eds. *Excluded Books of the New Testament.* London: E. Nash & Grayson, 1927. 403pp.

3.3.10 Reeves, John C., ed. *Tracing the Threads: Studies in the Vitality of Jewish Pseudepigrapha.* Society of Biblical Literature Early Judaism and Its Literature Series 6. Atlanta: Scholars, 1994. 296pp.

3.3.11 Rost, Leonhard. *Judaism Outside the Hebrew Canon.* Nashville: Abingdon, 1976. 205pp.

3.3.12 Russell, D. S. *The Old Testament Pseudepigrapha: Patriarchs and Prophets in Early Judaism.* Philadelphia: Fortress, 1987. 144pp.

3.3.13 Sparks, H. F. D. *The Apocryphal Old Testament.* Oxford: Clarendon, 1985. 990pp.

3.3.14 Torrey, Charles C. *The Apocryphal Literature: A Brief Introduction.* New Haven, Conn.: Yale University Press, 1945. 151pp.

See also the introductions to the several books of the Apocrypha and Pseudepigrapha published in the series Guides to the Apocrypha and Pseudepigrapha (Sheffield Academic Press).

3.4 Qumran and the Dead Sea Scrolls

H I G H L Y   R E C O M M E N D E D

3.4.1 Charlesworth, James H., ed. *The Dead Sea Scrolls: Hebrew, Aramaic, and Greek Texts with English Translations.* 10 vols. Princeton Theological Seminary Dead Sea Scrolls Project. Louisville: Westminster John Knox, 1994–. Vols. 1, 2, and 4 are available. Volumes average 160pp.

Reliable, comprehensive, critical edition of the Dead Sea Scrolls. Much more accessible and user friendly, more consistent in style and method, more interested in theology of the text, and more reasonably priced than *Discoveries in the Judean Desert* (§3.4.6). Gives less attention to linguistic matters and contains somewhat fewer notes than does *DJD.* Includes texts, English translation, and introductions. In contrast to *DJD,* excludes biblical materials, but devotes one volume to Qumran documents that are part of the Apocrypha and Pseudepigrapha. Introduction to each scroll includes discussion of text, language, provenance, history or historical events reflected in the scroll, major theological ideas, relation to other writings, especially Hebrew Bible, other Jewish literature, and the NT.

3.4.2 García Martínez, Florentino, and Eibert J. C. Tigchelaar, eds. *The Dead Sea Scrolls: Study Edition.* 2 vols. Leiden: Brill, 1997. 1361pp.

Overall the most usable and accessible edition of the scrolls for regular reading or study. Contains Hebrew and Aramaic transcription and literal English translation on facing pages. Each Q-number contains a brief heading with information on the text and very select bibliography. Omits unidentified and unclassified fragments, and omits also biblical materials among the scrolls. The translation is slightly corrected from that found in García Martínez's *The Dead Sea Scrolls Translated* (§3.4.18). Those who do not know Hebrew or Aramaic might prefer that less expensive volume.

3.4.3 Ringgren, Helmer. *The Faith of Qumran: Theology of the Dead Sea Scrolls.* Enl. ed. New York: Crossroad, 1995. 330pp.

Begins with a brief introduction to the history and literature of the community, but gives bulk of attention to analysis of the major theological concepts represented in the scrolls. Deals extensively with God, humanity, and eschatology, but gives some attention to other categories, including angels, sin, forgiveness, ethics, and Messianism. Systematic presentation of beliefs of the Qumran community as a whole could lead to enforcement of alien ideological unity on diverse material, but Ringgren acknowledges and generally allows for theological differences and tensions within the scrolls. Volume concludes with discussions on religious organization and practices of the community and relationship to other forms of religion, especially Christianity.

3.4.4 Schiffman, Lawrence H., and James C. VanderKam, eds. *Encyclopedia of the Dead Sea Scrolls.* 2 vols. Oxford: Oxford University Press, 2000. 1132pp.

Only reference work to bring all relevant information on Qumran and the scrolls together in one place. Presents lucid current discussion of every significant aspect of the scrolls. Treats all Judean desert texts, including those found at Wadi ed-Daliyeh and Masada. Each article emphasizes relevance for biblical scholarship, and each entry concludes with highly selective bibliography (sometimes with brief annotations).

3.4.5 VanderKam, James C. *The Dead Sea Scrolls Today.* Grand Rapids: Eerdmans, 1994. 208pp.

Eminently readable introduction to Qumran and the Dead Sea Scrolls. Covers all major aspects of the community and the scrolls on the basis of the most current findings and scholarly investigation. Describes the history and physical setting of the Qumran discoveries; provides brief surveys of the manuscripts; discusses the theology, practices, and history of the Qumran community (which VanderKam believes to be Essene); and relates the scrolls to the OT and NT. At several points develops major elements of the theology of the scrolls. Concludes each chapter with select annotated bibliography. Remarkable amount of useful information packed into this small volume.

3.4.6 Vaux, Roland de, et al., eds. *Discoveries in the Judean Desert.* 36 vols. thus far. Oxford: Clarendon, 1955–. Volumes average 200pp.

The most authoritative and complete edition of the Dead Sea Scrolls ever published. Individual volumes edited by the most prominent international authorities on the scrolls. Treatment of each portion of the scrolls includes (1) introduction describing condition and contents of the manuscripts, paleography, and orthography; (2) transcription of the original text; (3) translation (of nonbiblical materials); (4) textual notes; (5) commentary (mostly orthographical, grammatical, and lexical, or references to related biblical passages; some commentators clarify or explicate the meaning of the text); and (6) plates showing the actual fragments. Highly technical, with portions of each volume accessible only to those who are competent in Hebrew and Aramaic. Most of the volumes are in English; a few are in French.

P E R I O D I C A L

3.4.7 *Dead Sea Discoveries.* Leiden: Brill Academic Publishing, 1994–.

A L S O   S I G N I F I C A N T

3.4.8 Charlesworth, James H. *Graphic Concordance to the Dead Sea Scrolls.* Princeton Theological Seminary Dead Sea Scrolls Project. Louisville: Westminster John Knox, 1992. 529pp.

3.4.9 Charlesworth, James H., ed. *Jesus and the Dead Sea Scrolls.* Anchor Bible Reference Library. New York: Doubleday, 1992. 370pp.

3.4.10 Collins, John J., and Kugler, Robert A., eds. *Religion in the Dead Sea Scrolls.* Studies in the Dead Sea Scrolls and Related Literature. Grand Rapids: Eerdmans, 2000. 167pp.

3.4.11 Cross, Frank Moore. *Ancient Library of Qumran and Modern Biblical Studies.* 3d ed. Minneapolis: Fortress, 1995. 204pp.

3.4.12 Fitzmyer, Joseph A. *The Dead Sea Scrolls and Christian Origins.* Studies in the Dead Sea Scrolls and Related Literature. Grand Rapids: Eerdmans, 2000. 290pp.

3.4.13 ———. *The Dead Sea Scrolls: Major Publications and Tools for Study.* Rev. ed. Society of Biblical Literature Resources for Biblical Study 20. Atlanta: Scholars, 1990. 246pp.

3.4.14 Flint, Peter W., ed. *The Bible at Qumran: Text, Shape, and Interpretation.* Studies in the Dead Sea Scrolls and Related Literature. Grand Rapids: Eerdmans, 2001. 266pp.

3.4.15 Flint, Peter W., and James C. VanderKam, eds. *The Dead Sea Scrolls after Fifty Years: A Comprehensive Assessment.* Vol. 1. Leiden: Brill, 1998. 544pp.

3.4.16 Magness, Jodi. *The Archaeology of Qumran and the Dead Sea Scrolls.* Studies in the Dead Sea Scrolls and Related Literature. Grand Rapids: Eerdmans, 2002. 256pp.

3.4.17 García Martínez, Florentino. *A Bibliography of the Finds in the Desert of Judah 1970–1995.* Studies on the Texts of Judah 19. Leiden: Brill, 1996. 561pp.

3.4.18 ———.*The Dead Sea Scrolls Translated: The Qumran Texts in English.* 2d ed. Grand Rapids: Eerdmans, 1996. 519pp.

3.4.19 García Martínez, Florentino, and Julio Trebolle Barrera. *The People of the Dead Sea Scrolls: Their Literature, Social Organization and Religious Beliefs.* Leiden: Brill, 1994. 269pp.

3.4.20 Pate, C. Marvin. *Communities of the Last Days: The Dead Sea Scrolls, the New Testament, and the Story of Israel.* Downers Grove, Ill.: InterVarsity, 2000. 303pp.

3.4.21 Schiffman, Lawrence H. *Reclaiming the Dead Sea Scrolls: Their True Meaning for Judaism and Christianity.* Anchor Bible Reference Library. New York: Doubleday, 1995. 529pp.

3.4.22 Shanks, Hershel, ed. *Understanding the Dead Sea Scrolls: A Reader from the Biblical Archaeology Review.* New York: Random House, 1992. 336pp.

3.4.23 Shanks, Hershel. *The Mystery and Meaning of the Dead Sea Scrolls.* New York: Random House, 1998. 246pp.

3.4.24 Stegemann, Hartmut. *The Library of Qumran: On the Essenes, Qumran, John the Baptist, and Jesus.* Grand Rapids: Eerdmans, 1998. 299pp.

3.4.25 Ulrich, Eugene. *The Dead Sea Scrolls and the Origins of the Bible.* Studies in the Dead Sea Scrolls and Related Literature. Grand Rapids: Eerdmans, 1999. 309pp.

3.4.26 Vermes, Geza. *The Dead Sea Scrolls in English.* 4th ed. Sheffield: JSOT, 1995. 320pp.

3.4.27 ———. *An Introduction to the Complete Dead Sea Scrolls.* Minneapolis: Fortress, 1999. 256pp.

3.4.28 Wise, Michael, Martin Abegg Jr., and Edward Cook. *The Dead Sea Scrolls: A New Translation.* San Francisco: HarperSanFrancisco, 1996. 513pp.

3.5 Apocalyptic and Apocalypticism

3.5.1 Collins, John J. *The Apocalyptic Imagination: An Introduction to Jewish Apocalyptic Literature.* 2d ed. Biblical Resources Series. Grand Rapids: Eerdmans, 1998. 337pp.

Current and engaging introduction to apocalyptic literature. Argues that the essence of apocalypticism involved responding to crises not by offering reasonable solutions but by appealing to imagination and faith. Whereas Russell (§3.5.6) deals with apocalyptic literature as a whole, Collins gives separate treatment to each significant apocalyptic writing, including apocalyptic passages in the NT. In each case he discusses unity and structure, content, historical background (especially socioreligious factors), history of interpretation, and message. In the process, notes connections between the individual writings.

3.5.2 Collins, John J., Bernard McGinn, and Stephen J. Stein, eds. *The Encyclopedia of Apocalypticism.* 3 vols. New York: Continuum, 1998. 494/524/498pp.

Volume 1 deals with apocalypticism as a religious worldview or system involving belief "that God has revealed the imminent end of the ongoing struggle between good and evil in history." Understands this to be the central tenet of Judaism, Christianity, and Islam, and examines the origins of this belief system and the initial manifestations of it in the OT, intertestamental Judaism, and the NT. This is an encyclopedia, not a dictionary, in that it contains not brief articles identifying every person or document pertaining to apocalypticism, but rather a series of full-length articles detailing essential aspects of this belief system. Volumes 2 and 3 are not oriented to biblical data, but treat "Apocalypticism in Western History and Culture" and "Apocalypticism in the Modern Period and the Contemporary Age."

3.5.3 Hanson, Paul D. *The Dawn of Apocalyptic.* 2d ed. Philadelphia: Fortress, 1979. 444pp.

Focuses on the religious influences that gave rise to the apocalyptic movement. In contrast to prevailing scholarly opinion, argues that the forces behind the emergence of apocalypticism are to be found not in Persian or Greek circles but deep within the religious tradition (especially prophetic) of Israel. In the process, deals carefully with a number of OT prophetic books and passages so as to demonstrate their contribution to the development of apocalypticism. Shows how such an understanding of the development of apocalypticism within the OT illuminates the eschatological message of this vast and significant literature.

3.5.4 Hanson, Paul D. *Old Testament Apocalyptic.* Interpreting Biblical Texts. Nashville: Abingdon, 1987. 144pp.

Basic guide to apocalyptic material in the OT, written for the nonspecialist, and helpful for reflection on the use of this material for preaching and teaching within the church. Describes significance, identification and character, original theological message, and proper versus improper process of applying apocalyptic texts. Argues against "illegitimate and improper" applications (e.g., Hal Lindsey's *Late Great Planet Earth*). Treats several specific OT apocalyptic passages to show how they should be interpreted and how their proper interpretation can be creatively and compellingly applied to specific contemporary issues.

3.5.5 Minear, Paul S. *New Testament Apocalyptic.* Interpreting Biblical Texts. Nashville: Abingdon, 1981. 157pp.

Similar to Hanson's *Old Testament Apocalyptic* (§3.5.4) in that there is a concern to identify NT apocalyptic, discuss its character, and present examples of appropriate interpretation and contemporary application of key NT passages (in contrast to "illegitimate" use of these texts by some contemporary American movements, especially certain forms of the charismatic movement). But whereas Hanson focuses on the apocalyptic genre, Minear understands apocalyptic more broadly as constituting not only a type of literature but also a religious movement and a type of religious thinking. Consequently, Minear treats passages that represent apocalyptic thinking or themes, but are not apocalyptic in genre.

3.5.6 Russell, D. S. *The Method and Message of Jewish Apocalyptic: 200 BC–AD 100.* Old Testament Library. Philadelphia: Westminster, 1964. 464pp.

Remains the standard text for reliable, comprehensive treatment of Jewish apocalyptic literature. Limited to Jewish literature, and thus excludes Christian apocalyptic (yet constantly refers to NT passages). Gives no attention to the apocalyptic movement as a socioreligious phenomenon. Especially helpful is the discussion of the literary characteristics of apocalyptic and the analysis of apocalyptic theology. Explores theological categories that are of particular significance for Christianity and examines the influence of apocalyptic thought on subsequent Judaism and Christianity.

ALSO SIGNIFICANT

3.5.7 Carey, Greg, and Gregory L. Bloomquist, eds. *Vision and Persuasion: Rhetorical Dimensions of Apocalyptic Discourse.* St. Louis, Mo.: Chalice, 1999. 203pp.

3.5.8   Cook, Stephen L. *Prophecy and Apocalypticism: The Postexilic Social Setting.* Minneapolis: Fortress, 1995. 246pp.

3.5.9   Frost, S. B. *Old Testament Apocalyptic: Its Origins and Growth.* London: Epworth, 1952. 270pp.

3.5.10 Jones, Larry Paul, and Jerry L. Sumney. *Preaching Apocalyptic Texts.* St. Louis, Mo.: Chalice, 1999. 151pp.

3.5.11 Koch, Klaus. *The Rediscovery of Apocalyptic: A Polemical Work on a Neglected Area of Biblical Studies and Its Damaging Effects on Theology and Philosophy.* Studies in Biblical Theology 22. Naperville, Ill.: Allenson, 1970. 156pp.

3.5.12 Morris, Leon. *Apocalytpic.* Grand Rapids: Eerdmans, 1972. 105pp.

3.5.13 Reddish, Mitchell G., ed. *Apocalyptic Literature: A Reader.* Peabody, Mass.: Hendrickson, 1995. 352pp.

3.5.14 Rowland, C. *The Open Heaven: A Study of Apocalyptic in Judaism and Early Christianity.* New York: Crossroad, 1982. 562pp.

3.5.15 Russell, D. S. *Divine Disclosure: An Introduction to Jewish Apocalyptic.* Minneapolis: Fortress, 1992. 164pp.

3.5.16 Schmithals, Walter. *The Apocalyptic Movement: Introduction and Interpretation.* Nashville: Abingdon, 1975. 255pp.

3.5.17 VanderKam, James C., and William Adler, eds. *The Jewish Apocalyptic Heritage in Early Christianity.* Compendia Rerum Iudaicarum ad Novum Testamentum 3.4. Minneapolis: Fortress, 1996. 286pp.

4

THE NEW TESTAMENT

4.1 Bibliographic Helps

See also PERIODICALS (§4.2)

H I G H L Y   R E C O M M E N D E D

4.1.1 Carson, D. A. *New Testament Commentary Survey.* 5th ed. Grand Rapids: Baker, 2001. 144pp.

Annotated bibliography of significant NT resources, especially commentaries. Introduction provides suggestions for choosing a commentary. Treats commentary sets as well as individual volumes. Limited almost exclusively to English titles, and to exegetical works over against homiletical resources. Although written by a leading conservative evangelical scholar, works cited represent a variety of theological traditions. Brief but trenchant comments discuss reliability, usefulness for students or pastors, theological slant, and price.

4.1.2 Harrington, Daniel J. *The New Testament: A Bibliography.* Wilmington, Del.: Michael Glazier, 1985. 242pp.

Produced by a significant Catholic NT scholar and editor of *New Testament Abstracts,* represents what he considers to be those works that are most authoritative and useful for students, Christian educators, theologians, clergy, and interested laity. Includes both books and articles, almost entirely in English. Identifies especially recommended works. List is theologically ecumenical, but evangelical titles are not well represented. Includes a wide range of topics, not only concordances and commentaries, but also categories (e.g., eucharist, marriage and divorce, politics). Consequently, each section contains only a few titles, and there are no annotations.

4.1.3 Martin, Ralph P. *New Testament Books for Pastor and Teacher.* Philadelphia: Westminster, 1984. 152pp.

Compiled by a leading evangelical NT scholar, this volume is intended to be a companion to Brevard Childs's *Old Testament Books for Pastor and Teacher*

(§2.1.2), Martin employs the same format, discussing various types of reference works, from Bible dictionaries to New Testament theologies, but giving the bulk of attention to commentaries. Works cited are almost exclusively in English, and annotations emphasize assessment made on the basis of usefulness for preaching and teaching in the church. Comments are helpful but brief. Still useful in spite of its age.

4.1.4 Mills, Watson E., ed. *Bibliographies for Biblical Research: New Testament Series.* 21 vols. Lewiston, N.Y.: Mellen Biblical Press, 1993–. Volumes average 250pp, but vary greatly in length.

Includes citations of twentieth-century works that make important contributions to understanding the text and its backgrounds. Each volume has its own compiler, who assesses works to be included. Although this selection is necessarily subjective, the choices are judicious, reasonable, and fair, and few scholars would have serious problems with the majority of selections. Each volume includes three divisions: scriptural passages, subjects, and commentaries. There is some duplication between the first two categories. Lists works in all European languages, without annotations. All volumes presently available except vol. 20, dealing with the Johannine letters.

4.1.5 Wagner, Günter. *An Exegetical Bibliography of the New Testament.* 4 vols. Macon, Ga.: Mercer University Press, 1983–1996. 667/550/350/ 379pp.

Presumably this work will eventually cover the entire NT, but as yet only four volumes are available, covering Matthew-Mark (1983), Luke-Acts (1985), the Johannine Writings (1987), and Romans and Galatians (1996). Includes books and articles in major journals, in all the European languages. Moves through each biblical book passage by passage, giving rather complete bibliography for each. Gives little attention to works dealing with an entire biblical book or corpus.

ALSO   SIGNIFICANT

4.1.6 France, R. T. *A Bibliographic Guide to New Testament Research.* Sheffield: JSOT, 1979. 56pp.

4.1.7 Mills, Watson E. *Critical Tools for the Study of the New Testament.* Mellen Biblical Press Series 27. Lewiston, N.Y.: Mellen, 1995. 142pp.

4.1.8 Scholer, David M. *A Basic Bibliographic Guide for New Testament Exegesis.* Grand Rapids: Eerdmans, 1973. 94pp.

4.2 Periodicals

4.2.1 *Journal for the Study of the New Testament.* 1978–. Quarterly.

Published by Department of Biblical Studies, Sheffield, U.K. Consistently high-quality articles directed toward scholars and serious students, but written in lucid style and largely accessible to the nonspecialist. Represents balance between treatment of broad NT issues and specific interpretation of individual passages; in both cases, inclined to deal with issues that are relevant for theological understanding of the text. Articles tend to employ the more traditional historical-critical methods, with forays into literary or narrative criticism. Language: English. Book reviews: few and brief.

4.2.2 *New Testament Abstracts.* 1956–. 3 issues/year.

Like *Old Testament Abstracts* (§2.2.2), published by the Catholic Biblical Association in Cambridge, Mass. Abstracts more than two thousand articles per year from more than five hundred periodicals, and summarizes more than 850 books; these works represent all European languages. Makes no attempt to evaluate, but simply describes works in terms of content, argument, and method. Language: English.

4.2.3 *New Testament Studies.* 1954–. Quarterly.

Produced by Studiorum Novi Testamenti Societas (Society for the Study of the New Testament) and published by Cambridge University Press, Cambridge, U.K., this is the preeminent scholarly journal for NT studies. Articles from mostly European and North American scholars employing predominantly traditional higher-critical methods, with some of the newer literary approaches, but avoids especially political approaches, e.g., feminist and liberationist readings. Articles are technical, but often accessible to nonspecialists, and frequently deal with issues that are relevant for understanding the message of the text. Some articles focus on theological or hermeneutical issues. Language: English, German, and French. Book reviews: recent issues contain none.

4.2.4 *Novum Testamentum.* 1956–. Quarterly.

Published by Brill Academic Publishers in Leiden, the Netherlands, a premier scholarly journal. Articles are consistently technical and somewhat less accessible to nonspecialists than articles in *JSNT* or even *NTS,* tending to treat historical-critical, text-critical, and grammatical issues, with relatively little attention to specifically theological concerns. Language: English, German, and French. Book reviews: many, but brief.

4.3 History of the Canon and History of Interpretation

4.3.1 Epp, Eldon Jay, and George W. MacRae, eds. *The New Testament and Its Modern Interpreters*. The Bible and Its Modern Interpreters. Philadelphia: Fortress, 1989. 601pp.

Examines and evaluates the state of scholarly research in each major area of NT study, with a view toward suggesting how developments since the Second World War point to directions for future study. Groups individual chapters according to three broad areas: the world of the NT, methods (mostly traditional ones, e.g., textual criticism, form criticism, redaction criticism, and linguistics, but attends also to literary criticism), and NT literature. This last section includes the NT Apocrypha and Apostolic Fathers. Devotes considerable space to the synoptic problem and gospel genre but only a couple of pages to Matthew and Mark. Comprehensive in categories covered, but that means several categories are treated in very cursory fashion, ameliorated in part by an extensive bibliography concluding each chapter.

4.3.2 Kümmel, Werner Georg. *The New Testament: The History of the Investigation of Its Problems*. Nashville: Abingdon, 1972. 510pp.

A most authoritative text, virtually a standard for the history of NT interpretation. Because of the emphases of the period in which it was written and the convictions of its author, this volume treats the whole of the history of NT interpretation from the perspective of the rise of the historical-critical method. Considers everything prior to the eighteenth century as "prehistory." Emphasizes Continental, and especially German, scholarship. Gives scant attention to British and American scholars, and should therefore be supplemented with Neill-Wright (§4.3.4) or Epp-McCrae (§4.3.1), both of which give prominence to British and American scholarship (and are more current).

4.3.3 Metzger, Bruce M. *The Canon of the New Testament: Its Origin, Development, and Significance*. Oxford: Clarendon, 1987. 326pp.

Volume is divided into three parts: Part 1 surveys the literature on the canon, discussing almost every work that deals directly with the NT canon from 1650 to the present. Part 2 tracks the development of the NT canon in the church, dealing with the Apostolic Fathers, the various influences that led to the canon, the emergence of the canon in the east and west, and Christian apocryphal literature. This is the most careful, complete, and balanced presentation of the NT canon to be found anywhere. Part 3 explores the various problems the church confronted in the canonizing process, e.g., the criteria for canonicity, relationship between inspiration and canon, and the problem of four different Gospels. Here also are addressed several theological questions the canon raises for the church today. Metzger's discussion of these theological questions is helpful, but he is stronger when working with historical matters.

4.3.4 Neill, Stephen, and Tom Wright. *The Interpretation of the New Testament 1861–1986*. 2d ed. London: Oxford, 1988. 464pp.

Original edition written by Stephen Neill, covering 1861 through 1961, has been revised and updated by N. T. Wright to include developments through 1986. Written in engaging narrative style with personal touches, especially descriptions of the scholars discussed. Gives detailed treatment of selected scholars and works rather than a broad survey of all literature. Attends to British and American scholarship without diminishing the German contribution. Provides an understanding of the history of scholarship and points out key problems of NT interpretation.

ALSO SIGNIFICANT

4.3.5 Baird, William. *History of New Testament Research*. Vol. 1. *From Deism to Tübingen*. Minneapolis: Augsburg, 1992. 450pp.

4.3.6 ———. *History of New Testament Research*. Vol. 2. *From Jonathan Edwards to Rudolf Bultmann*. Minneapolis: Fortress, 2002. 592pp.

4.3.7 Gamble, Harry Y. *The New Testament Canon: Its Making and Meaning*. Guides to Biblical Scholarship. Philadelphia: Fortress, 1985. 95pp.

4.3.8 Grant, Robert M. *The Formation of the New Testament*. New York: Harper & Row, 1965. 194pp.

4.3.9 Harris, Horton. *The Tübingen School: A Historical and Theological Investigation of the School of F. C. Baur*. Grand Rapids: Baker, 1990. 288pp.

4.3.10 Riches, John K. *A Century of New Testament Study*. Valley Forge, Pa.: Trinity Press International, 1993. 246pp.

4.3.11 Westcott, Brooke Foss. *A General Survey of the History of the Canon of the New Testament*. 7th ed. Cambridge: Macmillan, 1896. 605pp.

4.4 History and Geography: Primary Sources

4.4.1 Barrett, C. K., ed. *The New Testament Background: Selected Documents.* Rev. ed. San Francisco: HarperSanFrancisco, 1989. 361pp.

Selection of passages from Roman imperial sources, the papyri, various inscriptions, philosophers, poets, gnostics, mystery religions, works of Jewish history, rabbinic literature, Qumran, Philo, Josephus, the Septuagint, Targums, apocalyptic literature, and mysticism. Intended to give the nonspecialist a sense of the world (Roman, Greek, Jewish) in which the NT was produced. Begins with a helpful bibliography of each of these areas, listing both primary and secondary sources. Introduces each area with a short paragraph, describing its history and significance, while brief annotations explain translation and historical significance. Selections are not chosen by reference to specific NT passages but because of their ability to provide a sense of the world that surrounded the NT.

4.4.2 Cartlidge, David R., and David L. Dungan, eds. *Documents for the Study of the Gospels.* Rev. ed. Minneapolis: Fortress, 1993. 298pp.

Passages chosen to demonstrate the diversity of the religious world that surrounded the NT. Selections from Jewish, Greek, Roman, Egyptian, Syrian, and early Christian sources are intended to illuminate the Christian acknowledgment of Jesus as Savior and God. Shows how the Gospels both reflected and differed from the worship of other savior gods, and provides insight as to how the Gospels arose and how their original readers understood them. Contains a brief but informative introductory chapter on savior gods in the Mediterranean world. Each subsequent chapter begins with a brief introduction, placing the work in its historical context and describing its significance for the NT, followed by a fresh translation produced by the authors, with a few concise explanatory annotations.

4.4.3 Kee, Howard Clark, ed. *The Origins of Christianity: Sources and Documents.* Englewood Cliffs, N.J.: Prentice-Hall, 1973. 270pp.

Careful selection of documents meant to illustrate how persons in the first and second centuries before and after Christ thought about and related to key aspects of life, e.g., religion, the gods, life and death, the future, and anxieties of everyday life. Represents a vast range of material, including literary works, letters, magical texts, and documents from rabbinic and sectarian Judaism. The purpose is to provide depth and clarity for understanding the NT as a whole and broad themes or issues within it; excerpts were not chosen in reference to specific NT passages. Introductions provide historical background to the documents, while notes offer helpful explanation to historical references and allusions.

A L S O   S I G N I F I C A N T

4.4.4 Layton, Bentley. *Gnostic Scriptures: A New Translation with Introduction and Notes.* New York: Doubleday, 1995. 576pp.

4.4.5 Robinson, James M., ed. *The Nag Hammadi Library.* 4th ed. Leiden: Brill, 1996. 549pp.

4.5 History and Geography: Secondary Sources

See also JUDAISM AND JEWISH CULTURE (§3.2)

H I G H L Y   R E C O M M E N D E D

4.5.1 Boring, M. Eugene, Klaus Berger, and Carsten Colpe, eds. *Hellenistic Commentary to the New Testament.* Nashville: Abingdon, 1995. 633pp.

Passage-by-passage commentary cites Hellenistic texts that provide relevant background for the passage. The most complete collection of Hellenistic texts correlated to the NT available in English. Contains 976 relatively extensive citations, each one annotated to describe ways in which the citation illuminates the passage. Introductory chapter describes the use and potential misuse of this information. Helpful supplement to Keener (§4.5.4), who gives prominence to Jewish background and does not explicitly cite sources when he does refer to Hellenistic material.

4.5.2 Evans, Craig A., and Stanley E. Porter, eds. *Dictionary of New Testament Background.* Downers Grove, Ill.: InterVarsity, 2000. 1328pp.

Articles deal with virtually every imaginable aspect of Jewish and Greco-Roman background to the NT. Articles are written by recognized experts in the field and are of consistently high quality. Reflects generally conservative perspective. All entries were selected and written with a view toward assisting in the interpretation of the NT. Each article concludes with extensive bibliography.

4.5.3 Ferguson, Everett. *Backgrounds of Early Christianity.* 2d ed. Grand Rapids: Eerdmans, 1993. 611pp.

Overall the best introduction to NT background. Deals with political, social, literary, and religious backgrounds of the Roman, Greek, and Jewish worlds. Gives somewhat more attention to Jewish background, reflecting the author's conviction that it is most significant. Written for college and seminary students, it will prove valuable also to pastors and even interested laypersons. Current, comprehensive, and informed, but written in clear, straightforward style. Frequently refers to NT texts to show relevance for NT interpretation. Of special value are the bibliographies to general works at the beginning of each chapter and to specialized works at the end of each subsection.

4.5.4   Keener, Craig S. *The IVP Bible Background Commentary: New Testament.* Downers Grove, Ill.: InterVarsity, 1994. 831pp.

Background information is essential for NT interpretation, but is diffuse and often difficult to find. Keener's verse-by-verse commentary focuses exclusively on cultural, social, and historical background. Concentrates on OT and Jewish background, providing explicit citations of the OT and OT Apocrypha and Pseudepigrapha, but notes also Greek and Roman background (which Keener tends to present in a general way, without citing references). Written in clear, nontechnical language. Includes a glossary of cultural terms and important figures, maps and charts, introductory essay on importance of cultural background, and bibliographies for each biblical book listing commentaries and other works that emphasize background.

4.5.5   Martin, Ralph P., and Peter H. Davids, eds. *Dictionary of the Later New Testament and Its Developments.* Downers Grove, Ill.: InterVarsity, 1997. 1289pp.

Covers all NT literature outside the Gospels and Paul (companion volumes treat these areas; see "The Gospels: Studies in the Gospels" [4.20] and "Paul" [4.30]). Offers comprehensive discussion of apostolic fathers and early Christianity through middle of the second century. Discusses topics specific to this portion of NT and thus in many cases missing from even the most comprehensive Bible dictionaries. Narrow focus of this dictionary permits relatively full treatment of the topics included. Contributors include prominent evangelical scholars who make responsible use of critical methods, and who represent North America, Europe, Australia, New Zealand, and Asia.

4.5.6   Schürer, Emil. *The History of the Jewish People in the Age of Jesus Christ.* 3 vols. Revised and edited by Geza Vermes, Fergus Millar, and Matthew Black. Edinburgh: T&T Clark, 1973–1987. 611/606/ 1014pp.

By far the most thorough and authoritative study of Jewish history, institutions, and literature between 175 B.C.E. and 135 C.E. ever produced. Originally published in 1874, with fourth edition in 1909. This new English edition is based on the German fourth. Retains the structure and information that continues to be valid from the original work but provides a fresh English translation with full revision of the material reflecting recent discoveries and the most current scholarly judgments. Highly technical, but most material accessible to nonspecialists.

A L S O   S I G N I F I C A N T

4.5.7 Bevan, Edwyn. *Jerusalem under the High Priests.* London: Arnold, 1904. 168pp.

4.5.8 Brown, Raymond E. *The Churches the Apostles Left Behind.* New York: Paulist, 1984. 156pp.

4.5.9 Brown, Raymond E., and Paul Meier. *Antioch and Rome: New Testament Cradles of Catholic Christianity.* New York: Paulist, 1983. 242pp.

4.5.10 Bruce, F. F. *New Testament History.* 4th ed. London: Pickering & Inglis, 1982. 434pp.

4.5.11 Charlesworth, James H., ed. *The Messiah: Developments in Earliest Judaism and Christianity.* First Princeton Symposium on Judaism and Christian Origins. Minneapolis: Fortress, 1992. 597pp.

4.5.12 Collins, John J. *The Scepter and the Star: The Messiahs of the Dead Sea Scrolls and Other Ancient Literature.* Anchor Bible Reference Library. New York: Doubleday, 1995. 270pp.

4.5.13 Deissmann, Adolf. *Light from the Ancient East: The New Testament Illustrated by Recently Discovered Texts of the Graeco-Roman World.* New York: Doran, 1927. 535pp.

4.5.14 Evans, Craig A. *Noncanonical Writings and New Testament Interpretation.* Peabody, Mass.: Hendrickson, 1992. 281pp.

4.5.15 Goppelt, Leonhard. *Apostolic and Post-Apostolic Times.* Grand Rapids: Baker, 1977. 238pp.

4.5.16 Hedrick, Charles, ed. *Nag Hammadi, Gnosticism and Early Christianity.* Peabody, Mass.: Hendrickson, 1983. 232pp.

4.5.17 Horsley, Richard A. *Archaeology, History, and Society in Galilee: The Social Context of Jesus and the Rabbis.* Harrisburg, Pa.: Trinity Press International, 1996. 240pp.

4.5.18 Horsley, Richard A., and John S. Hanson. *Bandits, Prophets, and Messiahs: Popular Movements at the Time of Jesus.* San Francisco: Harper, 1985. 271pp.

4.5.19 Jeffers, James S. *The Greco-Roman World of the New Testament Era: Exploring the Background of Early Christianity.* Downers Grove, Ill.: InterVarsity, 1999. 352pp.

4.5.20 Jeremias, Joachim. *Jerusalem in the Time of Jesus: An Investigation into Economic and Social Conditions During the New Testament Period.* Philadelphia: Fortress, 1969. 405pp.

4.5.21 Jonas, Hans. *The Gnostic Religions: The Message of the Alien God at the Beginnings of Christianity.* 3d ed. Boston: Beacon, 2001. 359pp.

4.5.22 MacMullen, Ramsay. *Paganism in the Roman Empire.* New Haven, Conn.: Yale University Press, 1981. 241pp.

4.5.23 Meer, Frederik van der, and Christine Mohrmann. *Atlas of the Early Christian World.* Edited by Mary F. Hedlund and H. H. Rowley. London: Thomas Nelson, 1958. 215pp.

4.5.24 Mowinkel, Sigmund. *He That Cometh.* New York: Abingdon, 1954. 528pp.

4.5.25 Osiek, Carolyn. *What Are They Saying about the Social Setting of the New Testament?* New York: Paulist, 1992. 127pp.

4.5.26 Perkins, Pheme. *Gnosticism and the New Testament.* Minneapolis: Fortress, 1993. 261pp.

4.5.27 Reicke, Bo. *The New Testament Era: The World of the Bible from 500 B.C. to A.D. 100.* Philadelphia: Fortress, 1974. 336pp.

4.5.28 Reitzenstein, Richard. *Hellenistic Mystery-Religions: Their Basic Ideas and Significance.* Pittsburgh: Pickwick, 1977. 572pp.

4.5.29 Roetzel, Calvin J. *The World That Shaped the New Testament.* Atlanta: John Knox, 1985. 120pp.

4.5.30 Rudolph, Kurt. *Gnosis: The Nature and History of Gnosticism.* San Francisco: HarperSanFrancisco, 1987. 411pp.

4.5.31 Sherwin-White, A. N. *Roman Society and Roman Law in the New Testament.* London: Oxford, 1963. 204pp.

4.5.32 Simon, Marcel. *Jewish Sects at the Time of Jesus.* Philadelphia: Fortress, 1967. 180pp.

4.5.33 Wilken, Robert Louis. *The Christians as the Romans Saw Them*. New Haven, Conn.: Yale University Press, 1984. 214pp.

4.5.34 Wilkinson, J. *Jerusalem as Jesus Knew It*. London: Thames and Hudson, 1978. 208pp.

4.5.35 Witherington, Ben, III. *New Testament History: A Narrative Account*. Grand Rapids: Baker, 2001. 430pp.

4.5.36 Yamauchi, Edwin. *Harper's World of the New Testament*. San Francisco: Harper & Row, 1981. 128pp.

See also the series The Library of Early Christianity, edited by Wayne A. Meeks:

4.5.37 Aune, David E. *The New Testament in Its Literary Environment*. Philadelphia: Westminster, 1987. 260pp.

4.5.38 Cohen, Shaye J. D. *From the Maccabees to the Mishnah*. Philadelphia: Westminster, 1987. 251pp.

4.5.39 Grant, Robert M. *Gods and the One God*. Philadelphia: Westminster, 1986. 211pp.

4.5.40 Kugel, James L., and Rowan A. Greer. *Early Biblical Interpretation*. Philadelphia: Westminster, 1986. 214pp.

4.5.41 Malherbe, Abraham J. *Moral Exhortation: A Greco-Roman Sourcebook*. Philadelphia: Westminster, 1986. 178pp.

4.5.42 Meeks, Wayne A. *The Moral World of the First Christians*. Philadelphia: Westminster, 1986. 182pp.

4.5.43 Stambaugh, John E., and David L. Balch. *The New Testament in Its Social Environment*. Philadelphia: Westminster, 1986. 194pp.

4.5.44 Stowers, Stanley K. *Letter Writing in Greco-Roman Antiquity*. Philadelphia: Westminster, 1986. 188pp.

For historical background (and history of interpretation) dealing with major NT characters, see the series, published originally by University of South Carolina Press and reprinted in paperback by Fortress Press, Studies on Personalities of the New Testament, ed. by D. Moody Smith:

4.5.45   Black, C. Clifton. *Mark: Images of an Apostolic Interpreter.* Minneapolis: Fortress, 2001. 400pp.

4.5.46   Culpepper, R. Alan. *John, the Son of Zebedee: The Life of a Legend.* Minneapolis: Fortress, 2000. 367pp.

4.5.47   Gaventa, Beverly Roberts. *Mary: Glimpses of the Mother of Jesus.* Minneapolis: Fortress, 1999. 164pp.

4.5.48   Painter, John. *Just James: The Brother of Jesus in History and Tradition.* Minneapolis: Fortress, 1999. 326pp.

4.5.49   Perkins, Pheme. *Peter: Apostle for the Whole Church.* Minneapolis: Fortress, 2000. 209pp.

4.5.50   Richardson, Peter. *Herod: King of the Jews and Friend of the Romans.* Minneapolis: Fortress, 1999. 360pp.

4.5.51   Roetzel, Calvin J. *Paul: The Man and the Myth.* Minneapolis: Fortress, 1999. 269pp.

4.6 Editions of the New Testament

H I G H L Y   R E C O M M E N D E D

4.6.1   Nestle, Eberhard, Barbara and Kurt Aland, Johannes Karavidopoulos, Carlo M. Martini, and Bruce M. Metzger. *Novum Testamentum Graece.* 27th ed. Stuttgart: Deutsche Bibelgesellschaft, 1993. 810pp.

4.6.2   ————. *The Greek New Testament.* 4th rev. ed. New York: United Bible Societies, 1998. 918pp.

These two volumes represent the same printed text, which is generally regarded as the most reliable presently available. *Novum Testamentum Graece* has a more extensive and detailed text-critical apparatus, while the textual apparatus in *The Greek New Testament* is limited to those textual variants about which there is some controversy and over which translators differ. The textual variants appearing in *The Greek New Testament* are discussed in Bruce M. Metzger, *A Textual Commentary on the Greek New Testament* (§4.11.3). See Kurt and Barbara Aland, *The Text of the New Testament* (§4.11.1), for discussion of other editions of the Greek New Testament.

4.7 Greek Grammars

4.7.1 Blass, F., and A. Debrunner. *A Greek Grammar of the New Testament and Other Early Christian Literature.* Edited by Robert W. Funk. Chicago: University of Chicago Press, 1961. 325pp.

"Blass and Debrunner" was a standard grammar in Germany, which Robert Funk translated, revised, and edited. Emphasizes the relationship of NT Greek to classical Greek, and explains the Greek of the NT by comparison and contrast with the classical models. Especially helpful are subsections that explore difficulties, rare or irregular features, and disputed points. In that it represents the German tradition of grammars, deals with grammatical issues somewhat differently (and at times more satisfactorily) than British and American counterparts. Somewhat more technical (and in some cases more arcane) than Robertson (§4.7.3), and its format and arrangement render it more difficult to use.

4.7.2 Moulton, James Hope, Wilbert Francis Howard, and Nigel Turner. *A Grammar of New Testament Greek.* 4 vols. Edinburgh: T&T Clark, 1976. 293/543/417/174pp.

Begun in 1906 by Moulton but, due to the unexpected deaths of both Moulton and Howard, brought to completion only in 1976 by Turner. The most comprehensive study of NT Greek ever produced by British scholars. Intended as a learned assessment that would be of value for scholars but would serve also as a practical guide for students and pastors in their work of NT exegesis. Discussion of syntax emphasizes relationship of NT Greek to the common Greek of the period ("Koine") and that of the Septuagint, over against classical Greek and in comparison with other Indo-European languages (which are stressed by Robertson (§4.7.3) and Blass-Debrunner [§4.7.1]). Unlike most other grammars offers valuable analysis of differences in construction and style between the various NT writers.

4.7.3 Robertson, A. T. *A Grammar of the Greek New Testament in the Light of Historical Research.* Nashville: Broadman, 1934. 1454pp.

Often called Robertson's "large grammar," this is the most comprehensive and detailed NT grammar available in English. Deals with every significant aspect of the language, including its relationship to other Indo-European tongues, its role within the history of the Greek language, accidence, and virtually every imaginable dimension of syntax. Emphasis is on the function of syntax for communicating exact and precise meaning, and thus the grammar is eminently useful for accurate and insightful interpretation. Although

discussions often reflect views of linguistics and the nature of the development of the NT that are now considered outdated, this volume remains indispensable for serious work in NT Greek.

4.7.4 Smyth, Herbert Weir. *Greek Grammar.* Revised by Gordon M. Mess-
ing. Cambridge, Mass.: Harvard University Press, 1956. 784pp.

Most authoritative, comprehensive, and detailed reference grammar on ancient Greek available. Brief explanations of forms and other grammatical features are extremely useful to readers of the Greek NT in that they serve to
place the grammatical phenomena of the Greek NT within the setting of the
Greek language of antiquity in general. This volume thus complements grammars that deal specifically with the Greek NT, but does not replace them, since
the latter deal with grammatical features of the Greek language that were
prevalent specifically at the time of the writing of the Greek NT.

4.7.5 Wallace, Daniel B. *Greek beyond the Basics: An Exegetical Syntax of
the New Testament.* Grand Rapids: Zondervan, 1996. 827pp.

An "exegetical grammar," intended for those who have a solid foundation in
the essentials of NT Greek and who wish to make serious use of syntactical
analysis in the exegesis of the NT. The most comprehensive of the exegetical
grammars presently available. Makes use of the most current linguistic theory.
Extremely detailed, analytical, and exact. Provides numerous illuminating examples from NT passages. Indeed, there is so much information that it is possible to become lost in the sheer mass of material. Wallace has therefore
produced an abridged version (*The Basics of New Testament Syntax* [§4.7.23])
that omits minor categories, some theoretical discussions, and many scriptural
examples, and is thus better adapted to regular readers of the Greek NT.

4.7.6 Zerwick, Maximilian. *Biblical Greek.* Scripta Pontificii Instititi Biblici
114. Rome: Pontifical Biblical Institute Press, 1963. 185pp.

Reliable and straightforward reference grammar. Selective, in that it makes no
attempt to deal with all of the grammatical phenomena of the Greek NT but
seeks rather to discuss briefly only those grammatical features that tend to be
of most significance for precise understanding of the Greek and for exegesis.

4.7.7 Zerwick, Maximilian, and Mary Grosvenor. *A Grammatical Analysis of
the Greek New Testament.* 5th ed. Rome: Pontifical Biblical Institute,
1996. 778pp.

Moves through the text of the Greek NT, parsing and defining each word. Oc-
casionally provides extremely brief (one sentence) description of background
or significance of the term. Constantly refers the reader to the appropriate

paragraph in Zerwick's *Biblical Greek* (§4.7.6) for fuller discussions of inflections or other grammatical points.

ALSO SIGNIFICANT

4.7.8 Black, David Alan. *It's Still Greek to Me: An Easy-to-Understand Guide to Intermediate Greek.* Grand Rapids: Baker, 1998. 191pp.

4.7.9 ———. *Linguistics for Students of New Testament Greek: A Survey of Basic Concepts and Applications.* 2d ed. Grand Rapids: Baker, 1995. 216pp.

4.7.10 Brooks, James A., and Carlton L. Winbery. *A Morphology of New Testament Greek: A Review and Reference Grammar.* Lanham, Md.: University Press of America, 1994. 468pp.

4.7.11 ———. *Syntax of New Testament Greek.* Lanham, Md.: University Press of America, 1979. 204pp.

4.7.12 Burton, Ernest De Witt. *Syntax of the Moods and Tenses in New Testament Greek.* Chicago: University of Chicago Press, 1900. 215pp.

4.7.13 Dana, H. E., and Julius R. Mantey. *A Manual Grammar of the Greek New Testament.* New York: Macmillan, 1927. 356pp.

4.7.14 Greenlee, J. Harold. *A Concise Exegetical Grammar of New Testament Greek.* 4th ed. Grand Rapids: Eerdmans, 1986. 79pp.

4.7.15 Guthrie, George H., and J. Scott Duvall. *Biblical Greek Exegesis: A Graded Approach to Learning Intermediate and Advanced Greek.* Grand Rapids: Zondervan, 1998. 173pp.

4.7.16 Moule, C. F. D. *An Idiom Book of New Testament Greek.* 2d ed. Cambridge: Cambridge University Press, 1959. 246pp.

4.7.17 Owings, Timothy. *A Cumulative Index to New Testament Greek Grammars.* Grand Rapids: Baker, 1983. 204pp.

4.7.18 Porter, Stanley E., and D. A. Carson, eds. *Biblical Greek Language and Linguistics: Open Questions in Current Research.* Journal for the Study of the New Testament Supplement Series 80. Sheffield: JSOT, 1993. 217pp.

4.7.19 Porter, Stanley E. *Idioms of the Greek New Testament.* Biblical Languages: Greek 2. Sheffield: JSOT, 1992. 339pp.

4.7.20 Porter, Stanley E., ed. *The Language of the New Testament: Classic Essays.*
Journal for the Study of the New Testament Supplement Series 60. Sheffield:
JSOT, 1991. 238pp.

4.7.21 Robertson, A. T., and W. Hersey Davis. *A New Short Grammar of the Greek
Testament.* 10th ed. New York: Harper & Bros., 1958. 454pp.

4.7.22 Robertson, A. T. *The Minister and His Greek New Testament.* New York:
Doran, 1923. 139pp.

4.7.23 Wallace, Daniel B. *The Basics of New Testament Syntax: An Intermediate
Greek Grammar.* Grand Rapids: Zondervan, 2000. 334pp.

4.7.24 Waugh, R. M. L. *The Preacher and His Greek Testament.* London: Epworth,
1953. 104pp.

4.7.25 Young, Richard A. *Intermediate New Testament Greek: A Linguistic and
Exegetical Approach.* Nashville: Broadman & Holman, 1994. 307pp.

POPULAR BEGINNING GRAMMARS

4.7.26 Adam, A. K. M. *A Grammar for New Testament Greek.* Nashville: Abingdon,
1999. 227pp.

4.7.27 Black, David Alan. *Learn to Read New Testament Greek.* Expanded ed. Nashville: Broadman & Holman, 1994. 236pp.

4.7.28 Hewett, James Allen. *New Testament Greek: A Beginning and Intermediate
Grammar.* Peabody, Mass.: Hendrickson, 1986. 234pp.

4.7.29 Jay, Eric. *New Testament Greek: An Introductory Grammar.* London: SPCK,
1958. 350pp.

4.7.30 Kubo, Sakae. *A Beginner's New Testament Greek Grammar.* Rev. ed. Washington, D.C.: University Press of America, 1995. 235pp.

4.7.31 LaSor, William Sanford. *Handbook of New Testament Greek: An Inductive Approach Based on the Greek Text of Acts.* 2 vols. Grand Rapids: Eerdmans,
1973. 260/231pp.

4.7.32 Machen, J. Gresham. *New Testament Greek for Beginners.* New York: Macmillan, 1923. 287pp.

4.7.33 Mounce, William D. *Basics of Biblical Greek.* Grand Rapids: Zondervan, 1999. 459pp.

4.7.34 Wenham, J. W. *The Elements of New Testament Greek.* Cambridge: Cambridge University Press, 1965. 267pp.

4.8 Greek Lexicons

H I G H L Y   R E C O M M E N D E D

4.8.1 Danker, Frederick W. *A Greek-English Lexicon of the New Testament and Other Early Christian Literature.* 3d ed. Revised and edited by Frederick William Danker. Based on Walter Bauer's *Griechisch-deutsches Wörterbuch zu den Schriften des Neuen Testaments und der frühchristlichen Literatur,* 6th edition, edited by Kurt Aland and Barbara Aland, with Viktor Reichmann, and on previous English editions by W. F. Arndt, F. W. Gingrich, and F. W. Danker. Chicago: University of Chicago Press, 2000. 1108pp.

The most current, complete, and authoritative NT lexicon available in English. Contains detailed definitions of each word found in the Greek NT and in much of other early Christian literature. Gives basic definition and, where applicable, groups occurrences of the term around the more specific ways it is used. Entries frequently list not only occurrences in early Christian literature, but also cite the term in Jewish writings (especially the Septuagint, Apocrypha, Pseudepigrapha, Philo, and Josephus). In keeping with most recent linguistic and translation theory, this new edition avoids simple one-word equivalents in favor of extended and specific definitions that provide a fuller explanation of the meaning. This third edition is often cited as "BDAG"; the second edition was "BAGD" [see §4.8.9].

4.8.2 Kubo, Sakae. *A Reader's Greek-English Lexicon of the New Testament.* Grand Rapids: Zondervan, 1975. 327pp.

Moves through the NT book by book, and within books passage by passage, giving the lexical form and basic definition of every word occurring fewer than fifty times in the NT. Each entry indicates the number of times the word appears in the particular book and in the NT as a whole. Words that occur fewer than fifty times in the NT but more than five times in a particular book are placed alphabetically at the beginning of that book in a special vocabulary, thus helping the student to identify the key themes and concerns of the book. Contains an appendix that lists words occurring more than fifty times in the NT, and a second appendix that lists unusual or irregular forms. Helpful for rapid reading of the NT.

4.8.3 Liddell, Henry George, and Robert Scott. *A Greek-English Lexicon.* Revised and augmented by Henry Stuart Jones and Roderick McKenzie. Oxford: Clarendon, 1940. 2111pp.

A massive work that treats the meaning of Greek terms appearing in literary texts from the beginning of literary Greek to 600 C.E. It is thus not a lexicon of NT Greek, but of ancient Greek language in general, although it does include many references to the Septuagint and the NT. Useful for identifying the original meaning of terms, the wide range of their use and their historical development in Greek literature, and their etymology (i.e., the history of the formation of the word as a means of discovering its essential meaning). Functions virtually as a concordance to literary Greek, with specific citations of passages. Very helpful in placing the meaning of NT words in broader semantic perspective and thereby providing depth and nuance to the significance of these terms.

4.8.4 Louw, Johannes P., and Eugene A. Nida. *Greek-English Lexicon of the New Testament Based on Semantic Domains.* 2 vols. New York: United Bible Societies, 1988. 843/375pp.

The first lexicon to make consistent, thoroughgoing use of the most recent developments in linguistic theory. Arranged according to "semantic domains," i.e., types or spheres of meaning, with various NT Greek terms of a particular domain listed and described so that the reader can ascertain how each of these Greek terms communicates and develops its own specific emphases within the larger area. For example, lists "Elevated Land Formations" as a semantic domain, and discusses five separate Greek terms that pertain to that concept. Avoids single-word definitions in favor of fuller, more expansive explanations of meaning. This approach provides a rich and precise understanding of terms and their relationship to associated words.

4.8.5 Moulton, James Hope, and George Millian. *The Vocabulary of the Greek Testament Illustrated from the Papyri and Other Non-Literary Sources.* Grand Rapids: Eerdmans, 1930. 705pp.

The work of Adolf Deissmann (e.g., *Light from the Ancient East* [§4.5.13]), who pioneered the study of everyday (Koine) Greek as represented in Egyptian papyri for understanding the Greek of the NT, was the impetus for this lexicon that explores the use of Greek terms in the papyri (and to a lesser extent in inscriptions) that were essentially contemporary with the NT. When one remembers that the Greek of the NT was in fact everyday spoken Greek, one recognizes the value of this volume, which is the only resource to make accessible this highly relevant information.

4.8.6 Perschbacher, Wesley J., ed. *The New Analytical Greek Lexicon.* Peabody, Mass.: Hendrickson, 1990. 449pp.

Represents the most thorough and accurate revision of George V. Wigram's *Analytical Greek Lexicon of the New Testament,* originally published in 1852. Lexicon gives basic definition of each word in its lexical form, but the real value of this volume is its function as a parsing guide, which offers complete parsing of every word that appears in the Greek NT (including variant readings). Includes paradigms of Greek declensions and conjugations, with explanatory grammatical remarks. Unusual or irregular forms in the lexicon are cross-referenced to explanatory grammatical remarks. Inclusion of Strong's numbers renders this volume accessible to those who do not know Greek well.

4.8.7 Thayer, Joseph Henry. *Greek-English Lexicon of the New Testament: Coded with the Numbering System from Strong's Exhaustive Concordance of the Bible.* Peabody, Mass.: Hendrickson, 1996.

For many years this lexicon, based on the earlier German work by C. G. Wilke and C. L. W. Grimm, was the standard NT Greek lexicon in the English-speaking world. This volume is a reprint of the fourth edition, originally published in 1896. In spite of its age and the fact that it has been superseded by the magisterial volume by BDAG (§4.8.1), it remains a basically reliable work and is often suggestive in its definitions. At points it offers nuances beyond even what can be found in BDAG. It often discusses the etymology of a term (i.e., the history of the formation of the term as providing insight into its essential meaning), which can be helpful, but one must remember that the original meaning of a term is not necessarily carried over into every occurrence, and significance must be determined by context. The inclusion of Strong's numbers makes this lexicon accessible to those who do not know Greek.

ALSO   SIGNIFICANT

4.8.8 Abbott-Smith, G. A. *A Manual Greek Lexicon and Supplement.* 3d ed. Edinburgh: T&T Clark, 1937. 512pp.

4.8.9 Arndt, William F., and F. Wilbur Gingrich. *A Greek-English Lexicon of the New Testament and Other Early Christian Literature: A Translation and Adaptation of the fourth revised and augmented edition of Walter Bauer's Griechisch-Deutsches Wörterbuch zu den Schriften des Neuen Testaments und der übrigen urchristlichen Literatur.* 2d ed. rev. and augmented by F. Wilbur Gingrich and Frederick W. Danker from Walter Bauer's 5th ed., 1958. Chicago: University of Chicago Press, 1979. 900pp.

4.8.10 Bullinger, Ethelbert W. *A Critical Lexicon and Concordance to the English and Greek New Testament*. London: Longmans, Green, 1877. 999pp.

4.8.11 Friberg, Timothy, Barbara Friberg, and Neva F. M. Miller, eds. *Analytical Lexicon to the Greek New Testament*. Grand Rapids: Baker, 2000. 439pp.

4.8.12 Hickie, W. J. *Greek-English Lexicon to the New Testament*. Grand Rapids: Baker, 1977. 213pp.

4.8.13 Mounce, William D. *An Analytical Lexicon to the Greek New Testament*. Grand Rapids: Zondervan, 1993. 542pp.

4.8.14 Newman, Barclay. *A Concise Greek-English Dictionary of the New Testament*. Stuttgart: United Bible Societies, 1993. 203pp.

4.8.15 Nida, Eugene A., and Johannes P. Louw. *Lexical Semantics of the Greek New Testament: A Supplement to the Greek-English Lexicon of the New Testament Based on Semantic Domains*. Society of Biblical Literature Resources for Biblical Study 25. Atlanta: Scholars, 1992. 155pp.

4.8.16 Whiton, James M. *A Lexicon Abridged from Liddell and Scott's Greek-English Lexicon*. New York: American Book Co., 1906. 831pp.

4.9 Theological Dictionaries (Wordbooks)

HIGHLY RECOMMENDED

4.9.1 Balz, Horst, and Gerhard Schneider, eds. *Exegetical Dictionary of the New Testament*. 3 vols. Grand Rapids: Eerdmans, 1990. 463/555/566pp.

Provides basic meaning and explores usage of every NT word in its various contexts for the purposes of providing insight into the exegesis of specific passages and of contributing to the theological understanding of the NT. Each entry includes transliteration, discussion of (usually) all NT occurrences, and bibliography (reference works, articles, monographs) that discusses the word and passages where the word plays a significant role. Most significant words are treated in longer articles that contain more extended bibliographies; fuller discussions of meanings and occurrences; background in classical Greek, the Septuagint, Judaism, and Hellenistic literature; exegetical problems that involve the word; and contribution to NT theology. More current than Kittel's *Theological Dictionary of the New Testament* (§4.9.3) in that it takes into account recent discoveries and newer trends in scholarly investigation and emerging insights into linguistic theory, without adopting any particular linguistic model. Contributors represent the most prominent critical NT scholars in German-speaking countries.

4.9.2   Brown, Colin, ed. *The New International Dictionary of New Testament Theology*. 4 vols. Grand Rapids: Zondervan, 1975–1979. 747/944/1223/592pp.

> Based on *Theologisches Begriffslexikon zum Neuen Testament,* translated, revised, and enlarged by Brown, with additional articles by (primarily) evangelicals from Britain and North America. Concise discussions of major NT theological terms are arranged in English alphabetical order. Discusses the use of each word in classical Greek, the OT, rabbinic literature, and the NT. Contains relatively extensive bibliographies of works in English, French, and German. More concise, more conservative in critical, historical, and theological outlook, and more accessible to the nonspecialist (i.e., less technical) than Kittel's *Theological Dictionary of the New Testament* (§4.9.3).

4.9.3   Kittel, Gerhard, and Gerhard Friedrich. *Theological Dictionary of the New Testament*. 10 vols. Grand Rapids: Eerdmans, 1964–1976. Volumes average 1000pp.

> Translated by Geoffrey Bromiley from *Theologisches Wörterbuch zum Neuen Testament,* this set is without peer among works in this category, although articles vary significantly in quality. The most authoritative, comprehensive, and detailed discussion of major NT terms ever published. Treats every significant NT term by discussing its secular Greek background, its use in the OT (both the Hebrew Bible and the Septuagint), in Jewish sources (especially Philo, Josephus, the Pseudepigrapha, and rabbinic material), and in the NT, often discussing differences among the various NT writers. The final volume comprises comprehensive indexes. The inclusion of discussion of coordinate Hebrew terms enables this set to be used for exploring the meaning of Hebrew terms for OT exegesis. Students should heed the warning of James Barr (*The Semantics of Biblical Language* [London: Oxford University Press, 1961]) that this set could encourage the false conclusion that the meaning of a term in one passage necessarily determines its sense in another passage. But if students are aware of this danger and give primary consideration to the way the word is used in the context of the passage they are interpreting, they will find this resource reliable. Recent printings include Strong's numbers.

A L S O   S I G N I F I C A N T

4.9.4   Barclay, William. *New Testament Words*. Philadelphia: Westminster, 1964. 301pp.

4.9.5 Cremer, H. *Biblico-Theological Lexicon of New Testament Greek.* 4th ed. New York: Scribner's, 1895. 943pp.

4.9.6 Earle, Ralph. *Word Meanings in the New Testament.* Kansas City, Mo.: Beacon Hill, 1986. 487pp.

4.9.7 Kittel, Gerhard, and Gerhard Friedrich. *Theological Dictionary of the New Testament: Abridged in One Volume by Geoffrey W. Bromiley.* Grand Rapids: Eerdmans, 1985. 1356pp.

4.9.8 Richards, Larry. *Expository Dictionary of Bible Words.* Grand Rapids: Zondervan, 1985. 720pp.

4.9.9 Spicq, Ceslas. *Theological Lexicon of the New Testament.* 3 vols. Peabody, Mass.: Hendrickson, 1994. 492/603/691pp.

4.9.10 Trench, Richard C. *Synonyms of the New Testament.* 9th ed. Grand Rapids: Eerdmans, 1953. [Originally published in 1880.] 405pp.

4.9.11 Turner, Nigel. *Christian Words.* Nashville: Thomas Nelson, 1981. 513pp.

4.9.12 Verbrugge, Verlyn. *The NIV Theological Dictionary of New Testament Words: An Abridgment of The New International Dictionary of New Testament Theology.* Grand Rapids: Zondervan, 2000. 1544pp.

4.9.13 Zodhiates, Spiros, ed. *The Complete Word Study Dictionary: New Testament.* Chattanooga, Tenn.: AMG, 1994. 1505pp.

4.10 Concordances to the Greek New Testament

HIGHLY RECOMMENDED

4.10.1 Aland, Kurt, ed. *Vollständige Konkordanz zum Griechischen Neuen Testament.* 2 vols. Berlin: Walter De Gruyter, 1975. 1352/557pp.

Despite the German title, use of this work does not require knowledge of German; terms are listed in Greek, and the introductory material appears in both German and English. Based on Nestle-Aland 26th edition. The work's distinctive value is its extremely detailed presentation of textual variants. Subdivides the occurrences of a word according to the major ways it is used in the NT. Citations are slightly longer than in Moulton-Geden (§4.10.3), thus providing more of the sense of context. Very accurate and complete, but expensive.

4.10.2 Bachmann, H., and W. A. Slaby, eds. *Computer Concordance to the Novum Testamentum Graece.* Edited by the Institute for New Testament Textual Research and the Computer Center of Münster University. Berlin: Walter De Gruyter, 1985. 1964pp.

Produced with the aid of electronic data processing, this concordance benefits from the accuracy and reliability of such technological assistance, while careful and competent work on the part of the editors has guarded against some of the unfortunate byproducts that accompany this kind of electronic searching. Employs Nestle-Aland 26th edition, and any variants appearing in the apparatus in the Nestle-Aland text are simply listed and identified with an asterisk (*), over against the comprehensive and complex identification of variants found in Aland's concordance (§4.10.1). Like Aland, gives more extensive citations than Moulton-Geden, but unlike Moulton-Geden, and especially Aland, does not subdivide occurrences according to the term's use in the NT.

4.10.3 Moulton, W. F., and A. S. Geden. *A Concordance to the Greek Testament.* 6th ed. Edited by I. Howard Marshall. New York: Continuum, 2002. 1120pp.

For many years the standard concordance to the Greek NT in the English-speaking world, it continues to be a valuable resource. The first five editions were based on the Westcott-Hort text, but the new sixth edition is based on the Nestle-Aland 27th edition (§4.6.1), lists important variants, and frequently subdivides occurrences on the basis of the various ways the term is used in the NT or on the basis of the various phrases in which it is found. Gives brief citations, usually long enough to give some basic sense of the immediate context. Recent printings are coded to Strong's numbers.

ALSO SIGNIFICANT

4.10.4 Clapp, Philip S., Barbara Friberg, and Timothy Friberg. *Analytical Concordance of the Greek New Testament.* Grand Rapids: Baker, 1991. 2619pp.

4.10.5 Hoffmann, Paul, Thomas Hieke, and Ulrich Bauer, eds. *Synoptic Concordance: A Greek Concordance to the First Three Gospels in Synoptic Arrangement, Statistically Evaluated, Including Occurrences in Acts.* 4 vols. Berlin: Walter de Gruyter, 1999–2000. 1034/957/997/1066pp.

4.10.6 Kohlenberger, John R., III, Edward W. Goodrick, and James A. Swanson, eds. *The Exhaustive Concordance to the Greek New Testament.* Grand Rapids: Zondervan, 1995. 1055pp.

4.10.7 ———.*The Greek-English Concordance to the New Testament: With the New International Version.* Grand Rapids: Zondervan, 1997. 1131pp.

4.10.8 Smith, J. B. *Greek-English Concordance to the New Testament: A Tabular and Statistical Greek-English Concordance Based on the King James Version with an English-to-Greek Index.* Scottsdale, Pa.: Herald, 1955. 430pp.

4.10.9 Wigram, George V. *The Englishman's Greek Concordance of the New Testament: Coded with Numbering System from Strong's Exhaustive Concordance of the Bible.* 9th ed. Peabody, Mass.: Hendrickson, 1998. [Concordance itself originally published in 1903.] 1020pp.

4.11 Textual Criticism

4.11.1 Aland, Kurt, and Barbara Aland. *The Text of the New Testament: An Introduction to the Critical Editions and to the Theory and Practice of Modern Textual Criticism.* 2d ed. Grand Rapids: Eerdmans, 1989. 366pp.

Thorough, current, and lucid introduction to all major aspects of textual criticism. Produced by two of Germany's most prominent authorities in the field. Enables beginning students to make practical use of the textual apparatus in modern editions of the Greek NT so as to form independent judgments regarding text-critical matters. Especially valuable are the overview of editions of the Greek NT from Erasmus to Nestle-Aland 26th ed., extensive explanation of the textual apparatus in modern editions, discussions of the major criteria for making text-critical decisions, and examples of text-critical analysis from specific NT passages. Gives basic but limited attention to most significant ancient versions and Greek manuscripts. Argues against practice among many NT text critics to make decisions largely on the basis of the "text-type" or "family" of texts to which a manuscript belongs; insists on a more dynamic approach that examines each reading on its own terms without primary attention to the quality of the "family" to which the manuscript belongs.

4.11.2 Metzger, Bruce M. *The Text of the New Testament: Its Transmission, Corruption, and Restoration.* 3d ed. Oxford: Oxford University Press, 1992. 310pp.

Like the Alands' *Text of the New Testament* (§4.11.1), intended as an introduction to NT textual criticism. Covers virtually all areas of the field, but gives special attention to ways in which ancient manuscripts were produced and transmitted, the major witnesses (versions and manuscripts) to the NT text, the various causes of errors in the transmission of the text, and the basic criteria for evaluating variant treadings. Gives examples of textual analysis from selected NT passages. In contrast to the Alands', gives significant role to "text-type" or "family" of manuscripts in the process of making decisions between variant readings.

4.11.3 Metzger, Bruce M., ed. *A Textual Commentary on the Greek New Testament.* 2d ed. Stuttgart: United Bible Societies, 1994. 696pp.

Designed to serve as companion to the fourth edition of the *Greek New Testament,* published by the United Bible Societies, but is of value to those who use other modern editions of the Greek NT. Discusses briefly the most significant textual variants listed in the apparatus of the fourth edition by describing the text-critical bases of the UBS committee's decision to adopt a particular reading and by exploring the interpretive (and sometimes theological) significance of the text-critical issues of the passage. Indeed, sometimes the discussion regarding the reasons why scribes attempted to "correct" the text can bring to light theological issues in passages that modern readers might tend to overlook.

4.11.4 Westcott, Brooke Foss, and Fenton John Anthony Hort. *Introduction to the New Testament in the Original Greek.* New York: Harper & Row, 1882. 324pp. + appendix.

Probably the most significant volume ever produced in the history of the field of textual criticism. Westcott and Hort produced the critical edition of the NT text that was the standard for almost a century, at least in the English-speaking world. In this volume they set forth the principles that remain the fundamental framework for the method of textual criticism. Here also they present their views (adopted by almost all subsequent text-critics) of the "genealogical" relationship between manuscripts, i.e., that virtually all ancient manuscripts and versions belong to a "text-type" or "family," and that judgments between variant manuscript readings should be based in large part on the general reliability or unreliability of the family to which the manuscript belongs. Concludes with a lengthy appendix discussing significant textual variants in specific NT passages.

ALSO SIGNIFICANT

4.11.5 Aland, Barbara, and Joël Delobel, eds. *New Testament Textual Criticism, Exegesis, and Early Church History: A Discussion of Methods.* Kampen: Pharos, 152pp.

4.11.6 Colwell, Ernest Cadman. *Studies in Methodology of Textual Criticism of the New Testament.* Leiden: Brill, 1969. 183pp.

4.11.7 Comfort, Philip Wesley. *The Quest for the Original Text of the New Testament.* Grand Rapids: Baker, 1992. 200pp.

4.11.8 Ehrman, Bart D., and Michael W. Holmes, eds. *The Text of the New Testament in Contemporary Research: Essays on the Status Quaestionis.* Grand Rapids: Eerdmans, 1995. 401pp.

4.11.9   Elliott, J. K. *A Bibliography of Greek New Testament Manuscripts.* 2d ed. Society for New Testament Studies Monograph Series 109. Cambridge: Cambridge University Press, 2000. 314pp.

4.11.10 ———. *Essays and Studies in New Testament Textual Criticism.* Estudios de
filología neotestamentaria. Cordoba: El Almendro, 1992. 172pp.

4.11.11 Elliott, Keith, and Ian Moir. *Manuscripts and the Text of the New Testament:
An Introduction for English Readers.* Edinburgh: T&T Clark, 1995. 111pp.

4.11.12 Epp, Eldon Jay, and Gordon D. Fee. *Studies in the Theory and Method of New
Testament Textual Criticism.* Studies and Documents 45. Grand Rapids: Eerdmans, 1993. 414pp.

4.11.13 Finegan, Jack. *Encountering New Testament Manuscripts: A Working Introduction to Textual Criticism.* Grand Rapids: Eerdmans, 1974. 203pp.

4.11.14 Greenlee, J. Harold. *Introduction to New Testament Textual Criticism.* Rev. ed.
Peabody, Mass.: Hendrickson, 1995. 100pp.

4.11.15 Metzger, Bruce M. *The Early Versions of the New Testament: Their Origin,
Transmission, and Limitations.* Oxford: Clarendon, 1977. 498pp.

4.11.16 ———. *Manuscripts of the Greek Bible: An Introduction to Paleography.* New
York: Oxford, 1991. 150pp.

4.11.17 Souter, Alexander. *The Text and Canon of the New Testament.* London:
Duckworth, 1913. 254pp.

4.11.18 Vaganay, Léon, and Christian-Bernard Amphoux. *An Introduction to New
Testament Textual Criticism.* 2d ed. Cambridge: Cambridge University Press,
1986. 227pp.

4.12 Exegetical Method/Hermeneutics

H I G H L Y   R E C O M M E N D E D

4.12.1   Black, David Alan, and David S. Dockery, eds. *Interpreting the New
Testament: Essays on Methods and Issues.* Nashville: Broadman &
Holman, 2001. 565pp.

Contains 22 essays by leading scholars, all evangelical, mostly younger, and almost all North American. Represents various theological traditions within evangelicalism, though Baptists are in the majority. Includes two fine introductory articles that place critical study of the NT in theological and historical perspective. Peter Davids's "Authority, Hermeneutics, and Criticism" is especially helpful in explaining how critical methods can be employed by those who adopt an evangelical view of the Bible's inspiration. The body of the book is divided into two sections. The first discusses each major critical method, including the newer literary and sociological ones, noting strengths and weaknesses. The second discusses major issues, e.g., the use of the OT in the NT, and the problem of pseudonymity, and describes significant issues for interpretation in various portions of the NT. Practical, reliable, and fair. Comprehensive in the scope of issues treated, but individual discussions are often quite brief.

4.12.2 Fee, Gordon D. *New Testament Exegesis: A Handbook for Students and Pastors*. 3d ed. Louisville: Westminster John Knox, 2002. 195pp.

Leading evangelical scholar offers straightforward step-by-step guidance for beginning students to move from initial encounter with a NT passage to the final stages of writing an exegesis paper or preparing a sermon. Discusses use of original language, but makes allowance for readers who do not know Greek. Describes most individual steps very briefly, but gives fuller treatment to the role of literary genre and analysis of grammatical structure of sentences. Gives almost no attention to critical methods, e.g., form criticism or redaction criticism, or to emerging literary approaches. Should be supplemented with volumes edited by Black-Dockery (§4.12.1), Green (§4.12.3), or Marshall (§4.12.4) that explain the use of these critical approaches in the overall exegetical process.

4.12.3 Green, Joel B., ed. *Hearing the New Testament: Strategies for Interpretation*. Grand Rapids: Eerdmans, 1995. 444pp.

The 19 contributors represent a variety of theological traditions, including but not limited to the evangelical. Contains lucid and nontechnical discussion of a series of hermeneutical issues and modern approaches to NT interpretation. Five NT passages are used as examples throughout, illustrating how each approach can illuminate the meaning of the text. Articles reflect diversity among the various approaches, a diversity that generally characterizes contemporary NT scholarship; an introductory article by Anthony Thiselton helpfully places this present methodological diversity in historical perspective. Each approach is set out by a practitioner (and therefore an advocate) of that approach, who gives little attention to weaknesses or shortcomings. The best introduction to the newer emerging methods and to the most current debates in NT hermeneutics.

4.12.4 Marshall, I. Howard, ed. *New Testament Interpretation: Essays on Principles and Methods*. Grand Rapids: Eerdmans, 1977. 406pp.

Similar to the more recent volume edited by Black-Dockery (§4.12.1) in that it covers many of the same topics and represents an evangelical perspective. The contributors to this volume, however, are mostly British. Articles assume a slightly more sophisticated audience, tend to be generally more supportive of the major critical approaches and less inclined to probe their weaknesses, and give greater attention to specific examples from the NT that illustrate the employment of these methods than is the case with Black-Dockery. Of course, this volume, produced in 1977, does not discuss the newer, emerging methods; for such discussions one should consult the volumes edited by Black-Dockery, and Green (§4.12.3).

4.12.5 Thiselton, Anthony C. *The Two Horizons: New Testament Hermeneutics and Philosophical Description.* Grand Rapids: Eerdmans, 1980. 484pp.

Written by a scholar who reveres the text as scripture, this groundbreaking work has significantly affected subsequent discussions on NT hermeneutics. Explores how philosophical assumptions affect the way NT scholars (and general readers) interpret and apply the text. Surveys modern philosophical thought pertaining to the nature of knowledge and of language and examines how this philosophical reflection can inform the hermeneutical process and illuminate the meaning of NT passages. Includes a number of examples from the study of specific NT passages. Argues that an informed, creative, and complex fusion of the world of the NT with the world of the interpreter is necessary. Highly technical, and assumes at least basic background in nineteenth and twentieth century philosophy. Written in heavy, turbid style. Still, the quality of the discussion and its importance make the effort to digest this book worthwhile.

ALSO SIGNIFICANT

4.12.6 Adam, A. K. M. *What Is Postmodern Biblical Criticism?* Guides to Biblical Scholarship. Minneapolis: Fortress, 1995. 81pp.

4.12.7 Bailey, James L., and Lyle D. Vander Broek. *Literary Forms in the New Testament: A Handbook.* Louisville: Westminster John Knox, 1992. 219pp.

4.12.8 Beardslee, William A. *Literary Criticism of the New Testament.* Guides to Biblical Scholarship. Philadelphia: Fortress, 1970. 86pp.

4.12.9 Collins, Raymond F. *Introduction to the New Testament.* Garden City, N.Y.: Doubleday, 1983. 449pp.

4.12.10 Conzelmann, Hans, and Andreas Lindemann. *Interpreting the New Testament: An Introduction to the Principles and Methods of New Testament Exegesis.* Peabody, Mass.: Hendrickson, 1988. 389pp.

4.12.11 Doty, W. G. *Letters in Primitive Christianity*. Guides to Biblical Scholarship. Philadelphia: Fortress, 1973. 84pp.

4.12.12 Duvall, J. Scott, and Daniel J. Hays. *Grasping God's Word: A Hands-On Approach to Reading, Interpreting, and Applying the Bible*. Grand Rapids: Zondervan, 2001. 429pp.

4.12.13 Elliott, John H. *What Is Social-Scientific Criticism?* Guides to Biblical Scholarship. Minneapolis: Fortress, 1993. 174pp.

4.12.14 Green, Joel B., and Max Turner, eds. *Between Two Horizons: Spanning New Testament Studies and Systematic Theology*. Grand Rapids: Eerdmans, 2000. 246pp.

4.12.15 Holmberg, Bengt. *Sociology and the New Testament: An Appraisal*. Minneapolis: Fortress, 1990. 173pp.

4.12.16 Horrell, David G., ed. *Social-Scientific Approaches to New Testament Interpretation*. Edinburgh: T&T Clark, 1999. 426pp.

4.12.17 Kennedy, George A. *New Testament Interpretation through Rhetorical Criticism*. Studies in Religion. Chapel Hill: University of North Carolina Press, 1984. 171pp.

4.12.18 Ladd, George Eldon. *The New Testament and Criticism*. Grand Rapids: Eerdmans, 1967. 222pp.

4.12.19 Mack, Burton L. *Rhetoric and the New Testament*. Guides to Biblical Scholarship. Minneapolis: Fortress, 1989. 110pp.

4.12.20 Malina, Bruce J. *Christian Origins and Cultural Anthropology: Practical Models for Biblical Interpretation*. Atlanta: John Knox, 1986. 230pp.

4.12.21 ———. *The New Testament World: Insights from Cultural Anthropology*. 3d ed. Louisville: Westminster John Knox, 2001. 256pp.

4.12.22 McKnight, Edgar V. *What Is Form Criticism?* Guides to Biblical Scholarship. Philadelphia: Fortress, 1969. 86pp.

4.12.23 McKnight, Edgar V., and Elizabeth Struthers Malbon, eds. *The New Literary Criticism and the New Testament*. Valley Forge, Pa.: Trinity Press International, 1994. 399pp.

4.12.24 Meyer, Ben F. *Reality and Illusion in New Testament Scholarship: A Primer in Critical Realist Hermeneutics*. Collegeville, Minn.: Liturgical Press, 1994. 244pp.

4.12.25 Osiek, Carolyn. *What Are They Saying about the Social Setting of the New Testament?* Rev. ed. Paulist: New York, 1992. 127pp.

4.12.26 Patte, Daniel. *What Is Structural Exegesis?* Guides to Biblical Scholarship. Philadelphia: Fortress, 1976. 90pp.

4.12.27 ———. *Structural Exegesis for New Testament Critics.* Guides to Biblical Scholarship. Minneapolis: Fortress, 1989. 134pp.

4.12.28 Perrin, Norman. *What Is Redaction Criticism?* Guides to Biblical Scholarship. Philadelphia: Fortress, 1969. 86pp.

4.12.29 Petersen, Norman R. *Literary Criticism for New Testament Critics.* Guides to Biblical Scholarship. Philadelphia: Fortress, 1978. 92pp.

4.12.30 Porter, Stanley E., ed. *Handbook to Exegesis of the New Testament.* New Testament Tools and Studies 25. Leiden: Brill, 1997. 638pp.

4.12.31 Powell, Mark Allan. *What Is Narrative Criticism?* Guides to Biblical Scholarship. Minneapolis: Fortress, 1990. 125pp.

4.12.32 Rohrbaugh, Richard L., ed. *The Social Sciences and New Testament Interpretation.* Peabody, Mass.: Hendrickson, 1996. 240pp.

4.12.33 Stegner, Werner. *Introduction to New Testament Exegesis.* Grand Rapids: Eerdmans, 183pp.

4.12.34 Tuckett, Christopher. *Reading the New Testament: Methods of Interpretation.* Philadelphia: Fortress, 1987. 200pp.

4.12.35 Wilder, Amon N. *Early Christian Rhetoric: The Language of the Gospel.* Cambridge, Mass.: Harvard University Press, 1971. 135pp.

4.13 New Testament Introductions

H I G H L Y   R E C O M M E N D E D

4.13.1 Achtemeier, Paul J., Joel B. Green, and Marianne Meye Thompson. *The New Testament: Its Literature and Theology.* Grand Rapids: Eerdmans, 2001. 544pp.

Synthesizes historical, sociological, cultural, literary, and theological considerations in so as to address the most significant issues that arise in the minds of modern readers of the NT. Reflects the most recent conclusions of the best scholarship in a readable, nontechnical fashion. Describes at points the history of interpretation, but mentions only the most significant figures. Analyzes the content and message of each book and discusses critical issues, e.g., author and date of writing, only insofar as they inform the message of the book. Usually accepts traditional views on date and authorship. Probes significant questions that emerge from the book, e.g., historicity, and examines the book's overall theological message. Provides very selective bibliographies. Probably the most accessible and engaging introduction for persons beginning NT studies.

4.13.2 Brown, Raymond E. *An Introduction to the New Testament*. Anchor Bible Reference Library. New York: Doubleday, 1997. 878pp.

Written by arguably the most prominent Roman Catholic NT scholar of the twentieth century. Produced for students rather than scholars, though scholars will take note of Brown's arguments and conclusions. Focuses on the final form of NT books rather than sources that lie behind the text (which Brown considers too speculative to be of much value, especially for beginning students). Carefully analyzes the content and development of thought within each book, discusses critical issues (e.g., authorship and date), explores theological issues, and offers extensive bibliography of works in English. Although a Roman Catholic, writes for an ecumenical audience. Tends toward moderate positions in critical issues, typically accepting the general critical consensus, but with sensitivity to and appreciation for conservative sentiment and arguments.

4.13.3 Guthrie, Donald. *New Testament Introduction*. 4th ed. Downers Grove, Ill.: InterVarsity, 1990. 1161pp.

Represents the best of British conservative scholarship. Discusses major critical issues for each NT writing, but focuses on authorship and date. Although consistently arrives at conservative conclusions, presents competing positions with clarity, detail, and fairness. Argues especially against pseudepigraphical writings in the NT. At points seems to move in the direction of conservative apologetics, as when he gives more than fifty pages to discussion of the Pastoral Epistles, almost twice the space given to Romans. Yet even those who disagree with certain conclusions will benefit from almost encyclopedic citations and rigorous reasoning.

4.13.4 Johnson, Luke Timothy. *The Writings of the New Testament: An Interpretation*. Rev. ed. Minneapolis: Fortress, 1999. 694pp.

Prominent Roman Catholic scholar explores the origin and shape of the NT in this comprehensive study that is at once both nontechnical and insightful. Written for students rather than scholars, discusses the most important critical issues for an understanding of the message of the NT texts. Presents his own informed conclusions, without referring to other scholars by name in the text, and without footnotes. Concludes each chapter with annotated bibliography of works almost exclusively in English. Incorporates the newest insights into NT origins and hermeneutics, dealing with introductory issues by a model that attends to anthropological, historical, literary, and religious aspects. Concludes with two helpful appendices on the new methods and on the historical Jesus.

4.13.5 Kümmel, Werner Georg. *Introduction to the New Testament.* Rev. ed. Nashville: Abingdon, 1975. 629pp.

A monumental work in the history of NT introductions. For several years has been the standard introduction representing critical German scholarship, and in spite of its age is still reliable and authoritative. Characterized by clear, concise explanations in which Kümmel sets forth the major positions and presents evidence for and against each, finally offering his own conclusion in such a way as to make transparent the process whereby he reached it. Conservatives will often disagree with Kümmel's critical conclusions, but he attempts to deal fairly with the evidence, and he sometimes surprises, as when he argues (against the general critical consensus) for Pauline authorship of Colossians. Especially valuable are his extended discussions on the synoptic problem, the development of the NT canon, and the history of textual criticism.

4.13.6 Wright, N. T. *The New Testament and the People of God.* Vol. 1 of *Christian Origins and the Question of God.* Minneapolis: Fortress, 1992. 535pp.

So sweeping are the concerns of this book that it is difficult to know under which category to classify it. It deals seriously with hermeneutical and methodological matters by discussing the challenge of NT interpretation in the current epistemological climate, and sets forth a hermeneutic that meets the tests provided by the nature of the text on the one hand and the intellectual demands of the modern (or postmodern) world on the other. It seeks to set the world of the NT within the context of Judaism and its interactions with the broader Greco-Roman world. And it shows how an appreciation of this setting, applied to the reading of the NT with methodological rigor and integrity, illuminates the theology of the NT. A truly groundbreaking work, and one that will expand the vision for the study and interpretation of the NT on the part of everyone who reads it, both student and scholar.

ALSO SIGNIFICANT

4.13.7 Carson, D. A., Douglas J. Moo, and Leon Morris. *An Introduction to the New Testament.* Grand Rapids: Zondervan, 1992. 537pp.

4.13.8 Childs, Brevard S. *The New Testament as Canon: An Introduction.* Philadelphia: Fortress, 1985. 572pp.

4.13.9 Drane, John. *Introducing the New Testament.* Minneapolis: Fortress, 1999. 480pp.

4.13.10 Ellis, E. Earle. *The Making of the New Testament Documents.* Biblical Interpretation Series 39. Leiden: Brill, 1999. 517pp.

4.13.11 Ehrman, Bart D. *The New Testament: A Historical Introduction to the Early Christian Writings.* 2d ed. New York: Oxford University Press, 2000. 465pp.

4.13.12 Goodspeed, Edgar J. *An Introduction to the New Testament.* Chicago: University of Chicago Press, 1937. 362pp.

4.13.13 Koester, Helmut. *Introduction to the New Testament.* 2d ed. 2 vols. New York: Walter de Gruyter, 1995. 416/364pp.

4.13.14 Marshall, I. Howard, Stephen Travis, and Ian Paul. *Exploring the New Testament.* Vol. 2. *A Guide to the Letters & Revelation.* Downers Grove, Ill.: InterVarsity, 2002. 300pp.

4.13.15 Martin, Ralph P. *New Testament Foundations.* Rev. ed. 2 vols. Grand Rapids: Eerdmans, 1986. 326/470pp.

4.13.16 McDonald, Lee Martin, and Stanley E. Porter. *Early Christianity and Its Sacred Literature.* Peabody, Mass.: Hendrickson, 2000. 708pp.

4.13.17 McNeile, Alan Hugh. *An Introduction to the Study of the New Testament.* Rev. ed. Oxford: Clarendon, 1953. 486pp.

4.13.18 Moffatt, James. *Introduction to the Literature of the New Testament.* 3d ed. International Theological Library. Edinburgh: T&T Clark, 1918. 659pp.

4.13.19 Moule, C. F. D. *The Birth of the New Testament.* 3d ed. Black's New Testament Commentaries. London: Adam & Charles Black, 1981. 382pp.

4.13.20 Perrin, Norman, and Dennis C. Duling. *The New Testament: An Introduction.* 2d ed. New York: Harcourt, Brace, Jovanovich, 1982. 516pp.

4.13.21 Porter, Stanley E., and Lee Martin McDonald. *New Testament Introduction.* IBR Bibliographies 12. Grand Rapids: Baker, 234pp.

4.13.22 Powell, Mark Allan, ed. *The New Testament Today.* Louisville: Westminster John Knox, 1999. 156pp.

4.13.23 Pregeant, Russell. *Engaging the New Testament: An Interdisciplinary Introduction.* Minneapolis: Fortress, 1995. 581pp.

4.13.24 Robinson, John A. T. *Redating the New Testament.* Philadelphia: Westminster, 1976. 369pp.

4.13.25 Schnelle, Udo. *The History and Theology of the New Testament Writings.* Minneapolis: Fortress, 1998. 573pp.

4.13.26 Schweizer, Eduard. *A Theological Introduction to the New Testament.* Nashville: Abingdon, 1991. 191pp.

4.13.27 Spivey, Robert A., and D. Moody Smith. *Anatomy of the New Testament: A Guide to Its Structure and Meaning.* 5th ed. Englewood Cliffs, N.J.: Prentice Hall, 1995. 513pp.

4.13.28 Strecker, Georg. *History of New Testament Literature.* Harrisburg, Pa.: Trinity Press International, 1997. 238pp.

4.13.29 Weiss, Bernhard. *A Manual of Introduction to the New Testament.* 2 vols. Foreign Biblical Library. London: Hodder & Stoughton, 1888. 420/426pp.

4.13.30 Wenham, David, and Steven Walton. *Exploring the New Testament.* Vol. 1. *A Guide to the Gospels & Acts.* Downers Grove, Ill.: InterVarsity, 2001. 302pp.

4.13.31 Wikenhauser, Alfred. *New Testament Introduction.* New York: Herder & Herder, 1958. 579pp.

4.13.32 Zahn, Theodor. *Introduction to the New Testament.* 3 vols. Edinburgh: T&T Clark, 1909. 564/617/539pp.

4.14 New Testament Theology

HIGHLY   RECOMMENDED

4.14.1 Bultmann, Rudolf. *Theology of the New Testament.* 2 vols. in 1. Scribner Studies in Contemporary Theology. New York: Scribner's, 1955. 366/278pp.

Although many scholars consider Bultmann's method and conclusions to be questionable, this book commands attention because of its great influence on the study of NT theology in the twentieth century. Rejects the notion that the teaching of Jesus is the center of NT theology, since the theology of the NT focuses on Christological claims made for Jesus, and (according to Bultmann) Jesus did not consider himself to be the Messiah. Thus, "the teaching of Jesus is the presupposition for NT theology but not part of that theology itself." New Testament theology is actually expressed in the major documents of the NT: the Pauline and Johannine materials. Bultmann attempts to understand NT theology in terms of its original cultural setting on the one hand, and its contemporary significance (i.e., its enduring significance for the human condition) on the other. Emphasizes the variety of theological views in the NT over against a coherent theology in the NT as a whole. Interprets NT theology according to the existentialism of Martin Heidegger, and inasmuch as Bultmann emphasizes the significance NT theology for the human condition he insists that it should be understood in terms of anthropology. Contains numerous profound insights, but weakened by its wholesale dependence on a particular philosophical model and on questionable historical-critical reconstructions.

4.14.2 Caird, G. B. *New Testament Theology.* Edited by L. D. Hurst. Oxford: Clarendon, 1994. 498pp.

Characterized by the comprehensive knowledge, balanced judgment, and critical reverence for the text that one associates with Caird. Edited and completed by Caird's student, L. D. Hurst, after Caird's untimely death in 1984. Hurst completed the unfinished portions of the book from Caird's lecture notes, articles Caird left behind, and informed conjectures. Yet there are no evident seams or disjunctions of thought; Hurst has presented the thinking of his teacher with great reliability. Adopts a dialogical model that sets forth the theological claims of the various NT authors in the form of a an imaginary roundtable discussion. Caird concludes with a discussion of the theology of Jesus. This roundtable approach has the advantage of recognizing both unity and diversity among the theologies of the NT writers (though Caird emphasizes the unity) and provides a dynamic interplay between their views that illuminates the theologies of the various NT writers and their relationship to one another.

4.14.3 Cullmann, Oscar. *The Christology of the New Testament.* New Testament Library. Rev. ed. Philadelphia: Westminster, 1963. 346pp.

Despite its age remains probably the most authoritative treatment of NT Christology, a central issue in NT theology. Examines the major titles used of Jesus in the NT in terms of their history in the OT and Judaism, in the general history of religion, and especially in the various NT writings. This emphasis on titles has limitations in that the NT presents its Christology in a variety of ways, not simply through titles. But Cullmann recognizes that the broader narrative descriptions of Jesus can in large part be understood in terms of one or more of these major titles. Acknowledges differences but emphasizes continuity and coherence in the employment of these titles among the various NT writers.

4.14.4 Guthrie, Donald. *New Testament Theology.* Downers Grove, Ill.: InterVarsity, 1981. 1064pp.

Written from a clearly evangelical perspective, seeks to present the theology of the NT in such a way as to stress its unity against the prevailing emphasis on the diversity and even incoherence of NT theology, and thus to serve as a "handbook to Christian doctrine." The volume is therefore arranged topically, according to major theological categories, e.g., "God," "Christology," "The Mission of Christ," and "The Future." Discusses the treatment of the theme by individual NT writers and concludes each category with a synthesis or summary. The introductory discussions of the major issues pertaining to NT theology are especially helpful, including such issues as the development of NT theology, the relationship between history and theology, and the tension between variety and unity within the NT.

4.14.5 Ladd, George Eldon. *A Theology of the New Testament.* Revised and edited by Donald A. Hagner. Grand Rapids: Eerdmans, 1993. 764pp.

The original 1974 edition of this comprehensive introduction to NT theology, something of a standard in evangelical circles, has been revised by Hagner, Ladd's student and successor at Fuller Theological Seminary. The value of the book is not limited to evangelicals, for it does not attempt to be novel but seeks to make the NT understandable and to show how the theology of the NT developed and coheres, and how it is distinctive in relation to its environment. An excellent introduction to NT theology: lucid, coherent, concentrating on the final form of the text, informed by critical discussion but not dependent on the more highly speculative critical theories. Argues that NT theology coheres around the concept of "salvation history." Revised edition includes two helpful new chapters dealing with the theology of each of the synoptic evangelists (by R. T. France) and with the issue of unity and diversity in the NT (by David Wenham).

4.14.6 Strecker, Georg. *Theology of the New Testament.* Edited by Friedrich Wilhelm Horn. Louisville: Westminster John Knox, 2000. 758pp.

Offers an alternative perspective and method to most of the other NT theologies recommended here. Emphasizes the diversity of the theology of the various NT witnesses virtually to the point of rejecting a unified or coherent "NT theology." Attempts to incorporate into the study of NT theology insights from a critical reconstruction of the development of the traditions within the NT. Volume is thus arranged historically, beginning with Paul, moving then to the synoptic tradition, then to the Johannine school, and concluding with Jude and James. Moreover, the study of the theology of each of these writers is based in part on the ways in which the NT writer has adapted and interpreted earlier traditions he inherited. Helpful in terms of understanding the distinctive theology of each NT writer, but insofar as Strecker sees continuity within NT theology only in terms of historical development rather than in terms of conceptual coherence, his presentation of NT theology as a whole will be of limited value for those readers who do not share his critical reconstruction of the NT.

A L S O   S I G N I F I C A N T

4.14.7 Adam, A. K. M. *Making Sense of New Testament Theology: "Modern" Problems and Prospects.* Studies in American Biblical Hermeneutics 11. Macon, Ga.: Mercer University Press, 1995. 238pp.

4.14.8 Balla, Peter. *Challenges to New Testament Theology: An Attempt to Justify the Enterprise.* Peabody, Mass.: Hendrickson, 1997. 279pp.

4.14.9 Bauckham, Richard. *God Crucified: Monotheism and Christology in the New Testament.* Grand Rapids: Eerdmans, 1998. 79pp.

4.14.10 Bauer, Walter. *Orthodoxy and Heresy in Earliest Christianity.* Philadelphia: Fortress, 1971. 326pp.

4.14.11 Boers, Hendrikus. *What Is New Testament Theology?* Guides to Biblical Scholarship. Philadelphia: Fortress, 1979. 95pp.

4.14.12 Cullmann, Oscar. *Christ and Time: The Primitive Christian Conception of Time and History.* Rev. ed. Philadelphia: Westminster, 1964. 253pp.

4.14.13 Dodd, C. H. *The Apostolic Preaching and Its Developments.* London: Hodder & Stoughton, 1936. 240pp.

4.14.14 Dunn, James D. G. *The Christ and the Spirit.* 2 vols. Grand Rapids: Eerdmans, 1998. 462/381pp.

4.14.15 ———. *Unity and Diversity in the New Testament: An Inquiry into the Character of Earliest Christianity.* Philadelphia: Westminster, 1977. 470pp.

4.14.16 Goppelt, Leonhard. *Theology of the New Testament.* 2 vols. Grand Rapids: Eerdmans, 1981. 292/348pp.

4.14.17 Hasel, Gerhard F. *New Testament Theology: Basic Issues in the Current Debate.* Grand Rapids: Eerdmans, 1978. 254pp.

4.14.18 Hultgren, Arland J., ed. *New Testament Christology: A Critical Assessment and Annotated Bibliography.* Bibliographies and Indexes in Religious Studies 12. New York: Greenwood, 1988. 485pp.

4.14.19 Jeremias, Joachim. *New Testament Theology*. Part 1. *The Proclamation of Jesus*. New Testament Library. London: SCM, 1971. 330pp.

4.14.20 Kümmel, Werner Georg. *The Theology of the New Testament according to Its Major Witnesses, Jesus—Paul—John*. Nashville: Abingdon, 1973. 350pp.

4.14.21 Morris, Leon. *New Testament Theology*. Grand Rapids: Zondervan, 1986. 368pp.

4.14.22 Räisänen, Heikki. *Beyond New Testament Theology: A Story and a Programme*. Philadelphia: Trinity Press International, 1990. 206pp.

4.14.23 Reumann, John. *Variety and Unity in New Testament Thought*. Oxford Biblical Series. Oxford: Oxford University Press, 1991. 330pp.

4.14.24 Richardson, Alan. *An Introduction to the Theology of the New Testament*. London: SCM, 1958. 423pp.

4.14.25 Schlatter, Adolf. *The Theology of the Apostles: The Development of New Testament Theology*. Grand Rapids: Baker, 1988. (Originally published, in German, in 1922.) 452pp.

4.14.26 ———. *The History of the Christ: The Foundation of New Testament Theology*. Grand Rapids: Baker, 1997. (Originally published in 1923, in German.) 426pp.

4.14.27 Schmithals, Walter. *The Theology of the First Christians*. Louisville: Westminster John Knox, 1997. 396pp.

4.14.28 Stauffer, Ethelbert. *New Testament Theology*. London: SCM, 1955. 373pp.

4.14.29 Via, Dan O. *What Is New Testament Theology?* Guides to Biblical Scholarship New Testament Series. Minneapolis: Fortress, 2002. 160pp.

4.14.30 Weiss, Bernhard. *Biblical Theology of the New Testament*. 2 Vols. Clark's Foreign Theological Library, new series, vols. 12–13. Edinburgh: T&T Clark, 1889–1892. 489/450pp.

4.15 New Testament Ethics

H I G H L Y   R E C O M M E N D E D

4.15.1 Hays, Richard B. *The Moral Vision of the New Testament: A Contemporary Introduction to New Testament Ethics*. San Francisco: HarperSanFrancisco, 1996. 508pp.

Probably the most important book on NT ethics to appear in a generation. Argues that the NT presents a unified ethical vision around the concepts of community, cross, and new creation. Discusses this ethical vision around four "tasks": (1) the "descriptive task" examines the moral vision presented by each of the NT writers; (2) the "synthetic task" attempts to identify the coherence of the NT's moral vision; (3) the "hermeneutical task" explores the method of appropriation of NT ethics to the contemporary scene and assesses the attempts of major theologians and biblical scholars to relate the NT to contemporary ethics; and (4) the "pragmatic task" illustrates the application of NT moral vision to the current issues of violence, divorce, homosexuality, ethnic conflict, and abortion. Valuable for its descriptions of the ethical teachings of the NT writers, although more incisive on the writings of Paul and John than on the other NT materials. Especially helpful in putting forth a comprehensive and coherent method for ethical appropriation.

4.15.2 Matera, Frank J. *New Testament Ethics: The Legacies of Jesus and Paul.* Louisville: Westminster John Knox, 1996. 325pp.

Lucid, nontechnical description of the ethical vision of Jesus and Paul as they are presented in the NT literature itself. Pursues literary analysis of the Gospels (in their final form) and the Pauline Epistles (both authentic and deutero-pauline) to explore the ethical visions of Jesus and Paul. Recognizes that the ethics of Jesus and Paul must be linked to the message and experience of salvation that they both proclaim. While acknowledging diversity in these presentations, finds also a core of unity that gives coherence to the ethics of both Jesus and Paul. In contrast to Hays (§4.15.1) and Verhey (§4.15.3), gives no attention to the method of contemporary ethical appropriation.

4.15.3 Verhey, Allen. *The Great Reversal: Ethics and the New Testament.* Grand Rapids: Eerdmans, 1984. 246pp.

Examines how the material of the NT bears on the church today as a community of moral discernment. Describes the moral teachings of the NT: the ethics of Jesus, of the developing Jesus traditions, and of the final form of the NT books. A survey of literature concerned with the method of using the NT for ethics is followed by a final section in which the author proposes a methodological model for the use of the NT in the church's task of moral discernment. Characterized by careful and informed analysis. Insightful judgment takes fully into account the complexities of the NT data and the process of appropriating them.

ALSO SIGNIFICANT

4.15.4 Dodd, C. H. *Gospel and Law: The Relation of Faith and Ethics in Early Christianity.* New York: Columbia University Press, 1951. 83pp.

4.15.5   Furnish, Victor Paul. *The Love Commandment in the New Testament*. Nashville: Abingdon, 1972. 240pp.

4.15.6   Houlden, J. L. *Ethics and the New Testament*. New York: Oxford University Press, 1977. 133pp.

4.15.7   Lohse, Eduard. *Theological Ethics of the New Testament*. Minneapolis: Fortress, 1991. 236pp.

4.15.8   Longenecker, Richard N. *New Testament Social Ethics for Today*. Grand Rapids, Eerdmans, 1984. 108pp.

4.15.9   Marxsen, Willi. *New Testament Foundations for Christian Ethics*. Minneapolis: Fortress, 1989. 319pp.

4.15.10 Sanders, Jack T. *Ethics in the New Testament: Change and Development*. London: SCM, 1986. 144pp.

4.15.11 Schnackenburg, Rudolf. *The Moral Teaching of the New Testament*. Rev. ed. New York: Herder & Herder, 1969. 387pp.

4.15.12 Schrage, Wolfgang. *The Ethics of the New Testament*. Minneapolis: Fortress, 1988. 369pp.

4.15.13 Yoder, John Howard. *The Politics of Jesus: Vicit Agnus Noster*. Rev. ed. Grand Rapids: Eerdmans, 1993. 252pp.

4.16 Use of the Old Testament in the New Testament

H I G H L Y   R E C O M M E N D E D

4.16.1   Ellis, E. Earle. *The Old Testament in Early Christianity: Canon and Interpretation in the Light of Modern Research*. Grand Rapids: Baker, 1992. 188pp.

Writes from the conviction that "the use of the OT by the NT writers is the primary key to their theology." Divides volume essentially into two parts. The first addresses the OT canon in the early church, its contents (virtually identical with the OT as Protestants acknowledge it), its authority (normative scripture), and its growth (adaptation of earlier traditions to meet contemporary needs). All of this discussion is foundational for the second part, dealing specifically with the use of the OT in the NT: OT quotations in the NT, exegetical methods employed by NT writers (and their relationship to Jewish exegetical practices), and perspectives and presuppositions relating to the NT writers' use of the OT. Informed and incisive analysis, illuminating the message of the NT and guiding contemporary exegetical practices, though tilted toward an evangelical Protestant perspective. Suggests that the NT's use of the OT is in continuity with the dynamics found within the OT itself and offers a model for Christians' contemporary use of Scripture.

4.16.2 Hays, Richard B. *Echoes of Scripture in the Letters of Paul.* New Haven, Conn.: Yale University Press, 1989. 240pp.

Although limited to Paul's use of the OT, this volume has significance for the broader question of the use of the OT by NT writers. Employs current literary insights concerning textuality to identify scriptural quotations or allusions ("echoes"), to determine their function (e.g., Does the writer intend that the reader should consider the original context of the OT passage in question?), and to discern their significance for the meaning of the Pauline text. Analyzes selected passages in Paul's undisputed letters, and concludes that Paul's approach is more church-centered than Christ-centered. Specifically, Paul employs Scripture not as fulfillment of prophecy pointing to Jesus as the Messiah, but as prefigurement of the church, a model for the way the church is to live. Concludes with practical discussion as to whether the modern church should read Scripture in the same way. Especially helpful are the seven tests for determining when OT echoes are present in NT texts.

4.16.3 Longenecker, Richard N., *Biblical Exegesis in the Apostolic Period.* 2d ed. Grand Rapids: Eerdmans, 1999. 238pp.

Engaging and lucid examination of the "exegetical procedures" of the NT writers toward the OT, i.e., explores the major ways in which the NT writers understood the OT, based on their quotations of OT scripture, and in comparison with the exegetical practices represented in Jewish documents from the same period (especially Talmud, Apocrypha, Dead Sea Scrolls, Targums, and Philo). Concludes with a brief but suggestive discussion on the normative character of these NT exegetical practices, i.e., considering whether NT exegetical practices obligate modern Christians to use the OT in the same way.

ALSO SIGNIFICANT

4.16.4 Bruce, F. F. *New Testament Development of Old Testament Themes.* Grand Rapids: Eerdmans, 1968. 122pp.

4.16.5 Dodd, C. H. *According to the Scriptures: The Substructure of New Testament Theology.* London: Nisbet, 1952. 145pp.

4.16.6 Ellis, E. Earle. *Paul's Use of the Old Testament*. Grand Rapids: Eerdmans, 1957. 204pp.

4.16.7 France, R. T. *Jesus and the Old Testament*. Downers Grove, Ill.: InterVarsity, 1971. 286pp.

4.16.8 Goppelt, Leonhard. *Typos: The Typological Interpretation of the Old Testament in the New*. Grand Rapids: Eerdmans, 1981. 264pp.

4.16.9 Juel, Donald. *Messianic Exegesis: Christological Interpretation of the Old Testament in Early Christianity*. Philadelphia: Fortress, 1988. 193pp.

4.16.10 Lindars, Barnabas. *New Testament Apologetic: The Doctrinal Significance of the Old Testament Quotations*. London: SCM, 1961. 302pp.

4.16.11 Moyise, Steve. *The Old Testament in the New: An Introduction*. New York: Continuum, 2002. 160pp.

4.16.12 Moyise, Steve, ed. *The Old Testament in the New Testament: Essays in Honor of J. L. North*. Journal for the Study of the New Testament Supplement Series 189. Sheffield: JSOT, 2000. 302pp.

4.17 New Testament Apocrypha

See also HISTORY AND GEOGRAPHY: PRIMARY SOURCES (§4.4)

H I G H L Y   R E C O M M E N D E D

4.17.1 Elliott, J. K., ed. *The Apocryphal New Testament: A Collection of Apocryphal Christian Literature in an English Translation*. Oxford: Oxford University Press, 1994. 747pp.

Complete revision of the classic work by Montague Rhodes James, originally published in 1924 and used for years as a reliable handbook for the most pertinent NT apocryphal literature. Does not attempt to be exhaustive, but includes those texts deemed to be the oldest, most important, influential, and popular. Yet unlike most other modern editions, is not limited to early texts but includes certain medieval texts considered to be significant for the history of Christian piety and devotion. Offers smooth, elegant, modern translations, along with formal introductions to each text that include fairly extensive bibliography of works in all European languages. Translations and especially introductions are more current than in Hennecke (§4.17.3).

4.17.2 Finegan, Jack. *Hidden Records of the Life of Jesus: An Introduction to the New Testament Apocrypha.* Philadelphia: Pilgrim, 1969. 320pp.

Introduction to the NT apocrypha and the communities through which these apocryphal writings were transmitted. Does not attempt to deal with all apocryphal writings, but selects material considered most likely to contain fragments of early, extracanonical tradition regarding Jesus. Begins with the most comprehensive description available of the communities responsible for the origin and transmission of apocryphal materials, then proceeds to the citation of texts (including both English translation and original Greek and Latin), with explanations pertaining to meaning of difficult elements and relationship to canonical passages.

4.17.3 Hennecke, Edgar. *New Testament Apocrypha.* Edited by Wilhelm Schneemelcher. 2 vols. Philadelphia: Westminster, 1963. 531/951pp.

The standard work on the NT apocrypha. Most comprehensive and authoritative collection of NT apocryphal texts available. Originally produced by Hennecke in 1904, revised by Schneemelcher, and further revised and translated by R. McL. Wilson. First volume contains translations of apocryphal gospels and related writings, while the second contains writings related to the apostles, apocalypses, and related subjects. Each volume includes introductory articles surveying the entire field, followed by brief introductions to and translations of specific apocryphal books or texts. Does not include original language, nor does it offer commentary on the text.

ALSO SIGNIFICANT

4.17.4 Cameron, Ron, ed. *The Other Gospels: Non-Canonical Gospel Texts.* Philadelphia: Westminster, 1982. 191pp.

4.17.5 Charlesworth, James H., and James R. Mueller, eds. *The New Testament Apocrypha and Pseudepigrapha: A Guide to Publications, with Excurses on Apocalypses.* ATLA Bibliography Series 17. Metuchen, N.J.: Scarecrow, 1987. 450pp.

4.17.6 Elliott, J. K., ed. *The Apocryphal Jesus: Legends of the Early Church.* Oxford: Oxford University Press, 1996. 214pp.

4.17.7 Grant, Robert M. *The Secret Sayings of Jesus.* Garden City, N.Y.: Doubleday, 1960. 206pp.

4.17.8 Pagels, Elaine. *The Gnostic Gospels.* New York: Random House, 1979. 182pp.

4.18 New Testament Commentaries: Multivolume

4.18.1 Alford, Henry. *The Greek Testament.* 7th ed. 4 vols. London:
Rivingtons, 1875. Volumes average 400pp.

Produced by an Anglican clergyman of erudition and piety. Commentary is
generally conservative on matters of authenticity and historical accuracy. Assumes some unusual positions, e.g., that the Synoptic Gospels were written in-
dependently of each other. Includes lengthy introductions dealing with critical
matters, with extensive attention to textual criticism. Places Greek text at top of
page, with text-critical notes and commentary on the Greek text below. Comments focus on linguistic matters (both lexical and syntactical), historical background, connections with other biblical passages (especially OT), and history of
interpretation, especially the Fathers whom Alford often quotes in the original
Greek or Latin. Attends seriously to theological implications.

4.18.2 Bengel, John Albert. *Gnomon of the New Testament.* Revised and
translated by Charlton T. Lewis and Marvin R. Vincent. 2 vols. Philadelphia: Perkinpine & Higgins, 1864. 925/980pp.

A true classic in the history of interpretation. Bengel (1687–1752) was a towering pietistic scholar, a professor at the renowned Tübingen University, a pioneer
in NT textual criticism, and the greatest commentator of his generation. Provides a brief introduction to each NT book, discussing its history and significance and offering a detailed outline of its contents. Comments themselves are
terse, but they give careful attention to the original Greek, to immediate context, to connections with other biblical materials, and to theological insights.

4.18.3 Lenski, R. C. H. *Commentary on the New Testament.* 12 vols. Peabody, Mass.: Hendrickson, 1998. Volumes average 1000pp.

Frequently insightful commentary on the final form of the text, making use of
context, lexical and syntactical analysis of original Greek, and canonical connections to determine theological meaning, with some attention to modern
significance. Represents strongly Lutheran orthodox position. Originally published in the 1930s and 1940s and now somewhat dated. Written particularly
for pastors to aid in preaching and teaching.

4.18.4 Nicoll, W. Robertson, ed. *The Expositor's Greek Testament.* 5 vols.
London: Hodder & Stoughton, 1897–1910. Volumes average 500pp.

Intended to be a successor to Alford's *Greek Testament* (§4.18.1), in that it presents commentary on the whole Greek NT accessible to educated English-speaking readers. Prints the text of the Greek NT at the top of the page and fills the
remainder of the page with brief comments on each verse. Contributors represent the most erudite British (especially Scottish) scholars of the period, all of

them churchmen who revered the text as scripture. The commentary therefore frequently offers theological and even pastoral and devotional insights. In spite of its brevity and age, continues to have value but, like Alford (§4.18.1) and Bengel (§4.18.2), should be supplemented with more recent resources.

4.18.5 Wesley, John. *Explanatory Notes upon the New Testament.* London: W. Bowyer, 1755. 1054pp.

Written for "plain, unlettered men" who possess no knowledge of the original language. Suggests alterations at points to the Authorized Version. Attempts to make notes as short and plain as possible, avoiding interpretive or critical difficulties. Based on Bengel (§4.18.2), as Wesley acknowledges, which he translated, abbreviated, and modified. Attempts a "reasonable interpretation" of the text, by construing individual verses in light of the flow of the book or of the broader passage. Although helpful and engaging, one learns more about Wesley's theology, his understanding of the NT bases for his distinct beliefs, and his hermeneutic than about the text itself.

4.19 New Testament Commentaries: Series

HIGHLY RECOMMENDED

4.19.1 Augsburg Commentary on the New Testament. Edited by Roy A. Harrisville, Jack Dean Kingsbury, and Gerhard A. Krodel. 15 vols. Minneapolis: Augsburg, 1980–1990. Volumes average 300pp.

Concise and readable, purpose is to set forth the basic meaning of the text for laypersons, pastors, and teachers. Introductions include brief discussions of background issues. Commentary moves section by section, giving thoughtful attention to contemporary significance as well as to original meaning. Written by Lutheran seminary and university professors.

4.19.2 The IVP New Testament Commentary Series. Edited by Grant R. Osborne. 15 vols. currently available. Downers Grove, Ill.: InterVarsity, 1992–. Volumes average 175pp.

This series, written from an evangelical perspective and intended for pastors and teachers within the church, attempts to join sound exposition based on solid exegesis of the text with implications for theological reflection and Christian devotion relevant for the contemporary church. Contributors include important NT scholars as well as prominent clergy with a reputation for serious biblical exposition. Concentrates on the primary message of larger passages, but at points attends to specific significant exegetical problems.

4.19.3 Black's New Testament Commentary. Edited by Henry Chadwick. Peabody, Mass.: Hendrickson, 1960–.

4.19.4 Harper's New Testament Commentaries. Edited by Henry Chadwick. New York: Harper & Row, 1957–1973.

4.19.5 New International Commentary on the New Testament. Edited by Ned B. Stonehouse (1946–1962), F. F. Bruce (1962–1990), and Gordon D. Fee (1990–). Grand Rapids: Eerdmans, 1951–.

4.19.6 New International Greek Testament Commentary. Edited by I. Howard Marshall, W. Ward Gasque, and Donald A. Hagner. Grand Rapids: Eerdmans, 1978–.

4.19.7 Proclamation Commentaries: The New Testament Witnesses for Preaching. Edited by Gerhard Krodel. Philadelphia: Fortress, 1975–1995.

4.19.8 Tyndale New Testament Commentaries. Edited by Leon Morris. Grand Rapids: Eerdmans, 1958–1989.

4.20 The Gospels: Studies in the Gospels

4.20.1 Burridge, Richard A. *What Are the Gospels? A Comparison with Graeco-Roman Biography.* Cambridge: Cambridge University Press, 1992. 292pp.

The issue of the genre of the Gospels (i.e., the nature of their literary form, and whether it was common in the first-century Mediterranean world or unique to these four NT books) has been disputed for hundreds of years. This volume is the most current, comprehensive, and compelling study of this key issue presently available. Traces the history of the debate, and carefully argues that the genre of our Gospels is not unique but that they share the form of Graeco-Roman biographies. Concludes with brief discussion of the hermeneutical implications of this finding.

4.20.2 Green, Joel B., Scot McKnight, and I. Howard Marshall, eds. *Dictionary of Jesus and the Gospels: A Compendium of Contemporary Biblical Scholarship.* Downers Grove, Ill.: InterVarsity, 1992. 933pp.

Worthy successor to the monumental *Dictionary of Christ and the Gospels* (§4.20.12). Attempts to make the most current Gospel scholarship accessible to students and pastors, but many of these articles also contribute to the scholarly discussion. Represents generally conservative perspective, but committed to responsible employment of critical tools and largely supportive of general critical consensus (e.g., two-source hypothesis for the relationship between synoptic Gospels). Complements more general Bible dictionaries by offering in-depth treatment of subjects that pertain specifically to the Gospels. Deals with theological topics (e.g., Holy Spirit, Son of David, Son of God), methods of interpretation, events (e.g., birth, temptation), each of the four Gospels, background (e.g., Pharisees, revolutionary movements), and items of general interest (e.g., historical reliability of the Gospels, preaching from the Gospels). Each entry concludes with brief bibliography of works mostly in English, but also in German and French.

4.20.3 Kingsbury, Jack Dean. *Jesus Christ in Matthew, Mark, and Luke.* Proclamation Commentaries. Philadelphia: Fortress, 1981. 134pp.

Lucid and concise presentation of the major aspects of the theology of the Synoptic Gospels and the hypothetical sayings-source Q. Deals with each Gospel in turn, discussing the "accomplishment" of the evangelist, i.e., what he set out to do and how he shaped his Gospel in such a way as to fulfill his theological and pastoral purposes in writing; the figure of Jesus; the mission of Jesus; discipleship; and soteriology. Emphasizes final composition of the Gospel, giving little attention to sources lying behind the Gospels or to the evangelists' redaction of these sources. Contains extensive footnotes.

4.20.4 Streeter, Burnett Hillman. *The Four Gospels: A Study in Origins.* London: Macmillan, 1926. 624pp.

A classic work, still considered the standard in its discussion of the synoptic problem (i.e., the literary and historical relationships between the first three Gospels) and synoptic origins (i.e., the date and place of origin of the Gospels). Although Streeter's text-critical discussion of the manuscript tradition is somewhat dated, his arguments for the two-source hypothesis for the synoptic problem (still by far the predominant scholarly position) have become the basis for all subsequent debate on this central issue.

ALSO SIGNIFICANT

4.20.5 Bauckham, Richard. *The Gospels for All Christians: Rethinking the Gospel Audiences.* Grand Rapids: Eerdmans, 1998. 220pp.

4.20.6 Blomberg, Craig L. *The Historical Reliability of the Gospels.* Downers Grove, Ill.: InterVarsity, 1987. 268pp.

4.20.7 ——. *Jesus and the Gospels: An Introduction and Survey.* Nashville: Broadman & Holman, 1997. 440pp.

4.20.8 Bultmann, Rudolf. *The History of the Synoptic Tradition.* Rev. ed. New York: Harper & Row, 1963. 462pp.

4.20.9 Dibelius, Martin. *From Tradition to Gospel.* Cambridge: James Clarke, 1971. 311pp.

4.20.10 Farmer, William R. *The Synoptic Problem: A Critical Analysis.* New York: Macmillan, 1964. 308pp.

4.20.11 Gerhardsson, Birger. *The Origins of the Gospel Traditions.* Philadelphia: Fortress, 95pp.

4.20.12 Hastings, James, ed. *A Dictionary of Christ and the Gospels.* 2 vols. Edinburgh: T&T Clark, 1906. 936/912pp.

4.20.13 Hengel, Martin. *The Four Gospels and the One Gospel of Jesus Christ.* Harrisburg, Pa.: Trinity Press International, 2000. 354pp.

4.20.14 Kingsbury, Jack Dean, ed. *Gospel Interpretation: Narrative-Critical and Social-Scientific Approaches.* Harrisburg, Pa.: Trinity Press International, 1997. 307pp.

4.20.15 Lightfoot, Robert Henry. *History and Interpretation in the Gospels.* London: Hodder & Stoughton, 1935. 236pp.

4.20.16 Malina, Bruce J. *The Social World of Jesus and the Gospels.* London: Routledge, 1996. 255pp.

4.20.17 Malina, Bruce J., and Richard L. Rohrbaugh. *Social Science Commentary on the Synoptic Gospels.* 2d ed. Minneapolis: Fortress, 2002. 448pp.

4.20.18 Mays, James Luther, ed. *Interpreting the Gospels.* Philadelphia: Fortress, 1981. 307pp.

4.20.19 McKnight, Scot, and Matthew C. Williams. *The Synoptic Gospels: An Annotated Bibliography.* IBR Bibliographies 6. Grand Rapids: Baker, 2000. 126pp.

4.20.20 Mills, Watson E. *Index to Periodical Literature on Christ and the Gospels.* New Testament Tools and Studies 27. Leiden: Brill, 1998. 959pp.

4.20.21 Rohde, Joachim. *Rediscovering the Teaching of the Evangelists.* New Testament Library. London: SCM, 1968. 278pp.

4.20.22 Stein, Robert H. *The Synoptic Problem: An Introduction.* Grand Rapids: Baker, 1987. 292pp.

4.20.23 Stonehouse, Ned B. *The Witness of the Synoptic Gospels to Christ.* Grand Rapids: Baker, 1979. Reprint of *The Witness of Matthew and Mark to Christ* (Philadelphia: Presbyterian Guardian, 1944, 269pp.) and *The Witness of Luke to Christ* (Grand Rapids: Eerdmans, 1951, 184pp.).

4.20.24 Talbert, Charles H. *What Is a Gospel? The Genre of the Canonical Gospels.* Philadelphia: Fortress, 1977. 147pp.

4.20.25 Taylor, Vincent. *The Formation of the Gospel Tradition.* London: Macmillan, 1960. 217pp.

4.20.26 Theissen, Gerd. *The Gospels in Context: Social and Political History in the Synoptic Tradition.* Minneapolis: Fortress, 1991. 320pp.

4.21 Studies in Specific Aspects of the Gospels

H I G H L Y   R E C O M M E N D E D

4.21.1 Brown, Raymond E. *The Birth of the Messiah: A Commentary on the Infancy Narratives in the Gospels of Matthew and Luke.* Rev. ed. Anchor Bible Reference Library. New York: Doubleday, 1993. 752pp.

Written by a leading Roman Catholic scholar, the most complete study ever produced on the infancy narratives in Matthew and Luke. Deals thoroughly with virtually every aspect of these passages, with encyclopedic citation of both ancient and modern sources. Focuses on the distinctive emphases of Matthew and Luke. Combines meticulous critical analysis with reverence for the text as the church's scripture. Gives significant attention to theological (and at points pastoral) issues. Although it deals only with the first two chapters of each of these Gospels, it sheds light on the theological purpose and message of the two Gospels as a whole.

4.21.2 Brown, Raymond E. *The Death of the Messiah: A Commentary on the Passion Narratives.* 2 vols. Anchor Bible Reference Library. New York: Doubleday, 1994. 1608pp.

Companion to Brown's *Birth of the Messiah* (§4.21.1). Again, probably the most complete examination of the passion narratives ever compiled. Focuses on the final form of the text, and analyzes each of the four accounts in terms of the distinctive theological and pastoral concerns of each of the evangelists. Also attends to the historical events that lie behind the accounts and to the development of traditions in the sources that were used by the final Gospel writers. Historical conclusions are informed by critical analysis of the texts, but are generally supportive of the historical reliability of the accounts. Since the passion narrative climaxes each of the Gospels, this study provides insight into the theology of the Gospels as a whole.

4.21.3   Dodd, C. H. *The Parables of the Kingdom.* New York: Scribner's, 1961. 176pp.

Extremely significant book in the history of parable interpretation, by a towering British NT scholar. Follows Jülicher (*Die Gleichnisreden Jesu,* 1899–1910) in his insistence that the parables, as Jesus spoke them, had one point only, and that the details of the story had no spiritual counterpoint but existed simply to give "color" to the story, with the consequence that Jesus' "explanations" to the parables (e.g., Matt 13:18–23) were later creations by the church or the evangelists. Dodd thus concentrates on the meaning the parables had for Jesus, and gives no attention to their function within their final Gospel contexts. Argues that the parables consistently proclaimed "realized eschatology," i.e., announced that the end-time kingdom of God was already coming to earth in the ministry of Jesus. While somewhat dated, Dodd's book reflects massive learning and continues to provide helpful insights from historical background and the analysis of the language of the parables.

4.21.4   Hultgren, Arland J. *The Parables of Jesus: A Commentary.* Grand Rapids: Eerdmans, 2000. 522pp.

Of the many books that have appeared recently offering commentary on all or most of the NT parables, this is the most comprehensive in scope, current in its employment of the most recent insights, interactive with both older and more recent scholarship, inclusive in target audience (scholars, students, and pastors), and insightful into the theological implications of the exegesis. Holistic in method, giving attention to historical background and development of the parables in the tradition. Introduction describes the methods for identifying and classifying parables, the distinguishing features of parables, and various interpretive approaches. Examines the 38 NT parables in depth. Line-by-line exegesis attends to the original form of each parable as Jesus spoke it, but concentrates on its meaning in its final Gospel context. In each case offers a fresh translation, notes on the text and translation, exegetical commentary, (brief) theological exposition, and select bibliography. Adopts critical methods, but conclusions are generally conservative.

4.21.5 Jeremias, Joachim. *Rediscovering the Parables.* New York: Scribner's, 1966. 191pp.

Like Dodd (§4.21.3), Jeremias is concerned to interpret the parables as Jesus understood them, and likewise follows Jülicher in insisting that these parables had one point only and contained no allegorical tendencies such as we find in the explanations to the parables the evangelists allegedly put into Jesus' mouth. Jeremias's academic focus was intertestamental and first-century Jewish background, and therefore he emphasized this setting much more than Dodd in his interpretation of the parables. He rejected as one-sided Dodd's insistence on "realized eschatology," and argued instead that we should interpret each parable in terms of the specific situation in Jesus' life that called it forth. Jeremias believed this almost always involved conflict, with the result that he saw the parables as "weapons of controversy." The continuing value of this work is its careful attention to the Jewish background of the details of each of Jesus' parables.

4.21.6 Scott, Bernard Brandon. *Hear Then the Parable: A Commentary on the Parables of Jesus.* Minneapolis: Fortress, 1989. 464pp.

Commentary on 25 parables of Jesus in the NT. This volume is set off from the many other commentaries on Jesus' parables by its creative synthesis of recent insights from the emerging literary, sociological, and cultural anthropological approaches with more traditional concerns for historical background, the authenticity of the parable, and the role of the parable within its final Gospel context. Characterized by original interpretations and fresh insights, especially from social history and from rabbinic and other Jewish sources. Even when the reader disagrees with the interpretation, it will often cause the reader to think in new ways about the parable and thus to obtain useful insights.

ALSO SIGNIFICANT

4.21.7 Bailey, Kenneth Ewing. *Poet and Peasant: A Literary Cultural Approach to the Parables in Luke.* Grand Rapids: Eerdmans, 1976. 238pp.

4.21.8 ———. *Through Peasant Eyes: More Lucan Parables, Their Culture and Style.* Grand Rapids: Eerdmans, 1980. 187pp.

4.21.9 Blomberg, Craig L. *Interpreting the Parables.* Downers Grove, Ill.: InterVarsity, 1990. 333pp.

4.21.10 Borsch, Frederick Houk. *Many Things in Parables: Extravagant Stories of New Community.* Philadelphia: Fortress, 1988. 167pp.

4.21.11 Carter, Warren, and Heil, John Paul. *Matthew's Parables: Audience-Oriented Perspectives*. Catholic Biblical Quarterly Monograph Series 30. Washington, D.C.: Catholic Biblical Association of America, 1998. 255pp.

4.21.12 Donahue, John R. *The Gospel in Parable: Metaphor, Narrative and Theology in the Synoptic Gospels*. Philadelphia: Fortress, 1988. 254pp.

4.21.13 Gowler, David B. *What Are They Saying about the Parables?* New York: Paulist, 2000. 150pp.

4.21.14 Jones, Ivor Harold. *The Matthean Parables: A Literary and Historical Commentary*. Supplements to Novum Testamentum 80. Leiden: Brill, 1995. 602pp.

4.21.15 Kingsbury, Jack Dean. *The Parables of Jesus in Matthew 13: A Study in Redaction Criticism*. London: SCM, 1969. 180pp.

4.21.16 Kissinger, Warren S. *The Parables of Jesus: A History of Interpretation and Bibliography*. Metuchen, N.J.: Scarecrow, 1979. 439pp.

4.21.17 Lambrecht, Jan. *Once More Astonished: The Parables of Jesus*. New York: Crossroad, 1983. 245pp.

4.21.18 ———. *Out of the Treasure: The Parables in the Gospel of Matthew*. Louvain Theological and Pastoral Monographs 10. Louvain: Peeters, 1991. 299pp.

4.21.19 Longenecker, Richard N., ed. *The Challenge of Jesus' Parables*. Grand Rapids: Eerdmans, 2000. 324pp.

4.21.20 Manson, T. W. *The Sayings of Jesus: As Recorded in the Gospels according to St. Matthew and St. Luke Arranged with Introduction and Commentary*. London: SCM, 1949. 347pp.

4.21.21 Shillington, V. George, ed. *Jesus and His Parables: Interpreting the Parables of Jesus Today*. Edinburgh: T&T Clark, 1997. 199pp.

4.21.22 Sider, John W. *Interpreting the Parables: A Hermeneutical Guide to Their Meaning*. Studies in Contemporary Interpretation. Grand Rapids: Zondervan, 1995. 283pp.

4.21.23 Theissen, Gerd. *The Miracle Stories of the Early Christian Tradition*. Philadelphia: Fortress, 1983. 322pp.

4.21.24 Tolbert, Mary Ann. *Perspectives on the Parables: An Approach to Multiple Interpretations*. Philadelphia: Fortress, 1979. 141pp.

4.21.25 Westermann, Claus. *The Parables of Jesus in Light of the Old Testament*. Edinburgh: T&T Clark, 1990. 211pp.

4.21.26 Young, Brad H. *The Parables: Jewish Tradition and Christian Interpretation*. Peabody, Mass.: Hendrickson, 1998. 332pp.

4.22 Studies in the Life of Christ

H I G H L Y   R E C O M M E N D E D

4.22.1 Crossan, John Dominic. *The Historical Jesus: The Life of a Mediterranean Jewish Peasant*. San Francisco: Harper, 1991. 507pp.

Written by the co-chair of the Jesus Seminar, this volume reflects in general the perspective of that group. Crossan contends that the basic problem with life-of-Jesus research lies with method. Crossan seeks to remedy this situation by presenting a complex process of historical reconstruction, employing cultural anthropology, history of first-century Mediterranean culture, and literary criticism (i.e., the procedure separating the actual words and deeds of Jesus from later expansions). The Jesus that emerges represents a social and political response on the part of the peasantry to economic, religious, and political exploitation of the ruling classes. Though not a revolutionary, he sought to relieve the plight of the peasant class by proclaiming that God reigns on behalf of the oppressed, even in the most brutal circumstances. Jesus challenged the ruling authorities in indirect as well as direct ways, such as providing healing to the people through the use of magic, thereby diverting the sick away from the usual channels of healing that came through temple rituals and authorities. This view rejects the notion that Jesus thought of himself in any way as the Jewish Messiah and repudiates the notion that one can speak historically of a bodily resurrection. This volume is included under "highly recommended" not because it offers significant help in our understanding of the historical Jesus (since many scholars consider it to be tendentious and extremely conjectural), but because it represents a major stream of recent history-of-Jesus research.

4.22.2 Meier, John P. *A Marginal Jew: Rethinking the Historical Jesus*. 3 vols. Anchor Bible Reference Library. New York: Doubleday, 1987, 1994, 2001. 496/1232/720pp.

The most massive, detailed, meticulous, and careful study available. Written by a leading American Roman Catholic scholar. Approach involves imagining an ecumenical group of historical critics (Catholic, Protestant, Jewish, Muslim) who were called upon to develop a reconstructed Jesus on whom they could all agree. Meier acknowledges that this reconstructed "historical Jesus" is not identical with the real Jesus, but a "scientific construct, a theoretical abstraction of modern scholars that coincides only partially with the real Jesus of Nazareth." Yet, according to Meier, this is the best scholarship can do. This "historical Jesus" is a prophet of the last days, which he proclaims as imminent and yet in some sense present in his own ministry; in recognition of that fact he called twelve disciples as a symbolic expression of the gathering of the twelve tribes of Israel, gave instruction regarding the true meaning of the Mosaic law, and performed exorcisms and healings.

4.22.3 Powell, Mark Allan. *Jesus as a Figure in History: How Modern Historians View the Man from Galilee.* Louisville: Westminster John Knox, 1998. 238pp.

The most comprehensive and balanced of all surveys of current Jesus research. Places the current interest in recovering the historical Jesus ("the third quest") in historical context by describing earlier attempts (beginning with Reimarus in 1774) and in methodological context by exploring the sources and criteria scholars employ in this task. Discusses in turn each of the major scholars or team of scholars involved in the current quest, describing their approach, summarizing their results (i.e., the portrait of Jesus they present), and identifying criticisms leveled by other historians. Concluding chapter identifies major issues that have emerged and presents likely future directions. Powell is descriptive throughout, and refuses to offer his own assessments; even evaluations of the various scholars are presented as reports of criticism leveled by others in the guild.

4.22.4 Sanders, E. P. *Jesus and Judaism.* Philadelphia: Fortress, 1985. 444pp.

Written by a leading authority on first-century Judaism. Adopts an approach that emphasizes critical reliance on canonical traditions (especially synoptic) and that depends heavily on the "social world" of first-century Judaism. Argues that Jesus adopted a restoration theology that insisted that God was about to restore Israel in fulfillment of covenant promises, and that Jesus considered himself the eschatological prophet who announced this restoration and who, along with his disciples, would be central to it. Jesus announced this restoration through his proclamation of the kingdom and his healings (a sign that God was already beginning to usher in his kingdom), and especially through the choosing of the twelve and the cleansing of the temple, which was the direct cause of his crucifixion. A highly regarded study, and one that significantly illumines the Jewish setting for Jesus' life and ministry. See also the author's abridged but more current study, *The Historical Figure of Jesus* (§4.22.30).

4.22.5 Schweitzer, Albert. *The Quest of the Historical Jesus: The First Complete Edition.* Edited by John Bowden. Minneapolis: Fortress, 2001. 608pp. (Originally published, in German, in 1906.)

A brilliant, groundbreaking work. Presents in engaging and elegant style a survey of the massive literature on the historical Jesus from Reimarus (1774) through Wrede (1901), who wrote just five years before the original German edition of Schweitzer's book. Schweitzer concluded that these scholars had not discovered the historical Jesus at all, but rather had created a Jesus in their own modern European image. Schweitzer himself insisted that the historical Jesus was committed to a "thoroughgoing eschatology," i.e., convinced that God was about to inaugurate the end-time kingdom and that his death would play a central role in that inauguration. This volume is of supreme importance in history-of-Jesus research, and in spite of its age it continues to have much to teach all subsequent Jesus research.

4.22.6 Wright, N. T. *Jesus and the Victory of God.* Vol. 2 of *Christian Origins and the Question of God.* Minneapolis: Fortress, 1996. 741pp.

This second volume in a projected five-volume project rests on the fundamental methodological and historical discussions of the first volume, *The New Testament and the People of God* (§4.13.6). Writes as a historian and a committed Christian, and insists that history and faith need not be separated in this search for Jesus; correspondingly, argues against Kähler's (*The So-Called Historical Jesus and the Historic Biblical Christ* [§4.22.22]) distinction (that often resurfaces) between the Jesus of history and the Christ of faith whom the church confesses. Insists that historians must take seriously the oldest traditions we have, i.e., those found within the synoptic Gospels, and arrive at a portrait of the historical Jesus that best explains these data in light of what we know about first-century Judaism and the development of the Jesus movement into the second century. Moves from a reconstruction of Jesus' acts (deeds and speech) to conclusions regarding his beliefs and mindset. Sees Jesus as an eschatological prophet who declared the inauguration of God's kingdom and who believed that he, as the Messiah, was the embodiment of this coming kingdom. Although his portrait of Jesus generally follows the synoptic framework, Wright frequently offers bold and original insights on Jesus' life, words, and deeds.

ALSO   SIGNIFICANT

4.22.7 Bock, Darrell L. *Studying the Historical Jesus: A Guide to Sources and Methods.* Grand Rapids: Baker, 2002. 224pp.

4.22.8 Borg, Marcus J. *Jesus: A New Vision.* San Francisco: Harper & Row, 1987. 216pp.

4.22.9 ———. *Meeting Jesus Again for the First Time: The Historical Jesus and the Heart of Contemporary Faith.* San Francisco: HarperSanFrancisco, 1994. 150pp.

4.22.10   Borg, Marcus J., and N. T. Wright. *The Meaning of Jesus: Two Visions*. London: SPCK, 1999. 290pp.

4.22.11   Bornkamm, Günther. *Jesus of Nazareth*. New York: Harper & Bros., 1960. 239pp.

4.22.12   Conzelmann, Hans. *Jesus*. Philadelphia: Fortress, 1973. 116pp.

4.22.13   Dalman, Gustaf. *The Words of Jesus: Considered in the Light of Post-Biblical Jewish Writings and the Aramaic Language*. Edinburgh: T&T Clark, 1902. 350pp.

4.22.14   DeJonge, Marinus. *Jesus: The Servant-Messiah*. New Haven, Conn.: Yale University Press, 1991. 115pp.

4.22.15   Dodd, C. H. *The Founder of Christianity*. New York: Macmillan, 1970. 181pp.

4.22.16   Dunn, James D. G. *The Evidence for Jesus*. Atlanta: John Knox, 1985. 113pp.

4.22.17   Evans, C. Stephen. *The Historical Christ and the Jesus of Faith: The Incarnational Narrative as History*. Oxford: Clarendon, 1996. 386pp.

4.22.18   Evans, Craig A. *Jesus*. IBR Bibliographies 5. Grand Rapids: Baker, 1992. 152pp.

4.22.19   Guthrie, Donald. *Jesus the Messiah: An Illustrated Life of Christ*. Grand Rapids: Zondervan, 1972. 386pp.

4.22.20   ———. *A Shorter Life of Christ*. Grand Rapids: Zondervan, 1970. 186pp.

4.22.21   Johnson, Luke Timothy. *The Real Jesus: The Misguided Quest for the Historical Jesus and the Truth of the Traditional Gospels*. San Francisco: HarperSanFrancisco, 1996. 182pp.

4.22.22   Kähler, Martin. *The So-Called Historical Jesus and the Historic Biblical Christ*. Philadelphia: Fortress, 1964. 153pp.

4.22.23   Keck, Leander E. *A Future for the Historical Jesus: The Place of Jesus in Preaching and Theology*. Nashville: Abingdon, 1971. 271pp.

4.22.24   ———. *Who Is Jesus? History in Perfect Tense*. Personalities of the New Testament. Minneapolis: Fortress, 2001. 207pp.

4.22.25 Kissinger, Warren S. *The Lives of Jesus: A History and Bibliography.* New York: Garland, 1985. 230pp.

4.22.26 Mack, Burton L. *A Myth of Innocence: Mark and Christian Origins.* Philadelphia: Fortress, 1988. 432pp.

4.22.27 Marshall, I. Howard. *I Believe in the Historical Jesus.* Grand Rapids: Eerdmans, 1977. 253pp.

4.22.28 O'Collins, Gerald. *What Are They Saying about Jesus?* Rev. ed. New York: Paulist, 1983. 77pp.

4.22.29 Robinson, James M. *A New Quest of the Historical Jesus.* Studies in Biblical Theology 25. London: SCM, 1959. 128pp.

4.22.30 Sanders, E. P. *The Historical Figure of Jesus.* New York: Penguin, 1994. 337pp.

4.22.31 Strauss, David Friedrich. *The Life of Jesus Critically Examined.* Lives of Jesus Series. Philadelphia: Fortress, 1972. 812pp. (Originally published 1835, in German.)

4.22.32 Stuhlmacher, Peter. *Jesus of Nazareth, Christ of Faith.* Peabody, Mass.: Hendrickson, 1993. 109pp.

4.22.33 Vermes, Geza. *Jesus the Jew: A Historian's Reading of the Gospels.* London: Collins, 1973. 286pp.

4.22.34 ———. *The Religion of Jesus the Jew.* Minneapolis: Fortress, 1993. 244pp.

4.22.35 Weiss, Johannes. *Jesus' Proclamation of the Kingdom of God.* Philadelphia: Fortress, 1971. 148pp. (Originally published 1892, in German.)

4.22.36 Witherington, Ben, III. *The Christology of Jesus.* Minneapolis: Fortress, 1990. 310pp.

4.22.37 ———. *Jesus the Sage: The Pilgrimage of Wisdom.* Minneapolis: Fortress, 1994. 436pp.

4.22.38 ———. *Jesus the Seer: The Progress of Prophecy.* Peabody, Mass.: Hendrickson, 1999. 427pp

4.22.39 ———. *The Jesus Quest: The Third Search for the Jew of Nazareth.* Downers Grove, Ill.: InterVarsity, 1995. 304pp.

4.23 Gospel Harmonies/Synopses

H I G H L Y   R E C O M M E N D E D

4.23.1 Aland, Kurt, ed. *Synopsis of the Four Gospels: Completely Revised on the Basis of the Greek Text of Nestle-Aland 26th Edition and the Greek New Testament 3d edition.* New York: United Bible Societies, 1985. 361pp.

Now generally considered the standard, it is the most complete and accurate Gospel synopsis, employing the best and most current Greek text. Greek and English (RSV) appear on opposite pages. Substantial text-critical notes (from Nestle-Aland, 26th ed.) are supplied under the Greek text with comparisons with readings of other major English translations under the English text. Presents parallel passages in columns, and (unlike Throckmorton [§4.23.3]) includes John along with the synoptics.

4.23.2 Huck, Albert. *A Synopsis of the First Three Gospels with the Addition of the Johannine Parallels.* 13th ed. Revised by Heinrich Greeven. Grand Rapids: Eerdmans, 1982. 298pp.

Huck's *Synopsis* appeared first in 1892. This most recent edition is based on Greeven's own recension of the Greek text. Includes extensive textual apparatus. Refers to parallels in apocryphal gospels and similar noncanonical sources. Notes are in German and English, but (unlike Aland [§4.23.1]) the NT text is entirely in Greek. Has some helpful features absent in Aland, but the use of Greeven's own Greek text and textual apparatus renders it less useful than Aland.

4.23.3 Throckmorton, Burton H. *Gospel Parallels: A Comparison of the Synoptic Gospels.* 5th ed. Nashville: Thomas Nelson, 1992. 212pp.

Arranges synoptic Gospels in parallel columns, employing the New Revised Standard Version. Does not include John, except in footnotes. Scriptural cross-references and selective current information on textual variants are helpful for those who know Greek. Notes all parallels with the Gospel of Thomas and other noncanonical writings, especially papyri, church fathers, and NT apocrypha. Includes index of Gospel and noncanonical parallels. The most complete and current synopsis based on the English Bible.

A L S O   S I G N I F I C A N T

4.23.4 Funk, Robert W., ed. *New Gospel Parallels.* 2 vols. Foundations and Facets: New Testament. Philadelphia: Fortress, 1985. 492/396pp.

4.23.5 ———, ed. *New Gospel Parallels.* Vol. 1.2. *Mark.* Rev. ed. Sonoma, Calif.: Polebridge, 1990. 271pp.

4.23.6 Orchard, John Bernard, ed. *A Synopsis of the Four Gospels: Arranged according to the Two-Gospel Hypothesis.* Macon, Ga.: Mercer University Press, 1982. 294pp.

4.23.7 Sparks, H. F. D. *The Johannine Synopsis of the Gospels.* New York: Harper & Row, 1974. 96pp.

4.23.8 ———. *A Synopsis of the Gospels: The Synoptic Gospels with the Johannine Parallels.* Philadelphia: Fortress, 1964. 248pp.

4.23.9 Stevens, William Arnold, and Ernest De Witt Burton. *A Harmony of the Gospels for Historical Study.* New York: Scribner's, 1932. 283pp.

4.23.10 Swanson, Reuben J. *The Horizontal Line Synopsis of the Gospels.* Dillsboro: Western North Carolina Press, 1975. 597pp.

4.23.11 Thomas, Robert L., and Stanley N. Gundry, eds. *The NIV Harmony of the Gospels: With Explanations and Essays.* San Francisco: Harper & Row, 1988. 341pp.

4.24 Matthew

See also STUDIES ON THE SERMON ON THE MOUNT (§4.25)

HIGHLY RECOMMENDED

4.24.1 Davies, W. D., and Dale C. Allison. *A Critical and Exegetical Commentary on the Gospel according to Saint Matthew.* 3 vols. International Critical Commentary. Edinburgh: T&T Clark, 1988–1997. 731/807/789pp.

Produced by two mature scholars who have written widely in NT studies, with particular attention to Matthew. The most detailed commentary available; the massive first volume covers only the introduction and chs. 1–7. The authors claim to opt for a holistic approach that takes seriously the traditional historical-critical analysis while also employing insights from the emerging literary- and canonical-critical methods. In fact, however, they typically focus attention on historical parallels (mostly Jewish) and the details of Matthew's redaction of his sources, with little notice of the flow of the narrative or the function of passages within the broader literary program of the canonical Gospel. Nevertheless, contains a wealth of background information, exhaustive citations of rabbinic and other Jewish parallels, and clear presentation of the history of interpretation.

4.24.2 France, R. T. *Matthew: Evangelist and Teacher.* Grand Rapids: Zondervan, 1989. 345pp.

Produced by a prominent British evangelical scholar, this volume is probably the most complete and helpful introduction to Matthew's Gospel. Deals with a range of introductory issues (including some theological ones) that France believes are most interesting to modern readers who approach the Gospel as the church's scripture and most significant for its interpretation. At certain points argues against easy acceptance of "critical orthodoxy," i.e., the tendency on the part of critical scholars to consider certain conclusions axiomatic. Even if one does not always agree with France (e.g., he thinks it likely, though not certain, that the Apostle Matthew wrote this Gospel), one will encounter informed and carefully reasoned arguments and a healthy reminder of the tentative character of many generally accepted critical conclusions.

4.24.3 Hagner, Donald A. *Matthew.* 2 vols. Word Biblical Commentary. Dallas: Word, 1993. 935pp.

Overall the most helpful commentary on Matthew presently available in English. Carefully considers Matthew's redaction of the traditions he inherited, especially Mark and Q, but gives greater attention to the final composition of the text. Consistently presents the major exegetical options and through lively interaction with the history of interpretation arrives at judicious and informed conclusions. In contrast to most volumes in this series, the "explanation" section develops theological issues that are of concern to contemporary Christians. Embraces critical methods, but conclusions are generally conservative, especially in regard to historical authenticity.

4.24.4 Kingsbury, Jack Dean. *Matthew: Structure, Christology, Kingdom.* New preface. Minneapolis: Fortress, 1989. 178pp.

Overall the most compelling presentation of Matthew's theology. Employs "composition criticism," an approach that considers Matthew's redaction of his sources but gives primary attention to the final composition of the Gospel. Argues for a tripartite structure to the Gospel (1:1–4:16; 4:17–16:20; 16:21–28:20), in which each major division reaches its climax in the declaration that Jesus is Son of God. On this and other grounds argues that Son of God is the major Christological category in Matthew. Discusses all Christological titles and develops their meaning and role. Insists also that Matthew has a bipartite view of salvation history, dividing this history into the time of preparation (prophets) and the time of fulfillment in Christ earthly and exalted, thus linking closely the ministry of the earthly Jesus to the present period of the church.

4.24.5 Luz, Ulrich. *Matthew 1–7: A Commentary.* Minneapolis: Augsburg, 1989. 460pp. *Matthew 8–20: A Commentary.* Hermeneia: A Critical and Historical Commentary on the Bible. Minneapolis: Fortress, 2001. 607pp.

A third volume, also in the Hermeneia series, is forthcoming. Originally published in German as part of the series, Evangelish-Katholischer Kommentar zum Neuen Testament, which adopts the interpretive method of *Wirkungsgeschichte,* usually translated "history of influence," and involves interpreting passages in light of the "history, reception, and actualizing of a text in media other than the commentary, e.g., in sermons, canonical law, hymnody, art, and in the actions and sufferings of the church." Thus, all the ways in which a passage has been appropriated can serve the heuristic function of helping readers discover meaning in the text that might otherwise be missed. Luz also attends to historical background (especially intertestamental and first-century Jewish writings) and history of the tradition towards its final form in Matthew, with special attention to Matthew's redaction of his sources. Luz masterfully integrates all these aspects into a holistic theological interpretation of the text.

A L S O   S I G N I F I C A N T

4.24.6 Aune, David E., ed. *The Gospel of Matthew in Current Study: Studies in Memory of William G. Thompson.* Grand Rapids: Eerdmans, 2001. 191pp.

4.24.7 Bacon, Benjamin W. *Studies in Matthew.* New York: Henry Holt, 1930. 533pp.

4.24.8 Balch, David L., ed. *Social History of the Matthean Community: Cross-Disciplinary Approaches.* Minneapolis: Fortress, 1991. 286pp.

4.24.9 Bauer, David R. *The Structure of Matthew's Gospel: A Study in Literary Design.* Journal for the Study of the New Testament Supplement Series 31. Sheffield: Almond, 1988. 182pp.

4.24.10 Bauer, David R., and Mark Allan Powell, eds. *Treasures New and Old: Contributions to Matthean Studies.* Society of Biblical Literature Symposium Series 1. Atlanta: Scholars, 454pp.

4.24.11 Beare, Francis Wright. *The Gospel according to Matthew.* San Francisco: Harper & Row, 1981. 550pp.

4.24.12 Bornkamm, Günther, Gerhard Barth, and Heinz Joachim Held. *Tradition and Interpretation in Matthew.* New Testament Library. Philadelphia: Westminster, 1963. 307pp.

4.24.13 Carter, Warren. *Matthew and the Margins: A Sociopolitical and Religious Reading.* Maryknoll, N.Y.: Orbis, 2000. 636pp.

4.24.14 ———. *Matthew: Storyteller, Interpreter, Evangelist.* Peabody, Mass.: Hendrickson, 1996. 322pp.

4.24.15 Garland, David E. *Reading Matthew: A Literary and Theological Commentary on the First Gospel.* New York: Crossroad, 1993. 269pp.

4.24.16 Gundry, Robert H. *Matthew: A Commentary on His Handbook for a Mixed Church under Persecution.* Grand Rapids: Eerdmans, 1994. 685pp.

4.24.17 Hare, Douglas R. A. *Matthew.* Interpretation: A Bible Commentary for Teaching and Preaching. Louisville: Westminster John Knox, 1993. 338pp.

4.24.18 Harrington, Daniel J. *The Gospel of Matthew.* Sacra Pagina. Collegeville, Minn.: Michael Glazier, 1991. 429pp.

4.24.19 Hill, David. *The Gospel of Matthew.* New Century Bible Commentary. Grand Rapids: Eerdmans, 1972. 367pp.

4.24.20 Keener, Craig S. *A Commentary on the Gospel of Matthew.* Grand Rapids: Eerdmans, 1999. 1040pp.

4.24.21 Kilpatrick, G. D. *The Origins of the Gospel according to St. Matthew.* Oxford: Clarendon, 1946. 150pp.

4.24.22 Kingsbury, Jack Dean. *Matthew.* 3d ed. Nappanee, Ind.: Evangel, 1998. 134pp.

4.24.23 ———. *Matthew as Story.* Rev. ed. Philadelphia: Fortress, 1988. 181pp.

4.24.24 Luz, Ulrich. *Matthew in History: Interpretation, Influence, and Effects.* Minneapolis: Fortress, 1994. 108pp.

4.24.25 ———. *The Theology of the Gospel of Matthew.* New Testament Theology. Cambridge: Cambridge University Press, 1995. 166pp.

4.24.26 McNeile, Alan Hugh. *The Gospel according to St. Matthew: The Greek Text with Introduction, Notes, and Indices.* London: Macmillan, 1938. 448pp.

4.24.27 Meier, John P. *The Vision of Matthew: Christ, Church, and Morality in the First Gospel.* New York: Paulist, 1979. 270pp.

4.24.28 Plummer, Alfred. *An Exegetical Commentary on the Gospel according to Matthew.* London: Robert Scott, 1909. 451pp.

4.24.29 Powell, Mark Allan. *God with Us: A Pastoral Theology of Matthew's Gospel.* Minneapolis: Fortress, 1995. 156pp.

4.24.30 Schweizer, Eduard. *The Good News according to Matthew.* Atlanta: John Knox, 1975. 572pp.

4.24.31 Senior, Donald. *What Are They Saying about Matthew?* Rev. ed. New York: Paulist, 1996. 136pp.

4.24.32 Stanton, Graham N. *A Gospel for a New People: Studies in Matthew.* Edinburgh: T&T Clark, 1992. 424pp.

4.24.33 Stanton, Graham N., ed. T*he Interpretation of Matthew.* Rev. ed. Issues in Religion and Theology 3. Philadelphia: Fortress, 1994. 164pp.

4.25 Studies on the Sermon on the Mount

H I G H L Y   R E C O M M E N D E D

4.25.1 Baumen, Clarence. *The Sermon on the Mount: The Modern Quest for Its Meanings.* Macon, Ga.: Mercer University Press, 1985. 440pp.

Detailed examination of the work of nineteen prominent thinkers who have shaped modern views regarding the Sermon, beginning with Tolstoy. Each entry includes a biographical sketch of the scholar so as to illuminate the role played by background, experience, and culture in that scholar's interpretation. Gives special attention to the role of presuppositions in determining the scholar's method and conclusions. Includes extended quotations from primary sources. Final synthetic chapters focus on major theological aspects. Illuminates the character of the Sermon and its contemporary significance for Christians.

4.25.2 Betz, Hans Dieter. *The Sermon on the Mount: A Commentary on the Sermon on the Mount, Including the Sermon on the Plain (Matthew 5:3–7:27 and Luke 6:20–49).* Hermeneia: A Critical and Historical Commentary on the Bible. Minneapolis: Fortress, 1995. 695pp.

One of the most massive studies of the Sermon ever produced. After presenting an introductory survey of the Sermon on the Mount and Sermon on the Plain, which includes discussion of the history of interpretation (beginning with the Fathers), source and tradition history, and genre of the Sermon, Betz offers a detailed commentary on each verse, giving more attention to Matthew's Sermon on the Mount than to Luke's Sermon on the Plain. Adopts the unusual source theory that the Sermon arose as a summary of Jesus' teachings

in the hypothetical sayings source Q in conversation with Hellenistic philosophy, and that this summary developed in two directions: for Jewish Christians
(adopted by Matthew), and for Gentile Christians (adopted by Luke). Consequently, Betz tends to ignore the broader context of Matthew's (and Luke's)
Gospel for the interpretation of the Sermon and to emphasize the Hellenistic
rather than Jewish background. The resultant portrait of Jesus in the Sermon is
at odds with that of Matthew's Gospel. Most scholars have rejected this
source theory. The value of the commentary lies in its minute attention to
every detail of the text, its in-depth exploration of exegetical problems, and
its presentation of Jewish, and especially Graeco-Roman, parallels.

4.25.3 Davies, W. D. *The Setting of the Sermon on the Mount.* Cambridge:
Cambridge University Press, 1966. 546pp.

Explores four contexts of the Sermon: (1) the world of Matthew's Gospel and of
Matthew's church (including the role of Jamnia and the rise of formative Judaism for Matthew's community); (2) Jewish messianic expectations and hopes of
a messianic teacher and lawgiver (including the relationship of Qumran's
"Teacher of Righteousness" to the Jesus of the Sermon); (3) the first-century
church, especially Paul, the hypothetical sayings source Q, and M (Matthew's
"special source"); and (4) the life of Jesus, i.e., the extent to which the Sermon
presents the actual teaching of Jesus. Somewhat dated in terms of issues
pursed, methods employed, and sources emphasized, but remains a helpful
analysis of pertinent background and an astute interpretation of the Sermon.

4.25.4 Guelich, Robert A. *The Sermon on the Mount: A Foundation for Understanding.* Waco, Tex.: Word, 1982. 451pp.

One of the few full-scale commentaries on the Sermon, and the most helpful
for the use of the Sermon in preaching and teaching within the church. Unlike Betz (§4.25.2), emphasizes the Sermon's role in Matthew's Gospel in
terms both of its literary development and its meaning, especially its theological message. Introduction offers a brief history of interpretation and discussions of Sermon's role in Matthew, its sources, and its structure. Verse-by-
verse commentary makes use of critical tools (e.g., text, source, form, and redaction criticism), historical background (especially Jewish, and particularly
rabbinic), and history of interpretation. Focuses on the final form of the text to
determine what the Sermon meant for the evangelist and his original audience. Full of rich theological discussion. Scholars will find it illuminating, and
students and pastors will find it accessible and engaging.

A L S O   S I G N I F I C A N T

4.25.5 Allison, Dale C. *The Sermon on the Mount: Inspiring the Moral Imagination.*
Companions to the New Testament. New York: Crossroad, 1999. 188pp.

4.25.6   Betz, Hans Dieter. *Essays on the Sermon on the Mount.* Philadelphia: Fortress, 1985. 170pp.

4.25.7   Bonhoeffer, Dietrich. *The Cost of Discipleship.* Rev. ed. New York: Macmillan, 1963. 352pp. (Originally published, in German, in 1937.)

4.25.8   Carson, D. A. *The Sermon on the Mount: An Evangelical Exposition of Matthew 5–7.* Grand Rapids: Baker, 1978. 157pp.

4.25.9   Carter, Warren. *What Are They Saying about Matthew's Sermon on the Mount?* New York: Paulist, 1994. 136pp.

4.25.10 Kissinger, Warren S. *The Sermon on the Mount: A History of Interpretation and Bibliography.* ATLA Bibliography Series 3. Metuchen, N.J.: Scarecrow, 1975. 296pp.

4.25.11 Patte, Daniel. *Discipleship According to the Sermon on the Mount: Four Legitimate Readings, Four Plausible Views of Discipleship and Their Relative Values.* Valley Forge, Pa.: Trinity Press International, 1996. 416pp.

4.25.12 Strecker, Georg. *The Sermon on the Mount: An Exegetical Commentary.* Nashville: Abingdon, 1988. 223pp.

4.25.13 Windisch, Hans. *The Meaning of the Sermon on the Mount: A Contribution to the Historical Understanding of the Gospels and to Their True Exegesis.* Philadelphia: Westminster, 1961. 224pp.

4.26 Mark

HIGHLY RECOMMENDED

4.26.1   Evans, Craig A. *Mark 8:27–16:20.* Word Biblical Commentary. Nashville: Thomas Nelson, 2001. 594pp.

This volume completes the Word Biblical Commentary on Mark, which began with Guelich's volume on 1:1–8:26 (§4.26.3). Evans is in essential agreement with Guelich's positions (especially regarding historical reliability of Mark's account), and his commentary is of the same character and high quality as the first volume. Emphasizes more than does Guelich the Graeco-Roman cultural background, and insists that the theological purpose of Mark is to challenge the claims of that culture and especially to repudiate the emperor cult by affirming that Jesus is king precisely in his role as crucified one, his royalty validated by God through the resurrection. Gives virtually no attention to contemporary application.

4.26.2 France, R. T. *The Gospel of Mark: A Commentary on the Greek Text.* New International Greek Testament Commentary. Grand Rapids: Eerdmans, 2002. 719pp.

Careful and detailed commentary by noted British evangelical scholar. Focuses on final form of the text, giving little attention to sources lying behind Mark's Gospel or the provenance or the original audience of Mark. Attends instead to the structure of the Gospel, ways in which individual passages contribute to the whole, and how intertextuality (especially OT passages) illumines the text. Draws heavily on historical and cultural context. Concerned to explain passages according to how a "Christian reader" would construe the text, but does little to develop the theology of passages or of the Gospel as a whole. Assumes knowledge of Greek.

4.26.3 Guelich, Robert A. *Mark 1–8:26.* Word Biblical Commentary. Waco, Tex.: Word, 1989. 454pp.

Because of Guelich's untimely death, only the first volume of his anticipated two-volume commentary is available (Craig Evans prepared the second volume [§4.26.1]). Gives meticulous attention to every detail of every verse, with special regard to linguistic analysis (both lexical and syntactic), Mark's sources, Mark's redaction of earlier traditions, the social and religious setting of the Gospel, the logical flow of the immediate context and the broader narrative context of the Gospel, and ways in which individual passages contribute to and are illuminated by Mark's purpose. Although he acknowledges growth of the tradition and Mark's creative hand, Guelich affirms the general reliability of Mark's Gospel as a report of Jesus' ministry. Highly technical commentary, and although there is concern for theological claims within the text, gives little attention to developing theological implications or continuing relevance for Christians.

4.26.4 Gundry, Robert H. *Mark: A Commentary on His Apology for the Cross.* Grand Rapids: Eerdmans, 1993. 1069pp.

Since Gundry believes that Mark was the first Gospel written and that we do not possess the earlier traditions that Mark used, concludes that a redaction-critical examination that seeks to analyze Mark's editing of earlier sources is inapplicable. Thus he pursues a close reading of the final form of the text, giving detailed attention to the literary structure of passages, linguistic analysis, and historical background. Follows each passage with thorough history of interpretation. Treats introductory matters (e.g., place and date of writing) at the end of the commentary, suggesting that these issues should be decided on the basis of the exegesis of individual passages. Concludes that the Gospel contains the recollections of Peter compiled by Mark (as Papias reported) before the trial of Paul (i.e., before 62 C.E.) for the evangelistic purpose of presenting to the population of Rome a defense of the Christian proclamation of Jesus' crucifixion. Since Gundry presents all this as a conclusion to his interpretation, setting and purpose play no role in his exegesis. Learned, judicious, and comprehensive.

4.26.5   Kingsbury, Jack Dean. *The Christology of Mark's Gospel.* Philadelphia: Fortress, 1983. 203pp.

Lucid, engaging, and illuminating study of the Christology of Mark, the major theological issue of the Gospel. Begins with the clearest survey of twentieth-century investigation into Mark's Christology available. Critically engages the two dominant scholarly perspectives on Mark's Christology. Corrects the contention of Wrede (§4.26.35) that Mark has shaped his Gospel so as to present Jesus as one who wishes to keep his messiahship a secret by pointing out that the secret in Mark is not that Jesus is the Christ but that he is Son of God. Corrects the contention of Weeden (§4.26.34) that Mark "corrected" an inappropriate understanding of Jesus' divine Sonship by de-emphasizing the title "Son of God" in favor of "Son of Man" by pointing out, on narrative grounds, that God himself affirms the appropriateness and centrality of "Son of God" in this Gospel. The remainder of the volume is devoted to an exegetically informed tracing of the narrative of the Gospel in order to provide specific content to both "Son of God," "Son of Man," and the other Christological titles.

4.26.6   Lane, William L. *Commentary on the Gospel of Mark.* New International Commentary on the New Testament. Grand Rapids: Eerdmans, 1974. 652pp.

In contrast to Gundry (§4.26.4), Lane, who shares Gundry's evangelical perspective, embraces a redaction-critical approach to this Gospel, analyzing how Mark's editing of earlier tradition provides an understanding of Mark's theological message and pastoral concerns. Also gives serious attention to the literary structure of passages, broader narrative of the Gospel, and historical background (especially Jewish). Gives less attention to details of the Greek language than does Guelich (§4.26.3) or Gundry, but more attention to theological reflection on the text. Much less technical than Guelich or Gundry.

4.26.7   Telford, W. R. *The Theology of the Gospel of Mark.* New Testament Theology. Cambridge: Cambridge University Press, 1999. 275pp.

Presents Mark's theology in its several historical contexts. First, sets Mark's theology in the context of his community and the broader Graeco-Roman world of which it was a part. Second, places Mark's theology in the context of the first-century church, noting points of continuity and discontinuity with other writings and theologies of the church as reflected in the various traditions and documents included in the NT. Third, discusses his own view of Mark's theology in dialogue with the history of interpretation (especially twentieth century). Fourth, probes the significance of Mark's theology for contemporary Christians in their own historical context. Written in technical style, with constant reference to details of history of interpretation, specific citations of Jewish and Graeco-Roman sources, and reconstructions of earlier tradition and of Mark's redaction of this earlier tradition. In contrast to Kingsbury (§4.26.5), who works exclusively with the final form of the text, Telford derives Mark's theological purposes both from the final composition and from Mark's shaping of earlier traditions.

4.26.8 **Witherington, Ben, III.** *The Gospel of Mark: A Socio-Rhetorical Commentary.* Grand Rapids: Eerdmans, 2001. 463pp.

Interprets Mark's Gospel by examining the dynamic interplay of the two "worlds" of Mark's Gospel: (1) The literary world involves the genre of Mark's Gospel (ancient biography of Jesus along the lines of other Graeco-Roman biographies) and Mark's use of ancient rhetoric. Draws on certain insights from emerging literary approaches (e.g., narrative criticism) but rejects a thoroughgoing narrative approach as inappropriately ahistorical, i.e., contrary to Mark's theological purpose to report events he was convinced had actually occurred, and contrary to Mark's pastoral purpose to address challenges facing his church in its historical setting. (2) The social world involves the structure of social life in the first-century Mediterranean world in general and Mark's church in particular, but Witherington emphasizes the Jewish and Graeco-Roman religious background. Of special value are the frequent excurses discussing specific exegetical, historical, and theological issues, and the applicable sections that explore points of continuing relevance for contemporary Christians.

A L S O   S I G N I F I C A N T

4.26.9 Achtemeier, Paul J. *Mark.* 2d ed. Proclamation Commentaries. Philadelphia: Fortress, 1986. 138pp.

4.26.10 Anderson, Hugh. *The Gospel of Mark.* New Century Bible Commentary. Grand Rapids: Eerdmans, 1976. 366pp.

4.26.11 Anderson, Janice Capel, and Stephen D. Moore. *Mark and Method: New Approaches in Biblical Studies.* Minneapolis: Fortress, 1992. 175pp.

4.26.12 Best, Ernest. *Mark: The Gospel as Story.* Edinburgh: T&T Clark, 1983. 155pp.

4.26.13 Bryan, Christopher. *A Preface to Mark: Notes on the Gospel in Its Literary and Cultural Settings.* New York: Oxford, 1993. 220pp.

4.26.14 Cranfield, C. E. B. *The Gospel according to St. Mark.* Cambridge Greek Testament Commentary. Cambridge: Cambridge University Press, 1977. 503pp.

4.26.15 Donahue, John R., and Daniel J. Harrington. *The Gospel of Mark.* Sacra Pagina. Collegeville, Minn.: Michael Glazier, 2002. 496pp.

4.26.16 Edwards, James R. *The Gospel according to Mark.* Pillar New Testament Commentaries. Grand Rapids: Eerdmans, 2002. 552pp.

4.26.17 Fowler, Robert M. *Let The Reader Understand: Reader-Response Criticism and the Gospel of Mark.* Minneapolis: Fortress, 1991. 279pp.

4.26.18 Hengel, Martin. *Studies in the Gospel of Mark.* Philadelphia: Fortress, 1985. 206pp.

4.26.19 Hooker, Morna D. *The Gospel according to St. Mark.* Black's New Testament Commentary. Peabody, Mass.: Hendrickson, 1991. 424pp.

4.26.20 Iersel, Bastiaan Martinius Franciscus van. *Mark: A Reader-Response Commentary.* Sheffield: Sheffield Academic Press, 1998. 556pp.

4.26.21 Kealy, Sean P. *Mark's Gospel: A History of Its Interpretation: From the Beginning Until 1979.* New York: Paulist, 1982. 269pp.

4.26.22 Kingsbury, Jack Dean. *Conflict in Mark: Jesus, Authorities, Disciples.* Minneapolis: Fortress, 1989. 150pp.

4.26.23 Lightfoot, Robert Henry. *The Gospel Message of St. Mark.* Oxford: Clarendon, 1950. 116pp.

4.26.24 Marcus, Joel. *Mark 1–8.* Anchor Bible. New York: Doubleday, 1999. 569pp.

4.26.25 Martin, Ralph P. *Mark: Evangelist and Theologian.* Contemporary Evangelical Perspectives. Grand Rapids: Zondervan, 1973. 240pp.

4.26.26 Matera, Frank J. *What Are They Saying about Mark?* New York: Paulist, 1987. 113pp.

4.26.27 Rhoads, David, Joanna Dewey, and Donald Michie. *Mark as Story: An Introduction to the Narrative of a Gospel.* 2d ed. Minneapolis: Fortress, 1999. 176pp.

4.26.28 Robbins, Vernon K. *Jesus the Teacher: A Socio-Rhetorical Interpretation of Mark*. New introduction. Minneapolis: Fortress, 1992. 249pp.

4.26.29 Schweizer, Eduard. *The Good News according to Mark*. Atlanta: John Knox, 1970. 395pp.

4.26.30 Taylor, Vincent. *The Gospel according to St. Mark: The Greek Text with Introduction, Notes, and Indexes*. London: Macmillan, 1952. 696pp.

4.26.31 Telford, William R., ed. *The Interpretation of Mark*. Rev. ed. Edinburgh: T&T Clark, 1994. 342pp.

4.26.32 Tolbert, Mary Ann. *Sowing the Gospel: Mark's World in Literary-Historical Perspective*. Minneapolis: Fortress, 1989. 336pp.

4.26.33 Watts, Rikki E. *Isaiah's New Exodus in Mark*. Grand Rapids: Baker, 2000. 479pp.

4.26.34 Weeden, Theodore J., Sr. *Mark: Traditions in Conflict*. Philadelphia: Fortress, 1971. 182pp.

4.26.35 Wrede, William. *The Messianic Secret*. Library of Theological Translations. Cambridge: James Clarke, 1971. 292pp. (Originally published 1901, in German.)

4.27 Luke and Luke-Acts

See also ACTS (§4.29)

H I G H L Y   R E C O M M E N D E D

4.27.1 Fitzmyer, Joseph A. *The Gospel according to Luke*. 2 vols. Anchor Bible. Garden City, N.Y.: Doubleday, 1981, 1985. 1642pp.

Most comprehensive and detailed commentary on Luke available in English. Employs a fully critical model, but often arrives at conservative conclusions (e.g., that the Gospel was probably written by Luke, the companion of Paul). Introduction includes discussion of historical and linguistic issues, and an illuminating and extensive presentation (130pp.) of Lucan theology. Commentary attends to Luke's redaction of his sources (Mark and Q), interpretative significance of forms or genres, linguistic analysis, and historical background for both the setting in the life of Jesus and the setting of the production of Luke's Gospel. All these considerations are employed to illuminate the final text. Thus gives most attention to the structure of passages and their role within the narrative of the whole of Luke-Acts, with a view toward identifying their theological theme and arriving at their essential message. A traditional commentary that makes no use of the emerging literary or sociological methods.

4.27.2 Franklin, Eric. *Christ the Lord: A Study in the Purpose and Theology of Luke-Acts*. Philadelphia: Westminster, 1975. 241pp.

Lucid, comprehensive, and (in the judgment of many) compelling discussion of Lucan theology and especially Christology. Argues that the purpose of Luke-Acts is to prompt readers to respond to the reality that is proclaimed in Jesus' ascension (according to Franklin, the central event in Luke's theology), viz., that Jesus is Lord and that the eschatological power of God was and is effective through him. Relates all the major aspects of Luke's two-volume work to this central theme. Concludes by discussing implications of this theological program for Luke's pastoral concerns and for the identification of the evangelist himself, identified as a former God-fearer who embraced Christianity, possibly a companion of Paul.

4.27.3 Green, Joel B. *The Gospel of Luke*. New International Commentary on the New Testament. Grand Rapids: Eerdmans, 1997. 928pp.

Recognizing that no commentary can do everything, Green limits the scope of this volume by pursuing "discourse analysis," i.e., correlation of "culture-critical" and narratological concerns. This approach involves the dynamic interplay of cultural insights from the critical examination of historical background (with special attention to religious and cultural issues), illuminated by modern social and cultural-anthropological studies, with insights pertaining to the nature of narrative derived from the new literary approaches. This process gives rise to a narrative theology that speaks directly to contemporary readers. Adopts sophisticated understanding of the nature and function of historical narrative; insists that there is a concern to present historical events, but for the purpose of persuasion, and thus all available rhetorical resources are employed to fulfill this persuasive function. Emphasizes how each passage functions in the narrative development of the whole of Luke-Acts, and thus provides many fresh insights and original perspectives that are at once engaging and compelling.

4.27.4 Johnson, Luke Timothy. *The Gospel of Luke*. Sacra Pagina. Collegeville, Minn.: Michael Glazier, 1991. 466pp.

Written by a Catholic layperson who has emerged as a leading American NT scholar, this commentary focuses on the final form of the text. Attends carefully to the ways in which each passage fits into the whole of Luke-Acts. Exclusively a literary analysis, with no attention given to the historical Jesus or the history of the tradition behind the final form. This restricted scope allows for examination of literary comparisons from the ancient world (especially classical Greek and Hellenistic) and to literary and rhetorical devices commonly employed in the ancient Mediterranean world and appropriated by Luke. Both the more technical "notes" and the more expository "interpretation" are rather brief, and the discussion of each passage concludes with a very select bibliography. One often wishes Johnson would have developed his interpretation more fully, especially his suggestive remarks on the theological message of passages.

4.27.5   Marshall, I. Howard. *The Gospel of Luke: A Commentary on the Greek Text.* New International Greek Testament Commentary. Grand Rapids: Eerdmans, 1978. 928pp.

If Johnson's commentary (§4.27.4) is literary, Marshall's is linguistic. Meticulously analyzes virtually every phrase with lexical and syntactical thoroughness. In the process, examines Luke's redaction of his sources (Mark and Q) and notes how Luke's theology can be discerned both by what he takes over from these sources, and how he alters them, omits from them, or adds from his own hand. Gives significant attention also to historical background (especially Jewish) and to canonical connections (especially Septuagintal). Interprets passages in light of Luke's overall purpose and often refers to other passages in Luke-Acts, but gives relatively little attention to the flow of the narrative. Although written for students, many will find it overwhelming and quite technical, as it assumes a solid knowledge of Greek. Those who can master it will find the commentary extremely helpful, especially in its analysis of the Greek text.

4.27.6   Marshall, I. Howard. *Luke: Historian and Theologian.* Rev. ed. Downers Grove, Ill.: InterVarsity, 1988. 252pp.

Like Franklin, presents a comprehensive and coherent understanding of Luke's theology. In contrast to Franklin, however, considers the concept of salvation to be central to Luke's theology and consistently presents all aspects of Luke's theology within the framework of this concept (e.g., Marshall describes the doctrine of God under the heading "God my Savior"). Insists that no wedge should be drawn between history and theology. As a historian who sees theological significance in the events he records, Luke is concerned with the reliable reporting of events, and is thus conservative in dealing with his sources. Indeed, argues that Luke creatively developed his theology from ideas already present in the traditions he inherited, over against the view the Luke was an innovator whose thought stood in stark discontinuity with earlier Christian convictions.

A L S O   S I G N I F I C A N T

4.27.7   Bock, Darrell L. *Luke.* Baker Exegetical Commentary on the New Testament. 2 vols. Grand Rapids: Baker, 1994. 2148pp.

4.27.8   Bovon, François. *Luke 1: A Commentary on the Gospel of Luke 1:1–9:50.* Hermeneia: A Critical and Historical Commentary on the Bible. Minneapolis: Fortress, 2002. 480pp.

4.27.9   Conzelmann, Hans. *The Theology of St. Luke.* New York: Harper & Row, 1960. 255pp.

X 4.27.10   Craddock, Fred B. *Luke.* Interpretation: A Bible Commentary for Teaching and Preaching. Louisville: John Knox, 1990. 298pp.

4.27.11   Darr, John A. *On Character Building: The Reader and the Rhetoric of Characterization in Luke-Acts.* Literary Currents in Biblical Interpretation. Louisville: Westminster John Knox, 1992. 208pp.

4.27.12   Fitzmyer, Joseph A. *Luke the Theologian: Aspects of His Teaching.* New York: Paulist, 1989. 250pp.

4.27.13   Green, Joel B. *The Theology of the Gospel of Luke.* New Testament Theology. Cambridge: Cambridge University Press, 1995. 170pp.

4.27.14   Green, Joel B., and Michael C. McKeever. *Luke-Acts and New Testament Historiography.* IBR Bibliographies 8. Grand Rapids: Baker, 1994. 148pp.

4.27.15   Keck, Leander E., and J. Louis Martyn, eds. *Studies in Luke-Acts.* Philadelphia: Fortress, 1980. 316pp.

4.27.16   Kingsbury, Jack Dean. *Conflict in Luke.* Minneapolis: Fortress, 1991. 180pp.

4.27.17   Kurz, William S. *Reading Luke-Acts: Dynamics of Biblical Narrative.* Louisville: Westminster John Knox, 1993. 261pp.

4.27.18   Maddox, Robert. *The Purpose of Luke-Acts.* Studies of the New Testament and Its World. Edinburgh: T&T Clark, 1982. 218pp.

4.27.19   Neyrey, Jerome H., ed. *The Social World of Luke-Acts: Models for Interpretation.* Peabody, Mass.: Hendrickson, 1991. 436pp.

4.27.20   Nolland, John. *Luke.* 3 vols. Word Biblical Commentary. Dallas: Word, 1989–1993. 1293pp.

4.27.21   Plummer, Alfred. *A Critical and Exegetical Commentary on the Gospel according to St. Luke.* International Critical Commentary. Edinburgh: T&T Clark, 1910. 592pp.

4.27.22 Powell, Mark Allan. *What Are They Saying about Luke?* New York: Paulist, 1989. 151pp.

4.27.23 Schweizer, Eduard. *The Good News according to Luke.* Atlanta: John Knox, 1984. 392pp.

4.27.24 Talbert, Charles H. *Reading Luke: A Literary and Theological Commentary on the Third Gospel.* New York: Crossroad, 1982. 246pp.

4.27.25 Tannehill, Robert. *The Gospel according to Luke.* Vol. 1 of *The Narrative Unity of Luke-Acts: A Literary Interpretation.* Foundations and Facets: New Testament. Philadelphia: Fortress, 1986. 334pp.

4.27.26 Tyson, Joseph B., ed. *Luke-Acts and the Jewish People: Eight Critical Perspectives.* Minneapolis: Augsburg, 1988. 160pp.

4.28 John and the Johannine School

See also JOHANNINE EPISTLES (§4.41)

H I G H L Y   R E C O M M E N D E D

4.28.1 Barrett, C. K. *The Gospel according to St. John: An Introduction with Commentary and Notes on the Greek Text.* 2d ed. Philadelphia: Westminster, 1978. 638pp.

Based on the Greek text, and not easily accessible to those who do not know Greek. Rejects much recent redaction criticism of the Gospel that posits several stages of editing in favor of treating it as a theological unity. Insists that John did not intend to supply historically verifiable information about the life and teaching of Jesus and that it is impossible to extract from the Gospel reliable historical traditions. Argues that John knew the Gospel of Mark and probably also Luke, and that he presents a creative theological interpretation based on these synoptic texts. Introduction contains helpful discussion of John's theology. Commentary focuses on linguistic analysis, textual variants, historical background (especially OT and Jewish), John's (supposed) development of synoptic passages and themes, and the theological meaning of the text.

4.28.2 Beasley-Murray, George R. *John.* Word Biblical Commentary. Waco, Tex.: Word, 1987. 441pp.

The word that best describes this commentary is "accessible." This British Baptist scholar who taught for several years in the United States writes for a varied audience (including scholars) but primarily for the average minister. Wishes to make available to nonspecialists the results of vast academic research into John along with the commentator's original insights. Like Barrett (§4.28.1), assumes the unity of the final form of the text. Refers to the Greek text, but gives primary attention to literary structure, historical background, and canonical connections. Relates each passage to broader-book context and John's overall purpose. Develops theology of each passage, and relates this theology to NT faith as a whole and to concerns of modern Christians.

4.28.3 Brown, Raymond E. *The Gospel according to John.* 2 vols. Anchor Bible. Garden City, N.Y.: Doubleday, 1966, 1970. 1208pp.

Discusses in depth major Johannine questions (e.g., authorship, composition, date, relationship to synoptics) in introduction, presenting major theories regarding these issues and assessing them in the light of the text itself and the historical setting of the book's production so as to arrive at a synthesis of relevant and reliable scholarly insights. Concludes that the Gospel originated in traditions of words and deeds of Jesus that were independent of the synoptic Gospels and that these traditions developed into characteristic Johannine patterns through years of preaching and teaching. The evangelist organized this material into a Gospel, and later revised it to meet the current needs of his congregation. A final redactor later inserted additional material. Commentary draws on this hypothetical reconstruction at points, but focuses on the meaning of the final form. Gives some attention to linguistic issues and to literary structure, but commentary is historically oriented, emphasizing historical background (mostly Jewish and first-century Christian), history of interpretation, and historical setting of original readers. Learned, detailed, and technical.

4.28.4 Morris, Leon. *The Gospel according to John.* New International Commentary on the New Testament. Rev. ed. Grand Rapids: Eerdmans, 1995. 824pp.

One of the most conservative commentaries on John, and one of the most popularly written of the commentaries in this series. But its popular style belies a subtle richness and depth. Sees no dichotomy between history and theology, insisting that John was master of expressing theology through accurate reportage of events. Includes a brief and salient introduction, treating only the most significant issues. Chief among these is apparently authorship, since Morris argues at great length, and in a careful and informed way, for Johannine authorship. Those who will disagree with his conclusions will recognize that his argument is hardly obscurantist. Interprets individual passages in light of this critical conclusion. Interpretation depends on a range of evidential considerations: historical background, broader-book context, canonical connections. Gives relatively less attention to linguistic analysis.

Commentary often breaks into theological reflection and considerations of contemporary application.

4.28.5 Schnackenburg, Rudolf. *The Gospel according to St. John*. 3 vols. New York: Crossroad, 1987. 638/556/510pp.

This German Roman Catholic NT scholar intends to present an "explanation" of the Johannine text understandable to modern persons, and to use "every available means" to do so. Thus, incorporates a wide range of interpretive considerations, especially literary structure, linguistic analysis, historical background, and canonical connections. Focuses on the theological meaning of the final form of the text, but gives some limited attention to earlier sources and the evangelist's redaction of them. Maintains that the earliest traditions stem from John the son of Zebedee and that the evangelist was one of his disciples. Similar in scope and character to Brown's commentary (§4.28.3), but gives greater attention to evidence from Qumran and Coptic Gnostic materials, and is more theologically reflective. Profound theological insights repeatedly burst forth from his exegesis.

4.28.6 Smalley, Stephen S. *John: Evangelist and Interpreter*. 2d ed. Downers Grove, Ill.: InterVarsity, 1998. 340pp.

Intended primarily for theological students, but also provides many insights for the scholar. Critically discusses virtually all significant issues and problems in the study of John's Gospel, giving special attention to origin and background, composition and purpose, points of commonality with Christian tradition in general, and unique aspects where John's Gospel makes its own contribution to NT theology. Thus moves from historical discussion (where Smalley argues that John's Gospel was based on generally historically accurate tradition independent of the synoptists), to literary analysis (where Smalley emphasizes the literary development of the narrative, "analyzed as a sustained piece of dramatic writing"), to an examination of the rich theological vision of John. Focuses almost entirely on the Gospel, saying very little about the Johannine epistles or their relationship to the Gospel.

A L S O   S I G N I F I C A N T

4.28.7 Ashton, John. *The Interpretation of John*. 2d ed. Edinburgh: T&T Clark, 1997. 329pp.

4.28.8 Barrett, C. K. *Essays on John*. Philadelphia: Westminster, 1982. 167pp.

4.28.9 Bernard, J. H. *A Critical and Exegetical Commentary on the Gospel according to St. John*. 2 vols. International Critical Commentary. Edinburgh: T&T Clark, 1928. 739pp.

4.28.10 Blomberg, Craig L. *The Historical Reliability of John's Gospel: Issues and Commentary.* Downers Grove, Ill.: InterVarsity, 2002. 396pp.

4.28.11 Brodie, Thomas L. *The Gospel according to John: A Literary and Theological Commentary.* New York: Oxford University Press, 1993. 625pp.

4.28.12 Brown, Raymond E. *The Community of the Beloved Disciple: The Life, Loves, and Hates of an Individual Church in New Testament Times.* New York: Paulist, 1979, 204pp.

4.28.13 Bruce, F. F. *The Gospel of John: Introduction, Exposition, and Notes.* Grand Rapids: Eerdmans, 1983. 425pp.

4.28.14 Bultmann, Rudolf. *The Gospel of John: A Commentary.* Philadelphia: Westminster, 1971. 744pp.

4.28.15 Carson, D. A. *The Gospel according to John.* Grand Rapids: Eerdmans, 1991. 715pp.

4.28.16 Cullmann, Oscar. *The Johannine Circle.* Philadelphia: Westminster, 1976. 124pp.

4.28.17 Culpepper, R. Alan. *Anatomy of the Fourth Gospel: A Study in Literary Design.* Foundations and Facets: New Testament. Philadelphia: Fortress, 1983. 266pp.

4.28.18 Dodd, C. H. *The Interpretation of the Fourth Gospel.* Cambridge: Cambridge University Press, 1954. 477pp.

4.28.19 Fortna, Robert T., and Tony Thatcher, eds. *Jesus in the Johannine Tradition.* Louisville: Westminster John Knox, 2001. 384pp.

4.28.20 Godet, Frederic Louis. *Commentary on John's Gospel.* Bible Student's Library. New York: Funk & Wagnalls, 1886. 1112pp.

4.28.21 Haenchen, Ernst. *John.* 2 vols. Hermeneia: A Critical and Historical Commentary on the Bible. Philadelphia: Fortress, 1984. 308/366pp.

4.28.22 Hengel, Martin. *The Johannine Question.* Philadelphia: Trinity Press International, 1989. 240pp.

4.28.23 Malina, Bruce J., and Richard L. Rohrbaugh. *Social-Science Commentary on the Gospel of John.* Minneapolis: Fortress, 1998. 326pp.

4.28.24 Painter, John. *The Quest for the Messiah: The History, Literature and Theology of the Johannine Community.* 2d ed. Nashville: Abingdon, 1993. 492pp.

4.28.25 Ridderbos, Herman. *The Gospel of John: A Theological Commentary*. Grand
         Rapids: Eerdmans, 1997. 719pp.

4.28.26 Segovia, Fernando F., ed. *What Is John?: Readers and Readings of the Fourth
         Gospel*. 2 vols. Society of Biblical Literature Symposium Series. Atlanta:
         Scholars, 1996–1998. 293/360pp.

4.28.27 Sloyan, Gerard. *John*. Interpretation: A Bible Commentary for Teaching and
         Preaching. Atlanta: John Knox, 1988. 239pp.

4.28.28 ———. *What Are They Saying about John?* New York: Paulist, 1991. 125pp.

4.28.29 Smith, D. Moody. *John Among the Gospels: Their Relationship in Twentieth-
         Century Research*. Minneapolis: Fortress, 1992. 210pp.

4.28.30 ———. *The Theology of the Gospel of John*. New Testament Theology. Cam-
         bridge: Cambridge University Press, 1995. 202pp.

4.28.31 Talbert, Charles H. *Reading John: A Literary and Theological Commentary on
         the Fourth Gospel and the Johannine Epistles*. New York: Crossroad, 1992.
         284pp.

4.28.32 Westcott, Brooke Foss. *The Gospel according to John: The Greek Text with In-
         troduction and Notes*. 2 vols. London: J Murray, 1908. 282/394pp.

4.28.33 Witherington, Ben, III. *John's Wisdom: A Commentary on the Fourth Gospel*.
         Louisville: Westminster John Knox, 1995. 411pp.

4.29 Acts of the Apostles

HIGHLY   RECOMMENDED

4.29.1 Barrett, C. K. *A Critical and Exegetical Commentary on the Acts of the
        Apostles*. 2 vols. International Critical Commentary. Edinburgh: T&T
        Clark, 1994–1998. 1272pp.

        Barrett has a well-deserved reputation for meticulous attention to detail, en-
        cyclopedic knowledge of almost everything pertaining to the text and world
        of the NT, sober judgment, and clear writing. This commentary only enhances
        his reputation. Introduction is postponed to the beginning of the second vol-
        ume since such issues can be decided only on the basis of careful exegesis.
        Typically moves through a passage by setting forth the interpretive issue, iden-
        tifying major possibilities, citing evidence (and sometimes quoting scholars,

both ancient and modern, often in original Greek, Latin, German, or French), and analyzing evidence thus presented so as to arrive at a reasonable conclusion, frequently appending observations regarding its theological significance. Often relates passages to other parts of Luke-Acts or other NT texts. Gives little attention to role within the sustained dramatic narration of Acts and draws not at all from current narratological or sociological insights. This last is not necessarily a weakness, but it does mark this work as a traditional commentary, full of engaging and compelling, if not always boldly original, insights.

4.29.2 Bruce, F. F. *Commentary on the Book of Acts.* Rev. ed. New International Commentary on the New Testament. Grand Rapids: Eerdmans, 1988. 541pp.

Bruce was a classicist by training and a historian by temperament, and both these impulses are manifested in this commentary. Comments are replete with illuminating discussions of historical background with citations from ancient writers, both Jewish and Graeco-Roman. Bruce gives some attention (mostly in footnotes) to nuances of the Greek. Treats Acts as essentially a history book whose purpose is to set forth the facts (with certain apologetic tendencies) of the emerging church. Consistently attempts to reconstruct and illuminate events herein recorded rather than attend to the narrative Luke has created and explore the theological message Luke thereby communicates. It is difficult to derive rich theological insights out of reconstructed historical events, explained without benefit of the theological purpose that the writer communicates by use of narrative strategies. Consequently, Bruce's commentary, though theologically suggestive in many ways, often lacks the theological depth it could have gained from attention to Luke's narrative and rhetorical strategies of persuasion.

4.29.3 Fitzmyer, Joseph A. *The Acts of the Apostles.* Anchor Bible. New York: Doubleday, 1998. 830pp.

Like Fitzmyer's commentary on Luke (§4.27.1), a traditional historical-critical commentary, giving no attention to newer narratological or sociological approaches, but rich in examination of the language and historical background. Allows for Lucan expansion and even free creation at points, and for nonhistorical accretions in the development of the tradition, but tends toward conservative conclusions on historical matters. Unlike his commentary on Luke, Fitzmyer was restricted here to a single volume, resulting in less attention to theological issues and the role of passages within the broader-book context. Apparently, Fitzmyer considered he had space to deal only with identification and illumination of events mentioned in the text, for he gives little attention to theological meaning, e.g., almost completely ignoring the often-noted literary and theological significance of money/possessions in Acts.

4.29.4 Johnson, Luke Timothy. *The Acts of the Apostles*. Sacra Pagina. Collegeville, Minn.: Michael Glazier, 1992. 568pp.

In some ways a continuation of Johnson's commentary on Luke (§4.27.4), to which he constantly refers in this commentary. Emphasizes continuity with the Gospel of Luke, taking seriously the literary unity of the two books. Treats both Luke's narrative artistry and his concern to present historical events, refusing to construe Acts as either a history book or as a work of fiction. Insists rather that all historical writing employs fictional techniques, and that Acts accords with standards and practices of ancient historiography. Thus Luke presents sustained narrative of events to communicate his theological message and purposes. Johnson traces these purposes through each passage of Acts.

4.29.5 Marshall, I. Howard, ed. *Witness to the Gospel: The Theology of Acts*. Grand Rapids: Eerdmans, 1998. 610pp.

Comprehensive survey of virtually all the major theological themes in Acts, presented in 25 essays written by some of the most prominent contemporary scholars in Lucan studies, many of whom have written whole books or seminal articles on the topic of their essay. Essays vary in perspective and method. Some naturally deal with more central issues and are more insightful than others; the essays on "The Plan of God" (Squires), "Salvation to the Ends of the Earth: God as the Savior in the Acts of the Apostles" (Green), "The Role of the Apostles" (Clark), and "The Spirit of Prophecy"(Turner) are especially helpful, as is the final synthetic article by David Peterson, "Luke's Theological Enterprise: Integration and Intent."

4.29.6 Willimon, William. *Acts*. Interpretation: A Bible Commentary for Teaching and Preaching. Atlanta: John Knox, 1988. 197pp.

In the history of interpretation, few commentaries on Acts have given serious consideration to theological meaning of the text, preferring to focus almost entirely on historical issues. Only recently have some major commentaries attended noticeably to the theological dimension, and most of these have dealt with the theological meaning as only one aspect of their exposition. This commentary complements these other works in that it assumes the kind of careful exegesis presented in the standard commentaries, but focuses on the theological and pastoral significance of these exegetical insights. Willimon is not himself a NT scholar, but an authority on preaching and pastoral care. At points his lack of thorough technical knowledge becomes evident to the trained eye, but this lack of personal exegetical expertise is compensated by his engaging connections between the original meaning and its contemporary theological and pastoral impact.

A L S O   S I G N I F I C A N T

4.29.7   Bauckham, Richard. *The Book of Acts in Its Palestinian Setting.* Vol. 4 of *The Book of Acts in Its First Century Setting.* Grand Rapids: Eerdmans, 1995. 526pp.

4.29.8   Conzelmann, Hans. *Acts of the Apostles.* Hermeneia: A Critical and Historical Commentary on the Bible. Philadelphia: Fortress, 1987. 287pp.

4.29.9   Foakes-Jackson, F. J., and Kirsopp Lake, eds. *The Acts of the Apostles.* 5 vols. London: Macmillan, 1920–1933. Volumes average 500pp.

4.29.10 Gasque, W. Ward. *A History of the Criticism of the Acts of the Apostles.* Rev. ed. Peabody, Mass.: Hendrickson, 1989. 359pp.

4.29.11 Gill, David W. J., and Conrad Gempf, eds. *The Book of Acts in its Graeco-Roman Setting.* Vol. 2 of *The Book of Acts in Its First Century Setting.* Grand Rapids: Eerdmans, 1994. 627pp.

4.29.12 Haenchen, Ernst. *The Acts of the Apostles: A Commentary.* Philadelphia: Westminster, 1971. 737pp.

4.29.13 Hemer, Colin J. *The Book of Acts in the Setting of Hellenistic History.* Winona Lake, Ind.: Eisenbrauns, 1990. 482pp.

4.29.14 Hengel, Martin. *Acts and the History of Earliest Christianity.* Philadelphia: Fortress, 1980. 149pp.

4.29.15 Jervell, Jacob. *The Theology of the Acts of the Apostles.* New Testament Theology. Cambridge: Cambridge University Press, 142pp.

4.29.16 Kee, Howard Clark. *Good News to the Ends of the Earth: The Theology of Acts.* Philadelphia: Trinity Press International, 1990. 122pp.

4.29.17 Kistemaker, Simon. *Exposition of the Acts of the Apostles.* New Testament Commentary. Grand Rapids: Baker, 1990. 1010pp.

4.29.18 Marshall, I. Howard. *The Acts of the Apostles.* Tyndale New Testament Commentaries. Grand Rapids: Eerdmans, 1980. 427pp.

4.29.19 Porter, Stanley E. *Paul in Acts.* Library of Pauline Studies. Peabody, Mass.: Hendrickson, 2001. 233pp.

4.29.20 Powell, Mark Allan. *What Are They Saying about Acts?* New York: Paulist, 1991. 147pp.

4.29.21 Rackham, Richard Belward. *The Acts of the Apostles: An Exposition.* 14th ed. Westminster Commentaries. London: Methuen, 1901. 524pp.

4.29.22 Rapske, Brian. *The Book of Acts and Paul in Roman Custody.* Vol. 3 of *The Book of Acts in Its First Century Setting.* Grand Rapids: Eerdmans, 1994. 512pp.

4.29.23 Soards, Marion L. *The Speeches in Acts: Their Content, Context, and Concerns.* Louisville: Westminster John Knox, 1994. 218pp.

4.29.24 Talbert, Charles H. *Reading Acts: A Literary and Theological Commentary on the Acts of the Apostles.* New York: Crossroad, 1997. 269pp.

4.29.25 Tannehill, Robert. *The Acts of the Apostles.* Vol. 2 of *The Narrative Unity of Luke-Acts: A Literary Interpretation.* Foundations and Facets: New Testament. Minneapolis: Fortress, 1986. 398pp.

4.29.26 Winter, Bruce W., and Andrew D. Clarke, eds. *The Book of Acts in Its Ancient Literary Setting.* Vol. 1 of *The Book of Acts in Its First Century Setting.* Grand Rapids: Eerdmans, 1993. 479pp.

4.29.27 Witherington, Ben, III. *The Acts of the Apostles: A Socio-Rhetorical Commentary.* Grand Rapids: Eerdmans, 1998. 874pp.

4.29.28 Witherington, Ben, III, ed. *History, Literature, and Society in the Book of Acts.* Cambridge: Cambridge University Press, 1996. 374pp.

4.30 Paul

HIGHLY RECOMMENDED

4.30.1 Beker, J. Christiaan. *Paul the Apostle: The Triumph of God in Life and Thought.* Philadelphia: Fortress, 1980. 452pp.

A groundbreaking work that has significantly influenced all subsequent studies of Pauline theology. Attempts to identify the basis of coherence of Paul's thought, and to explore how Paul has applied his theology to the churches under his care. Argues that the unifying theme of Paul's gospel is the apocalyptic concept of the triumph of God, i.e., "the hope in the dawning victory of God and in the imminent redemption of the created order, which he has inaugurated in Christ." In addition, claims that Paul adopted a hermeneutic that enabled him to apply this coherent theme to persons in a variety of conditions and circumstances (the "contingent particularities of the human situation").

Offers a learned, illuminating, and (in the judgment of many scholars) largely compelling portrait of the shape of Paul's thought.

4.30.2 Bruce, F. F. *Paul: Apostle of the Heart Set Free*. Grand Rapids: Eerdmans, 1977. 491pp.

Most comprehensive and informed account of Paul's life from a conservative evangelical perspective, lucidly written. Intended primarily for pastors and theological students, it nonetheless discusses issues of interest to the scholar. Takes Paul's undisputed letters as primary evidence, but has high regard for the historicity of Luke's presentation of Paul in Acts as strong secondary evidence. Deals with aspects of Paul's theology as they emerge from Paul's life.

4.30.3 Dunn, James D. G. *The Theology of Paul the Apostle*. Grand Rapids: Eerdmans, 1998. 808pp.

This prolific Pauline scholar presents the most complete and comprehensive theology of Paul since Ridderbos (§4.30.6), adopting recent insights from Sanders (§4.30.7) and Beker (§4.30.1). Offers lucid treatment of major themes (e.g., God, humankind, sin, Christian life and ethics), using Romans as a base but expanding on each theme with material from the other letters. Includes helpful discussion of methodological issues involved in developing a Pauline theology. Emphasizes the dynamic character of Paul's thought and the necessity to treat not only what Paul explicitly wrote but also Jewish and early Christian presuppositions of his thought, the role of transformative moments in Paul's life, and deeper issues involved in the situations Paul's letters attempt to address. This holistic approach gives the presentation breadth and depth.

4.30.4 Hawthorne, Gerald F., Ralph P. Martin, and Daniel G. Reid, eds. *Dictionary of Paul and His Letters: A Compendium of Contemporary Biblical Scholarship*. Downers Grove, Ill.: InterVarsity, 1993. 1038pp.

Most comprehensive reference work available for Pauline theology, literature, background, and scholarship. Contributors are prominent evangelical scholars from North America, Europe, Australia, and Asia. Clearly written, intended primarily for theological students and those engaged in preaching and teaching in the church, but authoritative, in-depth articles contribute to scholarly discussion. Articles pertain to Paul and all things associated with him, including theological themes (e.g., law, gifts of the Spirit, ethics, and Christology), hermeneutical methods (e.g., social scientific interpretation), and background (e.g., Graeco-Roman religions). Devotes specific articles to each of the Pauline epistles, to hermeneutics, and to preaching Paul today. Articles conclude with extensive bibliographies.

4.30.5 Murphy-O'Connor, Jerome. *Paul: A Critical Life.* Oxford: Clarendon, 1996. 416pp.

Whereas Bruce (§4.30.2) presents a portrait of Paul based on a surface reading of the entire NT and accepting Acts as a witness almost on a par with the undisputed epistles, Murphy-O'Connor insists on a critical procedure that largely dismisses Luke's Paul as hopelessly tendentious. Reads the undisputed epistles through the lens of rhetorical and epistolary criticism, exploring how knowledge of rhetorical strategies current in Paul's day and insights into the epistolary genre reveal deeper aspects of Paul's circumstances, thought, and personality. Begins with early life and conversion and concludes with Paul's last years, but the bulk of the book is arranged according to the churches Paul addressed, and throughout the emphasis is on ways in which the letters reveal how Paul's relationship with his churches prompted him to change or modify formulations of his theology. Thus, offers more of a literary history than a full-fledged biography, but such a work has value, for it provides helpful discussion of the dynamic between Paul's pastoral circumstances and the theology presented in his epistles. Indeed, the chapters could serve as a kind of "introduction" to the several letters.

4.30.6 Ridderbos, Herman. *Paul: An Outline of His Theology.* Grand Rapids: Eerdmans, 1975. 587pp.

The Reformed perspective of this leading Dutch scholar necessarily affects his reading of Paul, yet he seeks above all to be fair to the witness of the text. Based on careful exegesis and presented in constant interaction with the history of Pauline scholarship. Argues that Paul's central message is that the eschatological time of salvation has been inaugurated in the advent, death, and resurrection of Christ. Similar in some respects to Beker (§4.30.1), but significantly broader. A major difference is that Ridderbos accepts the Pauline authorship of all canonical epistles attributed to him, including the Pastorals. The center of Paul's theology as set forth by Ridderbos is not as sharp or as focused as Beker's, but neither is it as narrow, and thus it is arguably better able to account for the vast range of Paul's theological interests. Volume is arranged according to theological topics, beginning with sin and concluding with the doctrine of the future. One might learn more about the center (and coherence) of Paul's theology from Beker, but more regarding its specific aspects from Ridderbos.

4.30.7 Sanders, E. P. *Paul and Palestinian Judaism: A Comparison of Patterns of Religion.* Philadelphia: Fortress, 1977. 627pp.

Paul often articulates his faith in relationship to Judaism, and thus an understanding of Judaism and of Paul's relationship to it is essential for the interpretation of Paul's thought. Sanders, himself a leading authority on Palestinian Judaism, has produced here a watershed study that has revolutionized scholarly discussion on Paul's theology. His familiar assertion is that Judaism was characterized by "covenantal nomism": "one's place in God's plan is established on the basis of the covenant and the covenant requires as proper response obedience to its commandments," i.e., one enters the covenant relationship by grace, but maintains the covenant relationship by obedience. In contrast to this view, Paul adopts "participationist eschatology," "one participates in salvation by becoming one person with Christ, dying with him and sharing the promise of his resurrection." Thus, Paul has much in common with covenantal nomism, but his Christology marks differences in the overall pattern of his faith. Paul's critique of Judaism did not involve accusations of a legalistic righteousness that repudiated grace, but rather stemmed from his insistence that salvation is in Christ, and in nothing else.

4.30.8 Witherington, Ben, III. *The Paul Quest: The Renewed Search for the Jew of Tarsus*. Downers Grove, Ill.: InterVarsity, 1998. 347pp.

Clearly written introduction to the major issues in contemporary Pauline research and the various ways scholars are addressing these issues. Gives special attention to social history and cultural anthropology for understanding Paul. Witherington evaluates these scholarly options and offers his own arguments and conclusions. Attempts to integrate careful and critical examination of the biblical and historical evidence with the perspectives of each scholar discussed so as to arrive at a balanced and compelling portrait of Paul and of his thought. Stresses the Jewish background of Paul. Considers Acts to be fully reliable and develops the relationship between the chronology of Paul derived from Acts and from the epistles.

ALSO SIGNIFICANT

4.30.9 Ashton, John. *The Religion of Paul the Apostle*. New Haven, Conn.: Yale University Press, 2000. 261pp.

4.30.10 Barrett, C. K. *Essays on Paul*. Philadelphia: Westminster, 1982. 170pp.

4.30.11 ———. *From First Adam to Last: A Fresh Approach to Some Problems of Paul and the New Testament*. New York: Scribner's, 1962. 124pp.

4.30.12 ———. *Paul: An Introduction to His Thought*. Louisville: Westminster John Knox, 1994. 180pp.

4.30.13 Bassler, Jouette M., ed. *Pauline Theology*. Vol. 1. *Thessalonians, Philippians, Galatians, Philemon*. Minneapolis: Fortress, 1991. 287pp.

4.30.14 Becker, Jürgen. *Paul: Apostle to the Gentiles*. Louisville: Westminster John Knox, 1993. 513pp.

4.30.15 Bornkamm, Günther. *Paul.* New York: Harper & Row, 1971. 260pp.

4.30.16 Cousar, Charles B. *Reading Galatians, Philippians, and 1 Thessalonians: A Literary and Theological Commentary.* Macon, Ga.: Smyth & Helwys, 2001. 235pp.

4.30.17 Das, Andrew. *Paul, the Law, and the Covenant.* Peabody, Mass.: Hendrickson, 2001. 342pp.

4.30.18 Davies, W. D. *Paul and Rabbinic Judaism: Some Rabbinic Elements in Pauline Theology.* London: SPCK, 1948. 376pp.

4.30.19 Donfried, Karl P., and I. Howard Marshall. *The Theology of the Shorter Pauline Letters.* New Testament Theology. Cambridge: Cambridge University Press, 1993. 208pp.

4.30.20 Fee, Gordon D. *God's Empowering Presence: The Holy Spirit in the Letters of Paul.* Peabody, Mass.: Hendrickson, 1994. 967pp.

4.30.21 Hengel, Martin, and Anna Maria Schwemer. *Paul between Damascus and Antioch: The Unknown Years.* Louisville: Westminster John Knox, 1997. 530pp.

4.30.22 Hübner, Hans. *Law in Paul's Thought.* Studies of the New Testament and Its World. Edinburgh: T&T Clark, 1984. 186pp.

4.30.23 Jewett, Robert. *Paul the Apostle to America: Current Trends and Pauline Scholarship.* Louisville: Westminster John Knox, 1994. 178pp.

4.30.24 Johnson, E. Elizabeth, and David M. Hay, eds. *Pauline Theology, Volume 4: Looking Back, Pressing On.* Society of Biblical Literature Symposium Series 4. Atlanta: Scholars, 1997. 222pp.

4.30.25 Koperski, Veronica. *What Are They Saying about Paul and the Law?* New York: Paulist, 2001. 148pp.

4.30.26 Matera, Frank J. *Strategies for Preaching Paul.* Collegeville, Minn.: Liturgical Press, 2001. 186pp.

4.30.27 Meeks, Wayne A. *The First Urban Christians: The Social World of the Apostle Paul.* New Haven, Conn.: Yale University Press, 1983. 299pp.

4.30.28 Munck, Johannes. *Paul and the Salvation of Mankind.* Atlanta: John Knox, 1959. 351pp.

4.30.29 Neyrey, Jerome H. *Paul, In Other Words: A Cultural Reading of His Letters.* Louisville: Westminster John Knox, 1990. 263pp.

4.30.30 Plevnik, Joseph. *What Are They Saying about Paul?* New York: Paulist, 1986. 114pp.

4.30.31 Räisänen, Heikki. *Paul and the Law.* Rev. ed. Tübingen: Mohr, 1987. 320pp.

4.30.32 Segal, Alan. *Paul the Convert: The Apostolate and Apostasy of Saul the Pharisee.* New Haven, Conn.: Yale University Press, 1990. 368pp.

4.30.33 Seifrid, Mark A., and Randall K. J. Tan. *The Pauline Writings.* IBR Bibliographies 9. Grand Rapids: Baker, 2002. 150pp.

4.30.34 Stewart, James S. *A Man in Christ: The Vital Elements of St. Paul's Religion.* Grand Rapids: Baker, 1975. 331pp.

4.30.35 Thielman, Frank. *Paul and the Law: A Contextual Approach.* Downers Grove, Ill.: InterVarsity, 1994. 336pp.

4.30.36 Witherington, Ben, III. *Paul's Narrative Thought World: The Tapestry of Tragedy and Triumph.* Louisville: Westminster John Knox, 1994. 373pp.

4.30.37 Wright, N. T. *The Climax of the Covenant: Christ and the Law in Pauline Theology.* Minneapolis: Fortress, 1993. 316pp.

4.31 Romans

HIGHLY RECOMMENDED

4.31.1 Achtemeier, Paul J. *Romans.* Interpretation: A Bible Commentary for Teaching and Preaching. Atlanta: John Knox, 1985. 241pp.

Written by leading Presbyterian NT scholar, but his Reformed theological tradition does not determine his exposition (e.g., accepts a rather "Arminian" interpretation of chapter 7). Carefully examines Paul's theological argument, making use of "new avenues of investigation" from recent Pauline scholarship, especially the insight that Paul's thinking reflects his struggle over the role of the Jews as God's chosen people within God's whole plan for human salvation. Introduction provides helpful explanation of the structure of Paul's thought, particularly his Christian adaptation of Jewish apocalypticism. In view of this apocalyptic background, Achtemeier concludes that Paul is concerned not simply with the justification of the individual, but with the whole sweep of history and of creation. Relates this broad discussion of Paul's theology specifically to Romans, leading to a very helpful exposition of the shape of the theology of this epistle. Even more than is usually the case in this series, discusses specifically how passages (complex, and to the modern mind arcane) might be used for preaching and teaching.

4.31.2 Donfried, Karl P., ed. *The Romans Debate*. Rev. ed. Peabody, Mass.: Hendrickson, 1991. 372pp.

A standard work for exploring major issues pertaining to the study of Romans, especially the character, structure, historical setting, purpose, occasion, and theology of the book. Contains a series of essays, originally published elsewhere, by most prominent authorities in the field. Includes some classic older articles (e.g., by T. W. Manson, Günther Bornkamm, and F. F. Bruce), but primarily offers current discussion. Introductory essay by Donfried tracks major scholarly debates pertaining to Romans over the past half century. Includes extensive bibliography.

4.31.3 Dunn, James D. G. *Romans*. Word Biblical Commentary. 2 vols. Dallas: Word, 1988. 976pp.

Massive, detailed commentary that attempts to grasp the coherence of Paul's thought by carefully tracing the logic of the argument from the beginning of the letter to the end. Thus emphasizes the role of each passage within the flow of argument. Provides depth by exploring the lexical significance of Greek terms (does relatively little with grammatical analysis) and by considering Paul's broader theological program reflected in his other letters. Gives special attention to historical, cultural, and religious background, and is particularly concerned to explore the interaction in Paul's thought between his Jewish heritage and his Christian faith, considering this interface to be the primary religious and ideological background to the letter. By attending to the meaning of passages in the particularity of their original historical context Dunn is able to identify points of continuing relevance for contemporary Christians.

4.31.4 Fitzmyer, Joseph A. *Romans*. Anchor Bible. New York: Doubleday, 1993. 793pp.

First full-scale commentary on Romans written by an American Roman Catholic since 1934. Contains most complete bibliography of commentaries on Romans (from the Fathers to the present) available. In addition to usual treatment of authorship, date, occasion, and purpose, introduction includes illuminating sketch of the theology of this letter. Treatment of each passage begins with "comments," accessible to nonspecialists, with discussion of structure, main theological theme and the development of the theme in the passage, and role of passage within the letter's argument. "Notes" follow, offering detailed and technical discussions of exegetical issues, including linguistic evidence, relationship to the Pauline corpus, canonical connections, and historical background, some history of interpretation, and a bibliography of works on the passage or on matters pertaining to it. A model of fair, balanced, informed, and insightful interpretation.

4.31.5 Moo, Douglas J. *The Epistle to the Romans.* New International Commentary on the New Testament. Grand Rapids: Eerdmans, 1996. 1012pp.

A most complete and detailed commentary from a leading American evangelical scholar. A fair and balanced commentary that is at points quite independent from Moo's Reformed tradition, although his manner of framing issues and his conclusions generally reflect a traditional Protestant (and more specifically Reformed) perspective. Based on the English text, but gives extensive attention to the Greek. Interacts extensively with the history of interpretation, and vigorously challenges some of the new scholarly perspectives on Paul. Attends seriously to ways in which practical issues facing the Roman Christians affected the shape of Paul's theological arguments. Considers both the meaning for the original readers and the significance for contemporary Christians.

4.31.6 Sanday, William, and Arthur Headlam. *A Critical and Exegetical Commentary on the Epistle to the Romans.* International Critical Commentary. Edinburgh: T&T Clark, 1898. 450pp.

In spite of its age, remains one of the most insightful commentaries on Romans. Offers clear, crisp comments that are to the point and almost entirely free of confessional or theological bias. Maintains careful balance between concern for general flow of the argument and attention to exegetical details. Well ahead of its time in its emphasis on critical consideration of Paul's Jewish religious background. Develops meaning of major theological themes, placing them in the context of broader biblical thought.

ALSO SIGNIFICANT

4.31.7 Barrett, C. K. *The Epistle to the Romans.* Rev. ed. Black's New Testament Commentaries. Peabody, Mass.: Hendrickson, 1991. 278pp.

4.31.8 Barth, Karl. *The Epistle to the Romans.* London: Oxford, 1933. 547pp.

4.31.9 Boers, Hendrikus. *The Justification of the Gentiles: Paul's Letters to the Romans and Galatians.* Peabody, Mass.: Hendrickson, 1994. 334pp.

4.31.10 Bruce, F. F. *The Epistle to the Romans.* Tyndale New Testament Commentaries. Grand Rapids: Eerdmans, 1963. 288pp.

4.31.11   Byrne, Brendan. *Romans*. Sacra Pagina. Collegeville, Minn.: Liturgical Press, 1996. 503pp.

4.31.12   Cranfield, C. E. B. *A Critical and Exegetical Commentary on the Epistle to the Romans*. 2 vols. International Critical Commentary. Edinburgh: T&T Clark, 1975–1979. 927pp.

4.31.13   Godet, Frederic Louis. *Commentary on St. Paul's Epistle to the Romans*. New York: Funk & Wagnalls, 1883. 531pp.

4.31.14   Hay, David M., and E. Elizabeth Johnson, eds. *Pauline Theology, Volume 3: Romans*. Minneapolis: Fortress, 1995. 353pp.

4.31.15   Käsemann, Ernst. *Commentary on Romans*. Grand Rapids: Eerdmans, 1980. 428pp.

4.31.16   Johnson, Luke Timothy. *Reading Romans: A Literary and Theological Commentary*. New York: Crossroad, 1996. 224pp.

4.31.17   Murray, John. *The Epistle to the Romans*. New International Commentary on the New Testament. Grand Rapids: Eerdmans, 1959. 286pp.

4.31.18   Schlatter, Adolf. *Romans: The Righteousness of God*. Peabody, Mass.: Hendrickson, 1995. 287pp. (Originally published 1935, in German.)

4.31.19   Schreiner, Thomas R. *Romans*. Baker Exegetical Commentary on the New Testament. Grand Rapids: Baker, 1998. 919pp.

4.31.20   Stuhlmacher, Peter. *Paul's Letter to the Romans: A Commentary*. Louisville: Westminster John Knox, 1994. 269pp.

4.31.21   Wedderburn, A. J. M. *The Reasons for Romans*. Edinburgh: T&T Clark, 1991. 169pp.

4.32 Corinthian Epistles

H I G H L Y   R E C O M M E N D E D

4.32.1   Barnett, Paul. *The Second Epistle to the Corinthians*. New International Commentary on the New Testament. Grand Rapids: Eerdmans, 1997. 662pp.

Lucid and illuminating commentary. Based on the English text, but regularly refers to the Greek, both in the text and in footnotes bearing on text-critical and exegetical issues. Argues for the letter's unity and stresses the role of individual passages within the argument as a whole. Concludes that Paul responds to the triumphalism of the Corinthians by urging a theology of power-in-weakness, based on God's resurrection of the crucified one. Paul also addresses God's fulfillment of promise in Christ through the Spirit, and presents himself as a model of pastoral leadership. Concentrates on the meaning of text for the original audience, but gives specific (though brief) attention to contemporary significance. Accessible to nonspecialists, but stimulating for scholars.

4.32.2 Barrett, C. K. *The First Epistle to the Corinthians.* Harper's New Testament Commentaries. New York: Harper & Row, 1968. 410pp.

Clear, concise, insightful, authoritative, and engaging. Introduction includes a helpful sketch of the Corinthian church and the history of the relationship between the Corinthians and Paul leading up to the production of this letter. (Even more illuminating is Barrett's explanation of the confusing history of that relationship through 2 Corinthinas, in his introduction to the commentary on that epistle, cited in next entry.) Barrett is the master of economy here, including just enough information and comment to bring the meaning of the passage into sharp focus. Manages even to offer significant theological reflection at points. Includes little explicit discussion of contemporary significance, but by exploring the connection between Paul's theological arguments and the practical problems Paul attempts to address, Barrett enables readers to make connections to contemporary situations.

4.32.3 Barrett, C. K. *The Second Epistle to the Corinthians.* Harper's New Testament Commentaries. New York: Harper & Row, 1973. 353pp.

See Barrett's *First Epistle to the Corinthians* (§4.32.2).

4.32.4 Fee, Gordon D. *The First Epistle to the Corinthians.* New International Commentary on the New Testament. Grand Rapids: Eerdmans, 1987. 880pp.

Detailed and learned commentary, written primarily for theological students and those engaged in preaching and teaching in the church, but of value also for scholars. This evangelical and Pentecostal NT scholar gives meticulous attention to every word and phrase of the book, emphasizing (1) how every statement fits into the flow of its immediate context and every section fits into the development of the argument of the entire book; (2) ways in which the historical background of church, community, and culture illuminates each passage; (3) linguistic analysis of the Greek text; (4) interpretive significance of textual variants; and (5) contemporary significance, concluding each section with explicit suggestions for Christian application.

4.32.5 Hays, Richard B. *First Corinthians*. Interpretation: A Bible Commentary for Teaching and Preaching. Louisville: Westminster John Knox, 1997. 299pp.

Offers more substantial and innovative exegetical insights into the original significance of the text than is typical of this series. Insists that only by attending to the specifics of the text can we direct our imagination in such a way as to discover analogies between our own situation and that of the original addressees. Argues that the letter presents Paul as a model pastor and urges the "conversion of the imagination," i.e., the adoption of a radical new perspective that challenges inherited sociocultural norms and practices. Explores the role of social and economic factors in the development of theological problems in the church. Paul's innovative employment of Israel's scriptures must be appreciated in order to understand Paul's argument. Paul's use of Scripture encourages us to emulate his model in our own appropriation of Scripture.

4.32.6 Martin, Ralph P. *2 Corinthians*. Word Biblical Commentary. Waco, Tex.: Word, 1986. 527pp.

Addresses the complex scholarly issues of 2 Corinthians as well as the theological meaning of the final form of the text. Argues for the unity of chapters 1–9, which he believes left Paul's hands and was on the way to Corinth when he was informed of additional problems, addressed in a subsequent letter that now comprises chapters 10–13. Emphasizes linguistic analysis of the Greek. Explores ways in which the historical and theological situation at this point when Paul's apostolic leadership was under attack illumines the text, while acknowledging the somewhat speculative character of this historical reconstruction. Carefully analyzes how Paul's response to various crises in the Corinthian church illuminates problems of Christian faith in a hedonistic and cosmopolitan setting. Insists that Paul consistently challenges the Corinthians' theology of glory with a theology of weakness manifested in servanthood and selfless ministry.

4.32.7 Thiselton, Anthony C. *The First Epistle to the Corinthians: A Commentary on the Greek Text*. New International Greek Testament Commentary. Grand Rapids: Eerdmans, 2000. 1446pp.

Most current, comprehensive, and definitive commentary on this book presently available. Attempts to answer every question readers might reasonably be expected to raise regarding the meaning of the text. Gives special attention to Greek syntax and lexicography, sociohistorical background, Paul's use of rhetorical strategies, and history of interpretation. Incorporates insights from emerging approaches, e.g., cultural anthropology, study of semantic domains, and *Wirkungsgeschichte* (i.e., "history of influence" of a passage reflected not just in commentaries, but in art, literature, liturgy, hymnody, etc.). Includes expanded discussions on such key historical and theological issues as apostleship, divorce and remarriage, and speaking in tongues. Technical, but accessible to those who do not know Greek.

4.32.8 Thrall, Margaret E. *A Critical and Exegetical Commentary on the Second Epistle to the Corinthians*. 2 vols. International Critical Commentary. Edinburgh: T&T Clark, 1994–2000. 978pp.

Detailed and authoritative commentary characterized by highly technical discussion of the historical background and the linguistic evidence of the Greek. Includes the most extensive discussion of literary issues (i.e., unity or composite character of book) and chronology of Paul's relationship with the Corinthians to be found in any commentary, presenting both history of investigation into these questions and careful analysis of NT data. Concludes that 2 Corinthians includes three originally independent letters (chapters 1–8, 9, and 10–13). Recognizes that primary attention must be given to the emerging portrait of Paul and his theological thinking, but insists on the need to understand the viewpoint of the Corinthians as well. Almost exclusively historically oriented, with theological issues addressed only insofar as they are part of the exegesis of a text that has theological content and claims.

4.32.9 Witherington, Ben, III. *Conflict and Community in Corinth: A Socio-Rhetorical Commentary on 1 and 2 Corinthians*. Grand Rapids: Eerdmans, 1995. 492pp.

Presents in a lucid fashion the meaning of the final form of these two epistles primarily on the basis of a careful examination of sociological background and Paul's use of rhetorical devices that were frequently employed in his day. Takes seriously the flow of the argument, commenting on whole rhetorical sections over against the standard verse-by-verse approach. A significant advantage of this commentary over many others is that it deals in one volume with both Corinthian letters.

ALSO SIGNIFICANT

4.32.10 Best, Ernest. *Second Corinthians*. Interpretation: A Bible Commentary for Teaching and Preaching. Atlanta: John Knox, 1987. 142pp.

4.32.11 Bieringer, R., ed. *The Corinthian Correspondence*. Bibliotheca Ephemeridum Theologicarum Lovaniensium 125. Leuven: Leuven University Press, 1996. 791pp.

4.32.12 Bieringer, R., and J. Lambrecht, eds. *Studies on 2 Corinthians*. Bibliotheca Ephemeridum Theologicarum Lovaniensium 112. Leuven: Leuven University Press, 1994. 632pp.

4.32.13 Collins, Raymond F. *First Corinthians*. Sacra Pagina. Collegeville, Minn.: Liturgical Press, 2000. 695pp.

4.32.14 Conzelmann, Hans. *1 Corinthians*. Hermeneia: A Critical and Historical Commentary on the Bible. Philadelphia: Fortress, 1975. 323pp.

4.32.15 Furnish, Victor Paul. *2 Corinthians*. Anchor Bible. Garden City, N.Y.: Doubleday, 1984. 619pp.

4.32.16 Georgi, Dieter. *The Opponents of Paul in Second Corinthians*. Philadelphia: Fortress, 1986. 463pp.

4.32.17 Godet, Frederic Louis. *Commentary on St. Paul's First Epistle to the Corinthians*. Clark's Foreign Theological Library 27. Edinburgh: T&T Clark, 1889. 920pp.

4.32.18 Grant, Robert M. *Paul in the Roman World: The Conflict at Corinth*. Louisville: Westminster John Knox, 2001. 200pp.

4.32.19 Grosheide, F. W. *Commentary on the First Epistle to the Corinthians*. New International Commentary on the New Testament. Grand Rapids: Eerdmans, 1953. 415pp.

4.32.20 Harvey, A. E. *Renewal Through Suffering: A Study of 2 Corinthians*. Studies of the New Testament and Its World. Edinburgh: T&T Clark, 1996. 148pp.

4.32.21 Hay, David M. *Pauline Theology, Volume 2: 1 and 2 Corinthians*. Minneapolis: Fortress, 1993. 300pp.

4.32.22 Hering, Jean. *The Second Epistle of St. Paul to the Corinthians*. London: Epworth, 1967. 111pp.

4.32.23 Hughes, Philip Edgcumbe. *Commentary on the Second Epistle to the Corinthians*. New International Commentary on the New Testament. Grand Rapids: Eerdmans, 1962. 508pp.

4.32.24 Kistemaker, Simon. *Exposition of the First Epistle to the Corinthians*. New Testament Commentary. Grand Rapids: Baker, 1993. 649pp.

4.32.25 ———. *Exposition of the Second Epistle to the Corinthians*. New Testament Commentary. Grand Rapids: Baker, 1997. 495pp.

4.32.26 Lambrecht, Jan. *Second Corinthians*. Sacra Pagina. Collegeville, Minn.: Liturgical Press, 1999. 250pp.

4.32.27 Murphy-O'Connor, Jerome. *The Theology of the Second Letter to the Corinthians.* New Testament Theology. Cambridge: Cambridge University Press, 1991. 166pp.

4.32.28 Plummer, Alfred. *A Critical and Exegetical Commentary on the Second Epistle of St. Paul to the Corinthians.* International Critical Commentary. Edinburgh: T&T Clark, 1915. 404pp.

4.32.29 Robertson, Archibald, and Alfred Plummer. *A Critical and Exegetical Commentary on the First Epistle of St. Paul to the Corinthians.* International Critical Commentary. Edinburgh: T&T Clark, 1911. 424pp.

4.32.30 Savage, Timothy B. *Power through Weakness: Paul's Understanding of the Christian Ministry in 2 Corinthians.* Society for New Testament Studies Monograph Series 86. Cambridge: Cambridge University Press, 1996. 251pp.

4.32.31 Talbert, Charles H. *Reading Corinthians: A Literary and Theological Commentary on 1 and 2 Corinthians.* New York: Crossroads, 1987. 188pp.

4.32.32 Theissen, Gerd. *The Social Setting of Pauline Christianity: Essays on Corinth.* Philadelphia: Fortress, 1982. 214pp.

4.32.33 Thrall, Margaret E. *The First and Second Letters of Paul to the Corinthians.* Cambridge Bible Commentary. Cambridge: Cambridge University Press, 1965. 197pp.

4.32.34 Winter, Bruce W. *After Paul Left Corinth: The Influence of Secular Ethics and Social Change.* Grand Rapids: Eerdmans, 2001. 344pp.

4.32.35 Young, Frances, and David F. Ford. *Meaning and Truth in 2 Corinthians.* Grand Rapids: Eerdmans, 1987. 289pp.

4.33 Galatians

HIGHLY RECOMMENDED

4.33.1 Betz, Hans Dieter. *Galatians.* Hermeneia: A Critical and Historical Commentary on the Bible. Philadelphia: Fortress, 1979. 352pp.

Groundbreaking commentary on Galatians insofar as it introduced the significance of Graeco-Roman rhetoric and epistolography (i.e., study of function, structure, and forms of ancient epistles) into the interpretation of Galatians. Argues that this book is an example of an apologetic letter ("forensic rhetoric"),

and interprets the letter in light of that convention. The chief contribution of
this volume is its careful tracing of the argument of the letter, understanding
the letter primarily on the basis of its own internal dynamics and the historical
situation that occasioned it. Possible weakness is the tendency to impose the
concept of forensic rhetoric on the entire letter; many have argued that it is
plausible for chapters 1–2, but less persuasive for the remainder of the letter.

4.33.2   Longenecker, Richard N. *Galatians*. Word Biblical Commentary. Dallas: Word, 1990. 323pp.

Introduction offers the most detailed discussion available for the history of investigation into the key critical issues of destination and the relationship of
Galatians to Acts 11 and 15. Also explores the problems Paul faced in the Galatian churches, the message of the opponents, and the impact of this letter on
subsequent Christian thought and activity. Emphasizes the relationship between the doctrine of justification by faith and the vitality of Christian life
empowered by God's Spirit. Methodology stresses Paul's employment of Hellenistic epistolary conventions, Graeco-Roman rhetoric, and Jewish exegetical
practices. Makes selective and eclectic use of recent approaches, especially
epistolography (ancient letters in antiquity) and rhetorical analysis. Comments
include detailed and technical discussions of language, historical background,
and ancient rhetoric. "Explanation" sections synthesize main theological issues
and offer occasional brief suggestions for contemporary relevance.

4.33.3   Martyn, J. Louis. *Galatians*. Anchor Bible. New York: Doubleday,
1997. 614pp.

Emphasizes the relationship between Paul and the Galatians implicit in this
letter, including the roles played by Paul, the Galatians, and Paul's opponents
("the teachers"). Explores Paul's intentions by examining the understanding
and reception of the letter by various segments of the Galatian church. Encourages interpreters to place themselves in the position of the original readers, who had one ear tuned to Paul's instructions here and the other to the
sermons of "the teachers." In this way Martyn hopes to arrive at a scientific
(i.e., historically accurate) and empathetic interpretation. Maintains that lack
of attention to these dynamics have led some scholars to ascribe to Paul views
that actually belonged to his opponents. The employment of historical imagination is innovative and illuminating, though somewhat speculative at points.
Commentary is arranged as a series of "comments," extended discussions of
the most significant historical and theological issues in each passage, set
within a framework of "notes," brief, basic explanations of each verse.

4.33.4   Witherington, Ben, III. *Grace in Galatia: A Commentary on Paul's
Letter to the Galatians*. Grand Rapids: Eerdmans, 1998. 475pp.

Like the commentary by Betz (§4.33.1), this volume gives serious attention to the flow of the argument, Paul's rhetorical devices, and the rhetorical macrostructure of the book. In contrast to Betz, Witherington identifies Galatians as "deliberative discourse," rather than "forensic" or "apologetic." Paul is not primarily concerned to defend himself or his apostolic authority, but offers robust explication of the gospel and its implications. Incorporates insights from discoveries and scholarly discussions developing over the quarter century since the appearance of Betz's commentary. Hence there is significant concern for sociological background, an area that was just emerging in the 1970s. Rhetorical and historical discussion is employed in service of the theological message of the book and its meaning for today. Witherington concludes each chapter by drawing out the significance for contemporary Christians.

ALSO SIGNIFICANT

4.33.5 Barclay, John M. G. *Obeying the Truth: Paul's Ethics in Galatians*. Minneapolis: Fortress, 1991. 298pp.

4.33.6 Barrett, C. K. *Freedom and Obligation: A Study of the Epistle to the Galatians*. Philadelphia: Westminster, 1985. 120pp.

4.33.7 Bruce, F. F. *The Epistle to the Galatians: A Commentary on the Greek Text*. New International Greek Testament Commentary. Grand Rapids: Eerdmans, 1982. 305pp.

4.33.8 Burton, Ernest De Witt. *A Critical and Exegetical Commentary on the Epistle to the Galatians*. International Critical Commentary. Edinburgh: T&T Clark, 1921. 541pp.

4.33.9 Cousar, Charles B. *Galatians*. Interpretation: A Bible Commentary for Teaching and Preaching. Atlanta: John Knox, 1982. 158pp.

4.33.10 Dunn, James D. G. *The Epistle to the Galatians*. Black's New Testament Commentaries. Peabody, Mass.: Hendrickson, 1993. 375pp.

4.33.11 ———. *The Theology of Paul's Letter to the Galatians*. New Testament Theology. Cambridge: Cambridge University Press, 1993. 161pp.

4.33.12 Ebeling, Gerhard. *The Truth of the Gospel: An Exposition of Galatians*. Philadelphia: Fortress, 1985. 276pp.

4.33.13 Fung, Ronald Y. K. *The Epistle to the Galatians*. New International Commentary on the New Testament. Grand Rapids: Eerdmans, 1988. 342pp.

4.33.14 Hays, Richard B. *The Faith of Jesus Christ: The Narrative Substructure of Galatians 3:1–4:11*. 2d ed. Biblical Resource Series. Grand Rapids: Eerdmans, 2001. 304pp.

4.33.15 Howard, George. *Paul: Crisis in Galatia*. Society for New Testament Studies Monograph Series 35. Cambridge: Cambridge University Press, 1990. 113pp.

4.33.16 Lightfoot, J. B. *The Epistle of St. Paul to the Galatians*. London: Macmillan, 1865. 384pp.

4.33.17 Lührmann, Dieter. *Galatians*. Minneapolis: Fortress, 1992. 161pp.

4.33.18 Luther, Martin. *A Commentary on St. Paul's Epistle to the Galatians*. Grand Rapids: Zondervan, n.d. 252pp. (Originally published 1539, in German.)

4.33.19 Matera, Frank J. *Galatians*. Sacra Pagina. Collegeville, Minn.: Michael Glazier, 1992. 252pp.

4.33.20 Morris, Leon. *Galatians: Paul's Charter of Christian Freedom*. Downers Grove, Ill.: InterVarsity, 1996. 191pp.

4.33.21 Ridderbos, Herman. *The Epistle of Paul to the Churches of Galatia*. New International Commentary on the New Testament. Grand Rapids: Eerdmans, 1953. 238pp.

4.33.22 Smiles, Vincent M. *The Gospel and the Law in Galatia: Paul's Response to Jewish-Christian Separatism and the Threat of Galatian Apostasy*. Collegeville, Minn.: Liturgical Press, 1998. 286pp.

4.34 Ephesians and Colossians

See also PHILIPPIANS AND PHILEMON (§4.35)

H I G H L Y   R E C O M M E N D E D

4.34.1 Barth, Markus. *Ephesians*. 2 vols. Anchor Bible. Garden City, N.Y.: Doubleday, 1974. 849pp.

Virtually all scholars regard this as one of the best commentaries on Ephesians ever produced, notable especially for its breadth of learning, meticulous attention to detail, careful citation of evidence, fair and balanced presentation, and theological depth. Barth (son of theologian Karl Barth) maintains, against the majority of contemporary critical scholars, that the letter was written by Paul to Gentile Christians living in Ephesus. The "notes" provide brief explanations of the sense of each verse, based primarily on detailed examination of the Greek, historical background (both Jewish and Graeco-Roman), and canonical connections (especially Paul's letters). The "comments" are extended and insightful discussions on the most significant issues in each passage, focusing on the contribution of the passage to the presentation of the theme in the NT as a whole, its relationship to theological systems and the writings of theological thinkers in the history of the church, and significance for contemporary Christians.

4.34.2 Barth, Markus, and Helmut Blanke. *Colossians*. Anchor Bible. New York: Doubleday, 1994. 557pp.

Begun by Markus Barth and completed by his student Helmut Blanke as Barth's health failed. In spite of the dual authorship there are no evident seams and the volume flows evenly and coheres perfectly. Introduction contains extensive discussion of the nature of the Colossian "heresy," the relationship between Colossians and Ephesians, and the authorship of Colossians. Contends that Paul wrote this letter from Roman imprisonment around 60–61 to readers in acute danger of being led astray by a group largely outside the church. This group touted a religion involving Jewish and pagan elements synthesized in a remarkably complete, coherent, and therefore compelling system. Paul seeks to persuade readers of the ultimate and absolute sufficiency of Christ and the need to embrace a pattern of behavior that stems from affirmation of this ultimacy of Christ. Brief but specific notes explain the sense of each passage, with comments that expand on significant issues in each passage. The comments are eloquent even to the point of poetic, and offer rich theological insight and connections with historical and systematic theology.

4.34.3 Best, Ernest. *A Critical and Exegetical Commentary on Ephesians*. International Critical Commentary. Edinburgh: T&T Clark, 1998. 686pp.

Solid and detailed commentary, if not overly imaginative. Introduction includes lengthy discussion of authorship, concluding that Ephesians and Colossians were written by two separate representatives of a Pauline school; Ephesians was produced around 90 as a general letter addressed to churches throughout Asia Minor. Treatment of each passage includes select bibliography, general introduction (with description of the passage's structure, genre, and relationship to the book as a whole), and comments emphasizing linguistic analysis of the Greek, but with some attention to historical background and canonical connections, all with a view to clarification of the theological claims of the text.

4.34.4 Lightfoot, J. B. *Saint Paul's Epistles to the Colossians and to Philemon*. 6th ed. London: Macmillan, 1882. 430pp.

Lightfoot was one of the "Cambridge triumvirate," along with B. F. Westcott and F. J. A. Hort, who argued for the authenticity and early dating of NT documents over against the more radical positions of the "Tübingen school." All of Lightfoot's commentaries are erudite and insightful, but none has so influenced the history of interpretation as his commentary on Colossians. His analysis of the Colossian "heresy" is classic, and although his contention that the heresy arose out of the Essenes is generally rejected, his basic approach and many of his specific observations form the basis for all subsequent discussion. The Greek text appears at the top of the page, with notes below. Comments emphasize linguistic analysis of the Greek, contextual connections, ancient parallels, and history of interpretation (with quotes in the original Greek or Latin). Attends seriously to theological significance. In spite of its age remains extremely helpful.

4.34.5 Lincoln, Andrew T. *Ephesians*. Word Biblical Commentary. Dallas: Word, 1990. 494pp.

This evangelical scholar compares Ephesians with Colossians and other books in the Pauline corpus, concluding that Ephesians was written by a follower of Paul to a group of churches in Asia Minor after Paul's death. The author of Ephesians has redacted his sources (Colossians and other letters in the Pauline corpus) so as to apply the Pauline themes to the situation now facing his readers. Thus, explores the ways this redactional process illuminates the meaning of each passage. Also examines the lexical and syntactical significance of the Greek text, the employment of rhetorical strategies current at the time of writing, the structure of the passage, and the role of the passage in broader-book context. The purpose of the letter is to persuade readers to consider the role of the church (which includes the people of Israel) in the history of God's purposes, to embrace their Christian identity in a hostile socioreligious environment, and to recognize the ways in which this identity must be manifested in their behavior. Offers a more complete, coherent, and compelling portrait of the setting of this letter and of the letter's response to this setting than does Best (§4.34.3). Explanation sections synthesize the theology of each passage, but seldom address contemporary application.

4.34.6 O'Brien, Peter T. *Colossians, Philemon*. Word Biblical Commentary. Waco, Tex.: Word, 1982. 328pp.

Introduction provides illuminating history of interpretation into the Colossian "heresy," which O'Brien takes to be an admixture of Jewish and pagan elements, emphasizing mysticism and asceticism. To counter this teaching, Paul stresses realized eschatology, i.e., the aspects of salvation that Christians experience in the present, so as to insist that already Christ provides Christians with more than could possibly be offered by this competing religious system. Like Barth-Blanke (§4.34.2), contends that the letter was written by Paul during Roman imprisonment. But O'Brien's interpretation of individual passages often differs from Barth-Blanke, in some cases offering a more compelling interpretation. Emphasizes analysis of the Greek, religious and sociohistorical background, canonical connections, and history of interpretation. The "explanation" section synthesizes the theology of the passage and explores its significance for the religious experience of the original readers, but seldom addresses contemporary application.

4.34.7 Pokorný, Petr. *Colossians: A Commentary.* Peabody, Mass.: Hendrickson, 1991. 232pp.

Argues that Colossians is a pseudonymous letter written by a follower of Paul after the latter's death. Considers the theological significance of a pseudonymous canonical book, and concludes that the theological problems are manageable and that the letter "authentically renders apostolic witness." Reconstructs a plausible historical setting for the letter. Commentary focuses on the literary structure of whole book and of individual passages, and the structure of the theological argument. Gives secondary attention to linguistic analysis, historical background, and history of interpretation. Primarily concerned with theological exposition, and constantly relates the theological claims of specific passages in Colossians to the broader biblical witness. Gives no explicit attention to contemporary application.

4.34.8 Schnackenburg, Rudolf. *The Epistle to the Ephesians: A Commentary.* Edinburgh: T&T Clark, 1991. 356pp.

The author, a leading European Roman Catholic scholar, attempts to write for Protestants as well as Catholics. Considers Ephesians to be a post-Pauline pseudepigraphical work, a general letter addressed to a wide geographical area, whose author knew and used Colossians. Sees the focus of the letter as the church, and the purpose to persuade Christians in danger of conforming to their pagan environment to embrace decisively Christian commitment and behavior. Attends to the structure and form of each passage, its role within the argument of the whole work, linguistic analysis of the Greek, canonical connections, and contemporary significance.

ALSO SIGNIFICANT

4.34.9 Abbott, T. K. *A Critical and Exegetical Commentary on the Epistles to the Ephesians and to the Colossians.* International Critical Commentary. Edinburgh: T&T Clark, 1897. 315pp.

4.34.10 Bruce, F. F. *The Epistle to the Colossians, to Philemon, and to the Ephesians.* New International Commentary on the New Testament. Grand Rapids: Eerdmans, 1984. 442pp.

4.34.11 Dahl, Nils Alstrup. *Studies in Ephesians: Introductory Questions, Text- and Edition-Critical Issues, Interpretation of Texts and Themes*. Edited by David Hellholm, Vemund Blomkvist, and Tord Fornberg. Tübingen: Mohr Siebeck, 2000. 548pp.

4.34.12 Dunn, James D. G. *The Epistles to the Colossians and to Philemon: A Commentary on the Greek Text*. New International Greek Testament Commentary. Grand Rapids: Eerdmans, 1996. 388pp.

4.34.13 Francis, Fred O., and Wayne A. Meeks, eds. *Conflict at Colossae: A Problem in the Interpretation of Early Christianity Illustrated by Selected Modern Studies*. Missoula, Mont.: Scholars, 1975. 222pp.

4.34.14 Hoehner, Harold W. *Ephesians: An Exegetical Commentary*. Grand Rapids: Baker, 2002. 960pp.

4.34.15 Klein, William W. *The Book of Ephesians: An Annotated Bibliography*. New York: Garland, 1996. 312pp.

4.34.16 Lincoln, Andrew T., and A. J. M. Wedderburn. *The Theology of the Later Pauline Letters*. New Testament Theology. Cambridge: Cambridge University Press, 1993. 185pp.

4.34.17 Lohse, Eduard. *Colossians and Philemon*. Hermeneia: A Critical and Historical Commentary on the Bible. Philadelphia: Fortress, 1971. 233pp.

4.34.18 MacDonald, Margaret Y. *Colossians and Ephesians*. Sacra Pagina. Collegeville, Minn.: Liturgical Press, 2000. 390pp.

4.34.19 Martin, Ralph P. *Colossians and Philemon*. New Century Bible. Grand Rapids: Eerdmans, 1974. 174pp.

4.34.20 ———. *Ephesians, Colossians, and Philemon*. Interpretation: A Bible Commentary for Teaching and Preaching. Louisville: Westminster John Knox, 1991. 156pp.

4.34.21 Mitton, C. Leslie. *Ephesians*. New Century Bible Commentary. London: Oliphants, 1976. 235pp.

4.34.22 Moule, C. F. D. *The Epistles of Paul the Apostle to the Colossians and to Philemon*. Cambridge Greek Testament Commentary. Cambridge: Cambridge University Press, 1957. 169pp.

4.34.23 O'Brien, Peter T. *The Letter to the Ephesians*. Pillar New Testament Commentary. Grand Rapids: Eerdmans, 1999. 536pp.

4.34.24 Robinson, J. Armitage. *St. Paul's Epistle to the Ephesians*. London: Macmillan, 1922. 314pp.

4.34.25 Schweizer, Eduard. *The Letter to the Colossians: A Commentary*. Minneapolis: Augsburg, 1982. 319pp.

4.34.26 Thurston, Bonnie. *Reading Colossians, Ephesians, and 2 Thessalonians: A Literary and Theological Commentary*. New York: Crossroad, 1995. 197pp.

4.34.27 Westcott, Brooke Foss. *Saint Paul's Epistle to the Ephesians*. London: Macmillan, 1906. 212pp.

4.34.28 Wright, N. T. *Colossians and Philemon*. Tyndale New Testament Commentaries. Grand Rapids: Eerdmans, 1986. 192pp.

4.35 Philippians and Philemon

See also EPHESIANS AND COLOSSIANS (§4.34)

H I G H L Y   R E C O M M E N D E D

4.35.1 Barth, Markus, and Helmut Blanke. *The Letter to Philemon*. Eerdmans Critical Commentary. Grand Rapids: Eerdmans, 2000. 561pp.

Probably most comprehensive work on Philemon ever produced. Insists that Philemon is significant for its unique insights into the social setting of the NT and its creative and specific application of the central demand of the gospel, brotherly love. Presents extensive analysis of aspects of the ancient world relevant to Philemon, especially slavery, and compares references to slavery in Philemon with those in other Pauline letters. Verse-by-verse commentary gives special attention to such major Pauline theological themes as love, faith, Christian unity, and human responsibility. Surveys history of interpretation from antiquity to the most recent discussions. More detailed than Fitzmyer, especially in comments on individual passages, but bibliography is less thorough. Contains many excurses treating significant historical and theological issues in relation to their role within Philemon, Pauline theology, and biblical thought as a whole.

4.35.2 Bockmuehl, Markus. *The Epistle to the Philippians*. Black's New Testament Commentary. Peabody, Mass.: Hendrickson, 327pp.

One of the most methodologically reflective commentaries on Philippians or any other NT book. Considers methodological issues involved in the use of Acts for reconstructing the Philippian situation, concluding that a cautious, critical, but sympathetic employment of Acts is appropriate. Incorporates insights from sociological studies and investigations into ancient rhetoric, but rejects a heavy dependence on these recent approaches in favor of a more general historical approach that makes use of all relevant evidence for ascertaining the intended meaning of the text for its original readers and that in turn leads to theological understanding. Packs a remarkable amount of relevant information and theological insight into a small amount of space by focusing on those elements that are central to the agenda of the text and are of greatest concern to modern readers.

√4.35.3 Fee, Gordon D. *Paul's Letter to the Philippians.* New International Commentary on the New Testament. Grand Rapids: Eerdmans, 1995. 497pp.

Comprehensive and detailed commentary on the English text (NIV), but with constant reference to the Greek. Writes primarily for pastors and teachers, but with an eye also to the scholar. Argues for Pauline authorship and literary unity of the letter, which Fee takes to have been written from Roman imprisonment to a church facing opposition because of its commitment to Christ. Considers Philippians to have material and formal connections with two types of letters familiar to first-century readers: friendship, and moral exhortation. Introduction extensively discusses these two letter types, and commentary draws on literary and philosophical background of friendship and moral exhortation. Text of commentary is accessible to nonspecialist. Presents the theological meaning of the text, with references to original language, literary structure, and background of Paul's thought as discerned from his other letters all discussed more fully and technically in extensive footnotes.

4.35.4 Fitzmyer, Joseph A. *The Letter to Philemon.* Anchor Bible. New York: Doubleday, 2000. 138pp.

Deals in an informed and judicious manner with most significant issues in Philemon. The introduction, which comprises more than half of the volume, offers brief but illuminating discussions of slavery in antiquity, contemporary significance of this letter, theology, and complete bibliography. The "comments" on each passage, accessible to the nonspecialist, treat the literary structure of the passage, its function within the letter, and its basic meaning. The "notes" explore the meaning of each verse through linguistic analysis; social, political, economic, and religious background; and history of interpretation (both ancient and modern). Includes extensive bibliography on each passage.

4.35.5 Hawthorne, Gerald F. *Philippians.* Word Biblical Commentary. Waco, Tex.: Word, 1983. 232pp.

Solid and informed, though not particularly original, commentary written from an evangelical perspective. Argues that Philippians is a unity, written by

Paul from Caesarean prison around 60. Comments are lucid and clearly organized, typically listing major interpretive possibilities along with arguments for
and against each, concluding with Hawthorne's own considered judgment.
Generally discusses major issues or aspects of a passage, developing the
meaning of each and giving explicit citations of evidence, especially from
structure, linguistic analysis, other Pauline passages, and parallels from Jewish
and Graeco-Roman writings. Explicates theological meaning of each passage
and its pastoral significance for the original readers. Does little to address explicitly contemporary application.

4.35.6 O'Brien, Peter T. *Commentary on Philippians*. New International
Greek Testament Commentary. Grand Rapids: Eerdmans, 1991. 597pp.

Traditional commentary, focused on historical-critical and linguistic exegesis
of the Greek text and drawing little on the more recent literary, rhetorical, and
sociological approaches. O'Brien interacts fully with history of scholarship,
but gives primary attention to his own engagement with the text, often arriving at quite independent interpretive judgments. Deals with each passage by
exploring its structure, themes (overarching concerns and their specific development within the paragraph), function within the argument of the entire letter, and analysis of every phrase and word of the Greek text. Gives particular
attention to the background of the city of Philippi, Paul's opponents, and the
character and function within the book of the christological hymn in 2:5–11.
Focus is on the theological meaning of the text and how it relates to other biblical passages and to biblical theology as a whole.

4.35.7 Petersen, Norman R. *Rediscovering Paul: Philemon and the Sociology
of Paul's Narrative World*. Philadelphia: Fortress, 1985. 308pp.

This pioneer in the new literary criticism of the Gospels here integrates contemporary literary and sociological study with the traditional historical-critical
approach. Argues that letters have narrative substructures (i.e., that they assume and present a story), and that the "narrative world" presented in a letter
has the same kinds of social arrangements ("social structures underlying the
social relations comprised of the actions of the actors in Paul's letters and their
stories") and symbolic forms ("systems of knowledge, belief, and value, that
define these actors' identities and motivate their actions") as does the real
world. This volume is thus a groundbreaking work both in methodology and
in the study of Philemon, arguing that Paul relates the mundane experience of
a slave and the dynamics between this slave and his master to the story of the
transcendent divine world, in which God is Father, Christ is Lord, and love is
ultimate reality. Paul urges the church to submit this present temporal world
to the kingdom of God, which is already breaking in, and thus to function as
"antistructure," replacing the old order with new order after the image of

Christ. This vivid portrait of the church as the manifestation of the new order makes Philemon central to understanding Paul's theology as a whole.

A L S O   S I G N I F I C A N T

4.35.8 Bakirtzis, Charalambos, and Helmut Koester, eds. *Philippi at the Time of Paul and after His Death*. Harrisburg, Pa.: Trinity Press International, 1998. 87pp.

4.35.9 Beare, Francis Wright. *The Epistle to the Philippians*. Harper's New Testament Commentaries. New York: Harper & Row, 1959. 182pp.

4.35.10 Bloomquist, L. Gregory. *The Function of Suffering in Philippians*. Journal for the Study of the New Testament Supplement Series 78. Sheffield: JSOT, 1993. 235pp.

4.35.11 Caird, G. B. *Paul's Letters from Prison: Ephesians, Philippians, Colossians, Philemon, in the Revised Standard Version*. New Clarendon Bible. Oxford: Oxford University Press, 1976. 223pp.

4.35.12 Callahan, Allen Dwight. *Embassy of Onesimus: The Letter of Paul to Philemon*. Valley Forge, Pa.: Trinity Press International, 1997. 96pp.

4.35.13 Collange, Jean-Francois. *The Epistle of Saint Paul to the Philippians*. London: Epworth, 1979. 159pp.

4.35.14 Craddock, Fred B. *Philippians*. Interpretation: A Bible Commentary for Teaching and Preaching. Atlanta: John Knox, 1985. 84pp.

4.35.15 Eadie, John. *A Commentary on the Greek Text of the Epistle of Paul to the Philippians*. 2d ed. Edinburgh: T&T Clark, 1884. 296pp.

4.35.16 Knox, John. *Philemon among the Letters of Paul: A New View of Its Place and Importance*. 2d ed. New York: Abingdon, 1959. 110pp.

4.35.17 Lightfoot, J. B. *St. Paul's Epistle to the Philippians*. London: Macmillan, 1913. 350pp.

4.35.18 Martin, Ralph P. *Philippians*. 2d ed. New Century Bible Commentary. Grand Rapids: Eerdmans, 1987. 187pp.

4.35.19 Plummer, Alfred. *A Commentary on St. Paul's Epistle to the Philippians*. London: R. Scott, 1919. 115pp.

4.35.20 Silva, Moisés. *Philippians.* Baker Exegetical Commentary on the New Testament. Grand Rapids: Baker, 1992. 255pp.

4.35.21 Vincent, Marvin R. *A Critical and Exegetical Commentary on the Epistles to the Philippians and to Philemon.* International Critical Commentary. Edinburgh: T&T Clark, 1897. 201pp.

4.35.22 Witherington, Ben, III. *Friendship and Finances in Philippi: The Letter of Paul to the Philippians.* The New Testament in Context. Valley Forge, Pa.: Trinity Press International, 1995. 176pp.

4.36 Thessalonian Epistles

HIGHLY RECOMMENDED

4.36.1 Bruce, F. F. *1 and 2 Thessalonians.* Word Biblical Commentary. Waco, Tex.: Word, 1982. 228pp.

Careful, detailed exegesis, with special attention given to most problematic and difficult areas. Accepts unity and Pauline authorship of both letters. Emphasizes text-critical issues, linguistic analysis of the Greek, ideological background of Paul's thought as ascertained through his other letters, and historical background, especially Paul's relationship with the Thessalonians as this can be reconstructed from the letter itself and from Acts (which Bruce employs uncritically). Focuses on identifying and tracing the development of problems among the Thessalonians and Paul's response to these problems. Explores the contributions of theological claims in these letters to an understanding of Paul's thought and practice of pastoral care in general. Especially helpful are background articles treating Christianity in Macedonia, early Christian experience at Thessalonica, eschatology at Thessalonica, and the antichrist.

4.36.2 Donfried, Karl P., and Johannes Beutler, eds. *The Thessalonians Debate: Methodological Discord or Methodological Synthesis?* Grand Rapids: Eerdmans, 2000. 384pp.

Contains revised and, in some cases, translated seminar papers or responses to papers by some of the foremost authorities on Thessalonians, presented at the Seminar on Thessalonian Correspondence of the Studiorum Novi Testamentum Societas (SNTS). Focuses entirely on 1 Thessalonians. Especially helpful is Donfried's introductory article on the scope and nature of the debate. Each essay represents a major issue in contemporary discussion of the letter and interacts with the work of other prominent scholars. Greatest attention is given to rhetorical analysis and epistolography (study of ancient letters). Somewhat technical, but still accessible to nonspecialists.

4.36.3 Jewett, Robert. *The Thessalonian Correspondence: Pauline Rhetoric and Millenarian Piety.* Foundations and Facets: New Testament. Philadelphia: Fortress, 1986. 240pp.

Not a traditional commentary, but a careful exegetical study that attempts a comprehensive synthesis of historical-critical method with rhetorical and social-scientific critical approaches. Carefully analyzes significant issues in the interpretation of Thessalonians, including authorship, sequence, and literary integrity. Includes a rhetorical analysis of the letters that illuminates how Paul conceived the Thessalonian situation, the selection and evaluation of sociological models for the Thessalonian congregation, concluding that the millenarian model best explains the evidence. Suggests that Paul confronted a radical millenarianism unique in early Christianity, promoted by a group that grossly misunderstood Paul's apocalyptic gospel and proclaimed the "actual arrival of the millennium and proceeded to act on that assumption." Contains solid discussion of introductory matters and original insights, but volume becomes increasingly speculative and "experimental" as it proceeds.

4.36.4 Malherbe, Abraham J. *The Letters to the Thessalonians.* Anchor Bible. New York: Doubleday, 2000. 508pp.

Argues for unity and Pauline authorship of both letters, and maintains that 1 Thessalonians preceded 2 Thessalonians by a few months. Makes discriminating use of Acts for background pertaining to the Thessalonian situation. Employs linguistic analysis, historical background (especially Paul's ministry among the Thessalonians, Pauline thought as derived from his other letters, and Jewish and Graeco-Roman writings, with particular emphasis on Greek and Roman philosophical tradition, which Malherbe thinks had significant affinities with Thessalonians), and history of interpretation, both ancient and modern. Focuses on the theological meaning of the text, Paul as a model of pastoral care, and Paul's concern to address the moral, spiritual, and emotional needs of his converts.

✝ 4.36.5 Marshall, I. Howard. *1 and 2 Thessalonians.* New Century Bible Commentary. Grand Rapids: Eerdmans, 1983. 240pp.

Careful, solid exegesis by a leading evangelical British scholar. Lucid commentary, concise, straightforward, and accessible to the nonspecialist. Concerned throughout to present exposition relevant for those who read these letters as Christian scripture, emphasizing ways in which the theological claims encountered here relate to NT faith as a whole. Gives some consideration to contemporary application.

4.36.6 Wanamaker, Charles A. *Commentary on 1 and 2 Thessalonians.* New International Greek Testament Commentary. Grand Rapids: Eerdmans, 1990. 316pp.

Only major commentary to conclude that 2 Thessalonians preceded 1 Thessalonians, a position for which the author argues extensively. Recognizing that this is a minority view, Wanamaker presents his commentary in such a way that it is useful to those who accept the traditional sequence. Emphasizes linguistic analysis of the Greek, but is the first commentary on Thessalonians to integrate historical-critical methods with social-scientific and rhetorical-critical approaches. Employs sociological models both for Christianity in Thessalonica and for the "social character and functioning of Paul's letters within this context." Employment of sociological models generally leads interpreters to force a particular model on data of the text, but Wanamaker generally avoids this danger by cautious and restrained application of these models, and by beginning always with careful linguistic, historical, and literary analysis. Focus is on theological message, with occasional attention to contemporary significance.

ALSO   SIGNIFICANT

4.36.7 Best, Ernest. *A Commentary on the First and Second Epistles to the Thessalonians.* Harper's New Testament Commentaries. New York: Harper & Row, 1972. 391pp.

4.36.8 Collins, Raymond F. *The Birth of the New Testament: The Origin and Development of the First Christian Generation.* New York: Crossroad, 1993. 324pp.

4.36.9 ———. *Studies on the First Letter to the Thessalonians.* Leuven: Leuven University Press, 1984. 418pp.

4.36.10 Collins, Raymond F., ed. *The Thessalonian Correspondence.* Bibliotheca Ephemeridum Theologicarum Louvaniensium 87. Leuven: Leuven University Press, 1990. 546pp.

4.36.11 Donfried, Karl Paul. *Paul, Thessalonica, and Early Christianity.* Grand Rapids: Eerdmans, 2002. 347pp.

4.36.12 Frame, James Everett. *A Critical and Exegetical Commentary on the Epistles of St. Paul to the Thessalonians.* International Critical Commentary. Edinburgh: T&T Clark, 1912. 326pp.

4.36.13 Gaventa, Beverly Roberts. *First and Second Thessalonians.* Interpretation: A Bible Commentary for Teaching and Preaching. Louisville: Westminster John Knox, 1998. 138pp.

4.36.14 Green, Gene L. *The Letters to the Thessalonians.* Pillar New Testament Commentaries. Grand Rapids: Eerdmans, 2002. 416pp.

4.36.15 Malherbe, Abraham J. *Paul and the Thessalonians: The Philosophic Tradition of Pastoral Care.* Philadelphia: Fortress, 1987. 120pp.

4.36.16 Milligan, George. *St. Paul's Epistles to the Thessalonians.* London: Macmillan, 1908. 195pp.

4.36.17 Morris, Leon. *The First and Second Epistles to the Thessalonians.* Rev. ed. New International Commentary on the New Testament. Grand Rapids: Eerdmans, 1991. 278pp.

4.36.18 Richard, Earl J. *First and Second Thessalonians.* Sacra Pagina. Collegeville, Minn.: Liturgical Press, 1995. 409pp.

4.36.19 Smith, Abraham. *Comfort One Another: Reconstructing the Rhetoric and Audience of 1 Thessalonians.* Literary Currents in Biblical Interpretation. Louisville: Westminster John Knox, 1995. 160pp.

4.36.20 Weima, Jeffrey A. D., and Stanley E. Porter. *An Annotated Bibliography of First and Second Thessalonians.* New Testament Tools and Studies 26. Leiden: Brill, 1998. 292pp.

4.37 Pastoral Epistles

H I G H L Y   R E C O M M E N D E D

4.37.1 Collins, Raymond F. *I and II Timothy and Titus: A Commentary.* New Testament Library. Louisville: Westminster John Knox, 2002. 408pp.

Erudite and authoritative, yet readable, commentary from prominent Roman Catholic scholar. Agrees with the general critical consensus that these epistles were composed by a single post-Pauline hand around the end of the first century. Analyzes ways in which this author attempted to make relevant for his own generation the teaching of Paul. Collins attends especially to texts from Hellenism and rabbinic Judaism to shed light on the meaning of the Pastorals. Very helpful in providing background information, but gives little attention in the commentary proper to the history of interpretation or to theological reflection. Addresses select theological issues in excurses (extended discussions), e.g., Christians in the world, perspectives on women, and faith.

4.37.2 Johnson, Luke Timothy. *The First and Second Letters to Timothy.* Anchor Bible. New York: Doubleday, 2001. 494pp.

Insightful and original commentary in which this Roman Catholic scholar takes the position, unusual for contemporary critical scholars outside the evangelical tradition, that both letters were written by Paul. Consequently, Johnson reads 1 and 2 Timothy as real rather than fictional letters, to be understood within the framework of Paul's ministry and his relationship with Timothy. Attends seriously to the situation the letters purport to address, and interprets them in light of the Pauline corpus. Introduction contains extensive discussion of history of interpretation, from the Fathers to the present. Commentary consistently interacts with history of scholarship. Also makes use of linguistic analysis and Graeco-Roman rhetoric and moral philosophy, which Johnson takes to be significant for the interpretation of Paul's letters. Concerned with the theological meaning of the final text, and offers some suggestions regarding contemporary appropriation.

4.37.3 Knight, George W., III. *Commentary on the Pastoral Epistles.* New International Greek Testament Commentary. Grand Rapids: Eerdmans, 1992. 514pp.

This evangelical scholar argues that Paul authored all three Pastorals just prior to his death, possibly using Luke as an amanuensis. Gives some attention to the history of interpretation, but primarily presents Knight's own construal of the Greek text, paying particular regard to lexical and syntactical analysis of the Greek and to the flow of the argument. Notable for exploration of subtle nuances of meaning. Interpretive possibilities are clearly set out with arguments for and against each, followed by Knight's own cogent conclusions. Gives little explicit attention to contemporary application, and says virtually nothing regarding potential application of even the most difficult passages (e.g., 1 Tim. 2:8–15).

4.37.4 Marshall, I. Howard. *A Critical and Exegetical Commentary on the Pastoral Epistles.* In collaboration with Philip H. Towner. International Critical Commentary. Edinburgh: T&T Clark, 1999. 869pp.

Takes an unusual position for an evangelical by arguing against Pauline authorship, asserting that these letters were produced by close associates of Paul (perhaps Titus and Timothy) shortly after Paul's death. The letters were not intended to deceive, but were manifestly known to the audience as fictionalized expansions by Paul's associates of authentic Pauline tradition. Commentary thus is concerned to interpret them both according to their fictional framework as letters of Paul to his delegates and according to their actual intention of instructing the post-Pauline church and its leaders. Approaches these letters as literary wholes, interpreting passages as they relate to the form and structure of each letter and to the whole corpus of the Pastoral Epistles. Chiefly concerned to understand the theology of each passage on basis of detailed linguistic analysis of the Greek, historical background, and flow of argument. Gives little attention to history of interpretation or to contemporary application.

4.37.5   Mounce, William D. *Pastoral Epistles*. Word Biblical Commentary. Nashville: Thomas Nelson, 2000. 641pp.

Argues extensively for the Pauline authorship of all three letters, and gives great care to reconstruct the specific context of each letter within the life setting of Paul, Titus, Timothy, and the churches in Ephesus and Crete, showing how each letter responds specifically to particular problems or challenges. Derives this reconstruction from the Pastorals, Acts, and early Christian tradition. Emphasizes the uniquely Christian character and perspective of the letters, citing parallels with other canonical writings (especially Pauline) and contrasting them with Graeco-Roman literary and philosophical works. Provides immense bibliographies on individual passages. Focuses on the theological meaning of the text. This theological interpretation implicitly reflects contemporary concerns, but gives little explicit attention to application.

4.37.6   Quinn, Jerome D. *The Letter to Titus*. Anchor Bible. New York: Doubleday, 1990. 334pp.

This Roman Catholic scholar considers Titus to be post-Pauline, written around 82. Probably sent from Rome to all the churches in the central Mediterranean as a means of spanning the generation between the apostolic and post-apostolic periods. Introduction pertains to all three Pastoral Epistles, and offers a reconstructed historical setting that serves in the commentary as the definitive framework for interpretation. "Notes" contain citation of technical evidence (particularly linguistic analysis); parallels with canonical and extra-canonical literature (especially early church fathers); and historical background. "Comments" build upon the notes to reconstruct the theological meaning and pastoral significance for the original audience.

4.37.7   Quinn, Jerome D., and William C. Wacker. *The First and Second Letters to Timothy*. Anchor Bible. New York: Doubleday, 2000. 918pp.

Quinn had completed the manuscript through 1 Tim. 4:5 at the time of his death in 1988, leaving voluminous unedited notes on the rest. Wacker edited his teacher's material, adding very little of his own research. Consequently, this commentary, though published in 2000, dates essentially to 1988. As a companion to Quinn's commentary on Titus (§4.37.6), it shares the same format and character. Like that volume, it is notable for its originality, erudition, depth, and comprehensiveness. It is the most detailed commentary on these letters available in English. Includes the introduction to the Pastoral Epistles found in that commentary.

ALSO SIGNIFICANT

4.37.8   Barrett, C. K. *The Pastoral Epistles in the New English Bible*. New Clarendon Bible. Oxford: Clarendon, 1963. 151pp.

4.37.9   Dibelius, Martin, and Conzelmann, Hans. *The Pastoral Epistles*. Hermeneia: A Critical and Historical Commentary on the Bible. Philadelphia: Fortress, 1972. 175pp.

4.37.10 Guthrie, Donald. *The Pastoral Epistles*. 2d ed. Tyndale New Testament Commentaries. Downers Grove, Ill.: InterVarsity, 1990. 240pp.

4.37.11 Hanson, A. T. *The Pastoral Epistles*. New Century Bible Commentary. Grand Rapids: Eerdmans, 1982. 206pp.

4.37.12 Harding, Mark. *Tradition and Rhetoric in the Pastoral Epistles*. Studies in Biblical Literature 3. New York: Peter Lang, 1998. 253pp.

4.37.13 ———. *What Are They Saying about the Pastoral Epistles?* New York: Paulist, 2000. 176pp.

4.37.14 Houlden, J. L. *The Pastoral Epistles: I and II Timothy, Titus*. New Testament Commentaries. Philadelphia: Trinity, 1989. 166pp.

4.37.15 Kelly, J. N. D. *A Commentary on the Pastoral Epistles: I Timothy, II Timothy, Titus*. Harper's New Testament Commentaries. New York: Harper & Row, 1960. 263pp.

4.37.16 Johnson, Luke Timothy. *Letters to Paul's Delegates: 1 Timothy, 2 Timothy, Titus*. New Testament in Context. Valley Forge, Pa.: Trinity Press International, 1996. 263pp.

4.37.17 Lock, Walter. *A Critical and Exegetical Commentary on the Pastoral Epistles*. International Critical Commentary. Edinburgh: T&T Clark, 1924. 163pp.

4.37.18 Oden, Thomas C. *First and Second Timothy and Titus*. Interpretation: A Bible Commentary for Teaching and Preaching. Atlanta: John Knox, 1989. 190pp.

4.37.19 Prior, Michael. *Paul the Letter-Writer and the Second Letter to Timothy*. Journal for the Study of the New Testament Supplement Series 23. Sheffield: JSOT, 1989. 300pp.

4.37.20 Towner, Philip H. *The Goal of Our Instruction: The Structure of Theology and Ethics in the Pastoral Epistles*. Journal for the Study of the New Testament Supplement Series 34. Sheffield: JSOT, 1989. 346pp.

4.37.21 Verner, David C. *The Household of God: The Social World of the Pastoral Epistles*. Society of Biblical Literature Dissertation Series 71. Chico, Calif.: Scholars, 1983. 207pp.

4.37.22 Young, Frances. *The Theology of the Pastoral Epistles*. New Testament Theology. Cambridge: Cambridge University Press, 1994. 170pp.

4.38 Hebrews

H I G H L Y   R E C O M M E N D E D

4.38.1 Attridge, Harold W. *Hebrews*. Hermeneia: A Critical and Historical Commentary on the Bible. Minneapolis: Fortress, 1989. 437pp.

Careful, judicious, balanced, and lucid. Recognizing the limits of evidence pertaining to many disputed matters of background, the author refuses to accept positions that must, in his judgment, be speculative. Thus he dates the book between 60 and 100, and refuses to decide between a Jewish-Christian or Gentile-Christian audience. Insists that the book was a sermon or homily, and develops the significance of this conclusion for both the book's structure and its message. Exposition contains "analyses," presenting passages' form, structure, major themes, and function within entire book, while "comments" offers careful linguistic examination of the Greek and discussion of Jewish and Hellenistic background. Excurses deal helpfully with significant theological and literary issues. Meticulous, but accessible to the nonspecialist.

4.38.2 Bruce, F. F. *The Epistle to the Hebrews*. Rev. ed. New International Commentary on the New Testament. Grand Rapids: Eerdmans, 1990. 426pp.

The best of Bruce's many commentaries. Makes use of his background in classical Greek, his intimate familiarity with the thought of the OT, and his encyclopedic knowledge of Jewish and early Christian background to explore the homiletical intention of the book for its original readers. Gives little explicit attention to contemporary application. Regularly cites background material, but focuses on the theology of the text. Consistently relates the teaching of Hebrews to other biblical passages, at times uncritically reading passages in Hebrews in the light of other NT passages, thereby running the risk of obscuring the unique perspective of Hebrews.

4.38.3 Ellingworth, Paul. *Commentary on Hebrews*. New International Greek Testament Commentary. Grand Rapids: Eerdmans, 1993. 764pp.

No commentary on Hebrews gives more attention to lexical, syntactical, and text-critical concerns. But the supreme value of this volume is its balance between meticulous attention to detail and its relating individual passages to the broad context of the book, other early Christian writings, and the OT. Concern for sound methodology is expressed in regular discussion of methodological issues and explicit articulation of the methodological bases of the interpretive processes used. Commentary assumes knowledge of Greek. Gives little attention to contemporary application.

4.38.4   Koester, Craig R. *Hebrews*. Anchor Bible. New York: Doubleday, 2001. 512pp.

Current and original. Argues that the book was written between 60 and 90, and insists that the social setting of the community is more significant for the book's interpretation than a precise decision regarding date. Introduction offers a comprehensive survey of interpretation from the Fathers to the present, a thorough investigation into the social and religious circumstances of the community, and a helpful discussion of the book's theology, which Koester understands to center around God's intentions for humanity. Commentary is accessible to students and pastors, but contains a wealth of technical information valuable to scholars. Employs historical background, history of interpretation, and linguistic analysis (primarily lexical, with less emphasis on syntax) to produce a rich theological exposition. Emphasizes sociological insights and ancient rhetoric, at times in ways that seem to superimpose these categories on the text.

4.38.5   Lane, William L. *Hebrews*. 2 vols. Word Biblical Commentary. Dallas: Word, 1991. 617pp.

Written primarily for scholars, but large portions are accessible to pastors and teachers, who will find it eminently useful. Offers comprehensive treatment of every phrase. Attends to the broad argument of Hebrews in an introduction to each of the book's five main units. Employs insights from emerging disciplines of genre criticism, sociological studies, and discourse analysis, but refuses to be bound to a rigid application of any of these methods. Emphasizes the book's sermonic character and pastoral purpose, but gives little explicit attention to contemporary application; for helpful suggestions in this area one should consult Lane's *Hebrews: A Call to Commitment* (§4.38.20).

4.38.6   Lindars, Barnabas. *The Theology of the Letter to the Hebrews*. New Testament Theology. Cambridge: Cambridge University Press, 1991. 155pp.

Remarkably clear and satisfying study of the difficult and (to modern readers) arcane theology of Hebrews. Discerns the book's theology through careful tracing of its argument, examination of its rhetoric, and consideration of its pastoral purpose. Addresses several theological issues, but gives primary attention to Christ's priesthood and sacrifice. Discusses Hebrews' contribution to NT theology and considers its contemporary significance.

4.38.7   Westcott, Brooke Foss. *The Epistle to the Hebrews: The Greek Text with Notes and Essays*. London: Macmillan, 1892. 504pp.

A classic work from one of the greatest NT commentators of the modern period. Concludes the book was written to Jewish Christians in Palestine about the time of the destruction of Jerusalem in order to address their overwhelming disappointment and despair, and to use this occasion as an opportunity to present to them "a larger hope through a new revelation of the glory of Christ." As such, Hebrews has relevance for all succeeding generations, especially as they experience severe upheavals in their corporate or personal lives. Gives minute attention to every detail of the Greek text, demonstrates how the structure of passages informs their meaning, presents relevant quotations from patristic and medieval interpreters in original Greek and Latin, relates the teachings of Hebrews to other biblical writings, and reflects on the theology of the text. Numerous excurses discuss in depth the most significant theological issues.

A L S O   S I G N I F I C A N T

4.38.8   Buchanan, George Wesley. *To the Hebrews*. Anchor Bible. Garden City, N.Y.: Doubleday, 1972. 282pp.

4.38.9   Delitzsch, Franz. *Commentary on the Epistle to the Hebrews*. 2 vols. Edinburgh: T&T Clark, 1871. 401/499pp.

4.38.10 DeSilva, David A. *Perseverance in Gratitude: A Socio-Rhetorical Commentary on the Epistle "to the Hebrews."* Grand Rapids: Eerdmans, 2000. 560pp.

4.38.11 Dunnill, John. *Covenant and Sacrifice in the Letter to the Hebrews*. Society for New Testament Studies Monograph Series 75. Cambridge: Cambridge University Press, 1992. 297pp.

4.38.12 Guthrie, George H. *The Structure of Hebrews: A Text-Linguistic Analysis*. Grand Rapids: Baker, 1994. 161pp.

4.38.13 Hughes, Graham. *Hebrews and Hermeneutics: The Epistle to the Hebrews as a New Testament Example of Biblical Interpretation*. Society for New Testament Studies Monograph Series 36. Cambridge: Cambridge University Press, 1979. 218pp.

4.38.14 Hughes, Philip Edgcumbe. *A Commentary on the Epistle to the Hebrews*. Grand Rapids: Eerdmans, 1977. 623pp.

4.38.15 Hurst, L. D. *The Epistle to the Hebrews: Its Background of Thought.* Society for New Testament Studies Monograph Series 65. Cambridge: Cambridge University Press, 1990. 209pp.

4.38.16 Isaacs, Marie E. *Reading Hebrews and James: A Literary and Theological Commentary.* Macon, Ga.: Smyth & Helwys, 2002. 259pp.

4.38.17 ———. *Sacred Space: An Approach to the Theology of the Epistle to the Hebrews.* Journal for the Study of the New Testament Supplement Series 73. Sheffield: Sheffield Academic Press, 1992. 253pp.

4.38.18 Käsemann, Ernst. *The Wandering People of God: An Investigation of the Letter to the Hebrews.* Minneapolis: Augsburg, 1984. 255pp.

4.38.19 Kistemaker, Simon *Hebrews.* Grand Rapids: Baker, 1984. 464pp.

4.38.20 Lane, William L. *Hebrews: A Call to Commitment.* Peabody, Mass.: Hendrickson, 1985. 184pp.

4.38.21 Lehne, Susanne. *The New Covenant in Hebrews.* Journal for the Study of the New Testament Supplemental Series 44. Sheffield: JSOT, 1990. 183pp.

4.38.22 Long, Thomas G. *Hebrews.* Interpretation: A Bible Commentary for Teaching and Preaching. Louisville: Westminster John Knox, 1997. 153pp.

4.38.23 Manson, William. *The Epistle to the Hebrews: An Historical and Theological Reconsideration.* London: Hodder & Stoughton, 1951. 204pp.

4.38.24 Milligan, George. *The Theology of the Epistle of Hebrews.* Edinburgh: T&T Clark, 1899. 233pp.

4.38.25 Moffatt, James. *A Critical and Exegetical Commentary on the Epistle to the Hebrews.* International Critical Commentary. Edinburgh: T&T Clark, 1924. 264pp.

4.38.26 Montefiore, Hugh. *The Epistle to the Hebrews.* Harper's New Testament Commentaries. New York: Harper & Row, 1964. 272pp.

4.38.27 Nairne, Alexander. *The Epistle of Priesthood: Studies in the Epistle to the Hebrews.* Edinburgh: T&T Clark, 1913. 446pp.

4.38.28 Peterson, David. *Hebrews and Perfection: An Examination of the Concept of Perfection in the Epistle to the Hebrews.* Society for New Testament Studies Monograph Series 47. Cambridge: Cambridge University Press, 1982. 313pp.

4.38.29 Scholer, John M. *Proleptic Priests: Priesthood in the Epistle to the Hebrews.* Journal for the Study of the New Testament Supplemental Series 49. Sheffield: JSOT, 1991. 243pp.

4.38.30 Thompson, James W. *The Beginnings of Christian Philosophy: The Epistle to the Hebrews.* Catholic Biblical Quarterly Monograph Series 13. Washington, D.C.: Catholic Biblical Association of America, 1982. 184pp.

4.38.31 Wilson, R. McL. *Hebrews.* New Century Bible Commentary. Grand Rapids: Eerdmans, 1987. 268pp.

4.39 James

See also PETRINE EPISTLES AND JUDE (§4.40) AND HEBREWS (§4.38)

H I G H L Y   R E C O M M E N D E D

4.39.1 Davids, Peter H. *The Epistle of James: A Commentary on the Greek Text.* New International Greek Testament Commentary. Grand Rapids: Eerdmans, 1982. 226pp.

Argues that the core of this book was produced by James the Just in the 40s and later edited either by him, with the assistance of others, or by his followers. In practice, Davids makes little of this two-stage development in his exposition of the text. Insists that the book is carefully structured, against many who, like Luther, consider its arrangement "chaotic." Makes significant use of his understanding of the book's structure in the commentary, along with linguistic analysis of Greek and Hellenistic, Jewish, and early Christian parallels. Introduction discusses the book's major theological issues at length.

4.39.2 Johnson, Luke Timothy. *James.* Anchor Bible. New York: Doubleday, 1995. 412pp.

Lucid, elegantly written, and theologically profound. Arguably the best commentary available on James. Argues at length that the book was written by James the Just and that it is one of the earliest NT writings. Offers the most comprehensive examination of the history of interpretation of James available in English. Commentary emphasizes linguistic analysis and the logic of the letter. Includes selective interaction with modern scholarship and fuller interaction with ancient commentators. Relates individual passages and themes to one another in an attempt to identify the dynamic structure of James' thought. Probes beneath the surface of the text to underlying theological issues that have continuing relevance for Christian thought and behavior.

4.39.3 Martin, Ralph P. *James.* Word Biblical Commentary. Waco, Tex.: Word, 1988. 240pp.

Useful for the scholar, and suggestive for those who preach and teach within the church. Characterized by thorough and current bibliographies, careful grammatical analysis employed to clarify theological meaning of the text), and extensive allusions to ancient materials. Engages in serious dialogue with other interpreters, although focuses almost entirely on modern scholars. Identifies discernible structure in the book. Argues that sayings from James the Just, originally directed to Palestinian churches, or perhaps to non-Christian Palestinian Jews, were arranged in the form of a letter by James's disciples after his death in order to address concerns of a primarily Jewish church in Antioch.

4.39.4 Mayor, Joseph B. *The Epistle of St. James: The Greek Text with Introduction, Notes, Comments and Further Studies in the Epistle of St. James.* 3d ed. London: Macmillan, 1913. 291/264/41pp.

Comprehensive and authoritative, still valuable after nearly a century. Contains massive compilation of technical historical, linguistic, and text-critical information that is often simply adopted by later commentators. Introduction of nearly three hundred pages concludes that the book was produced by James the Just in the 40s. Meticulously examines every Greek word or phrase, with attention to flow of argument, historical setting of original readers, ancient parallels, and history of interpretation. Quotations typically appear in original Greek and Latin. Attends also to the significance of James's teaching for NT theology and, to a lesser extent, for contemporary application. Highly technical; assumes knowledge of Greek.

ALSO SIGNIFICANT

4.39.5 Adamson, James B. *The Epistle of James.* New International Commentary on the New Testament. Grand Rapids: Eerdmans, 1976. 227pp.

4.39.6 ———. *James: The Man and His Message.* Grand Rapids: Eerdmans, 1989. 553pp.

4.39.7 Bauckham, Richard. *James: Wisdom of James, Disciple of Jesus the Sage.* New Testament Readings. London: Routledge, 1999. 246pp.

4.39.8 Cadoux, A. T. *The Thought of St. James.* London: James Clarke, 1944. 101pp.

4.39.9 Dibelius, Martin. *James.* Rev. by Heinrich Greeven. Hermeneia: A Critical and Historical Commentary on the Bible. Philadelphia: Fortress, 1975. 285pp.

4.39.10   Hartin, Patrick J. *A Spirituality of Perfection: Faith in Action in the Letter of James*. Collegeville, Minn.: Liturgical Press, 1999. 192pp.

4.39.11   Hort, Fenton John Anthony. *The Epistle of St. James*. London: Macmillan, 1909. (Several sections have separate pagination.)

4.39.12   Kistemaker, Simon. *Exposition of the Epistle of James and the Epistles of John*. New Testament Commentary. Grand Rapids: Baker, 1986. 425pp.

4.39.13   Laws, Sophie. *A Commentary on the Epistle of James*. Harper's New Testament Commentaries. San Francisco: Harper & Row, 1981. 273pp.

4.39.14   Mitton, C. Leslie. *The Epistle of James*. London: Marshall, Morgan & Scott, 1974. 255pp.

4.39.15   Moo, Douglas J. *The Letter of James*. Pillar New Testament Commentary. Grand Rapids: Eerdmans, 2000. 271pp.

4.39.16   Penner, Todd C. *The Epistle of James and Eschatology: Re-reading an Ancient Christian Letter*. Journal for the Study of the New Testament Supplement Series 191. Sheffield: Sheffield Academic Press, 1996. 331pp.

4.39.17   Ropes, James H. *A Critical and Exegetical Commentary on the Epistle of St. James*. International Critical Commentary. Edinburgh: T&T Clark, 1916. 319pp.

4.39.18   Wall, Robert W. *Community of the Wise: The Letter of James*. New Testament in Context. Valley Forge, Pa.: Trinity Press International, 1997. 354pp.

4.40 Petrine Epistles and Jude

H I G H L Y   R E C O M M E N D E D

4.40.1   Achtemeier, Paul J. *1 Peter*. Hermeneia: A Critical and Historical Commentary on the Bible. Minneapolis: Fortress, 1996. 423pp.

Cautiously concludes that the letter is pseudonymous, and offers a brief discussion of pseudonymity in the NT in an attempt to clarify the phenomenon and explain the motives behind it. Introduction includes a brief but helpful discussion of theology. Especially useful is the analysis of the coherence and structure of the thought of the letter. Focuses on linguistic analysis, parallels from Jewish and Hellenistic literature (citing many passages not known by or accessible to earlier scholars), and historical background (especially social and cultural considerations). Extensive footnotes offer interaction with history of interpretation, largely limited to modern scholars. Commentary gives more attention to theology than is typical of volumes in this series, but does not explicitly address contemporary application.

4.40.2 Bauckham, Richard J. *Jude, 2 Peter*. Word Biblical Commentary. Waco, Tex.: Word, 1983. 357pp.

The most authoritative and current commentary on these books. Although recognizing the literary dependency of 2 Peter on Jude, insists that each letter must be understood on its own terms, and that each has its own contribution to make to NT theology. Argues that Jude authored the letter bearing his name in the 50s, but insists that 2 Peter is pseudepigraphical, dating from the end of the first century. Interpretation depends largely on genre and literary structure, but also utilizes lexical and syntactical analysis, historical background, and history of interpretation, especially modern interpreters. Theologically oriented commentary is suggestive of modern significance, but does not directly address contemporary appropriation.

4.40.3 Davids, Peter H. *The First Epistle of Peter*. New International Commentary on the New Testament. Grand Rapids: Eerdmans, 1990. 266pp.

Argues that Peter was ultimately responsible for the production of this letter, though probably commissioned Silvanus to write in his name. Understands the letter to be a model for the way the early church applied the OT and Jesus' teachings to specific problems calling for pastoral response. Introduction contains relatively extensive discussion of the letter's theology, with an especially helpful excursus on suffering in 1 Peter and in the NT. Interprets passages largely on the basis of literary structure and flow of argument, and in relation to other biblical passages. Gives less attention to linguistic analysis, history of interpretation, or historical background. Contains some new insights valuable to the scholar, but clearly written and understandable by the nonspecialist. Concern for theology and pastoral issues makes it useful for teaching and preaching.

4.40.4 Elliott, John H. *I Peter*. Anchor Bible. New York: Doubleday, 2000. 956pp.

Most thorough, comprehensive, and current commentary on this letter, which Elliott takes to be pseudonymous, written between 73 and 92. Elliott builds on his earlier sociological study of 1 Peter, which pioneered sociological interpretation of NT epistles (see his *Home for the Homeless* [§4.40.16]). Although emphasizing sociological considerations in this commentary, Elliott sets the epistle in a variety of contexts, attending to literary, historical, linguistic, and theological issues, as well as the history of interpretation (both ancient and modern). Includes exhaustive bibliography comprising 150 pages. The study of each passage also concludes with a bibliography. Commentary is highly technical but written in a clear style, and thus much of it is accessible to nonspecialists.

4.40.5 Goppelt, Leonhard. *A Commentary on 1 Peter.* Grand Rapids: Eerdmans, 1993. 385pp.

This highly regarded German NT scholar completed this commentary shortly before his death in 1973. The substance of the volume is Goppelt's, but bibliographies have been updated to 1993. Introduction contains detailed and comprehensive discussions of background issues, concluding that Peter and Silvanus were responsible for the traditions behind the letter but were not its authors. Commentary is full of original exegetical insights and rich theological reflections. Attends to situation of the original community, Jewish and Hellenistic background, and history of interpretation, and to a lesser extent flow of argument and linguistic analysis. Emphasizes Peter's contribution to Christian ethics in a socially complex environment and marginalized existence.

4.40.6 Mayor, Joseph B. *The Epistle of St. Jude and the Second Epistle of St. Peter: Greek Text with Introduction, Notes, and Comments.* London: Macmillan, 1907. 239pp. + extensive Introduction.

Mayor was a trained classicist and therefore gives primary attention to language, especially grammar. Attends also to text-critical issues, Jewish and Hellenistic parallels, and history of interpretation, giving citations in original Latin and Greek. All of this highly technical discussion is in the service of a theological explication of the text that at points borders on devotional. Immense introduction (two hundred pages) thoroughly presents evidence bearing on authorship, date, and the relationship between 2 Peter and Jude. Concludes that 2 Peter is a pseudonymous second-century writing, while Jude authored letter bearing his name. Contains a mass of technical information that has become foundational for all subsequent scholarship.

4.40.7 Michaels, J. Ramsey. *1 Peter.* Word Biblical Commentary. Waco, Tex.: Word, 1988. 337pp.

Michaels refutes the longstanding perception that this letter simply echoes generally held beliefs of early Christianity and makes no unique contribution to NT theology, insisting instead that 1 Peter offers a distinctive non-Pauline Christianity. Cautiously accepts Petrine authorship, and suggests that Peter might have written it as late as the 70s. Focuses on lexical and syntactical analysis and historical background (especially Jewish and Hellenistic literature, and sociocultural situation), and gives relatively little attention to history of interpretation. Emphasizes Peter's mixture of theology and ethics (i.e., ethically applied theology), but says little regarding contemporary application.

4.40.8 Neyrey, Jerome H. *2 Peter, Jude*. Anchor Bible. New York: Doubleday, 1993. 287pp.

In much the same way that Bauckham (§4.40.2) emphasizes literary aspects of genre and structure, Neyrey stresses the role of ancient rhetoric and the social, political, and economic setting of these pseudonymous letters, produced at the turn of the second century. Employs five social-scientific models as "templates" to help readers see and understand significant facets of the text. Grounds the use of these models in cultural anthropology and historical examination of ancient Greek, Roman, and Jewish literature. While providing important insights, these models at times seem to be imposed on the text and materially influence its interpretation. Tends to emphasize social and cultural phenomena rather than theological issues. Yet there are many original and illuminating interpretations, and Neyrey gives some attention to theological and pastoral concerns.

4.40.9 Selwyn, Edward Gordon. *The First Epistle of St. Peter: The Greek Text with Introduction, Notes and Essays*. 2d ed. London: Macmillan, 1947. 517pp.

For years considered the most authoritative commentary on this letter in English, it remains indispensable. Argues that letter was drafted by Silvanus at Peter's direction. Introduction contains extensive discussion of the letter's theology and ethics. Commentary focuses on the Greek text, which appears at the top of the page. Attends also to flow of argument, Jewish and Hellenistic parallels, and history of interpretation, especially the Fathers. Citations are in original Greek and Latin. Contains several "additional notes," dealing in detail with significant interpretive and theological issues. Assumes knowledge of Greek.

ALSO SIGNIFICANT

4.40.10 Bauckham, Richard. *Jude and the Relatives of Jesus in the Early Church*. Edinburgh: T&T Clark, 1990. 459pp.

4.40.11 Beare, Francis Wright. *The First Epistle of Peter: The Greek Text with Introduction and Notes*. 3d ed. Oxford: Basil Blackwood, 1970. 184pp.

4.40.12 Best, Ernest. *I Peter*. New Century Bible Commentary. Grand Rapids: Eerdmans, 1971. 188pp.

4.40.13 Bigg, Charles. *A Critical and Exegetical Commentary on the Epistles of St. Peter and St. Jude*. International Critical Commentary. Edinburgh: T&T Clark, 1901. 353pp.

4.40.14 Chester, Andrew, and Ralph P. Martin. *The Theology of the Letters of James, Peter, and Jude*. New Testament Theology. Cambridge: Cambridge University Press, 1994. 189pp.

4.40.15 Earl, Richard. *Reading 1 Peter, Jude, and 2 Peter: A Literary and Theological Commentary*. Macon, Ga.: Smyth & Helwys, 2000. 394pp.

4.40.16 Elliott, John H. *A Home for the Homeless: A Sociological Exegesis of I Peter, Its Situation and Strategy*. Philadelphia: Fortress, 1981. 306pp.

4.40.17 Green, Michael. *The Second Epistle General of Peter and the General Epistle of Jude*. 2d ed. Tyndale New Testament Commentaries. Grand Rapids: Eerdmans, 1987. 208pp.

4.40.18 Kelly, J. N. D. *A Commentary on the Epistles of Peter and of Jude*. Harper's New Testament Commentaries. New York: Harper & Row, 1969. 387pp.

4.40.19 Kistemaker, Simon. *Expositions of the Epistles of Peter and the Epistle of Jude*. New Testament Commentary. Grand Rapids: Baker, 1987. 443pp.

4.40.20 Luther, Martin. *Commentary on Peter and Jude*. Grand Rapids: Kregel, 1990. (Originally published 1523, in German.) 303pp.

4.40.21 Lyle, Kenneth R., Jr. *Ethical Admonition in the Epistle of Jude*. Studies in Biblical Literature 4. New York: Peter Lang, 1998. 152pp.

4.40.22 Perkins, Pheme. *First and Second Peter, James, and Jude*. Interpretation: A Bible Commentary for Teaching and Preaching. Louisville: Westminster John Knox, 1995. 204PP.

4.40.23 Reese, Ruth Anne. *Writing Jude: The Reader, the Text, and the Author in Constructs of Power and Desire*. Biblical Interpretation Series 51. Leiden: Brill, 2000. 182pp.

4.40.24 Reicke, Bo. *The Epistles of James, Peter, and Jude*. 2d ed. Anchor Bible. Garden City, N.Y.: Doubleday, 1985. 221pp.

4.40.25 Richard, Earl J. *Reading 1 Peter, Jude, and 2 Peter: A Literary and Theological Commentary*. Macon, Ga.: Smyth & Helwys, 2000. 394pp.

4.40.26 Talbert, Charles H., ed. *Perspectives on First Peter*. Special Studies Series 9. Macon, Ga.: Mercer University Press, 1986. 151pp.

4.40.27 Watson, Duane Frederick. *Invention, Arrangement, and Style: Rhetorical Criticism of Jude and 2 Peter.* Society of Biblical Literature Dissertation Series 104. Atlanta: Scholars, 1988. 214pp.

4.41 Johannine Epistles

H I G H L Y   R E C O M M E N D E D

4.41.1 Brown, Raymond E. *The Epistles of John.* Anchor Bible. Garden City, N.Y.: Doubleday, 1982. 812pp.

Argues that these letters must be understood in relation to John's Gospel. They demonstrate division within the Johannine community over the meaning of the Gospel of John. The portion of the community responsible for these letters is attempting to force its construal of John's Gospel on the community as a whole. Commentary is based on this reconstruction of the history of the Johannine community and of the adversaries described in these letters. Although this reconstruction is arguably as plausible as any, there is no consensus on these matters, and Brown's interpretation is thus rendered speculative. Nevertheless, careful explication of every interpretive problem, exhaustive linguistic analysis, and thorough interaction with history of interpretation (ancient and modern) makes this volume invaluable.

4.41.2 Marshall, I. Howard. *The Epistles of John.* New International Commentary on the New Testament. Grand Rapids: Eerdmans, 1978. 274pp.

Maintains that these letters come from the author of the Fourth Gospel, probably either John the apostle or a follower of the apostle known as "the elder." They were written to urge members of the Johannine community to avoid the appeals of a heretical group that had recently seceded from the community. Commentary characterized by careful argumentation, balanced judgment, and clear and understandable presentation of current scholarly discussions and of complex exegetical issues. Relegates technical discussion to extensive footnotes. Addresses contemporary significance.

4.41.3 Schnackenburg, Rudolf. *The Johannine Epistles: Introduction and Commentary.* New York: Crossroad, 1992. 320pp.

Against Brown (§4.41.1), insists that the relationship between these letters and John's Gospel remains unanswerable; it is impossible to determine which came first. Consequently, Schnackenburg interprets these letters on their own terms, using John's Gospel as evidence, but not relying on a specific reconstruction of the Johannine community. Attends to linguistic analysis of the Greek, though less rigorously than Brown. Emphasizes the literary structure of the letters, the theological structure of John's thought, historical background, Jewish and Hellenistic parallels, and history of interpretation (ancient and modern). Excurses offer full discussion of theological issues. Provides richer theological reflection than any other commentary on these letters.

4.41.4 Smalley, Stephen S. *1, 2, 3 John.* Word Biblical Commentary. Waco, Tex.: Word, 1984. 386pp.

Understands emphasis of these letters to be Christology and its implications for Christian behavior. Smalley detects a balanced understanding of Jesus' person, presenting him as both fully human and fully divine. Concludes that the letters were written later than John's Gospel, and by a different author. Introduction is very brief, but commentary offers meticulous lexical and syntactical analysis of every phrase, and gives thorough attention to the flow of argument, relationship of passages within Johannine corpus, and historical background, especially the situation of the original audience. Focuses on theological meaning, and is particularly concerned to resolve apparent theological contradictions and tensions within the letters. Gives little explicit attention to contemporary application.

4.41.5 Strecker, Georg. *The Johannine Letters.* Hermeneia: A Critical and Historical Commentary on the Bible. Minneapolis: Fortress, 1996. 319pp.

Insists that 2 and 3 John shared a common author and were produced first, followed by 1 John and the Gospel, which were written by different authors. Argues against any literary dependence between these writings. Insists rather that various members of the "Johannine school" shared a common (mostly oral) tradition and each employed this tradition in his own way in the process of addressing complex theological struggles within the Johannine community. Consequently, the commentary is especially concerned to explore ways in which writers of these letters edited the Johannine tradition so as to deal with the theological and pastoral challenges they faced. This approach renders the commentary somewhat speculative. Attends also to linguistic analysis of the Greek and to historical background (especially Jewish and Hellenistic). Excurses deal with key terms. Consistently probes theological significance.

4.41.6 Westcott, Brooke Foss. *The Epistles of St. John: The Greek Text, with Notes and Addenda.* London: Macmillan, 1883. 245pp.

Attends to even the minutest details of the Greek. Quotes relevant sources from classical antiquity and Church Fathers in original Greek and Latin. Carefully analyzes structure of the entire letter and individual passages. Regularly cites other biblical passages, exploring points of continuity and discontinuity. Excurses provide detailed discussion of theological issues. Insists that these letters, along with the Fourth Gospel, were written by the apostle John, although refuses to take a stand on the sequence of their production. In spite of its age and its tendency to overdo analysis of Greek prepositions and particles, it remains a standard work. Highly technical, assumes knowledge of Greek.

ALSO SIGNIFICANT

4.41.7 Brooke, A. E. *A Critical and Exegetical Commentary on the Johannine Epistles.* International Critical Commentary. Edinburgh: T&T Clark, 1912. 242pp.

4.41.8 Bultmann, Rudolf. *The Johannine Epistles.* Hermeneia: A Critical and Historical Commentary on the Bible. Philadelphia: Fortress, 1973. 143pp.

4.41.9 Dodd, C. H. *The Johannine Epistles.* Moffatt New Testament Commentary. London: Hodder & Stoughton, 1946. 168pp.

4.41.10 Houlden, J. L. *A Commentary on the Johannine Epistles.* Rev. ed. Black's New Testament Commentaries. London: A. & C. Black, 1994. 107pp.

4.41.11 Kruse, Colin G. *The Letters of John.* Pillar New Testament Commentary. Grand Rapids: Eerdmans, 2000. 255pp.

4.41.12 Lieu, Judith. *The Second and Third Epistles of John.* Studies of the New Testament and Its World. Edinburgh: T&T Clark, 1986. 264pp.

4.41.13 ———. *The Theology of the Johannine Epistles.* New Testament Theology. Cambridge: Cambridge University Press, 1991. 130pp.

4.41.14 Painter, John. *1, 2, and 3 John.* Sacra Pagina. Collegeville, Minn.: Liturgical Press, 2002. 416pp.

4.41.15 Smith, D. Moody. *First, Second, and Third John.* Interpretation: A Bible Commentary for Teaching and Preaching. Louisville: Westminster John Knox, 1991. 164pp.

4.42 Book of Revelation

HIGHLY RECOMMENDED

4.42.1 Aune, David E. *Revelation.* 3 vols. Word Biblical Commentary. Dallas: Word, 1997–1998. 1354pp.

Most current, authoritative, and comprehensive commentary on Revelation available in any language. Introduction of 250 pages explores especially his-

torical matters (concluding that the book was written by an otherwise unknown "John," a Christian prophet who had no significant connection with
the Johannine community), literary issues (genre and syntax), and sources (arguing for a two-stage editing process that the author pursued over a 30-year
period). Commentary emphasizes literary structure, genre, linguistic analysis,
historical background, literary precursors, and text-critical issues. Gives little
attention to the history of interpretation. Emphasis on literary and historical
considerations leaves little room for probing theological reflection. Highly
technical; encyclopedic in amount of material assembled.

4.42.2 Bauckham, Richard. *The Climax of Prophecy: Studies on the Book of
Revelation.* Edinburgh: T&T Clark, 1993. 550pp.

A helpful introduction to the most significant literary, historical, and theological issues. Series of essays cohere around "a single sustained enterprise of understanding both the form and the message of the Apocalypse in its literary
and historical contexts." Essays emphasize (1) the literary unity of Revelation
(over against focus on earlier sources) and significance of literary techniques
and structure; (2) the author's constant and disciplined allusions to the OT,
employing Jewish exegetical methods in an attempt to produce a "work of
prophetic scripture, the climax of prophetic revelation"; (3) the relationship
between Revelation and other apocalyptic writings; and (4) the historical context in which Revelation was produced, and especially religious, political, social, and economic circumstances. Literary and historical study serves to
explicate the theology of Revelation.

4.42.3 Beale, G. K. *The Book of Revelation.* New International Greek Testament Commentary. Grand Rapids: Eerdmans, 1999. 1245pp.

Comprehensive and learned commentary that emphasizes the use of the OT
according to Jewish exegetical traditions as a major key to unfolding the meaning of Revelation. Attends also to historical background and careful analysis of
the development of argument. Gives less attention to linguistic analysis than is
typical of volumes in this series. Slightly more theologically oriented than
Aune's commentary (§4.42.1). Introduction includes helpful discussion of
major approaches to Revelation and of methodological issues pertaining to the
interpretation of symbolism. Excurses deal in depth with significant interpretive
issues. Allows that Revelation could have been written by John the apostle (author of the Fourth Gospel) or by another "John," but insists that identification of
the author is unnecessary for the book's interpretation.

4.42.4 Caird, G. B. *The Revelation of St. John the Divine.* Harper's New Testament Commentaries. New York: Harper & Row, 1966. 316pp.

Recognizing the inherent difficulty of Revelation for modern readers, Caird
offers a lucid and straightforward exposition of this book, which he takes to

have been written by an otherwise unknown Christian leader around the end of the first century to address pastorally urgent challenges facing congregations under his care. Presents an extremely short introduction, preferring to give primary attention to explication of text itself. Stresses the use of the OT and historical background, gives less consideration to genre and literary structure, and says virtually nothing about linguistic analysis or history of interpretation. Its brevity, narrow focus, and lack of technical discussion belies a depth of learning that results in a rich and theologically suggestive exposition.

4.42.5 Mounce, Robert H. *The Book of Revelation.* Rev. ed. New International Commentary on the New Testament. Grand Rapids: Eerdmans, 1998. 439pp.

Lucid commentary, solid, reliable, and balanced, if not particularly original or probing. Posits that Revelation was written by John the apostle during reign of Domitian. Adopts a generally premillennial eschatological perspective, but allows that much of chs. 4–22 describe events that were contemporary to the original audience or are symbolic representations of realities pertaining to the entire period of the church. Emphasizes historical background, flow of argument, and relationship to other biblical materials, giving less attention to linguistic analysis or to history of interpretation. Focuses on the basic meaning of the text, with little development of its theological richness and few suggestions regarding contemporary application.

ALSO SIGNIFICANT

4.42.6 Bauckham, Richard. *The Theology of the Book of Revelation.* New Testament Theology. Cambridge: Cambridge University Press, 1993. 169pp.

4.42.7 Beasley-Murray, George R. *The Book of Revelation.* New Century Bible Commentary. Grand Rapids: Eerdmans, 1981. 352pp.

4.42.8 Beckwith, I. T. *The Apocalypse of John.* New York: Macmillan, 1922. 794pp.

4.42.9 Boring, M. Eugene. *Revelation.* Interpretation: A Bible Commentary for Teaching and Preaching. Atlanta: John Knox, 1989. 236pp

4.42.10 Charles, R. H. *A Critical and Exegetical Commentary on the Revelation of St. John.* 2 vols. International Critical Commentary. Edinburgh: T&T Clark, 1920. 373/497pp.

4.42.11 Ellul, Jacques. *Apocalypse: The Book of Revelation.* New York: Seabury, 1977. 283pp.

4.42.12 ————. *The Meaning of the City.* Grand Rapids: Eerdmans, 1970. 209pp.

4.42.13 Farrer, Austin M. *The Revelation of St. John the Divine.* Oxford: Clarendon, 1964. 233pp.

4.42.14 Fiorenza, Elisabeth Schussler. *The Book of Revelation: Justice and Judgment.* 2d ed. Minneapolis: Fortress, 1998. 243pp.

4.42.15 Guthrie, Donald. *The Relevance of John's Apocalypse.* Grand Rapids: Eerdmans, 1987. 121pp.

4.42.16 Harrington, Wilfrid J. *Revelation.* Sacra Pagina. Collegeville, Minn.: Michael Glazier, 1993. 271pp.

4.42.17 Hemer, Colin J. *The Letters to the Seven Churches of Asia in Their Local Setting.* Biblical Resources Series. Grand Rapids: Eerdmans, 2001. 338pp.

4.42.18 König, Adrio. *The Eclipse of Christ in Eschatology.* Grand Rapids: Eerdmans, 1989. 248pp.

4.42.19 Ladd, George Eldon. *A Commentary on the Revelation of John.* Grand Rapids: Eerdmans, 1969. 308pp.

4.42.20 Malina, Bruce J. *On the Genre and Message of Revelation: Star Visions and Sky Journeys.* Peabody, Mass.: Hendrickson, 1995. 317pp.

4.42.21 Mulholland, M. Robert, Jr. *Revelation: Holy Living in an Unholy World.* Grand Rapids: Zondervan, 1990. 376pp.

4.42.22 Muse, Robert L. *The Book of Revelation: An Annotated Bibliography.* New York: Garland, 1996. 352pp.

4.42.23 Osborne, Grant R. *Revelation.* Baker Exegetical Commentary on the New Testament. Grand Rapids: Baker, 2002. 896pp.

4.42.24 Pate, C. Marvin, ed. *Four Views on the Book of Revelation.* Counterpoints Series. Grand Rapids: Zondervan, 1998. 252pp.

4.42.25 Ramsey, William M. *The Letters to the Seven Churches of Asia.* Revised and updated by Mark W. Wilson. Peabody, Mass.: Hendrickson, 1994. 317pp.

4.42.26 Resseguie, James L. *Revelation Unsealed: A Narrative Critical Approach to John's Apocalypse.* Leiden: Brill, 1998, 233pp.

4.42.27 Roloff, Jürgen. *Revelation*. Continental Commentaries. Minneapolis: Fortress, 1993. 275pp.

4.42.28 Smalley, Stephen S. *Thunder and Love: John's Revelation and John's Community*. Milton Keynes, U.K.: Word, 1994. 223pp.

4.42.29 Swete, Henry Barclay. *Commentary on Revelation: The Greek Text with Introduction, Notes and Indexes*. London: Macmillan, 1911. 338pp.

4.42.30 Wainwright, Arthur W. *Mysterious Apocalypse: Interpreting the Book of Revelation*. Nashville: Abingdon, 1993. 293pp.

INDEX